SUDDEN JUSTICE

SUDDEN JUSTICE

AMERICA'S SECRET DRONE WARS

CHRIS WOODS

OXFORD
UNIVERSITY PRESS

OXFORD
UNIVERSITY PRESS

Oxford University Press is a department of the University of
Oxford. It furthers the University's objective of excellence in research,
scholarship, and education by publishing worldwide.

Oxford   New York
Auckland   Cape Town   Dar es Salaam   Hong Kong   Karachi
Kuala Lumpur   Madrid   Melbourne   Mexico City   Nairobi
New Delhi   Shanghai   Taipei   Toronto

With offices in
Argentina   Austria   Brazil   Chile   Czech Republic   France   Greece
Guatemala   Hungary   Italy   Japan   Poland   Portugal   Singapore
South Korea   Switzerland   Thailand   Turkey   Ukraine   Vietnam

Oxford is a registered trademark of Oxford University Press
in the UK and certain other countries.

Published in the United States of America by
Oxford University Press
198 Madison Avenue, New York, NY 10016

Cataloging-in-Publication data is on file at the Library of Congress
ISBN 978–0–19–020259–0

1 3 5 7 9 8 6 4 2
Printed in the United States of America
on acid-free paper

For my family.
Always there.

CONTENTS

ACKNOWLEDGMENTS

My particular thanks are due to the Bureau of Investigative Journalism, the London-based not-for-profit which funded and supported my investigations into the use of armed drones over a 30-month period. In particular, I would like to thank Alice Ross, my co-reporter on a number of investigations, and Jack Serle for his excellent assistance and data analysis. Thanks must also go to former editor Iain Overton and to deputy editor Rachel Oldroyd. My gratitude as well to Manuela Lanza for her work on the death of Raquel Burgos Garcia; to Nina Schick for her forensic unpacking of German deaths in Pakistan; and to Emma Slater for her commendable work on an Iranian TV station's faked drone strike claims. While I draw heavily on the data and research of the Bureau here, the invaluable work of the New America Foundation and Long War Journal in mapping and scrutinizing US covert drone strikes also deeply informs this book.

In Pakistan I was able to draw on the advice and assistance of journalists Rahimullah and Mushtaq Yusufzai. Their courage and determination, along with that of many other Pakistani and Western journalists and researchers in the region, helps ensure our better understanding of those events some would wish remained secret. Lawyer Mirza Shahzad Akbar has also been patient in the face of my many questions over the years, and Christopher Rogers was kind enough to share details of his time in Islamabad. I also received the generous assistance of many present and former senior Pakistani military and intelligence officials, and while many must remain anonymous I would particularly like to thank former ISI Brigadier Asad Munir for helping me better understand US–Pakistani counterterrorism cooperation after 9/11. Lieutenant General Asad Durrani, former head of the ISI, was also kind enough to share his views during a London trip. The assistance of the Pakistan military's media office, the ISPR in facilitating my field trips to South Waziristan and Swat was much appreciated, and I would also like to thank Channel 4 News foreign editor Nevine Mabro for enabling that trip. My particular thanks go to Tahir Khan, a reporter with the BBC's Pashtun Service who was my companion and translator in both Waziristan and Swat.

In Yemen I benefited greatly from the insights of many fine specialists, and I would particularly like to thank reporters Iona Craig, Saeed al-Batati, and Hakim Almasmari. Vivian Salama not only shared with me her insights from a research trip to Yemen, but has also generously allowed the reproduction of two of her striking photographs for this book. I am grateful too for the work of those NGOs seeking to understand counterterrorism operations inside the country—often at some risk to their own staff. In particular, my appreciation goes to HOOD, to the Alkarama Foundation, to Reprieve's local team, and to Letta Tayler and her colleagues at Human Rights Watch.

The assistance of USAF's Book Support Program has been much appreciated, as has that of Lieutenant General Bob Otto, the present head of USAF's ISR Agency, and his staff. My thanks too to Air Combat Command and to Langley AFB for its hospitality. In particular, I would like to thank Colonel Lourdes Duvall, Vice Commander of the 480th Intelligence, Surveillance and Reconnaissance Wing, who with her team so patiently explained the complexities of modern battlefield intelligence-gathering. USAF clinical psychologist Dr. Wayne Chappelle was generous with his insights into stress among drone operators. I would also like to thank the many serving and former intelligence analysts, pilots, sensor operators, mission controllers, and other key RPA personnel (some of whom have asked to remain anonymous) who gave so much of their time. Many of these are Special Forces personnel, sharing their experiences for the first time. I have also benefited greatly from the knowledge and insights of many former US military, intelligence, and diplomatic officials with a deep knowledge of remotely piloted aircraft (RPA). These include General Chuck Wald, Lieutenant General Dave Deptula, Major General Kenneth Israel, Major General James Poss, and Major General George Harrison. I also much appreciated the helpful notes provided by the Predator's inventor Abe Karem. State Department officials providing their wise counsel include former Deputy Secretary of State Richard Armitage and Ambassador Cameron Munter, and Professor Lawrence Wilkerson.

For their invaluable aid in facilitating my understanding of Britain's own armed RPA programme, my thanks go to the Royal Air Force. Greatly appreciated too have been the gatherings organized by Sir Mike Aaronson and his team at the University of Surrey's Centre for International Intervention. Professor Anatol Lieven of King's College London was also generous with his expertise, while Professor David Cortright at the University of Notre Dame's Kroc Institute in Chicago has my thanks for his insights and patience. Professor Eyal Weizman and Dr. Susan Schuppli of Forensic Architecture were also kind enough to share their important modeling of the physical impact of armed drone strikes from an early stage. Professor Dapo Akande at Oxford University, Professor Amos Guiora at Utah and Professor Greg McNeal at Pepperdine have all been generous with their time. So too have been the law centers of Stanford and NYU, and especially Professors Sarah Knuckey and Jim Cavallaro; while Dr. Naureen Shah (now with Amnesty International) has also been a great help. UN special rapporteurs Ben Emmerson QC and Professor Christof Heyns were both kind enough to allow me to observe key aspects of their investigations for the United Nations. My thanks are also due to their legal team, including Iain Morley QC, Annie O'Riley, and Leonard Cuscoleca. I would also like to thank Norwegian documentary film-maker Tonje Hessen Schei and her team, who for their film Drone followed my work for three years, and also allowed me access to their own findings. The investigation into the role of the CIA's secret drone squadron described here was very much a joint enterprise.

Much of this book covers events and actions which remain highly classified. This has led in turn to a cottage industry of lawyers, academics, NGOs, and journalists seeking to deepen our understanding of this novel form of warfare. Their research and publications inform this work throughout. I would like to thank Reprieve (and, in particular, Clive Stafford Smith, Jennifer Gibson, and Cori Crider); Clara Gutteridge for her outstanding work on renditions; Amnesty International and, in particular, Mustafa Qadri for his work on Pakistan; Code Pink's Medea Benjamin and Colonel Ann Wright; Chris Cole of Drone Wars UK for his dogged pursuit of the facts on British RPA operations; and at the ACLU the tireless work of Jameel Jaffar and Hina Shamsi. I have also benefited often from the forensic writings of Marcy Wheeler at Emptywheel, and those of journalists Glenn Greenwald and Jeremy Scahill. Jemima Khan has also been supportive, in particular allowing me to quote from the unedited manuscript of her New Statesman interview with General Pervez Musharraf. There are many insights within this book (and others) that were only made possible by the actions of Chelsea Manning, Edward Snowden, and WikiLeaks, to whom I offer my sincere and particular thanks.

Michael Dwyer at publishers Hurst has been a patient and diligent editor, and I am also grateful to Alexandra Dauler at Oxford University Press for her faith in *Sudden Justice*, along with her insightful suggestions. For their invaluable constructive criticism, my final thanks go to readers and friends Kinda Haddad, Sebastian Sandys, and James Hirst.

INTRODUCTION

★

Almost daily from September 2014, US Air Force Reaper and Predator drones—remotely piloted aircraft in Pentagon jargon—had begun bombing targets across Syria associated with rampant Al Qaeda offshoot the Islamic State. Weeks earlier, President Obama had already ordered the return of armed drones to Iraq's skies after an absence of three years, in an effort to halt the advance of radical Islamists there. What he was not prepared to do, Obama told the American public, was to put "large numbers of US troops on the ground" in the Middle East during this latest crisis. Instead, armed drones represented a new warfare model which "is going to be part of the solution," the president insisted.[1] For policymakers and planners in Washington, weaponized drones were the first tool they often reached for.

Their success was an accident of history. The slow-flying, ungainly remote aircraft had not emerged from the design boards of prestigious US arms manufacturers. Instead they were the vision of a genius American-Israeli, backed by two maverick brothers with little experience of weapons manufacturing. Enabling the United States to track and analyze targets in real time—and then to strike immediately—the Predator in effect was the world's first airborne sniper rifle. Indeed, the aircraft was weaponized with the explicit purpose of enabling the CIA to assassinate Osama bin Laden at his remote home in Afghanistan, before the Al Qaeda leader ever launched his murderous attacks in September 2001.

The Predator's battlefield debut was not an auspicious one—allowing the Taliban's supreme leader to escape unscathed in the opening minutes of the Afghan war. Yet in the days which followed, the CIA's few drones ably demonstrated their revolutionary potential as they helped to drive Al Qaeda and the Taliban from power. The new weapon system might then have been expected to transition swiftly to military control. Yet these were not ordinary times. In its zeal to pursue Al Qaeda globally, the Bush administration played fast and loose with international law—the Guantanamo camp, extraordinary rendition, and torture were all hallmarks of this period. So too was the US program of assassinating terrorist suspects beyond the hot battlefield—a tactic which armed drones proved particularly adept at. In the first such operation, in November 2002 six men were targeted and killed in Yemen—one an American whose presence was, it seems, known to the CIA. The survival of a seventh man perfectly highlighted the problem of the United States acting as judge, jury, and executioner, after the suspect was later acquitted of any terrorism charges by a Yemen military court.

Despite major objections by the United Nations—and by some of the United States' closest allies—that first strike would prove to be the first of hundreds of secret US targeted killings by drone. Between them they had killed more than 3,000 people at the time of writing—most of them likely terrorists or militants, but also including hundreds of civilians. When Barack Obama assumed the presidency in 2009, he acted swiftly to end the worst excesses of his predecessor. Yet one Bush Era program proved too tempting to relinquish. Obama had come to power determined to secure victory in Afghanistan—and that meant heavily expanding a secret US drone war inside Pakistan which was already in its fifth year. Within days, the CIA had carried out its first strikes there on Obama's orders, which thanks to poor intelligence led to the deaths of numerous civilians. Even so, Obama would steeply escalate targeted killings away from the battlefield, carrying out eight times more strikes than Bush in Pakistan alone—and opening new fronts in Yemen and Somalia. This was not the "reluctant warrior" of popular imaginings.

For many in Washington, this novel form of warfare appeared risk-free. The killing of terrorist leaders proved particularly valuable in what was otherwise a grinding, seemingly endless fight against Al Qaeda and its allies. Yet over time, an international backlash against targeted killings beyond the battlefield risked undermining any potential longer term US benefits. Even within the US military and intelligence communities, senior leaders were questioning Obama's overreliance on drones. The CIA's actions in

Pakistan came under particular scrutiny, with concerns raised at the historically high number of civilians killed, and at the Agency's more brutal tactics there. With allegations of CIA war crimes as a result of an investigation by this author and others, a UN team began looking into the deliberate targeting of first responders and funeral-goers in Pakistan—tactics which were likened to those of Al Qaeda itself.

Controversial though drone civilian casualties were, they were still few in number when compared with previous conflicts. The relative precision of armed drones—and their ability to "slow down war" in the words of one pilot—meant that noncombatants were likely to be at less risk of death or injury than from most other weapon systems. The closest parallel to Washington's drone targeted killing program could be found three decades earlier. During the Vietnam conflict, the United States had also secretly bombed two neighboring states. The scale of those attacks was staggering. Between 1965 and 1973 during carpet-bombing raids on Cambodia and Laos, the United States had released more than 4.7 million tons of ordnance in over half a million sorties.[2] At least 100,000 civilians are credibly reported to have died alongside Viet Cong insurgents. In contrast, some 500 secret US bombings in Pakistan, Yemen, and Somalia between 2002 and 2014 had resulted in no more than 250 tons of precision-guided ordnance being released, according to the author's calculations, causing an estimated 500 noncombatant deaths. While still troubling, this was a far remove from the indiscriminate bombings of earlier wars.[3]

While most controversy focused on America's secret wars, the drone's primary impact had actually been on the conventional battlefield—where an estimated four out of five of all remote strikes had taken place. It was above Afghanistan and Iraq where the US Air Force and its British allies learned how best to use this revolutionary weapons system. Friendly troops on the ground were originally fearful, concerned that operators thousands of miles distant would be less able to protect them. Yet over time—and as armed drones became ubiquitous—the Predator and Reaper emerged as key assets. Convoys of troops and materiel would often be accompanied by a drone providing top cover, seeking out ambushes or tell-tales for improvised explosive devices (IEDs) along the route. The aircraft were also crucial to the intelligence revolution now taking place in US warfighting. Terabytes of surveillance data were being sucked up daily from the War on Terror's many battlefields, with armed drones often at the forefront of that program. Uniquely they were then able to act immediately on any findings, a situation which led to the increased use of targeted killings on the regular battlefield. According to former military intelligence officers, assassinations became commonplace in both Afghanistan and Iraq.

Back home in the United States, the Air Force readily embraced the remote warfare revolution. Many conventional warplane squadrons were transitioned to unmanned aircraft, with thousands of remote operators and intelligence analysts now fighting their wars from concrete boxes, far from the frontlines. With recruitment difficult, the Pentagon thought this to be a plus—surely personnel able to fight their wars by day then return home to families at night would be happier? They were not. Removed from the battlefield, remote operators were unable to decompress from difficult missions. Working hours were grueling. A six-month stint in Afghanistan for manned crews could be as long as three years for those in Nevada or New Mexico. And the very intimacy which drone operations allowed—the ability to observe unseen the most intimate of human acts—also carried its own horrors, with operators forced to watch powerless as atrocities were committed far away. Psychologists are having to invent a new language to describe the damaging effects of this remote warfare on military personnel.

For a few short years, the United States and Israel had enjoyed an extraordinary duopoly in the manufacture and use of armed drones. It was a select club, with only Britain invited to join. Yet proliferation was inevitable, with dozens of nations aggressively pursuing their own programs. More ominously, so too were terrorist and militant groups. In the hours before the United States began its own attacks on Syria, a little-noticed announcement by Hezbollah in August 2014 claimed that the Lebanese militia had itself successfully fired missiles from a drone at Sunni radicals across the border.[4] The future of drone warfare promised to be far more chaotic—and far more deadly. America's own use of armed drones during the War on Terror would likely set the template—for good and for bad—of what would follow.

VIEW TO A KILL
Armed Drones on the Battlefield

In early 2011, the 284th and final Predator remotely piloted aircraft came off the California production line of makers General Atomics, prompting the company to throw a celebratory party. There that March day to receive the last Predator for the US Air Force (USAF) was Colonel Jim Beissner, a veteran pilot with 400 hours of combat experience—many of them in Afghanistan. He recalls an enjoyable day of events and speeches at General Atomics' private Gray Butte airfield: "It was a great ceremony. They had the last MQ-1 sitting in the hangar, a huge crowd of General Atomics folks out there, and then spread throughout were military folks who'd worked on the program or who had flown the aircraft."

Beissner believes that by the time of this last handover, the MQ1-Predator had already secured its place in aviation history, up there with iconic aircraft like the P-51 Mustang and the F-16: "The MQ-1 was the statement-maker for the unmanned aerial vehicles because it was armed and operational, and that rang throughout the whole ceremony. The capability of the airplane, and the fact that though it was our last, it certainly wasn't going away." Indeed, the 100 or so remaining Predators in the Air Force fleet would be worked relentlessly in the years to come as the War on Terror ground on. By late 2013, they had amassed between them more than 1.5 million flying hours during an estimated 60,000 combat missions over Afghanistan, Iraq, Yemen, Pakistan, Somalia, and Libya (only a fraction of which had ended in violence).[1] Unlike many of his colleagues, Beissner had resisted transitioning to unmanned aircraft. Yet his was likely to be the last generation in which the majority of Air Force pilots physically flew combat planes. By 2010, USAF had already begun training more drone pilots than fighter and bomber pilots combined.[2] As for the final Predator, tail number 268 was eventually based out of Washington State, where as one Air Force press officer joked to the author, it was "probably spying on Vancouver."

Only a little longer than the average station wagon, the Predator's light-weight composite skin helped it remain airborne for up to 24 hours. With its modified snowmobile engine, early versions of the remotely piloted air-craft rarely passed speeds of 85 mph. Although the word "Predator" had swiftly become media shorthand for any action by an armed drone, the aircraft itself was fast being replaced by the MQ-9 Reaper (also manufac-tured by General Atomics). At almost twice the size, the Reaper carried many more weapons—usually four Hellfire missiles and a pair of 500 lb precision-guided bombs. With a cruising speed of around 200 mph, it could also reach targets faster, though with three times the weight it could rarely stay aloft for more than 18 hours. Neither was a particularly sophisticated airframe, with operators comparing them to early Wright Brothers models. Where that comparison ended was with the technology crammed onto the platforms themselves. The sensor ball carried by every armed drone was packed with full-motion video cameras; infra-red capa-bilities; tracking technologies and a laser targeting designator. Each drone also carried sophisticated and highly classified electronic warfare pods attached to reinforced hard points on the wings. These were used to scoop up intelligence from the ground—from cellphones, Wi-Fi signals, or tiny hidden tracking devices—information which might then be used to target and kill those being spied on.

Despite the fearsome reputation of armed drones, their lethal use on the battlefield was at first uncommon. Known as hunter-killers in Air Force parlance, even in 2014 their focus still remained mostly on intelligence, surveillance, and reconnaissance (ISR). Predators and Reapers were just some of the manned and unmanned aircraft traversing US theaters of war daily, in search of information on the enemy. At its 2011 peak, more than 38,000 of these ISR sorties were flown in Afghanistan. "In the twenty-first century, intelligence, surveillance, and reconnaissance is operations. It's not support to operations," insists retired USAF Lt. General Dave Deptula, who oversaw a massive expansion in US armed drones between 2006 and 2010.

> We've spent the past 100 years trying to figure out how to hit any target anywhere on the surface of the earth, all weather, day or night, rapidly and with precision. Guess what—we can do that. In other words we figured out the Finish part of the Find, Fix, and Finish equation. The real challenges are in the Finding and the Fixing, or the determining of what kinds of effects you want to achieve through kinetic or non-kinetic action.[3]

Of all of those ISR assets, only the Predator and Reaper had the ability not only to Find and Fix but also directly to Finish targets in real time. "If you're a terrorist and I am an intelligence expert, I generally need to know not where you are but where you're going to be at flight time plus preparation time plus approval time from my strike asset," says counterterrorism adviser David Kilcullen. "But if my strike asset is the same drone that's surveilling you, I could have a two second, three second turnaround and I can strike now."[4] For those few countries with access to the technology, the embracing of armed drones had been swift. Britain's Ministry of Defence revealed that by 2014, four out of five of its airstrikes in Afghanistan were now being carried out by remotely piloted aircraft.[5]

Even when not directly responsible for a strike, on thousands more occasions drones helped facilitate attacks from other air assets, by providing intelligence and by guiding other aircraft to target. As Charles Blanchard, General Counsel for the Department of the Air Force noted in 2011, "Most of the strikes that are occurring in Afghanistan right now are not by MQ-1s [Predators] or MQ-9s [Reapers], they are being done by other air platforms. That being said, it's very likely that the reconnaissance, surveillance and intelligence assets of the Reaper and Predator were instrumental in virtually every one of those strikes."[6]

To exploit this tremendous asymmetric battlefield advantage, two overlapping drone campaigns have evolved since 2001. According to

Table 1.1 US drone strikes: Minimum estimates by conflict 2001–2013

Year	Afghanistan 2001–2013	Iraq 2003–2011	Pakistan 2004–2013	Yemen 2002; 2011–2013	Somalia 2011–2013	Libya 2011	Total
	1,670	158	381	64	8	145	2,426

Note: Iraq and Afghanistan data includes some missions crewed by British military personnel. Sources include CENTCOM, British MoD, NATO, and monitoring organizations the Bureau of Investigative Journalism, and New America Foundation.

data gathered by the author, of an estimated 2,500 drone strikes carried out by the United States and Britain over a 12-year period, some three-quarters—around 1,900 strikes—took place on the conventional battlefields of Afghanistan, Iraq, and Libya (see table 1.1). Most of those were in turn the work of regular USAF drone squadrons and their Royal Air Force allies, flying in support of Coalition forces on the ground. Yet hundreds more attacks by armed drones had been carried out in secret by US Special Forces and the CIA, often far from the hot battle-field. The particular suitability of these remotely piloted aircraft for one task—assassination—ensured that they would become one of the most controversial weapons of modern times.

Path to a Drone Killing

In 2013 the United States was still embroiled in Afghanistan, a dozen years after it had first invaded the impoverished nation in the hunt for Al Qaeda. With the public back home now tired of the longest war in US history, President Barack Obama had insisted most troops would withdraw by the end of the following year. Yet the United States was not completely through. The Pentagon's Joint Special Operations Command, its elite force, still ran major intelligence operations to identify key insurgents whose removal from the battle space was thought likely to cripple Taliban operations. Drone strikes were deemed particularly effective in suppressing militant activity. The Obama administration's plan in 2013 was that even if most of its remaining 39,000 US troops departed, this clandestine Afghan war would continue. Washington did not want to see the Taliban, or worse Al Qaeda, back in power.[7]

To ensure a continued military presence, the United States needed to conclude a Bilateral Security Agreement with Kabul. Talks had become bogged down, with President Hamid Karzai balking at some of Washington's conditions—most controversially the demand for a permanent exemption of any remaining US forces from potential prosecution under Afghan domestic law.[8] Two years earlier, Iraq had refused what it deemed similarly onerous terms, and so instead of leaving behind a planned contingent of Predators and Special Forces, the United States had left. Now in late 2013, Baghdad was calling for the return of those same armed drones. Islamic State, the Al Qaeda-backed group, had carved out a major base of operations in northern Syria during that country's civil war, and it now threatened to overrun many of Iraq's own cities.[9] The Obama administration was keen to conclude the Afghan agreement and so prevent a similar fiasco. Yet a botched US drone strike was about to hand President Karzai fresh negotiating leverage.

On a clear November morning in 2013, Nazir Gul was making his way by motorbike through southern Helmand province. Allegedly a mid-level Taliban commander, according to local officials, Gul was also a proficient smuggler of weapons and explosives. As he approached the village of Faqiran, Gul was oblivious to the MQ-9 Reaper 18,000 feet above him, which was now tracking his every move. He could also not know he had been marked for death. The same armed drone observing Gul—the successor to the Predator—was able to strike thanks to onboard software which could lock onto moving vehicles. With the remotely piloted aircraft's laser invisibly "painting" the motorbike, one of the drone's Hellfire missiles was fired. It should have been a straightforward operation, one of many hundreds of targeted killings carried out by USAF drones since 9/11. Instead, Gul was blown off his motorbike as the first missile hit nearby. A young boy named Jamil was instead killed and two women seriously injured. Undeterred, perhaps even unaware of the civilian casualties thanks to their restricted view of the terrain below, the Reaper's distant operators continued their pursuit of Nazir Gul, now escaping on foot. A second Hellfire killed him as he ran.

After so many years of war in Afghanistan, the killing of Jamil and the alleged Taliban commander would usually have warranted little media interest. The intervention of the country's long-serving president changed that equation "This attack shows that American forces are not respecting the life and safety of Afghan people's houses," Hamid Karzai protested. He expressed particular anger that the United States had authorized the drone strike without consulting his own government. As a Pentagon report had noted just days beforehand, Afghan security forces "now conduct 95% of conventional operations and 98% of special operations in Afghanistan."[10] Why then had Kabul not been informed of this mission? While most American combat personnel were grouped alongside those of other nations within the International Security Assistance Force (ISAF), America's elite troops were instead part of Operation Enduring Freedom. Here, far less restrictive Rules of Engagement meant that Special Forces could operate in Afghanistan with little regard for the democratically elected government—or even for allied Western forces. "You could not tell them anything," recalls Mike Martin, who served as an intelligence officer in Afghanistan with the British Army. "They continuously got it wrong and killed the wrong people—or even killed the right people, but they shouldn't have killed them because actually we were talking to them at the same time."[11]

Angered by this latest unilateral American Special Forces action, Hamid Karzai used the death of one child in a single US drone strike to bring bilateral negotiations to a complete halt: "There will be no security agreement between Kabul and Washington, if these unilateral military operations by arrogant and oppressive foreign troops on our people continue," he threatened.[12] Aides to the top US commander in Afghanistan insisted that General Joseph Dunford "talked to President Karzai directly, expressed deep regrets for the incident and any civilian casualties, and promised to convene an immediate joint investigation to determine all the facts of what happened."[13] The apology had little effect: Karzai chose to leave any bilateral agreement decision to whichever candidate eventually succeeded him, leaving US policy in crisis. A deal was eventually signed with his successor in late 2014, just 12 weeks before US troops would have had to pull out entirely.[14]

Afghanistan's people had paid a high price in the ongoing struggle between the Taliban and pro-government forces, with at least 19,000 civilian deaths resulting from six years of fighting from 2007 alone.[15] By a significant margin, most of these fatalities were the work of the Taliban according to the United Nations Assistance Mission in Afghanistan (UNAMA). Insurgent actions accounted for three-quarters of civilian deaths in 2013, for example, including over 700 people assassinated in the Taliban's own targeted killing campaign.[16] Yet just a few years earlier,

pro- and anti-government forces had been killing almost as many civilians as each other.[17] "What we've seen is a large, significant reduction
in civilian casualties by pro-government forces, mainly international
forces," noted a senior UNAMA official. She attributed that steep fall to
three factors. The accurate documenting of deaths was crucial in holding
parties to account, as was a realization by the international Coalition that
"the counter-insurgency effort is not advanced with civilian casualties."
The third factor was a continuing public pressure from Afghanistan's
government.

Some critics had represented Karzai's concern at the death of civilians
in drone strikes as a ploy to gain leverage in talks with Washington.[18] This
was unfair, given that his intervention was part of an eight-year long skir-
mish with the United States and its allies over noncombatant deaths.[19] The
president's official spokesman had complained in summer 2013, for example, that "we are strongly against drone strikes in our territory—it is not
an effective way to fight terrorists. We cannot allow airstrikes to target one
or two insurgents because of the sheer number of civilian casualties they
result in."[20] According to the senior UN official, "if Karzai had not been so
vocal about civilian casualties, there would not have been such a reduction
in civilian casualties caused by international forces and the greater attention paid to the issue by them."[21]

When civilians were killed by the Coalition, airstrikes were most often
responsible. And there were concerns at the increasingly violent role that
US and British drones were now playing in such operations. In response,
the United Nations had begun separately tracking drone strikes and related
casualties. The indications were alarming. While overall civilian deaths
caused by Coalition aircraft fell by a tenth to 125 killed in 2013, noncombatant casualties from drone strikes alone had actually tripled, to at least
45 fatalities. A Pentagon-funded study of classified Afghanistan airstrike
data by Dr. Larry Lewis had also found that drone strikes "were an order
of magnitude more likely to result in civilian casualties per engagement"
than manned aircraft.[22] Something about the way armed drones were
being used in Afghanistan was becoming a problem. A significant number of these RPA bombings were offensive actions, pre-planned operations
focused on targeted strikes or killings. Nazir Gul and 8-year-old Jamil had
died in just such an attack. UN officials began publicly expressing worries

that as the US draw-down neared, Washington risked a greater dependence on these secretive and less accountable drone strikes:

> UNAMA notes the lack of transparency and accountability on the use of UAVs [unmanned aerial vehicles] to carry out targeted killings and/or that resulted in civilian casualties. In spite of requests to international military forces, UNAMA has not received information on the legal framework and operational policies used to guide pre-engagement targeting criteria . . . and measures in place to prevent civilian casualties.[23]

As ISAF later privately confirmed to the United Nations, the mission which targeted and killed Nazir Gul in November 2013 had been run by the Combined Joint Special Operations Task Force (CJSOTF)—an elite command headquartered at Bagram Air Base which ran most US counterinsurgency and counterterrorism operations in Afghanistan.[24] One of its core units was Joint Special Operations Command (JSOC.) The main operational emphasis here had once been on capturing targets to harvest their intelligence potential. "One of our mottos was 'A dead terrorist is one we can't talk to,'" says retired Colonel Pete Forrest, who helped pioneer the use of Predator remotely piloted aircraft (RPAs) by Special Forces.[25] Yet now, US ground forces had handed over much of their work to their Afghan equivalents. And despite southern Helmand province being under supposed government control, its districts ranked among the most dangerous in Afghanistan.[26] US Special Forces, unwilling to attempt a capture of Nazir Gul, instead dispatched a Reaper to target and kill him.

President Bush had once boasted of America's newfound ability to deliver "sudden justice" to its enemies beyond the battlefield, with the Predator developed as an assassination tool for the CIA expressly to deliver that capability (see chapter 2).[27] Yet over time, the use of armed drones for targeted killings had become a mundane reality even on the regular battlefield. The British RAF—which only flew conventional drone missions in Afghanistan—has admitted to carrying out at least seven targeted killings in 2012, for example.[28] "Having identified the insurgent, the crew were given authority to attack but elected not to do so as they had observed him entering a Bazaar. The Reaper crew followed this individual for a further 7 hours before carrying out a successful attack," the RAF reported in one case.[29] On the same day that Gul was killed in Helmand, a second alleged Taliban commander was also killed by a drone nearby, without controversy.[30]

In seeking out alleged militants solely for killing, US and British tactics had begun resembling more closely those in neighboring Pakistan. There, for a decade, the CIA had carried out hundreds of targeted assassinations by drone—a controversial policy which had helped bring relations between Washington and Islamabad to the point of collapse (see chapter 10). Karzai was determined not to see the same tactic become dominant in Afghanistan. In this he had some surprising allies. General Stanley McChrystal, the former JSOC commander who had also once led US and Coalition forces in Afghanistan, later emerged as a potent critic of an overdependence on armed drones. Warning there was a danger that a drone strike "lowers the threshold for taking operations because it feels easy," McChrystal summarized his concerns:

> There's a perception of arrogance, there is a perception of helpless people in an area being shot at like thunderbolts from the sky by an entity that is acting as though they have omniscience and omnipotence. And you can create a tremendous amount of resentment inside populations, not even the people that are themselves being targeted but around, because of the way it appears and feels. So I think that we need to be very, very cautious. What seems like a panacea to the messiness of war is not that at all. . . . And wars are ultimately determined in the minds of populations.[31]

Yet in a climate of military draw-downs and unpopular wars, the potential of armed drones held great appeal not only within Washington's vast military-intelligence machine but within government itself. As counterterrorism expert David Kilcullen notes, for the Obama administration their ability to provide tactical victories while keeping boots off the ground was "making the drones as addictive as catnip."[32]

AIR FORCE SPECIAL OPERATIONS COMMAND

The Reaper which carried out the lethal strike on Nazir Gul that November 2013 morning had been physically launched from the major Coalition airfield at nearby Kandahar. Yet its remote operators were based some 7,600 miles away, part of the elite Air Force Special Operations Command, or AFSOC. Cannon Air Force Base in New Mexico was home to the 3rd and 33rd Special Operations Squadrons, respectively, the Predator and Reaper drone units of AFSOC. The isolated base was unpopular with some of the hundreds of aircrew there, thanks in part to its proximity to the vast cattle ranges of nearby west Texas. "There's no oxygen out there, just cow poop," one long-serving operator jokes. Yet Cannon lay at the heart of a clandestine US program, which had majorly impacted the Afghan Taliban, and before them Al Qaeda in Iraq.

Housed in reinforced buildings on the base was a cluster of individual rooms known as ground control stations (GCS), each home to a two-person crew "flying a line"—Air Force-speak for an individual mission. While the pilot remotely flew the aircraft and the sensor operator handled all of the onboard technologies, both were responsible for any missile strike. Resembling a claustrophobic flight simulator, crews spent most of their eight hours a day, six days a week shifts confined within their GCS "boxes."[33] As Brandon Bryant, a former Predator sensor operator with AFSOC has described it, "Your 'office' is 8 feet wide, 7.5 feet tall, and 30 feet long. Most of it is filled with computers. You need a special code to get into each box, and you're pretty much alone with your partner for the duration of the shift. It's always kept at 68 degrees [Fahrenheit], so you're cold. And the lights are typically off."[34]

The idea behind the GCS was to create a unique sense of place and time. Midnight at the New Mexico air base was 11.30 a.m. in Afghanistan, and crews were not just limited to one theater. Major Chad Bruton, a pilot who flew with AFSOC for two years up to 2008, might find himself in two different wars on the same shift: "We would show up, we would get a briefing then we'd go to whichever box was ours. I usually did Afghanistan first, and we'd be in there for 4 hours and then we got a break. Then we might go to a different box in the other theater, Iraq, and do a 4 hour mission there. The magic of satellites."[35]

The pilot and sensor operator were just two of scores of personnel involved in any mission. The Air Force measured its fleet of armed drones in Combat Air Patrols (CAPs), referring to the number of simultaneous missions it could field over any 24-hour period. Directly serving any one CAP could be as many as 200 people.[36] Up to 50 aircrew were involved in remotely flying the aircraft. Separately, as many as 80 intelligence analysts and associated staff might also contribute, offering real-time analysis of the drone's feeds. Meanwhile on the ground, 70 Air Force and contractor personnel provided the maintenance and launch teams needed to keep each Reaper or Predator CAP almost permanently airborne. At its 2013 peak the Air Force was able to field 63 simultaneous armed drone missions in any one 24-hour period, remotely operated from eight air bases across the United States. What proportion of those were Special Forces CAPs—and where they flew—remained classified. However the Air Force bundled Cannon's missions (along with those of the CIA's own drone squadrons) into its overall tallies, with officials admitting in 2012 to CAPs "mostly in Afghanistan, Pakistan and areas around Yemen and the Africa coast."[37]

Despite the apparent isolation of pilots and sensor operators in their boxy rooms, feeds from every mission or "line" were piped in real-time to the base's nearby Operations Cell. "In the center of this huge room was a sort of stage where the Flight Operation Supervisor and the Mission Intelligence Coordinator would sit, and where Weather would be monitoring Afghanistan and other theaters," recalls a former analyst. Here additional operators were on permanent standby for when missions went "kinetic," or to cover those needing bathroom and meal breaks: the screens of a ground control station could never be left unattended. Live video feeds from a Reaper or Predator mission could also be seen by others. Forward air controllers and combat troops on the ground were able to direct a drone to target using a handheld ROVER, a military-grade tablet device which received data direct from an overhead drone.[38] More than a dozen remote intelligence hubs in the United States, Europe, and Asia could also receive the feeds, enabling analysts to provide expert advice in real time. Linked up too might be the Central Intelligence Agency, the National Security Agency, or the Pentagon. On rare occasions, senior officials all the way up to the president might also be watching.

"The good news about the Predator is it's got a full motion video sensor that can get a picture to anywhere on earth within three seconds. The bad news is the Predator's got a full motion video sensor on its nose that can get a picture anywhere in three seconds," jokes Major General Jim Poss, who retired as Director of Air Force Intelligence at the end of 2012. In the early the days of the Predator the ability of commanders and politicians to see live feeds of missions had been a problem says Poss. "The issue was our higher-ups were demanding that this real time feed go everywhere. It could be at CENTCOM, it could be at the White House, it could be the Pentagon. We eventually had to evolve rules and put positions in place to make sure that, you know, this is an exaggeration, to make sure the president didn't call the Predator pilot up."[39] Defense Secretary Donald Rumsfeld shared those concerns, refusing to have Predator feeds piped into his own office at the Pentagon and asking "that they be turned off in any offices that had no compelling reason to receive them."[40]

To prevent drone operators being overwhelmed by these multiple observers, the Air Force evolved a system of using text-only chat rooms rather than voice communications. Each mission featured up to a dozen such digital conversations. Command and control by the forward "customer" occupied the key chat room, with others for remote intelligence analysis. Military lawyers would also be monitoring up to 20 different missions, on hand to advise when needed.[41] To help insulate USAF crews further, a gate-keeper position was created—the Mission Intelligence Co-ordinator (MC), whose role was to interface between the pilot and sensor operator in their room and the world outside. Only the MC, for example, could usually talk by voice to the pilot and sensor operator, while also directly speaking with the "customer" and with intelligence analysts elsewhere. Every drone mission had a dedicated MC, and each sat at a screen in the Operations Cell. "My job is to be the pilot's computer bitch," jokes Janet Atkins, who served as an MC with AFSOC for three years.

All drone missions worked for a customer. For conventional operations this would generally be the local military ground commander. For those Air Force personnel flying secret missions in Pakistan or Yemen, the CIA would call the shots. And for Air Force Special Operations Command's fleet, the customer was often JSOC. Yet despite being part of a Special Forces squadron, Cannon's operators would sometimes be told little about a job. "It depended on how open they were being with us," recalls Chad Bruton, a former AFSOC pilot. "Sometimes you'd get a really good one that would really tell you what was going on and would give you a brief of what they had done on this target previously, and what specific kind of stuff they were looking for, what the higher objectives were. Then you had other ones who didn't feel like sharing anything." For some of those on the Special Forces customer side, a Reaper or Predator was simply there to do what it was told. Often JSOC analysts had little knowledge—or interest—in where a drone was being remotely piloted from: "The pilot has very little say-so in what happens. Yes they pull the trigger and they will sometimes have to say if there's a problem with the bird. If it's going to crash that's kind of their responsibility to make sure it doesn't," one former intelligence analyst for JSOC told the author. "But even those decisions can be over-ridden. They can be told, 'Hey, you better fly this until it does crash.' And they'll have to do that."[42]

Like hundreds of others in Afghanistan, Nazir Gul had been designated a figure in the Taliban insurgency whose removal was deemed crucial to the war effort. In Iraq, similar tactics had been used to drive Sunni insurgents to the negotiating table. "The idea is, identify the 1% or 2% of people that are absolutely irreconcilable, kill only them, but do it so heavily that everybody who is reconcilable wants to make peace. And then give the people that want to make peace such a good deal that you suck oxygen from the irreconcilables," recounts David Kilcullen, one of that campaign's architects.[43] Analysts from across the military and intelligence communities would profile targets. "You've got a bunch of agent handlers who gather the intelligence, then that goes to an intelligence cell that fuses it and comes up with the answer; we need to kill this guy. Then the Special Forces go out and actually kill him," says one former ISAF military intelligence officer of the process.[44] According to another, a former JSOC analyst, "the target development process for someone in Afghanistan, once they've gotten to the point where they're determined they're going after this person, once it gets to the tactical phase it's usually a matter of weeks—those people come off the battlefield relatively quickly."[45]

The Afghanistan Kill/Capture program was run from a large, reinforced shed-like building at Bagram Airfield, known as the Joint Operations Center: "The JOC is kind of like a conference center where everyone's looking in one direction, and that one direction is just a bunch of different screens, displaying a different feed from a different sensor on a different asset in a different part of the country," recalls Daniel Hale, who worked as an intelligence analyst with CJSOTF, the Combined Joint Special Operations Task Force. "Within that space there are people doing all sorts of things: asset management, collection managers, weather monitors, people making sure planes don't run into each other. There were liaisons from just about every intelligence agency. Reps of every military branch," says Hale. "So it was a central part of the mission in Afghanistan: there would be no mission without it." Also vital to CJSOTF's drone missions were the "screeners," Special Forces analysts with the 11th Intelligence Squadron based back at Hurlburt Field in Florida, who would pore over video images and other field intelligence to build up target profiles. The decision to kill Gul would have been approved by the JOC's commanding officer, in consultation with Pentagon lawyers.

The Reaper's upgraded high-definition cameras were still incapable of picking an alleged insurgent out from a crowd. Instead Nazir Gul was almost certainly betrayed either by human intelligence or by his mobile phone signal, which a special pod on the Reaper known as the GMESH (short for Gilgamesh) could target with ease. Former Special Forces analysts, while aware of the pod's purpose, were unwilling to discuss its precise abilities with the author. However in early 2014 journalists Glenn Greenwald and Jeremy Scahill, citing leaked NSA documents and "a former JSOC operator," reported that "the [GMESH] device locates the SIM card or handset that the military believes is used by the target." The duo also revealed the existence of a second secret NSA pod system, codenamed "Shenanigans," which "utilizes a pod on aircraft that vacuums up massive amounts of data from any wireless routers, computers, smart phones or other electronic devices that are within range."[46]

In preparation for any attack, the Operations Cell back at Cannon AFB would already have sent a second pilot to the ground control station flying the mission. Their job was to be the safety observer. Local airspace coordinators had to be informed of a possible missile strike, and a check made that there were no "friendlies" or civilians in the area—a check which on this occasion clearly failed. Finally, the drone would be cleared to engage. The Reaper which attacked Gul fired two Hellfire missiles, the first of which missed its target and hit nearby civilians. Safety procedures should have prevented this. Even during what was usually a 15 to 20 second flight, a Hellfire missile could still be forced off-course to a pre-decided "safe" point for detonation. A former AFSOC sensor operator describes the process: "The pilot gives us a safety brief, a ready brief and says, 'Well if we're told to abort the fire shot, this is where you're going to drag the crosshair and you're going to guide the missile over to this location.' And we sit there and he asks if everyone is ready to fire and the safety observer says 'Go ahead and fire if you've completed all these tasks.' The pilot checks everything and if everything looks fine he counts down to missile rifle, he rifles the missile, counts down to impact and splash."[47] The Reaper would have remained for a time to carry out a Battle Damage Assessment, and would then have been assigned to another mission or have returned to base.

Despite the gung-ho media image of US Special Operations Forces, armed drones flown by AFSOC had traditionally been far less likely to fire on a target than those operated by conventional USAF squadrons. The emphasis instead was on forensic intelligence-gathering, at least until Barack Obama wanted AFSOC's drones to begin more regular targeted killings. The contrast with conventional units could be stark. The Nevada-based 15th Reconnaissance Squadron was one of the Air Force's heavy-workhorse conventional drone units, and its Predators frequently saw combat, often while protecting troops below. "The year [2006] that I was in the 15th, there were about 140 missiles fired. There was one sensor operator that had 14 shots just to their name," says former sensor operator Brandon Bryant. "When we got to the 3rd [Special Operations Squadron] I think there were 6 shots fired that first year by the entire squadron, total."

Many pilots and sensor operators assigned to AFSOC's elite squadrons report personally carrying out only one or two lethal strikes in their entire time there. The impact of killing a child was therefore likely to have been particularly strongly felt by any crew involved. Once an error was suspected, "everything freezes that has to do with that particular incident, including the GCS and all the tapes, and everything is frozen and kept as evidence," according to retired Lt. Col. Bruce Black, who for many years flew with conventional Predator squadrons. "Then a separate group—not from that squadron—somebody from somewhere else comes and reviews the evidence and reviews everything that is going on, both on the side of the Air Force and on who we were supporting if there was Special Operations, or if it's Army or it's Navy." Steve, a former Predator pilot, insists that lessons were learned from such situations: "You take that and you actually do train within the squadron, you take those lessons and you go through it and say, 'Where could we have helped? Where could we have done this better? How did things fall through the cracks here?' "[48]

However, by 2013, many of AFSOC's drone operations now more closely resembled those of the CIA in neighboring Pakistan—not only in the sharply escalating use of targeted killings but also in the obsessive secrecy which surrounded such operations when they went wrong.

Despite a proclaimed US inquiry into the death of a child in the Nazir Gul attack, whatever lessons were learned remained secret. Both the Pentagon and ISAF have refused to discuss any aspect of the drone strike. Noting that "US Forces-Afghanistan has release authority for the investigation into this incident" (tacit acknowledgment that the bombing was the work of US Special Forces), ISAF's spokesman declared that "the command has decided not to release the investigation due to operational security and classification concerns."[49] Subsequent Freedom of Information requests were rebuffed. It remained publicly unknown what had gone wrong in the attack on Gul; what lessons might have been learned; and even what compensation had been paid to affected families. Improved transparency by ISAF forces had played a key role in driving down civilian deaths in Afghanistan, according to UN monitors. Yet if, as many anticipated, Washington left behind only armed drones and troops under Special Forces command after any draw-down, such transparency and accountability appeared unlikely to survive.

THE CIA'S DRONE SQUADRONS

Whatever the controversies caused by the battlefield use of drones, it had been their use elsewhere by the CIA which had caught the public's imagination. As a result of the rapid shift toward remote warfare, by 2014 the Air Force had stood up almost two dozen armed drone squadrons across eight different US states, remotely crewed by thousands of USAF airmen, reservists, and Air National Guard. Even so, the core of the drone program remained at Creech Air Force Base near Las Vegas, Nevada. Creech housed four of the most active conventional Predator and Reaper squadrons in the Air Force, as well as its main training unit.[50] Yet there was also another, far more secretive cluster of squadrons at the Nevada base. The 732nd Operations Group blandly stated that it "employs remotely piloted aircraft in theaters across the globe year-round." In reality its own four drone squadrons worked with the Central Intelligence Agency.[51] The 30th Reconnaissance Squadron "test-flew" the RQ-170 Sentinel, the CIA's stealth drone which made headlines after one was captured over Iran in December 2011.[52] The 22nd and 867th Reconnaissance Squadrons each flew Predators and Reapers: little was known about their activities by

2014, though they may have been tasked with CIA operations in Yemen (the souvenir coffee mug for the 22nd RS carried the motto "Seek and Destroy"). The Air Force would confirm only that each of the squadrons was operational.[53]

Most crucial of all to the CIA was the 17th Reconnaissance Squadron, a USAF unit which over the course of more than a decade had remotely conducted hundreds of targeted killings outside conventional warzones. Operating from an ultra-secure inner compound at Creech, the 17th RS, as it was better known, was made up of some 300 aircrew. Estimates of the number of armed drones which the CIA had access to across its squadrons—all still "owned" by the Air Force—ranged from 45 to 80 aircraft, a significant proportion of an estimated 400 USAF armed Reapers and Predators.[54] Established in 2002,[55] the 17th RS has carried out more "kills" than perhaps any other drone unit in the Air Force, with an estimated 2,400 directly attributed deaths in Pakistan by mid-2014. According to one former drone operator at Creech, "Everyone talks about CIA over Pakistan, CIA double-tap, CIA over Yemen, CIA over Somalia and Mogadishu. But I don't believe that they deserve the entirety of all that credit for the drone program. They might drive the missions, they might say that these are the objectives, accomplish it. They don't fly it. Probably makes it easier for them to give the [kill] order you know?"[56]

Even for other Air Force operators at the base, secrecy around the CIA's drone squadrons was absolute. On one occasion, the 17th RS needed to make use of a Ground Control Station belonging to a regular unit. "They wouldn't even let us walk by it, they were just so protective of it," says Michael Haas, a former sensor operator and trainer at Creech. "From what I was able to gather, it was pretty much confirmed they were flying missions almost exclusively in Pakistan with the intent to strike. And that's about really all I could gather from it." Even military VIPs were unable to access the squadron's secure compound when visiting the base: "They were treating that little squadron like the Crown Jewels or something. They don't let anybody in there unless they have the patch and the badge. Makes you wonder what they were trying to hide, really," says Haas.[57]

In Creech's Operations Cell, which received video feeds from every drone operation flown from the base, mission coordinators (MCs) from the 17th RS were kept segregated from all others. "They set up their MC in the same building as our squadron but they had a special room that they closed off just for him or her," recalled another MC. "It was an odd time, we kept being told 'Don't ask what they're doing! Don't ask what they're doing!'" Further firewalling the CIA's operations, Air Force pilots and operators were never forward-deployed to launch and land drones from the Agency's forward bases. Instead, private contractors carried out that work. Blackwater's former president Erik Prince has confirmed the company's erstwhile role in maintaining the CIA's secret Pakistan drone fleet role, though he denied ever supplying launch and recovery crews: "I didn't have any drone pilots. We loaded them, we protected them in secret bases, and we were hanging Hellfires on them."[58]

Air Force personnel were closely directed by civilian analysts at the CIA and had little direct input into their missions according to one former USAF officer with knowledge of the unit. "Their customer's more closed: 'Just go here, just watch that, be ready when I tell you!' . . . Their [the CIA's] intel analysts were really the job."[59] There were other hints at the unit's role. An early squadron leader later outlined his job as "Commanded military, government employees, and contractors in conduct of continuous worldwide global War on Terror combat operations in support of DoD and other government agencies."[60] And a sensor operator who left the squadron in 2012 has described their own role as "non-traditional ISR operations" in which they conducted "operations tasked by senior US government officials using unique advanced tactics for target tracking and destruction. Operates RPA to collect intelligence on national priority targets and accurately guide precision weapons to target."[61]

The revelation that regular Air Force personnel were carrying out lethal strikes on the orders of civilian intelligence officials was a cause of concern for some.[62] "It will come as a surprise to most Americans if the CIA is directing the military to carry out warlike activities. The agency should be collecting and analysing foreign intelligence, not presiding over a massive killing apparatus," complained the American Civil Liberties Union's Hina Shamsi. "We don't know precisely what rules the CIA is operating under, but what we do know makes clear that it's not abiding by the laws that strictly limit extrajudicial killing both in and out of traditional battlefields. Now we have to ask whether the regular military is violating those laws as well, under the secrecy that the CIA wields as sword and shield over its killing activities."[63] This use of regular USAF personnel to carry out targeted killings on behalf of a civilian intelligence agency did not sit well with some fellow airmen either. Former AFSOC sensor operator Brandon Bryant decided to speak out about the CIA's squadron after hearing that the Obama administration aimed to "transfer" control of the CIA's secret drones program to the military: "There is a lie hidden within that truth. And the lie is that it's always been the Air Force that has flown those missions. CIA might be the customer, but the Air Force has always flown it," he says. "I think they're gonna be like, 'We're gonna create a squadron at Creech Air Force Base that is flying these missions. And then these people that have always been there are magically gonna show up, and they're gonna officially take over and everyone's going be cheering because transparency is being pretended to be given to the public. That's how I see it.' "[64]

The National Security Council and the CIA declined to comment to the author on the role of the 17th RS, although a spokesman for Creech AFB confirmed that the four squadrons of the 732nd Operations Group were all active, that each was involved in "global operations" and that "their mission is to perform high-quality, persistent, multi-role intelligence, surveillance, and reconnaissance in support of combatant commanders' needs."[65]

AFSOC's Secret Pakistan Missions

Despite the widespread portrayal of many US drone operations as the work solely of the CIA or of JSOC, in reality the US targeted killing program had always involved multiple players. Personnel from the military, the CIA, the NSA, and other intelligence agencies would jointly assess terabytes of data gathered in the field by drones and other assets every day. On the ground, US Special Forces might assist with CIA missions. The targeted assassination of Al Qaeda leader Osama bin Laden in June 2011 was actually carried out by JSOC troops under CIA leadership, for example. Three months later this was echoed when an Agency drone killed US citizen Anwar al Awlaki. Investigative reporter Jeremy Scahill has described the complex logistics involved:

> As the vehicles made their way over the dusty, unpaved roads, US drones, armed with Hellfire missiles, were dispatched to hunt them down. The drones were technically under the command of the CIA,

though JSOC aircraft and ground forces were poised to assist. A team of commandos stood at the ready to board V-22 helicopters. As an added measure, Marine Harrier jets scrambled in a backup manoeuvre.[66]

One enduring mystery had been what role, if any, JSOC played in lethal drone operations within Pakistan. The elite unit had certainly been responsible for a number of deadly ground incursions there. Its troops had also played a key role in keeping secure Pakistan's nuclear arsenal. Then in 2009, Scahill claimed the existence of "a secret US military drone bombing campaign [in Pakistan] that runs parallel to the well-documented CIA Predator strikes."[67]

Any lethal JSOC drone missions in Pakistan would have been carried out by personnel from AFSOC's 3rd and 33rd Special Operations Squadrons. Yet according to a number of former operators spoken to by the author, no such strikes occurred. Instead they have detailed for the first time how AFSOC carried out much of the mundane surveillance of CIA targets in Pakistan. The missions remain so sensitive that none of those with direct knowledge were prepared to be named for this book. One stated they had "no intention of wearing an orange jumpsuit for the next 20 years by talking about this." As President Bush's drone campaign began to escalate toward the end of his second term, the few Predator lines of the 17th RS—now secretly flying from two Pakistani airbases though remotely operated from Creech—risked being overwhelmed. The Agency turned to AFSOC for help. From 2007 onward many hundreds of surveillance-only missions were flown inside Pakistan by the 3rd Special Operations Squadron's Afghanistan-based Predators. Flights always took place just inside Pakistan—"no more than 15 or 20 miles in"—and some operators believe that Pakistan's military was aware of operations. On occasion Predators had to be steered away from local Pakistan Air Force activity, they note. None of these drone missions went "kinetic," since the aim was only to gather signals intelligence for the CIA. AFSOC operators were kept almost completely in the dark about the true purpose of their missions:

> Our job was just to watch. Interesting thing about those is that they don't have very many people in 17th Squadron, so they just basically made us do their bitch work. So we watched, they could see everything

that we were doing, and then they would just take over. They'd be like, "OK, turn your cameras off or stow your [observation] ball and look up at the sky and we're gonna take over."[68]

These missions supporting the CIA's top secret war in Pakistan might have been gathering intelligence deemed vital to US national security, but for AFSOC crews locked in their New Mexico rooms, unable even to look at their own sensors for hour upon hour, they were crushingly dull: "After a while I was really like, I hope I'm not on that line today! Towards the end of when I was there, I can remember thinking God, it's going to be so boring," says one former crew member. "If something was happening close to you [in Afghanistan] you could be called off the mission to go help out and that's what all of us strived for. We would all be praying 'Please please please approve us,' then be bummed out when told we had to stay on target."

Boring or not, this gathering of signals intelligence—SIGINT—appears to have been a crucial element of emerging "pattern of life" analysis in Pakistan, which the CIA could then employ in its controversial signature strikes—the killing of alleged militants on the basis of their behavior rather than any knowledge of their identities: "What those SIGINT missions were targeted at was intercepting not necessarily a full-on call but to pinpoint locations. And follow them and get a hold of their habit patterns. The impression I got was that those people were arms runners and messengers," says one former crew member. Often target locations would appear unchanged when AFSOC crews were finally allowed to look again, as another former operator recalls: "It would look like nothing happened. Working with them was really weird, getting these orders saying 'Do this, do that,' and not having them explain. But we did a lot of their extra [Pakistan] ISR that they couldn't maintain or didn't have the resources to do."

Other missions were far more focused. Another former crew member recalls spending months observing a religious school in Waziristan run by the militant Haqqani Network: "Supposedly that's where UBL [bin Laden] was for a long time. But I remember watching that thing for a whole summer and it's burnt into my brain. We just saw the compound and we just stared at it and it was like, Can you give us more information about this? 'No.' Can you tell us what we're looking for? 'No, just watch.'" Although bin Laden was publicly codenamed Geronimo in the operation which killed him in 2011, these AFSOC hunting missions always referred to the Al Qaeda leader as Objective Beast—"As in 666 Mark of the Beast is how they labeled it, so take that as you will." An AFSOC spokesman declined to discuss drone surveillance operations over Pakistan when contacted by the author.

The armed drone had repeatedly proven its worth to the United States in Afghanistan and Pakistan—not only in targeting and killing key militants but in patiently gathering the intelligence needed for those strikes. Yet for all of its revolutionary capabilities, the Predator's lethal debut back in 2001 had been a disaster, allowing one of America's greatest enemies to escape.

BIRTH OF A PREDATOR
The Origins of Lethal Drones

"Who the fuck did that?" The words greeting the first ever combat strike by a remotely piloted aircraft were not in praise but in anger. A botched Hellfire missile attack by a CIA Predator had just cost the United States a likely chance to kill Taliban supreme commander Mullah Mohammed Omar. In response, the US Air Force General in charge of airstrikes in Afghanistan was about to threaten to call off the entire opening campaign of the War on Terror, unless he was given control of the CIA's secret weapon.

It was the night of October 7, 2001, and from the United States' new Combined Air Operations Center (CAOC) in Saudi Arabia, it was the job of Lt. General Chuck Wald and his one-star deputy Dave Deptula to coordinate every aspect of the unfolding Afghan air war. Less than a month earlier, Al Qaeda terrorists had massacred almost 3,000 people in the United States in the 9/11 atrocities. Operation Enduring Freedom—the campaign to rid Afghanistan of Al Qaeda and its Taliban hosts—was the first offensive of a global conflict which would eventually consume many tens of thousands of lives and trillions of dollars, and see more than two and a half million US personnel sent into battle.[1] Yet this longest of American wars had small beginnings. In autumn 2001, the United States had few assets in a region 7,000 miles from home and was unwilling to launch a full-scale land invasion. Instead, a plan was evolved to send into Afghanistan a small number of CIA agents and Special Forces in support of anti-Taliban militias. In turn, they would be aided by the United States Air Force (USAF).

That first October night was a powerful display of coordinated precision. A pair of B-2 bombers flew westwards for 36 straight hours from their US mainland base before delivering laser-guided bombs precisely at their designated time. From the island of Diego Garcia in the Indian Ocean came B-1 and B-52 bombers. F-14 and F/A-18 fighters flew in from a carrier group in the Arabian Sea, while 50 Tomahawk cruise missiles were let loose by other US and British naval assets.[2] According to CENTCOM commander General Tommy Franks, the assault involved in total some 40,000 personnel, 393 aircraft, and 32 ships.[3] Yet one aircraft did not feature at all in USAF's complex planning: a tiny, CIA-controlled propeller-driven spy plane, which had crept into Afghanistan some hours earlier. Predator tailfin number 3034 now hangs suspended in the Smithsonian Air and Space Museum in Washington, DC, its place in history assured. Yet its actions that first night of the war—in which numerous agencies in the vast US military-intelligence machine each played sharply contradictory roles—remain steeped in controversy.

The southern city of Kandahar was the epicenter of Taliban power in Afghanistan in 2001. US intelligence agencies had already identified Mullah Omar's home in the city and were watching unseen as a convoy of vehicles left the building complex: "We observed Mullah Omar, or 98% probable it was he, coming out of his facility in an entourage," recalls General Deptula.[4] The United States tracked Omar using the CIA's Predator drone as he journeyed south-west of the city. When the Taliban's leader finally stopped, he unwittingly presented an opportunity to the United States to deliver a devastating blow to its enemies in the opening minutes of the war. According to Deptula the CAOC already had on standby "fighter aircraft with a couple of 1,000-lb bombs holding 20 miles south so the noise wouldn't tip off Mullah Omar and his gang. And we wanted to use those weapons against the facility where Mullah Omar and his senior Taliban staff were hiding."

But there was a problem. The line of command which governed the Predator now shadowing Mullah Omar was blurred and untested. Armed with two lightweight Hellfire air-to-ground missiles, and launched from Khanabad airbase in southern Uzbekistan, the drone was remotely piloted by USAF operators, working from a mobile station in the carpark of the CIA's headquarters at Langley. Yet Agency analysts overseeing the mission did not have full control. In the days after 9/11 a "joint ownership" deal had been cut between Defense Secretary Donald Rumsfeld and CIA Director George Tenet: "We came to an agreement over who owned and paid for the assets, where they would operate, and who would 'pull the trigger' on the very few UAVs that were armed at the time," according to Rumsfeld.[5] In later years, as the targeted killing program developed, the CIA could consult its own legal advisers when preparing for a strike. Yet for now "CENTCOM had operational control over CIA activities in the theater of war, including the armed Predator."[6] That deal included CENTCOM's military lawyers. At his Tampa, Florida, headquarters, supreme commander General Tommy Franks received legal advice that there was a risk of civilian casualties if he attacked. There was also concern that Omar was inside a religious building—and President Bush had explicitly ordered that no mosques be attacked during the battle for Afghanistan, recalls General Wald:

> After a 90-minute briefing on the coming air campaign, the only thing President Bush said was: "I want to give you three pieces of guidance. One, we're going to fight through Ramadan. Two, I don't want you to bomb any mosques, and three, this is your fight, and fight it the way you see fit."[7]

After some debate, Bush had nevertheless signed off on a strike against Mullah Omar: even with the possible risk to civilians, the laws of war allowed reasonable leeway when such high-value targets were involved.[8] Yet instead of calling in the nearby F-16s to kill Omar, it was decided to use the untested Predator. Air Force personnel at the sophisticated CAOC in Saudi Arabia—supposedly in charge of the entire air campaign—insist they were kept completely out of the strike loop, "whether out of malice or incompetence I still don't know," says General Chuck Wald today. A senior Pentagon official recalls a less fractious but still "a very challenging night.

We had the right tools in place but it was the process that had to be worked on. I watched all those day's missions, and now that CENTCOM was in the decision matrix, it was the combatant commander's decision as to how we break these things out. And we had to go with that."[9]

Instead of striking the building in which Omar was thought to be located, a convoy vehicle outside was targeted and destroyed by the Predator and a number of bodyguards killed—the first ever lethal action by a remotely piloted aircraft.[10] When Predator pilot Scott Swanson finally broke his silence 13 years later to describe his role in the attack, he described the sight of a body thrown through the air as still "burned into my memory."[11] The strike was aimed at drawing Omar outside: but in the chaotic moments which followed, the Taliban leader escaped. "Mullah Omar and his senior staff piled out of that building and here we are 13 years later and we don't know where he is," says Wald's number two that night, General Dave Deptula. He is still angry at the failed opportunity. "What was the rationale of shooting an empty truck when the leadership was in an adjacent building, and where we had two minutes away aircraft that could have sent Mullah Omar and the senior Taliban leadership to the nether regions? It was a significant lost strategic opportunity—to put it mildly."

The botched Predator strike led to an immediate three-way fight between the Air Force, CENTCOM, and the CIA, which risked bringing the first night of the War on Terror to a shuddering halt. "The first I knew that Predator was there," says General Wald, "was when I heard an unknown voice on my radio say 'You are cleared to fire.'" Deptula recounts the anger both men felt as they sat next to each other in the CAOC: "To this day there is a degree of uncertainty over just who issued that fire order. We both watched the weapon impact and both turned to each other simultaneously and said 'Who the fuck did that?' General Wald got on the line to talk to General Franks, and I got on the line to talk to the individual who actually was in charge of the unit controlling the Predator, to try to find out just what the heck was going on."

So furious was Wald that he threatened to call off the first night's bombings unless he was given direct control of the CIA's new weapon: "The minute I heard that radio call I stopped the air op, I called CENTCOM and said, 'We're going to bring everybody out of the theater, we're going to stop bombing, and we're going to send everybody home until we find out where this is coming from,'" recalls Wald.[12] Fifteen minutes later, the General got his wish, and for that night at least, the CIA's armed Predator was placed under CAOC control. As Deptula now concedes, in the rush to go to war "there had not been a lot of attention paid to ascertaining command and control relationships between OGA [Other Government Agencies, often shorthand for the CIA] and the combatant commander. So this led to complications when the first weapons were released." Tommy Franks has put it more bluntly. "In combat there has to be one line of authority. But in this goat rope there had been CENTCOM, the Pentagon, the White House, [and] the CIA." The armed Predator's debut had not been auspicious. Yet in the War on Terror which followed, it would become one of the most effective and feared weapons in America's arsenal. Indeed, US foreign policy would increasingly shape itself to the Predator's unique selling point—its effectiveness as an assassination tool.

GENERAL ATOMICS

The Aeronautical Systems branch of arms manufacturer General Atomics sits on 85 acres of scrubby industrial estate in Poway, San Diego. Nearby neighbors have included golf suppliers Aldila ("A hellofa fine place to work") and divorce lawyers Kershek & Shular ("Going the extra mile"). Yet the big employer here is General Atomics Aeronautical Systems Inc. (GA-ASI as it is officially known). Inside four vast, air-conditioned hangars, more than 3,500 staff spend their shifts building the Reaper (the Predator's more powerful successor) and the Avenger, a jet-powered version in advanced development. For more than a decade, General Atomics maintained an absolute and lucrative monopoly on the production of US armed drones. It appeared a good place to work, with employee feedback websites suggesting most were happy in their jobs. "Opportunities to learn from the team—great benefits—amazing product," one worker reported in 2013, with another noting "By GOD, We helped get Ben Lauden [sic]." Others griped about a "Conservative, military environment, a Good ole boys club," and of "too many government auditors."[13] Those auditors were doubtless keen to see that the US government was getting value for money. Little has been published regarding the financial situation at GA-ASI, despite the company having been in receipt of billions of US tax dollars over 20 years. There are clues. The US military planned to purchase up to 400 Reapers on top of the 284

Predators eventually produced.[14] A 2013 assessment for the Government Accountability Office (GAO) placed the development and purchase cost of the Reaper project alone at $12.4 billion.[15] And the USAF spent a further $2.8 billion buying its Predator fleet, with undeclared millions more spent on research and development.[16]

Where any profits had ended up proved harder to follow (GA-ASI declined to be interviewed for this book or to respond to any factual queries). Court papers prepared by the Army in 2003 describe the business as a "privately held company" where 80% to 90% of revenues came from government contracts: "At any given time since 1991 [the company] was involved in between 40 and 50 ongoing contracts with the United States Government," the documents noted.[17] GA-ASI was itself part of the much larger industrial group General Atomics (GA), with interests ranging from nuclear fusion research and Australian uranium mines to hi-tech military equipment. Perhaps uniquely for a major US arms manufacturer, GA appeared to have remained entirely in private hands, those of the Blue family. General Atomics was owned fully by General Atomic Technologies Corporation (GATC), registered in Wyoming and with recent annual revenue estimates at around $1 billion.[18] According to court documents published in the 1990s, GATC in turn was 80% owned by Tenaya Corporation, a holding company based in Delaware and controlled by James Neal Blue, aged 77, and his family. The other 20% of GATC appears to have been controlled by Neal's brother Linden.[19]

The business acumen of these Colorado-born brothers, who had put the world's first armed drone into production, was clear even while they were students at Yale. As Linden later noted, "At that time, you couldn't drive around Latin America. We hatched this plan to learn to fly so we could go into business somewhere in Latin American after we graduated." In 1957 the pair convinced *Life* magazine to sponsor them for $8,000 on a South American adventure, flying in a tiny borrowed Tri-Pacer plane they nicknamed "Blue Bird."[20] The brothers made the cover that April, two all-American boys squashed into a tiny cockpit under the headline *Great Adventures: Over Andes by Light Plane.* The extraordinary trip took them 25,000 miles in 110 days through much of South America: "Once you have that kind of experience, it does give you confidence that maybe you can do almost anything you want," Linden later told journalist Di Freeze.[21]

After leaving university, the pair first tried their hand at farming in Nicaragua. They had met and interviewed the late father of the country's president and dictator Luis Somoza Debayle on their *Life* magazine trip.[22] Now, in a reported joint venture with Somoza's family the Blue brothers set up a ranch—complete with airstrip—on Nicaragua's Caribbean coast, with the aim of cultivating cocoa and bananas according to a detailed profile by Charles Duhigg for the *New York Times*.[23] The project was a failure, the bananas blighted by disease. But that first business outing did place the brothers in close proximity to one of the most notorious US blunders of the twentieth century. In 1961, Somoza allowed the CIA's mercenaries to embark from Nicaragua's east coast as part of the disastrous "Bay of Pigs" invasion of Cuba. Just weeks before the attack, Linden Blue's light plane was forced down by Cuban fighter jets over the island. In his 2005 interview with Freeze, he insisted that the timing was a coincidence and that he was returning to Nicaragua with agricultural parts for the farm: "I ended up in jail for 12 days. Anybody can go through 12 days, but it was an intense period, because that was right before the Bay of Pigs invasion. If I hadn't gotten out when I did, I probably would never have gotten out." He says he later learned the invasion was to take place from Nicaragua: "They wouldn't have let me out, once they learned that it was coming from there, because they were very suspicious of my connection with Nicaragua in the first place."[24]

By the end of 1961, both brothers had been called up by the USAF. While serving their country, they lost the ranch they had invested so much time and money in. Undeterred, on returning to civilian life, they first followed in their parents' footsteps by setting up a successful real estate business in Denver. Soon they diversified into construction, ranching, and gas. As Neal grew the business, Linden spent a number of years working with aviation companies Learjet and Beech, where he became an expert in composite materials—knowledge which would later serve him well with the Predator. In 1986, the duo bought nuclear and defense contractor General Atomics from Chevron for a knock-down $50 million. The Blue brothers were keen to expand their energy interests. But there was also a more personal agenda. Their friends the Somozas had been deposed by the revolutionary Sandinistas in 1979, and the Reagan administration had authorized the CIA to assist a secret war against Nicaragua's new leaders. The Blues were keen to help, since "the Contras were resisting communism and the domination of the Soviet Union," as Linden put it.[25] According to Neal, the brothers were "enthusiastic supporters," though not formally involved in the secret war.[26]

It was Neal who began considering the possibility of using primitive unmanned aircraft on kamikaze missions against Nicaragua's gasoline infrastructure: "You could launch them from behind the line of sights you would have total deniability," he told *Fortune* magazine years later.[27] When asked by the *New York Times* if either brother had ever worked for the CIA, Neal Blue declined to discuss the matter.[28] The duo wanted to use their new General Atomics company to research these kamikaze drones, calling bemused staff together in 1986 to tell them the news. That early project went under the name "Predator," though would prove a dead end. It would be another six years before the Blue brothers would snare the prototype of the armed drone which now bears that name, acquired from an Israeli-American design genius.[29]

Abe Karem—"the Moses of modern drones" according to one senior Pentagon official[30]—had served as an aeronautical engineer with the Israel Air Force before running a team of radical innovators at state-owned Israel Aircraft Industries (still a world leader in drone design). In the wake of the Yom Kippur War in 1973, the country had "an emerging operational need for real time intelligence on the front lines," Karem recalls. It was the perfect place for a young designer obsessed with the potential of unmanned aircraft capable of surveillance. On leaving Israel Aircraft Industries, Karem set up his own company aimed at making "robust, reliable, high performance and affordable UAV [unmanned aerial vehicle] systems." Unable to break into Israel's close-knit defense world, he instead moved his family and business to California where (with echoes of Apple and Microsoft) he built early models of his new drone designs in his three-car Los Angeles garage. Karem views Predator's can-do origins as part of a historic tradition: "We owe aviation to the bicycle shop of the Wright brothers, and many of the early inventors built cars and aircraft in sheds and barns," he says.[31]

His garage designs soon caught the attention of the CIA and the Pentagon's shadier departments. Over 300 US and French peacekeepers had died in Beirut in terrorist attacks in 1983, starkly highlighting the need to keep closer tabs on radicals in areas like the Bekaa Valley.

Yet such places were difficult to access and harder still to insert human spies into. Satellites and U2 reconnaissance planes could provide photographs at specific times, but the process was cumbersome and technically limited. What was needed was an unobtrusive aircraft that could fly at lower altitude, could loiter at the scene unobserved, and which could then quickly deliver pictures from the scene. At first, the CIA held secret discussions with Israel about developing a joint drones program. The solution lay closer to home. Karem's Leading Systems was contracted as part of a $40 million "black" Pentagon project to develop its UAV technology. Specifications for the new drone were clear: it would need to operate at between 15,000 and 25,000 feet; be able to carry cameras and other sensor equipment; and crucially, be able to loiter over a target and so provide the fabled "persistent stare" needed by military and intelligence analysts. What no one gave any thought to at the time was arming such a platform. Major General George Harrison, former head of the Air Force's Operational Test and Evaluation Center, recalls huge institutional opposition at the Pentagon and CIA to the idea of arming any surveillance aircraft: "This reconnaissance mafia was dead set against armed, because if you were armed it would divert you from your primary job of target development. So there was strong resistance, I mean strong resistance, I can't overstate it."[32]

Karem developed two prototypes, the Amber and the Gnat, which both included the inverted V-tail later made famous by the Predator.[33] They first successfully flew in 1986, and Leading Systems appeared destined for success.[34] Off the back of an expected contract for up to 200 Ambers, Karem expanded the business rapidly, taking on a 200,000-square-foot factory and buying a lease on the El Mirage airfield in California.[35] Yet design success was not enough to save the business. The Pentagon froze the project as a result of inter-services bickering and post-Cold War cuts, and Leading Systems went bankrupt in 1990 after the bank called in a $5 million loan. In a particular irony, Pakistan at one point considered buying the mothballed prototype Predator fleet. Bankrupt or not, the CIA and Pentagon still needed their new drone. The company chosen to save the day was General Atomics: "The Blue brothers were looking for a UAV company to buy and so they saw the potential of what Abe Karem had," recalls Major General Ken Israel, who was sent to visit the pair to see if they would pick up the drone project. "And they had deep pockets."[36] Neal and

Linden acquired the bankrupt business in 1991, hiring Karem and eight other key designers.[37] The Predator was back in business.

FRIENDS IN HIGH PLACES

When Bill Clinton assumed the US presidency in January 1993, a key priority was the escalating conflict across former Yugoslavia. A lack of good intelligence, surveillance, and reconnaissance (ISR) was hampering US efforts to understand and, if possible, contain the civil wars. Chuck Wald, then an Air Force colonel, recalls that the Serbs were proving particularly difficult to monitor: "They were pretty clever at hiding in tree lines and stuff; there was this cat and mouse game that was going on. The [Air Force] fighters would go out there and a forward air controller would try to talk the pilot onto the target. But you're moving at 300 plus miles per hour at 20,000 feet looking into a tree line: it was a very difficult task."[38] What was needed was something which could loiter at the scene and gather real-time intelligence. General Atomics CEO Neal Blue met with senior officials at the Pentagon. Asked how long it would take to produce a flight-ready version of the prototype drone, Blue insisted he could deliver in just six months.[39] The CIA too needed its spies in the sky, focused as it was at the time on pure intelligence-gathering. Agency director James Woolsey played an important role in the Predator's early success. Briefed about the drone's potential at an early 1993 meeting—and concerned at the quality of satellite coverage over the Balkans—the CIA chief is said to have personally flown to California to inspect the new system.[40] Impressed, the Agency bought five Gnats on the spot, instructing Abe Karem to re-engineer the drone's modified snowmobile engine to make it quieter.[41]

The Agency also brought into play its own expertise. Independently of Karem and General Atomics, the CIA's Directorate of Science and Technology had been working on how to remotely pilot aircraft from thousands of miles away. Former senior technician Frank Strickland has described how "Agency employees were working on a cutting edge operations concept using unmanned and manned aircraft for testing, often with risk to the lives of the test pilots."[42] That CIA know-how was now merged with General Atomics' expertise. The CIA's development role had strong precedents, not least the U2 spy plane which the Agency had bankrolled in the 1950s. "Unconventional users, like the CIA or the Special Forces, are essential to rapidly testing and maturing any new military capability," Karem notes. "We certainly would not have Predator today without a great team from the CIA, willing to take the risks of rapidly modifying and deploying the Gnat 750 system, and willing to experiment with a reasonably complex new technology."[43] Major General Jim Poss, who rose to become USAF's Director of Intelligence, says that so many innovative US reconnaissance platforms have had direct CIA development input—from U2 spy-planes to the first weather satellites—that "it's probably quicker to talk about the reconnaissance aircraft the US Air Force and CIA didn't co-develop than the ones they did."[44]

There was now immense pressure on General Atomics to deliver. A new Pentagon organization had been created to drive unmanned military aircraft forward, known as the Defense Airborne Reconnaissance Office (DARO), headed up by Air Force Major General Kenneth Israel. There was certainly no shortage of cash to fund development. As Israel now recalls, "they [General Atomics] had tremendous support on the Hill. There was not one year that I did not get more money than I requested. I was thinking, 'Who the hell is talking to these people?' "[45] Some of that largesse was down to the persuasive talents of former US Rear Admiral Tom Cassidy, recently recruited by the company. He sold Karem's design hard, winning over influential supporters in Washington, DC, and Virginia. Cassidy was aided by aggressive lobbying.[46] A 2006 report found that General Atomics "had spent $660,000, more than any other company, sending Congressional staff members on trips," as the New York Times put it. Cassidy was dismissive, saying only that "everyone else was doing it, so we did, too."[47] The downside to this success was that it became difficult at times for the Pentagon's bureaucracy to handle. A retired USAF General involved in the early days recalls his surprise at how vertically integrated the structures of the tiny company were: "It wanted to make everything."[48] Another recalls confronting General Atomics: "I went nuts, and said 'Look, there are other people who make these subsystems a lot cheaper and have a track record of reliability. You guys are learning.' But then there was more profit if they vertically integrated."[49]

That company structure was deliberate. Neal Blue had told colleagues back in 1986, when he acquired General Atomics, that he wanted it to be similar to entrepreneur Howard Hughes's pioneering aviation business of the 1930s. As well as hothousing radical designs, it would mean keeping all related business (and profits) in-house where possible. Blue also hoped that a small, nimble defense contractor could avoid the mistakes and slow workup times of bigger rivals, something on which he and Karem agreed: "They get overcome by bloated bureaucracy aimed at avoiding risk, and focused on the process of running their business and not on creation of market-winning products," the designer still believes. It appears unlikely that a major arms manufacturer could have produced, and adapted quickly enough, the ISR system Washington now sought for former Yugoslavia.

In record time, General Atomics' prototypes were approved for deployment in the escalating Balkan wars. Just as with the War on Terror seven years later, the CIA's drones got there first. The Agency flew its classified Bosnian missions from the semi-derelict Gjader airfield in Albania, reportedly rented with two truckloads of blankets and other basic supplies.[50] A year later and the Pentagon's own drones arrived in the shape of four modified Gnats (newly christened "Predators"), which operated from Taszar airfield in Hungary and which were controlled by the US military.[51] The early Predator had major limitations, many of which were ironed out in a literal trial by combat since they were easy prey for Serbian anti-air defenses. At least two were shot down. Wings would also freeze up, sometimes causing a drone to drop expensively from the sky, and video was only being transmitted every third or fourth second: "It basically made it impossible for the guy to steer the payload," Frank Pace of General Atomics later recalled. "It wasn't at all the system we have now."[52] Missing too was the facility to fly the RPAs from any distance via satellites. Instead the pilots, sensor operators, and intelligence analysts were all crammed into huts beside the runways. This was barely over-the-hill technology, never mind the over-the-horizon capability which the Pentagon had demanded.

Yet with its ability to stay in the air for almost 24 hours, the Predator was still proving an effective reconnaissance machine. "The bad guys used to just wait for our fighter pilots to leave," recalls Ken Israel. "They didn't have that option anymore." The new drones also helped reveal some of the horrors of the conflict: "We saw mass graves, so the Serbs could no longer deny them. With the kind of sensors we had on board, with IR [infra-red], we could tell if the earth had been moved and we were able to send forensic teams where they needed to be."[53] Israel was given the job of summing up the Predator's first battlefield contribution. In a now-declassified Pentagon report, he cited the ancient Greek poet Homer in praise: "I've seen the cities of men and understand their thoughts." Flying 159 missions over Bosnia in its first year "Predator helped determine the course of the Bosnia conflict," the paper boasted. "This single resource gave NATO commanders the key piece of intelligence that underlay their decision to resume the bombing campaign that, in turn, led to the Dayton peace accord."[54]

The unarmed Predator had proven its worth, but "ownership" was still unclear. The Air Force was eventually ordered to take control. Its Chief of Staff did not take much convincing—if only to keep the Predator out of "enemy" hands. As General Ronald Fogleman later noted, "If the Army took Predator, they would just screw it up and the program would go down the tubes. If anyone was going to make it work, we were."[55] One major shift after Bosnia was that pilots and analysts no longer needed to be stationed near the battlefield. Incorporating the CIA's new remote satellite technology, General Atomics added a bulbous nose to the Predator which allowed it to transmit and receive data via military satellites. Crews could now be thousands of miles away, instead of just a few kilometers.

Back in the United States, remote analysts moved in to Langley Air Force Base in Virginia, where they formed Distributed Ground System One, the first of what would eventually become more than a dozen Air Force hubs employing thousands of real-time intelligence specialists. For the pilots and sensor operators, Fogleman reactivated the 11th Reconnaissance Squadron (better known as 11th RS), which after conducting thousands of manned reconnaissance missions in Vietnam had trialed early Air Force drones in the 1970s.[56] The chosen home for the squadron was Indian Springs AFB in Nevada, soon renamed Creech after a local Air Force dignitary.[57] Fogleman also insisted that officer pilots would operate his drones, noting that if USAF Predators failed it would not be because of who was flying them.[58] Sensor operators and other key posts were instead filled by enlisted men and women, a move which created tensions for some in the new Ground Control Stations—the metal boxes from which RPA missions were first flown. "You go through basic training in tech school and they're like 'Officers are a thousand times better than you. They don't give a shit about you. You do everything that they say. Don't become friends with officers because then you're fraternizing with them,'" recalls former sensor operator Brandon Bryant. "So when I first joined that was my thought process, I was just like—stay quiet." Former mission controller Janet Atkins also recalled some tensions, particularly within conventional drone squadrons: "I just remember some pilots were very brash and very cruel, as far as our role as an MC. Though some were really cool and laid back, 'We're all just doing our part,' and didn't make me feel less of a person. I just remember one pilot with the 15th saying a monkey could do my job."[59]

By the end of the Predator's second Bosnian tour, the USAF was beginning to think beyond routine surveillance. As Steve Hampton, the first commander of the new drone squadron later noted: "At first, we fell into the trap of 'reporting the news.' We were on the 'scene of the crime,' showing what was happening . . . [We learned] our job is to ignore that, go over the horizon, and find out what's not happening yet."[60] In 1999 the Predator also played a valuable role in the Kosovo conflict, though it still had major shortcomings. One was that "customers" found it hard to identify where exactly a Predator was beaming its pictures from, since one valley might look very much like the next. Eventually a GPS mapping overlay was developed for customers, which could show exactly where any Predator was. And in the final days of the Kosovo war, the Pentagon successfully field-trialed a laser designator within a Predator's sensor ball—using it to "light up" a hut which an A-10 Warthog then destroyed.[61]

Supporters of the Predator now pushed hard to get one of the drones assigned to the Middle East. Operations Southern and Northern Watch were no-fly zones above Saddam Hussein's Iraq, enforced by US and allied aircraft. One of the biggest challenges was dealing with Iraq's air defenses—with the regime continually testing pilots. Surveillance was carried out by U2s, satellites, *and other surveillance aircraft*, yet these provided only intermittent, static images. According to Jim Poss, then director of intelligence for Air Force CENTCOM, the Iraqis soon realized that all they needed to do was sit out any overflights: "They switched to the greatest counter to Coalition airpower that's ever existed, the ignition key." One mobile anti-aircraft radar vehicle, in particular, had eluded the Coalition for months. "Every time we got a fix on him and got strike aircraft there, he'd be gone," recalls Poss. "Unless we could reacquire him again, assure ourselves that there was no possibility of collateral damage, and know that it was that radar, we just wouldn't strike. Enter Predator." A single unmanned RPA operating out of Kuwait crept over the border unseen, with its full-motion, real-time video. The mobile radar was then tricked into revealing itself, only to be laser-targeted by the Predator for other

Coalition aircraft to destroy: "We bagged that radar we'd been after for nine months on just our second mission," says Poss.[62] Yet the drone was still dependent on other aircraft to deliver the killing blow. One question now began to dominate: could the Predator itself be weaponized?[63]

ARMING THE PREDATOR

The targeted killing of terrorism suspects—and their secret rendition to interrogation and torture facilities in allied nations—were key policies which helped define the presidency of George W. Bush. Yet it was his Democratic predecessor Bill Clinton who had not only begun the rendition program against Al Qaeda-linked suspects—but who also partially lifted a decades-long ban on US assassinations. As Bosnia-Herzegovina collapsed into civil war in the mid-1990s, thousands of Muslim fighters had flocked to help, among them battle-hardened veterans of Afghanistan and Chechnya. Just as with Syria two decades later, Washington was deeply concerned at the national security risk some of these men posed. One US response was particularly brutal. In the words of a former CIA commander, "Al-Qaeda leaders and other Sunni Islamists" would be "taken off the street" before being secretly handed over to third party nations—some of which were untroubled by concerns over legal process or torture.[64] The policy helped fuel a lethal tit-for-tat between Al Qaeda and the CIA, which continued for two decades. The first known operation took place in September 1995, when Ta'lat Fu'ad Qassim was captured in Croatia at the urging of the CIA. Wanted for his alleged role in President Anwar Sadat's assassination, the 38-year-old Egyptian had been granted political asylum by Denmark, one of hundreds of radicals who had fled the subsequent Mubarak regime's crackdown on Islamic militancy in the 1980s.

Al-Qassim—who US officials would later claim was also linked to Al Qaeda—was questioned on a US military vessel, then secretly handed over to Cairo's security services. The Egyptians interrogated, tortured, and then executed al-Qassim. Three years later and this time in the Albanian capital Tirana, four more Egyptian alleged militants were seized with the aid of the CIA and handed over to Cairo. Two were then killed. All were claimed to have links with Islamic Jihad.[65] Ayman al-Zawahiri was the founder of that terrorist group, as well as being Al Qaeda's second in command.[66] He warned in a letter to the London-based *Al Quds* newspaper on August 5,

1998, that America's "message has been received" and that there would be a response "in a language they will understand."[67]

Two days later a suicide bomber detonated his explosives-packed truck at the gates of the US embassy in central Nairobi, Kenya's capital. Ten minutes later and 400 miles away, a second truck bomb blew up the embassy in Dar-es-Salaam, Tanzania. Twelve Americans died in the coordinated attack, among them two CIA agents whose true status was kept secret for 13 years.[68] A further 212 people were killed alongside them, with 4,500 more wounded. Most casualties were local passers-by. The dual embassy bombings were the work of Islamic Jihad, the FBI later concluded, in an attack sponsored by al-Zawahiri and Osama bin Laden. Both were now living in chaotic Afghanistan, a land-locked nation controlled by the radical Taliban movement.[69] As Clinton struggled with the Monica Lewinsky affair at home, he obtained legal opinions authorizing covert attacks against Al Qaeda abroad.[70] The first response saw cruise missiles fired at supposed Al Qaeda assets in Afghanistan and Sudan on August 20, 1998.[71] Washington quickly found itself mired in controversy, when the Sudanese site was found to be a pharmaceutical factory—and not the "chemical weapons facility" the CIA had claimed.[72]

If the United States wanted to deal with Osama bin Laden directly, it first had to find him. Yet daily satellite and U2 spy-plane passes over Afghanistan could only offer a time-stamped glimpse of possible locations. As Richard Clarke, Clinton's chief counterterrorism adviser later explained: "The problem we had was that we wanted to kill him but we never knew where he was until after he had left that place. We would always know where he had been yesterday."[73] For a time, the Pentagon considered placing a giant, hidden telescope on an Afghan mountain in the hope of spotting Al Qaeda's gaunt leader.[74] More sensible heads turned to the Predator, by now field-tested over Bosnia, Kosovo, and southern Iraq. Not only could the unmanned aircraft help find bin Laden, it could also laser-illuminate his location so that Tomahawk cruise missiles could be launched from a submarine in the Gulf. Under pressure from Clarke—and despite some internal misgivings—the CIA agreed to Predator intelligence missions.[75]

A joint Pentagon-CIA operation dubbed "Afghan Eyes" was born, which went live on September 7, 2000, when the first unarmed RPA crossed into

Afghanistan.[76] The CIA had convinced the government of post-Soviet Union Uzbekistan to allow it use of Khanabad airfield near the Afghan border. Locally based CIA "contractors" (supplied by General Atomics and the Air Force) piloted the unarmed Predator as it trundled down the runway. As the drone banked south, control was then handed via satellite to operators at the US Air Force base in Ramstein, Germany.[77,78] A video link to CIA headquarters also allowed Langley to analyze and observe, and senior national security officials were frequent visitors.[79] Over the next few weeks the Predator made ten successful flights into Afghanistan. Its task was simple: find bin Laden. On September 25, 2000, and against all expectations, it apparently did. Circling high and unseen above Tarnak Farms near Kandahar, the Predator fed back live pictures of a tall, white-robed man surrounded by a security detail. "I can remember seeing the Predator imagining of Osama bin Laden and several other of his colleagues," recalls Richard Armitage, Deputy Secretary of State at the time. "It was pretty compelling to me because you can tell—according to those who know these things—by the length of the shadow approximately how tall this fellow was."[80]

According to one senior Pentagon official with close knowledge of the operation, in total Al Qaeda's leader was directly observed by the CIA's drones for four hours and 23 minutes over a number of missions. Yet there was still no guarantee that any cruise missiles would find the terrorist still there by the time it reached the target. This proved a catalyst for arming the Predator: "We showed that [bin Laden] video to the Secretary of the Air Force, the Chief of Staff of the Air Force and the Assistant Vice-Chief and someone mentioned, 'Let me take Hellfire quick, black and dirty.' That direction was given, so we moved money and notified Congress."[81] The CIA had developed the Predator as a spying platform. Now the rush was on to turn it into an assassination tool.[82] On January 23, 2001—just three days into the Bush presidency—an inert anti-tank missile was successfully and secretly fired at a target by Predator tailfin number 3034 (the same drone which would later make history with the failed attack on Mullah Omar). The drone had always theoretically been able to carry and fire weapons, designed as it was with "hard points" on its wings meant for sensor pods.[83] But theory was not practice. The chosen munition was manufacturer Lockheed Martin's

Hellfire, a lightweight anti-tank missile which could be laser-guided onto its target. "We selected Hellfire because 175 lbs. or more on a Predator wing and the wing comes off. Hellfire and its whole kit weigh 154 lbs. It was very Darwinian," recalls a Pentagon official who worked with General John Jumper to weaponize the drone. Declassified film footage released to the author shows the Predator weighted down with concrete blocks for its momentous first launch. As the Hellfire missile streaks from the drone to the words "Item away! Item away!" the composite wing is left shuddering but intact.[84] The US government finally had its assassination tool.

Over the coming months, the Predator successfully test-fired live Hellfires onto various targets, controlled both locally and by satellite uplink. The CIA had also been hard at work in the Nevada desert, building a mock-up of bin Laden's four-room Afghan house.[85] In early June 2001, the replica starred in what many hoped would be a dress rehearsal for the Al Qaeda leader's death. High above the desert, an armed Predator controlled by a joint CIA and USAF team fired a Hellfire missile into the "bin Laden compound," destroying it. As former National Security Council official Roger Cressey later told reporter Peter Bergen: "I'm looking at the video of this big fucking explosion packed in there and I'm like, 'I can't believe anybody would have survived that.' "[86] Despite this apparent success, the CIA rejected the results as inconclusive, unsure whether a Hellfire missile could kill all of those inside. The Predator's early weapons trials should have been the start of a long process of evaluation and improvement on what was still a prototype system. Certainly the Pentagon's independent Operational Test and Evaluation unit was not much of a fan. In a damning report, director Thomas Christie judged that "As tested the Predator UAV system is not operationally effective or suitable." With poor communications and "unable to operate in less than ideal weather," the RPA's new laser designator was also inaccurate, registering "target location errors approximately twice what the accuracy requirement allows."[87] Those comments should have seen the Predator undergo major new trials. Yet by the time the OTE report landed on Pentagon desks in late September 2001, General Atomics' newly armed drone had already been crated up and shipped off to the impending war in Afghanistan, where its capabilities and shortcomings would instead be determined in the heat of battle.

AFGHANISTAN, 2001

The failure to kill the Taliban's supreme leader Mullah Omar in October 2001, a primary goal of the US war in Afghanistan, owed as much to ignorance among senior personnel of the Predator's revolutionary capabilities as to poorly thought-out command and control systems. After all, the CIA's drone that night could have loitered for many more hours, waiting for a better opportunity to kill the Taliban's leader. "The beauty of force application is now you have on one aircraft all the Find, Fix and Finish capability that had always been separated on different systems. You can now observe and take an action to engage in a matter of minutes, seconds quite frankly, which you never had before," explains Lt. General Dave Deptula, co-architect of the Afghan air campaign. "In World War II, on many occasions target evaluation took months. Today it's single-digit minutes." The slow-moving drone, with its small-yield missiles, was poorly equipped to carry out air-strikes against conventional battlefield targets. Yet as one former senior air force commander notes, within 30 minutes of the air war beginning in Afghanistan, almost all fixed targets such as air defenses or command and control buildings had already been destroyed: "It took a while for the system to understand that the real mission had changed rapidly from fixed targets to a counterterrorism model of going after individuals."[88] What the Predator turned out to be good at was secretly observing, tracking, and, if necessary, killing those individuals.

The CIA had shipped out its three prototype armed Predators (tailfins 3034, 3037, and 3038) and a crate of ten Hellfire missiles on September 16, 2001. Freshly designated as MQ-1s (the "M" denoting their new multipurpose role, the "Q" a signifier for remote-piloting), the CIA's drones were joined above the battlefield by every unarmed RQ-1 Predator the regular Air Force could ship to Pakistan.[89] Forward aircrews operated from Shamsi and Jacobabad airbases (both of which would later play a crucial role in the CIA's targeted killing project) while intelligence analysis was provided by remote teams in Virginia and California. "The Pakistanis did us a huge favor by letting us into Jacobabad, but every pilot we could keep back we needed to, because they were very sensitive to the numbers we were putting on the ground," recalls Jim Poss, then a colonel with Air Force Intelligence who helped coordinate operations from Pakistan. Only some USAF drones carried the laser designators successfully trialed in Kosovo. Most were politely referred to as "Classic Predators," equipped only with poorer quality cameras. Afghanistan's mountainous geography also presented enormous problems: the RPAs were at risk of icing up and falling to the ground. After some were lost this way, each Predator was eventually retrofitted with a five-gallon drum of de-icing fluid which could be used just once. "It was almost as big a decision whether to squirt the de-icing fluid as it was to release weapons, just because doing either meant you had to come home," recalls Poss.[90] The drones could also only fly at 90 knots, and some days the winds were so strong that the Predators would find themselves going backward.

As the Air Force fought to get its assets in place, the CIA was given the lead on the ground in Afghanistan. The first team in, codename Jawbreaker 6, was given a briefing by Cofer Black, director of the Agency's Counter Terrorist Center, in which he demanded to see Al Qaeda "heads on pikes." Team leader Gary Schroen later said that it was the first time he had been ordered to kill rather than capture a target, though this would become a regular event for some CIA personnel.[91] Ultimately the Agency sent 110 agents into Afghanistan in 2001, accompanied by 300 elite Special Forces supplied by the Pentagon. Backed by the USAF and the wider intelligence community, these 400 would effectively win the initial war, working with the Northern Alliance to rout Al Qaeda and the Taliban in weeks.[92] Intelligence was key, and each day, Air Force intelligence officers worked with CENTCOM to decide which of the Special Forces teams would get Predator support. "That was our big life and death decision every day: who was going to get that Predator?" says Poss. Even USAF's unarmed Predators had lethal potential in Afghanistan's uncontested airspace, where in theory at least they could use laser designators and real-time video to direct in other assets. Yet few other strike aircraft so far had the ability to receive these feeds: "We had intelligence of a senior Taliban leadership meeting in Kabul. We knew the specific building it was to be held in, and we directed the Predator over there and watched it," recalls Lt. General Deptula. "But because there wasn't a satcom capability in the aircraft, nor could we directly relay the picture to the aircraft, we were literally talking the fighter pilot to the building through radio relay. So we're watching the picture and we're going, 'OK, you see the traffic circle in north east of Kabul? OK, take the northern route off of that, go up three blocks, take a left and it's the third structure on the right.' That was the birth of, 'OK let's pipe this ISR directly to the users.' "93

Although the Air Force made as much as it could of its weaponless drones, only the CIA's Predators had teeth during the Afghan invasion—a situation which remained in place until 2004. It was a shaky start. On October 12—just five days after the Mullah Omar incident—a CIA forward team was almost bombed by an Agency drone. Commander Gary Schroen has recalled how analysts described to him looking down on "two men dressed in Western-style clothing, walking around on the [air]strip. They are definitely not Afghans and we think they may be al-Qaida." In fact, the men were two oblivious CIA agents five miles inside Northern Alliance territory at a clearly labeled friendly base. Schroen instructed the Predator to stand down, noting in his memoirs: "I could understand that the US military might not know [the base's location], but how could the CIA not know about it?"94 Two weeks later, a Predator was caught up in a strategic disaster when Abdul Haq was killed. A former mujahideen commander, he had been touted by some as a possible leader for Afghanistan after the war. But the Taliban had located Haq and his small force and was in pursuit. A desperate attempt was made to save him. With no ground forces anywhere nearby a lone Predator was sent to assist. "The UAV finally showed up and we could see that they had grabbed this guy, took him down the hill and hung him," recalls General Chuck Wald. "We blew up their pickups after that but we weren't able to save Abdul Haq."95

Other CIA strikes had more success. At 1.00 a.m. Afghan time on November 16, the United States found Mohammed Atef, Al Qaeda's military commander. Only Osama bin Laden and Ayman al-Zawahiri were more senior. The 57-year-old Egyptian, once an agricultural engineer, had fought the Soviets in Afghanistan. One of a handful of jihadists present at the birth of Al Qaeda in 1988, he was so close to the terror organization's leader that in January 2001, his daughter married bin Laden's 17-year-old son Mohammed. At the ceremony, bin Laden recited a poem eulogizing the USS *Cole* attack.96 Atef had been involved in multiple deadly plots against the United States going back more than a decade. Reportedly involved in preparations for the 1998 Africa embassy bombings and for the 9/11 attacks, Atef had remained behind to help direct Kabul's defenses. But the city fell to the Northern Alliance on November 13, and Atef was on the run. US intelligence tracked him to a meeting in a small-town hotel some miles outside Kabul. A Predator was feeding live video images back to CENTCOM in Tampa, and to the CIA's headquarters in Langley. Senior Administration officials looked on as General Franks personally gave the order to kill. Lessons had clearly been learned from the Mullah Omar debacle. Three F-15 Strike Eagles, on stand-by some miles off, dashed in and each dropped a 2,000-lb. GBU-15 "bunker buster" bomb on the hotel. The Predator also fired its own small Hellfire as back-up. The building was destroyed, killing Atef and six colleagues as phone intercepts later confirmed. The surrounding area too was devastated: "Almost everyone at the scene was incinerated, with close to 100 people killed," the *Sunday Times* reported. Initially it was noted that Al Qaeda's strategist had simply died in a US "air raid," though Predator's role soon emerged.[97]

By mid-November the CIA's drones had reportedly fired 40 Hellfire missiles throughout Afghanistan, although this should be measured against an estimated 6,500 airstrikes by all platforms during the three-month air war. As former CIA commander Gary Berntsen has noted, after the initial confusion over who was in control, the Agency's drone had integrated well into the US battle plan: "The Predator over-head and Special Forces soldiers on the ground directed one precision bombing run after another on Taliban positions."[98] Those Air Force crews flying the CIA's drones out of a trailer in the Agency's Virginia grounds—part of a secret unit known as the 32nd Expeditionary Air Intelligence Squadron according to aviation historian Richard Whittle—could never discuss their work publicly.[99] Yet internally at least they were honored. CIA Director George Tenet personally awarded the squadron a National Intelligence Meritorious Unit Citation, noting its "exemplary accomplishments."[100]

By December 2001, President Bush would himself come out strongly as a Predator fan. Describing what was still a secret CIA weapon, he spoke of how drones were now "able to circle over enemy forces, gather intelligence, transmit information instantly back to commanders, then fire on targets with extreme accuracy." Bush boasted to the assembled military cadets that "the conflict in Afghanistan has taught us more about the future of our military than a decade of blue ribbon panels and think-tank symposiums."[101] The armed Predator had made a powerful debut on the modern battlefield.

THE RISE OF TARGETED KILLING
Yemen and Palestine

Following the success of the air war against the Taliban and Al Qaeda, the CIA's few armed Predators spent the early part of 2002 scouring the Afghan countryside for remnant forces now hiding among a civilian population. What began emerging here were the rudiments of a US targeted killing program. The successful arming of the Predator had made it a potent assassination tool thanks to its relative precision, persistence, and low detectability—though such accuracy never diminished the need for high-quality intelligence. In his memoirs Donald Rumsfeld describes remotely observing the final stages of a drone preparing an attack on a man thought to be Al Qaeda's leader. Suddenly something spooked the target, the former Defense Secretary recalls:

> He took off, running like a gazelle over rocky, rugged terrain. He couldn't have been more than 20 years old. Bin Laden was in his mid-forties in 2001. Intelligence later confirmed that the man we were absolutely convinced was bin Laden was not.[1]

Others mistaken for the gaunt terrorist were not so lucky. Munir Ahmad, Jehangir Khan, and Daraz Khan were three friends who one cold February morning were scavenging for scrap metal at the site of recent fighting. The drone operators and analysts thousands of miles away were not privy to this knowledge, peering at their narrowly focused camera feed with its poor quality images. In what amounted to an early "signature strike" it was decided that Daraz Khan, the tallest of the trio, again looked very like Osama bin Laden—despite his being five inches shorter than the Al Qaeda leader. Somehow the command chain agreed, and permission was given for the unseen Predator to attack. All three men died, though Washington brushed off the targeting error. Despite comprehensive field evidence of civilian deaths, a Pentagon spokesman insisted there were "no initial indications that these were innocent locals."[2] Two weeks after the attack no US official had yet explained to relatives why the three had been slain. "Surely, it was a big mistake of the Americans. They should know that there are no Al Qaeda here," complained the brother of Daraz Khan.[3]

Other strikes were more focused. In May 2002, the Agency attempted to kill Afghan warlord Gulbudin Hekmatyar in a Predator bombing which the *New York Times* described as "the first confirmed mission to kill a factional leader who was not officially part of the fallen Taliban government or Al Qaeda terrorist network."[4] In his monumental study of the CIA's activities in Afghanistan prior to 9/11, Steve Coll notes that "both at headquarters and in the field, CIA officers . . . [had] embraced Hekmatyar as their most dependable and effective ally" in the fight against the Soviet occupation.[5] Millions of dollars of CIA covert funding had been funneled to the warlord and his movement Hezb-i-Islami. With the rise of the Taliban in the 1990s Hekmatyar had gone into exile in Iran, only returning a month before the US attempt to kill him. Linked to an alleged plot to overthrow the Karzai government, the warlord was also reportedly offering bounties for the deaths of US military personnel in Afghanistan. "While foreign troops are present, the interim government does not have any value or meaning. We prefer involvement in internal war rather than occupation by foreigners and foreign troops," Hekmatyar had told reporters just before his return.[6]

Unable to reconcile with their old ally, the CIA decided instead to assassinate him. As Hekmatyar's vehicle convoy traveled through the Shegal Gorge in his home province of Kunar, a tracking Predator fired a Hellfire missile. The warlord survived the attempt on his life, remaining an implacable foe of the United States even as its forces drew down more than a decade later. Others were killed.[7] Although the drone strike was the work of the CIA, it was a Pentagon official who would announce that "we had information that he [Hekmatyar] was planning attacks on American and Coalition forces, on the interim government and on Karzai himself." Even with the "hot" war now over, the dual Pentagon-CIA control of armed Predators remained in place.

Before September 2001, the CIA had been reluctant to carry out targeted killings, even once the Predator's potential as an aerial sniper rifle had begun to be realized. The 9/11 Commission chronicles how then-CIA Director George Tenet insisted he had no authority to "pull the trigger":

> This was new ground. What is the chain of command? Who takes the shot? Are American leaders comfortable with the CIA doing this, going outside of normal military command and control?[8]

Armed Predators would instead require a new command and control structure "that could respond to fleeting opportunities while ensuring the right level of leadership control over the operation," believed Tenet, since a potential "kill chain" of hours would soon shrink to minutes. He stressed that the CIA needed the president and the NSC to know "from the beginning" the implications of the Predator's use.[9]

After more than a decade of CIA targeted killings—and thousands of deaths—Tenet's protests may now appear quaint. Yet assassination by US agencies had been banned since 1976, when President Gerald Ford issued Executive Order 11905. This stated bluntly that "no employee of the United States Government shall engage in, or conspire to engage in, political assassination."[10] That ban had come in the wake of grim disclosures to the Senate's Church Committee of CIA lethal excesses in South America and elsewhere. Jimmy Carter and Ronald Reagan had later gone further, plugging loopholes by ruling out killings by contractors.[11] The principle and the law seemed clear, though some officials began seeking flexibility. Reagan's Defense Secretary Caspar Weinberger argued that only "murder by treacherous means" was forbidden, and a 1986 air attack on Libya (a country with which the United States was not at war) and the deliberate targeting of leader Muammar Gaddafi certainly appeared to sidestep the orders.[12] In 1989, President George Bush Senior received a "clarification" on the no-assassination ruling which concluded: "Acting consistent with the Charter of the United Nations, a decision by the President to employ clandestine, low visibility or overt military force would not constitute assassination if US military forces were employed against the combatant forces of another nation, a guerrilla force, or a terrorist or other organization whose actions pose a threat to the security of the United States."[13]

More direct US moves toward a targeted killing program away from the battlefield preceded both 9/11 and President Bush, though in a stop-start fashion. Provoked by escalating attacks from Al Qaeda including a fatwa urging "all Muslims . . . to kill the Americans and their allies—civilians and military," Bill Clinton's administration had toyed with empowering the CIA to kill Osama bin Laden.[14] In his memoirs John Rizzo, the Agency's longtime Acting General Counsel, recounts drafting three separate Memoranda of Notification (MON) for the president between May 1998 and February 1999—each with contradictory positions. With the first, "the Clinton White House was only talking about capturing bin Laden, not knocking him off." A second MON signed after the US embassy bombings allowed the CIA "to kill bin Laden only if capture was not 'feasible.'" Yet with his last Memorandum, says Rizzo, Clinton personally "scratched out" an acknowledgment that bin Laden might be killed, "taking the concept of 'mixed presidential signals' to a new and perilous level."[15] According to a later highly critical internal report, "CIA managers refused to take advantage of the ambiguities that did exist."[16] The 9/11 Commission also noted that as late as December 1999, a Northern Alliance plot to rocket-attack bin Laden was vetoed since it "might cross the line into violation of the assassination ban."[17] Paul Pillar, deputy chief of the CIA's Counter Terrorism Center (CTC) in the late 1990s, recalls the chaotic effect these mixed messages had:

> It probably was understood [at CTC] that there were at least some circumstances, involving resistance by the target or difficulty in capturing him, where lethal force would be permitted. But just how extenuating circumstances would have to be before bin Laden could be killed was a grey area. There was a sense that the White House did not want to put clearly on paper anything that would be seen as an authorization to assassinate, but instead preferred more of a wink-and-nod to killing bin Laden.[18]

George W. Bush's government was still operating by these ambivalent no-kill rules in the months before 9/11, though there were "desultory" internal talks on formally adopting a targeted assassination program using the newly armed Predators. "We wanted the ability not for assassination—we hadn't even thought that far ahead—we wanted to be able to deal a blow against terrorism," recalls Deputy Secretary of State Richard Armitage.[19] "The bureaucratic aspect would often cause people to leave meetings shrugging their shoulders and muttering under their breath—it simply couldn't be decided," adds Lawrence Wilkerson, later Chief of Staff to Colin Powell. Senior administration officials finally met on September 4, 2001, a week before 9/11, to discuss the proposed targeted killing by a Predator of Osama bin Laden. It was almost a year to the day since an unarmed RPA had first observed the Al Qaeda leader at the Tarnak Farms site. National Security Adviser Condoleezza Rice, on the advice of her staff, wanted to hold off on deploying armed Predators to Afghanistan until "spring 2002," while Colin Powell at State and Paul Wolfowitz at Defense supported weaponizing the Predator immediately. The Pentagon and the CIA argued until the last about who might fire any missile.[20] As Richard Clarke later noted: "The CIA said it wasn't their job to fly airplanes with missiles on them. That was the Air Force's job. The Air Force said it wasn't their job to fly their aircraft without pilots in them. I think both were just avoiding what they thought would be a potentially controversial weapon and a weapon that they thought would get them into political trouble."[21]

That ambivalence toward assassinations—or targeted killings as they would soon be known—was something Bush was determined to change immediately following Al Qaeda's September 11 atrocities. As the President later recalled, "George [Tenet] proposed that I grant broader authority for covert actions, including permission for the CIA to kill or capture al Qaeda operatives without asking for my sign-off each time. I decided to grant the request."[22] On September 17, 2001, Bush signed a 12-page MON which among other authorizations cleared the way for the CIA to kill any members of Al Qaeda or other global terrorist networks— including American citizens—who appeared on a "high value target list."[23] Former CIA chief lawyer John Rizzo has described this in his memoirs as "the most comprehensive, most ambitious, most aggressive, and most risky Finding or MON I was ever involved in."[24]

It was long assumed that this secret memorandum, coupled with Congress's signing of the sweeping Authorization for Use of Military Force three days earlier, had provided the domestic enabling framework for US targeted killings. Yet Armitage's recollection is that an additional order was issued early in 2002 which explicitly related to targeted killings using the Predator. "It would have been shared with our intelligence committees so my suspicion is it was either a draft executive order or a finding," he says. "I don't recall necessarily the words, 'Targeted Killings,' but it was clearly that. It was loosening the [Executive Order] 12333 against assassinations. And the reasoning as I recall was, its wartime, it's not an assassination, its war." Armitage himself was not troubled by the order's implications: "I felt this was just. Didn't like it particularly, but we were at war. I saw this myself as not unlike the six years I spent in Vietnam where if you came across an enemy, and you could, you'd kill him. So once this was declared a war, and as a war on terrorism, that cleared up a lot of things for me."[25]

Although world attention was focused on Afghanistan in the autumn of 2001, the United States had also begun hunting down Al Qaeda suspects globally. It struck hard against known and alleged militants in Europe, Africa, Asia, and the Pacific. Some actions were military in nature, while others saw suspects arrested by local law enforcement partners. Elsewhere, targets were secretly renditioned by the CIA to "friendly" countries such as Egypt, where they were questioned under coercion or torture.[26] Yemen had long been of particular concern to Washington. On October 12, 2000, a small explosives-laden boat had rammed the missile destroyer USS *Cole* as it sat in Aden's harbor, killing 17 American sailors aboard. The suicide mission had been backed by Osama bin Laden, a Yemeni by descent. Al Qaeda's agents appeared able to operate with impunity in the unstable southern Gulf country—not least because Yemen's autocratic President Ali Abdullah Saleh had drawn on support from the terrorist group during a brief civil war in 1994.[27] Eleven weeks after 9/11, Saleh had traveled to Washington to offer his full support for the emerging War on Terror, doubtless conscious of the fate already befalling Afghanistan. As a secret cable wryly noted shortly before his trip: "It would be helpful if Ambassador could reassure President Saleh . . . that the USG [United States Government] sees Yemen as a partner in CT [counterterrorism], not a target."[28] The United States had a list of Al Qaeda operatives it wanted dealt with, and near the top was Qa'id Salim Sinan al-Harithi, described by CIA officials as "the godfather" of Al Qaeda in the region. In an account of a meeting between the two presidents, academic Gregory Johnsen reports Bush as telling Saleh that if he "couldn't arrest or kill the men on the CIA's list of names . . . he would be more than happy to send in US Special Forces."[29]

Even before September 2001, the FBI had begun a joint inquiry into the *Cole* bombing with Yemen's feared security service, the Political Security Organization (PSO), and numerous suspects were incarcerated. Yet, as Johnsen notes, so many were swept up that "the Yemenis had no idea who they held," including some members of the *Cole* attack team. Helping to sift through these suspects, Bureau agents were allowed to be present during some PSO interrogations.[30] At this stage of the US War on Terror then, capture remained a viable option. As with Pakistan, Yemen had proven reasonably effective at rolling up Al Qaeda cells and at bringing alleged terrorists into the criminal justice system. Some of these suspects and convicts would go on to be imprisoned at the Guantanamo Bay facility, where Yemenis eventually made up one-third of all detainees.

A leaked US diplomatic cable dated October 20, 2002, shows the extent to which the United States was influencing detentions and trials relating to the USS *Cole* bombing. The memo suggests, for example, that the New York District Attorney's Office be drafted in to aid Yemen's Attorney General with the imminent prosecution of nine suspects. In a further three cases, the United States wanted trials delayed to allow it time to prepare indictments against other suspects: "We expect the Yemeni government will continue to accede to the US request to hold in abeyance going to trial for these three." Even in autumn 2002 then, the State Department and FBI viewed those accused of the *Cole* bombing within a criminal justice framework. Yet as the secret cable also noted, "The key US objective in this is to see that the guilty are convicted and punished, but this goal is likely to be satisfied only partially by Yemen's decisions."[31] Two weeks later the Pentagon and CIA presented their own solution: the assassination or targeted killing of one of those allegedly involved in the *Cole* bombing, along with six other suspects. As the Agency knew at the time, one of them was an American citizen.

Israel: A Template for Targeted Killings

While Washington began to explore the potential for "targeted assassinations," as Secretary of State Colin Powell would later term them, there were concerns in some quarters regarding the legality of any such program—or even how it might operate.[32] The arming of the Predator had been driven by a secret pre-9/11 plot to assassinate Osama bin Laden. Yet what was now being proposed was a more regularized program against numerous Al Qaeda-related targets. For many years, close ally Israel's intelligence agencies had assassinated Palestinians allegedly linked with terrorist actions. University of Utah professor Amos Guiora was a lawyer with the Israel Defense Forces (IDF) between 1994 and 1997. There he found himself providing advice on at least one targeted killing mission in the Gaza Strip: "It's 3am," Guiora has written, recalling an incident: "Most people are sleeping or at least are trying to. Perhaps a few are having one last drink. But few ever hear the following words and fewer hear them at 3am: 'We need to talk. The window of opportunity to neutralize the target is only open for a few minutes.' "[33]

With the beginning of the Second Intifada in autumn 2000, Israel had begun a far more systematic assassination program, two years before the first known US targeted killing by drone.[34] Operations were carried out by the IDF, though were often based on intelligence provided by the domestic security service Shin Bet. Between 2000 and early 2014, human rights group B'Tselem recorded 270 Israeli targeted killing operations in the Palestinian Territories, which between them killed 455 people. Of these, according to the Israeli monitoring group, 177 were noncombatants.[35] It was only after the killing by snipers in early 2001 of Dr. Thabet Ahmad Thabet that senior IDF lawyers were asked by their commanders for an opinion on the lawfulness of such actions. There had been a public outcry at the killing of Thabet, with some insisting he was instead focused on Israeli-Palestinian reconciliation.[36] "We called him Dr. Jekyll and Mr. Hyde, because during the day he was a peace activist and a physician, but in the night he actually operated terrorist squads," claims one former senior IDF legal official with close knowledge of the case. "As a result of this incident, the Chief of Staff actually turned to us and said, 'Is it legal for us to specifically target identified terrorists?' "[37] Lawyers at the IDF's International Law Branch were tasked in early 2001 with drawing up a secret opinion, which—according to Middle East counterterrorism expert Daniel Byman—concluded that targeted killings were lawful under the following conditions:

> The target is a combatant, the target cannot be arrested, the operation is approved by senior civilian officials, efforts are taken to reduce civilian casualties (that is they must adhere to the principle of proportionality), and the operation occurs in areas Israel does not control. Perhaps most important the target has to be a future threat, not just someone who committed crimes in the past.[38]

As a key architect of those guidelines noted to the author, underlying the new Israeli rules was a novel interpretation of international humanitarian law: "All of that was premised on the legal assumption that this [Intifada] had been transformed from a law enforcement scenario, to an armed conflict scenario. Because we could now look at these terrorists as enemy combatants: criminals you can't kill, you have to arrest."[39]

Prior to 9/11, Washington had no truck with such claims. Former US Senator George Mitchell was the lead author of an April 2001 report into the Second Intifada, commissioned by Bill Clinton and inherited by the Bush administration. This concluded that "The IDF should abandon the blanket characterization of the current uprising as 'an armed conflict short of war,' which fails to discriminate between terrorism and protest."[40] As the former senior IDF legal official notes, "when Senator Mitchell rejected that premise, he was in fact rejecting the underlying logic of all of Israel's targeted killing policies." In July 2001, US Ambassador Martin Indyk added to the pressure, declaring on Israeli TV that "the United States Government is very clearly on record as against targeted assassination. . . . They are extrajudicial killings, and we do not support that."[41] Even after Al Qaeda's suicide attacks on New York and Washington and with the United States now mobilizing for war, a State Department official was still insisting that "we oppose the policy of targeted killings. . . . That has not changed."[42] In truth everything was changing. Behind the scenes Bush administration officials were consulting with both the Pentagon and the intelligence community on how best to move forward with the US's own targeted killing program.[43] Lawrence Wilkerson, later Chief of Staff to Secretary of State Colin Powell, recalls the issue coming up frequently at State Department meetings: "After 9/11 it seemed like we were going to more or less adopt the same kind of policy. And it frustrated our ability to bring any pressure on the Israelis because the response we got from them was, 'Ha! Are you shitting me? You do it!' "[44]

Now that the two countries were pursuing similar policies, it might have seemed logical for the United States to turn to its ally for advice on the legal, ethical, and practical challenges of targeted killings. Certainly former officials recall a flurry of visits to discuss broader counterterrorism cooperation. "I think the military in particular—but the CIA also—was involved in a constant dialogue with the Israelis, especially post-9/11 when it all becomes counterterrorism and 'Tell us what you know,' " says Wilkerson, now a politics professor at William & Mary University. "And this caused a great exchange of information. Most of it at the beginning like a torrent from the Israelis to us." Amos Guiora, by now commander of the IDF's School of Military Law, also recalls a visit by Pentagon officials in 2002 to discuss potential aspects of US-Israeli cooperation: "They asked me to meet with them on a very specific issue that I was working on which from my perspective was not related to drones, but perhaps in retrospect tangentially was," he says now.[45]

Whether there was any formal dialogue on targeted killings is less clear. The New York-based *Jewish Daily Forward* claimed in early 2003 that "the Bush administration has been seeking Israel's counsel on creating a legal justification for the assassination of terrorism suspects. . . . Legal experts from the United States and Israel have met in recent months to discuss the issue."[46] Reporter Ori Nir has described his source to the author as an Israeli government official.[47] If any dialogue did occur, it may have been directly between intelligence agencies. As former Deputy Secretary of State Richard Armitage puts it, "My understanding was it would have been the CIA who had these discussions with the Israelis, and that's my strong suspicion." If there were direct discussions, the IDF's senior lawyers were not privy to them. "I'd actually expected an engagement with the US on these issues and to be called on," says a former senior IDF legal adviser. "But after September 11th we were informed that under US government policy, they are not coordinating, or at least not with us." Instead, as another senior IDF legal official from the time notes, given the complex emerging legal debate around targeted killings there was a continuous dialogue over many years and in many forums such as international conferences, between US and

Israeli military law specialists: "We ourselves were struggling with forming our legal positions, so it took us time too. And we changed our positions, not dramatically, but they evolved as we grew, because it was like on-the-job training. . . . So the whole year of 2002 was for us an ongoing learning process, and for the US too."[48] For both nations this was clearly uncharted legal territory.

YEMEN

The name of Qa'id Salim Sinan al-Harithi, Yemen's Al Qaeda leader, had been added to the CIA's emerging potential "kill or capture" list in late 2001. Yet finding the terrorist leader and other Al Qaeda threats would not be easy. "You had the FATA [Pakistan's tribal areas], Yemen and Somalia as kind of the poster children for inaccessible and ungoverned. The tools we had to go after Al Qaeda became more limited," says a former senior US intelligence official whose agency was actively involved in the hunt for al-Harithi.[49] One of those key tools was the MQ-1 Predator. The chosen base for what was expected to be a lengthy secret campaign was a former French Foreign Legion post next to Djibouti City's airfield. The tiny east African state of the same name was strategically positioned at the mouth of the Red Sea, right next to Somalia and a short hop from southern Yemen. Yet Djibouti was also a stable ally with little history of radical Islam. The US presence began rapidly expanding. By mid-2002, 800 troops from the 13th Marine Expeditionary Unit were stationed at Camp Lemonnier. They were not alone: "There were Air Force guys there and there were a lot of techy guys, people who knew their shit," recalls former US Marine Corps sniper Matthew Mardan. "We had one little small area of the base and we kind of had to stick to it. We weren't supposed to tell people even that Camp Lemonnier existed, we couldn't call directly home."

One piece of equipment commanders were keen for the Marines not to discuss were the CIA's armed Predator drones recently shipped in. Also present were Special Operations Forces from Fort Campbell, Kentucky, whose job was to assist the CIA on the ground in Yemen. Members of Mardan's scout-sniper platoon were tipped at one point to accompany to Yemen an elite unit known as an Operational Detachment Alpha, or ODA. Although the Marines would go on to take part in Fallujah in some of the fiercest US fighting since World War II, few had any combat experience back in 2002: "We were stationed there ready to go in with an ODA team and they basically just left us behind. I don't blame 'em either because they don't want to go in with the rookies. They went ahead and ran all the missions and didn't tell us about it, sent a couple of their guys in," Mardan recalls today.[50]

The search for al-Harithi finally yielded results in early November 2002, the product of hard work by multiple US military and intelligence agencies. In the words of one senior Pentagon official with detailed knowledge of the covert drones program, there was often a public misunderstanding when it came to attributing US covert drone strikes to the CIA: "The best way to view this thing is holistically, as the work of the United States government."[51] Troops from the US 5th Special Forces Group, with some assistance from their Yemeni counterparts, had been hunting for al-Harithi on the ground. The State Department's in-country ambassador reportedly also paid tribal leaders for information.[52] Predator RPAs had helped search from above, remotely flown by regular Air Force pilots and sensor operators back in Nevada. Detailed mapping of the terrain was provided by the then-National Imagery and Mapping Agency.[53] The National Security Agency at Fort Meade played perhaps the most crucial role, monitoring the signals of multiple phones linked to Yemen's Al Qaeda leader. According to investigative reporter Dana Priest, this electronic intelligence eventually led to the location and killing of al-Harithi after he used one of his cellphones on November 3. The method, trialed a year earlier in Afghanistan, now enabled the CIA to use a phone "as a targeting beacon to kill its owner." A special team had since been established at the NSA, known as the Geolocation Cell and with the informal motto "We Track 'Em, You Whack 'Em."[54]

Lt. General Michael DeLong was at CENTCOM's Tampa, Florida, headquarters when news came in that al-Harithi had been positively identified on a desert road in Marib, a landlocked central province. The continuing threat represented by Al Qaeda in Yemen had been emphasized that same day when terrorists tried to bring down a US helicopter.[55] Just as during the 2001 Afghan offensive, the Agency's drones required the legal say-so of CENTCOM's judge advocates-general (JAGs) rather than the CIA's own lawyers. With al-Harithi firmly in the Predator's sights, authorization for an attack was obtained from President Bush. DeLong, the deputy commander of CENTCOM, then made his way to a secure room receiving live video feeds from Yemen. The terrorist suspects in the vehicle convoy below were unaware a decision had already been taken to kill them. Interviewed by PBS years later, DeLong recalled speaking by phone to CIA Director George Tenet as he watched the video wall: "Tenet goes 'You going to make the call?' And I said, 'I'll make the call.' He says, 'This SUV over here is the one that has Ali in it.' I said, 'OK, fine.' You know, 'Shoot him.' They lined it up and shot it."[56] Eight thousand miles away and moments later, six alleged terrorists were dead. Among them was a US citizen. A seventh injured man only survived because the solitary Predator had already fired both missiles.[57]

The decision to kill al-Harithi and the vehicle's other occupants was a momentous one. After all, this was an assassination or targeted killing beyond the hot battlefield, exactly the kind of operation Bush officials had been so vociferously opposing with Israel. The State Department was certainly caught off guard. In a tetchy exchange with journalists two days later, spokesman Richard Boucher was still insisting that "Our policy on targeted killings in the Israeli-Palestinian context has not changed." Pushed to declare whether Washington now had "one rule for one conflict and another rule for another," Boucher replied: "If you look back at what we have said about targeted killings in the Israeli-Palestinian context, you will find that the reasons we have given do not necessarily apply in other circumstances."[58] There was, of course, no discernable distinction, and in the months ahead the United States would quietly end its criticism of Israeli targeted killings.

More than a decade on, many of the legal and ethical issues raised by that first strike remained unresolved, as did questions regarding who was knowingly targeted. Uncontested was the fact that al-Harithi and five others died in a Hellfire missile attack, all allegedly linked to terror conspiracies. Four were reported to be local members of the Aden-Abyan Islamic Army, an Al Qaeda affiliate group said to have assisted in the USS *Cole* bombing. Yemen's government would later claim to the United Nations that Harithi and the other occupants could not have been arrested:

> The Government stated that it had made every effort to bring these accused persons to justice and had promised them that they would not be harmed if they had come forward voluntarily to stand trial. The group however refused to comply and persisted in its resistance to, and evasion of, justice and in planning new acts of terrorism.[59]

Yet in killing the men they had been denied a criminal trial, and their guilt could not be assumed. Sole survivor Abdul Rauf Nassib was finally apprehended by Yemeni troops in February 2004, but was later acquitted by Yemen's Special Penal Court over his alleged peripheral role in the USS *Cole* bombing.[60] Despite his acquittal Yemen continued to hold Nassib, under US pressure, for two additional years. By the time he was re-apprehended in 2012 he had allegedly risen to become a local commander with Al Qaeda.[61]

Could al-Harithi and the others realistically have been apprehended in November 2002? The United States already had an active hand in Yemen's extensive criminal justice investigation into the USS *Cole* bombing, with more than a dozen senior Al Qaeda suspects incarcerated. The CIA also had al-Harithi and the other occupants of the SUV under direct observation at the time of the killing, and with the cooperation of Yemen might have tried to seize the men at a later stage. Similar joint operations in Pakistan had already netted many senior Al Qaeda figures (see chapter 5), and any intelligence obtained would have proven invaluable. Indeed, just days after the CIA's first Yemen drone strike, Al Qaeda's overall architect of the USS *Cole* bombing—Abd al-Rashim al-Nashiri—had been secretly picked up by the Americans in Dubai.[62] Yet the FBI appears to have had no knowledge of any impending lethal CIA operation in the Gulf. As the *New York Times* reported at the time, "although [US] investigators wanted to question Mr. Harethi [sic] about the *Cole* bombing, the CIA did not consult law enforcement officials before the Yemeni operation, a senior law enforcement official said."[63] It is important to note, however, that there would have been clear risks to any capture attempt. Efforts by Yemeni troops to apprehend al-Harithi a year earlier had ended disastrously, when 19 soldiers were killed by local tribesmen interceding on the Al Qaeda leader's behalf.[64]

Question marks have also remained over whether al-Harithi was the only intended target that day. There appeared little doubt he was a significant terror threat to both Western and Yemeni interests. Strongly linked to the USS *Cole* bombing, al-Harithi also reportedly coordinated an Al Qaeda attack on French-registered oil tanker the LV *Limburg* on October 6, 2002, which had killed a Bulgarian merchantman.[65] Yet American citizen Kamel Derwish was also a significant figure, and at the time of his death was high on a list of US priority targets. Sometimes known as Abu Ahmad al-Hijazi, he was the son of a Yemeni steelworker, born in upstate New York at Buffalo's Mercy Hospital in 1973. The suspect's family had moved back to Yemen in 1978—but when Derwish's father died in a car crash the boy was sent to Saudi Arabia to live with relatives. There he came under the sway of the extremist doctrines of Wahabist Islam, and he later claimed to have fought in Bosnia as a young man.

In 1997 Derwish was deported by the Saudis for alleged radical activities; and a year later he had turned up in Lackawanna, NY, where he gained a reputation as a fiery preacher at his local mosque. He was also a recruiter for Al Qaeda and played a key role in convincing half a dozen local men to travel to Afghanistan, where they received weapons training at Al Qaeda's notorious al-Farooq camp in spring 2001.[66] The Lackawanna Six, as they became known, were rounded up in simultaneous raids in early September 2002 and portrayed as the most significant terror threat on US soil since 9/11 by officials from Bush downwards. "We've broken Al Qaeda cells in Hamburg and Milan and Madrid and London and Paris—as well as Buffalo, New York. We've got the terrorists on the run," the President later told the nation.[67] While the "Lackawanna Six" were eventually convicted of lesser charges of materially supporting terrorism, evidence emerged during the investigation of Kamel Derwish's alleged involvement with operational elements of Al Qaeda—including some of those linked to the bombing of the USS *Cole*.

By autumn 2002, a massive international manhunt was underway, with Derwish's name placed on the FBI's "Most Wanted Terrorist" list—though missing from the same list was al-Harithi's name. Numerous press reports from late September onward, based on briefings by US federal officials, said that Derwish was "on the run in Yemen." A *Guardian* story six weeks prior to the killings, titled "US elite force gets ready for Yemen raid," even directly named Derwish as a possible target.[68] Al-Harithi and Derwish were therefore both of major interest to US authorities. Yet Washington had always indicated that Kamel Derwish was "just in the wrong place at the wrong time" when he was killed by a Predator, and few questioned this in 2002.[69]

In fact Derwish's presence in the vehicle was known to US intelligence officials at the time of the attack as the *Washington Post*'s Dana Priest discovered eight years later, reporting that "Killed with [Harithi] was a U.S. citizen, Kamal Derwish, who the CIA knew was in the car."[70]

As Priest later noted to the author, "My recollection is that Harithi was the primary target and their attitude was, that he was such a big deal and it was such a difficult thing to arrange that whoever else was there with him was a legitimate target too." She recalled her discussions with former US intelligence officials for the 2010 story: "They just felt like the primary target, whoever was with him, was guilty too you know? And they were taking the risk. That's what they used to say about even women and children who were in convoys that they struck: 'It's too bad, but they are traveling with really bad people and we gotta get them.'"[71] When Attorney General Eric Holder released information on the targeted killing of US citizens in covert drone strikes in 2012, he limited himself to those attacks carried out by the Obama administration. In doing so, coincidentally or not Holder avoided having to clarify the circumstances of Derwish's death.[72] Public knowledge back in 2002 of any deliberate targeting of an American citizen would likely have had major implications for the nascent targeted killing project. After all, US citizens were constitutionally assured the right not to be "deprived of life, liberty, or property, without due process of law."[73]

There was one further mystery: whether Yemen had consented to this first US targeted killing on its territory. President Saleh had certainly approved secret Predator intelligence-gathering operations some months beforehand, after CIA officials showed him "an animated video demonstrating how the drones worked" according to journalist Mark Mazzetti.[74] Yet at least some senior Yemeni officials were unhappy with the al-Harithi attack. "We tried to make it clear that we did not want the Americans to do it themselves. They are just here to get their enemies and get out," General Yahya al-Mutawakel told a reporter.[75] Many years later a former senior official under Saleh admitted to Human Rights Watch that there had never been more than a "gentleman's agreement" governing US strikes—the same vague formula underpinning the early years of CIA strikes in Pakistan.[76] Whether Saleh directly approved the al-Harithi killing or not, both nations agreed to remain publicly silent: the deaths were at first blamed on a "terrorist bomb" self-detonating in their car. But with US mid-term elections taking place just two days after the killings, at least one Bush official could not resist speaking out. US Deputy Defense Secretary Paul Wolfowitz discussed the CIA strike with CNN on the day of the election, noting that a "successful tactical operation [has] gotten rid of somebody dangerous."[77] In response, a furious President Saleh banned US armed Predators from operating over the country. "This is why we are reluctant to work closely with them. They don't consider the internal circumstances in Yemen," a close ally of Saleh complained.[78] Although US targeted killings employing manned aircraft would finally resume with Barack Obama in late 2009, armed Predators only returned to Yemen's skies as President Saleh's long grip on power began faltering in the Arab Spring two years later.

ASSERTIONS OF LEGALITY

Despite such an extraordinary precedent having been set by the United States in Yemen, there was little hint of the scale of killings to come. *Time* magazine even reported that such attacks were "unlikely to become a norm."[79] That was certainly the hope at the State Department, where officials initially proposed flagging the drone deaths as extrajudicial killings in their annual report on Yemen's human rights record. As a secret cable from the US Ambassador to Yemen, Edmund Hull, to the State Department's Near Eastern Affairs section tartly noted: "In President Bush's State of the Union address, the Predator attack on November 3 against al-Qaeda was highlighted as a significant success in the War on Terror. It is inconsistent that a report from the Department of State would indicate that the same killing is extrajudicial or unlawful."[80] The final version of the State Department report makes no mention of the killing of al-Harithi and Derwish, adopting instead the exact language proposed by Hull: "There were no reports of arbitrary or unlawful deprivation of life committed by the Government [of Yemen] or its agents."[81]

Was the killing of al-Harithi and five others by a US Predator drone lawful? Deployed conventionally, remotely piloted aircraft represented a weapon system little different from an F-16 or a B-1 bomber—if rather more precise. All but one of the CIA's drone strikes since 2001 had so far taken place on the regular battlefield. Here combat was overtly regulated both by the laws of war and by international human rights law. While any individual strike might be in breach of one or both, the general presumption for drone strikes used in armed conflict was that they were lawful. Indeed there could be a preference for any aerial attacks—including targeted killings—to be carried out on the regular battlefield by RPAs given their precision capabilities and lower-yield warheads: "The law of armed conflict requires a State to use the most precise weapon available in preference to the least precise weapon available," notes Ben Emmerson QC, an expert for the United Nations on human rights in the context of counterterrorism operations.[82] War fighters themselves also argue that RPAs have brought advantages to the battlefield: "We now have, I think, a weapon system that is not only compliant with international humanitarian law but actually delivers two key fundamental tenets of IHL [international humanitarian law] better than our existing platforms. Proportionality and distinction," claims Wing Commander Richard Mason of the RAF, who has made a study of the moral implications of remote-piloted warfare. "Provided there is an acceptance that armed forces have a moral, legal, and ethical right to deliver violence on behalf of the State, then we actually have a way of doing that in a more acceptable way, that is more compliant with IHL."[83]

More challenging was the issue of drone targeted killings beyond the hot battlefield—the actions of the CIA and later JSOC in Yemen for example, or of Israel in the Gaza Strip. Domestic US legal authority for such targeted killings was generally claimed from the Authorization for Use of Military Force Against Terrorists (AUMF), a response to "acts of treacherous violence . . . committed against the United States and its citizens" which was passed by a joint session of Congress just a week after the Twin Towers fell. As the AUMF proclaimed:

> The President is authorized to use all necessary and appropriate force against those nations, organizations, or persons he determines planned, authorized, committed, or aided the terrorist attacks that occurred on September 11, 2001, or harbored such organizations or persons, in order to prevent any future acts of international terrorism against the United States by such nations, organizations or persons.[84]

What of international law? Whether Washington's targeted killing in Yemen and those which followed were lawful or not depended to a significant degree on whether the United States was involved in a recognized conflict. Washington asserted just that, insisting that such operations were a part of "an armed conflict against Al Qaida" as Secretary of State Colin Powell described it, one "governed by the Laws of Armed Conflict." This meant in turn that "al Qaida terrorists who continue to plot attacks against the United States may be lawful subjects of armed attack in appropriate circumstances." It was Al Qaeda's actions which were unlawful, Powell insisted to the United Nations, not those of the United States.[85]

According to the International Committee of the Red Cross, the laws of war distinguish only two forms of armed conflict, noting that "legally speaking, no other type of armed conflict exists."[86] International armed conflicts were fights between two or more sovereign states, while the term "non-international armed conflict" had at the time only been used to describe nations fighting insurgencies on their own territories, or struggles between "non-governmental armed groups" within the borders of a country. Both forms of conflict were simultaneously governed by international humanitarian law (IHL)—summarized as "outlawing excessive human suffering and material destruction in the light of military necessity"—and international human rights law, or IHRL, which "provides non-discriminatory treatment to everybody at all times, whether in peacetime or in times of war or other upheaval."[87]

While the Bush administration had clearly embarked on a major war with Al Qaeda after 9/11, it broke with all precedent by claiming the United States was in neither internationally recognized form of armed conflict. Bush accepted that the war was not one between States. Yet his government also refused to accept that it was in a non-international armed conflict since the war was taking place outside US territory.[88] As a consequence, while Washington claimed some of the privileges which being a party to a conflict brought—for example, the applicability of the laws of war or IHL—it simultaneously denied others. It asserted, for example, that the Geneva Conventions did not apply to Al Qaeda prisoners in its custody, a crucial element of the US torture or "enhanced interrogation" program. Little wonder this unprecedented situation was described by scholars of international law as a "legal black hole."[89] Only in June 2006 would the US Supreme Court rule that the overall US War on Terror was "a conflict not of an international character," a decision which would help bring to an end some of the worst abuses of the Bush era.[90]

While the broader US war against Al Qaeda would come to be recognized as a conflict by much of the international community, drone targeted killings beyond the hot battlefield generally were not. The CIA's covert drone strikes occurred on the territories of (usually) consenting nations with which the United States was not at war, and where law enforcement operations against terror suspects remained feasible. There was little precedent for treating such actions as falling within the definition of a conflict. Were Washington ever to concede that point, it would have to accept that most drone targeted killings beyond the regular battlefield must be unlawful, since only the more proscriptive international human rights law would then be in effect.[91] It was this view which informed much of the international response to the CIA's first targeted killing. Sweden's Foreign Minister complained of "a summary execution that violates human rights" for example,[92] while Amnesty International demanded that "the United States should issue a clear and unequivocal statement that it will not sanction extra-judicial executions in any circumstances, and that any US officials found to be involved in such actions will be brought to justice."[93] Others were more circumspect. Kenneth Roth, executive director of Human Rights Watch, would later state that "treating [Harithi] as an enemy combatant and resorting to lethal force was appropriate,"[94] while countries such as Russia—which had allegedly targeted and killed dissidents beyond its own borders—remained silent.

Nevertheless, the consensus position within the international community was that US (and later Israeli) drone targeted killings beyond the hot battlefield were of significant concern, and the United Nations Human Rights Council, or UNHRC, decided to engage.[95] As its leading expert now warned, "an alarming precedent might have been set for extrajudicial execution by consent of Government."[96] Those comments, just days after the killing of al-Harithi, helped lead to a decade-long stand-off between the United Nations and Washington. The UNHRC's special rapporteurs were independent legal experts with the authority to advise and report on human rights issues. Pakistani barrister Asma Jahangir's own UN brief covered extrajudicial, summary, or arbitrary executions. In her view, the CIA's drone strike constituted "a clear case of extrajudicial killing," since the United States and Yemen had failed to act "in accordance with international human rights and humanitarian law." Jahangir wrote to the Yemen and US governments seeking answers. Sana'a was the first to reply, stating that all of those killed by the Predator "were being sought by the judicial authorities on charges of involvement in terrorist activities."[97] Four months later in April 2003 the Bush administration also engaged, rejecting outright the view that it had carried out "extrajudicial executions" and insisting the Special Rapporteur and UNHRC lacked the competence to consider the United States' actions.[98]

"At its most extreme the conflict follows the fighter," says UN investigator Ben Emmerson. "To put it another way, the United States considers itself entitled to adopt the targeting rules of IHL against a non-state armed group with which it is engaged in a non-international armed conflict, wherever those individuals are—whether they be in Yemen or Somalia or Waziristan. Or in Afghanistan."[99] Yet Washington's assertion that its targeted killings beyond the hot battlefield were part of a lawful conflict under international humanitarian law were never more than a "legal theory," one former high-ranking US intelligence official told the author, adding that "we are the only country on Earth who thinks that we're in a global war with Al Qaeda and that we have the right to take the fight to the enemy outside of internationally agreed theaters of conflict."[100] Despite having such "a peculiar, unique definition of the conflict," for more than a decade the United States had nevertheless maintained a consistent position. "Under two incredibly different Presidents our behavior hasn't changed at all, and if anything has become more on the targeted killing side under the constitutional lawyer president than it was under the cowboy oil man. So clearly there's a great comfort level in doing this," notes the former official.[101]

Even were the United States to have reached consensus with the rest of the world on a legal framework for targeted killings away from the hot battlefield, Washington may have believed itself to be under no obligation to respect this. In frank testimony provided to the Senate Select Committee on Intelligence in December 2013, new CIA General Counsel Caroline Krass noted that while covert actions by the Agency cannot "violate the Constitution or any statute of the United States . . . Congress did not prohibit the President from authorizing a covert action that would violate a non-self-executing treaty or customary international law." Clarifying further, Krass claimed that only where international treaty provisions had been incorporated into domestic statute would the United States "need to comply." In summary, she noted that "as a general matter, and including with respect to the use of force, the United States respects international law and complies with it to the extent possible in the execution of covert action activities."[102] In effect, covert action by the Agency—including drone strikes—could be in breach of international law or treaty, so long as US domestic law was upheld.

Israel: A Different Path

Israel's own advanced remotely piloted drones had at first only assisted other aircraft or troops with targeted killings.[103] Emulating the US success in arming the Predator, missiles were later placed on Israel's own Hermes and Heron RPAs, with Israeli drone strikes reportedly beginning by the summer of 2004, around the same time that the CIA's covert bombing campaign had begun in Pakistan. "If you confront the terrorist while he's executing his mission this is too late," the former commander of the Israel Air Force, Eitan Ben Eliyahu, later explained to Al Jazeera. "The idea is to prevent the terrorist operation from even starting. And these things cannot be done by jet aeroplanes or even helicopters."[104] Eyewitness Abd Al-Karim Abd Allah, who lived in the West Bank town of Jenin, described at the time how "I saw a small plane and then a flash of light, then I heard a huge explosion and a car went up in flames"—a fair description of a drone strike.[105] Although US RPA attacks were often limited to employing variants of a single munition—the Hellfire missile—Israel's remotely piloted warfare independently developed its own weapons and tactics. One method employed by Israel, for example, was "knocking"—the firing at a building's roof of a small inert missile described by the IDF as "loud but non-lethal bombs." Their role was to warn those inside to leave prior to a major attack, although on occasion the knocking missiles themselves caused fatalities.[106]

In contrast with US drone strikes, which tended to occur in rural areas of Pakistan, Israel's targeted killings usually took place in densely packed urban centers within the Palestinian Territories. Often generating high noncombatant casualties, Israel found itself under sustained international criticism. "The Special Rapporteur reiterates that aerial bombing or targeted assassinations in areas populated by civilians resulting in deaths would constitute extrajudicial or summary executions," Special Rapporteur Philip Alston told the UN General Assembly in 2004.[107] Even close allies were critical, with high-ranking British officials protesting Israeli strikes (though not American ones) that same year: "It goes without saying that the Prime Minister also condemns today's killing. We have repeatedly made clear our opposition to Israel's use of targeted killings and assassinations," Tony Blair's official spokesman told journalists following the death of Palestinian spiritual leader Sheikh Ahmed Yassin.[108]

While the United States had sought to block its courts from scrutinizing targeted killings, Israel instead actively sought higher court approval. In 2002 the IDF's lawyers had gone public with their assertions of legality for such operations, successfully fighting a case to the Supreme Court. As the landmark ruling of December 2006 noted:

> It cannot be determined in advance that every targeted killing is prohibited according to customary international law, just as it cannot be determined in advance that every targeted killing is permissible according to customary international law. The law of targeted killing is determined in the customary international law, and the legality of each individual such act must be determined in light of it.[109]

In short the IDF would need to make a unique legal assessment of each planned operation. The Supreme Court ruling was welcomed by the IDF's senior lawyers. As one of those closely associated with the case notes, "it was proof positive that we were supervised. And also, when you write such a legal opinion, no matter how many lawyers you consult, it's still a very lonely thing to do. But when you have the Supreme Court of the State of Israel checking what you did and coming up with fine tuning, even if changing some of the things we wrote . . . that's absolutely fine, because it gives you the confidence that you are no longer alone."[110]

In the wake of that ruling and Israel's general openness about the legal basis of its targeted killing program (if not an operational openness) they "consider themselves to have, if you like, a gold standard in targeting terms and in accountability terms," according to Emmerson, "And in principle at least, and in terms of black-letter law, the standards are pretty high under Israeli law."[111] This had led to harsh comparisons by some with the United States' own campaign: "My Israeli friends say, how was it that the Americans can literally act with impunity and get away with it?" notes Professor Amos Guiora. "The legal structure in the United States is fundamentally distinct and different from the Israeli legal system [and] the lack of Congressional oversight and the lack of judicial review is a major downfall of this thing called separation of powers in checks and balances."[112] Yet in practice Israeli targeted killings, often by armed drones, had proven highly controversial. During the four-week Operation Cast Lead in Gaza in 2008-2009, significant numbers of civilian deaths occurred. As a later report to the UN General Assembly noted:

> Israel has acknowledged that its military operation resulted in "many civilian deaths and injuries, and significant damage to public and private property in Gaza." Israel has not to date released disaggregated civilian casualty estimates in a form that would enable an analysis of the specific impact of remotely piloted aircraft (either as a direct weapons-delivery system or for the purposes of target acquisition).[113]

That monitoring work fell instead to NGOs. Human Rights Watch in its report *Precisely Wrong* examined the deaths of 29 civilians it said had died in Israeli RPA strikes during Cast Lead, concluding that "Drones, much like sniper rifles, are only as good at sparing civilians as the care taken by the people who operate them. The accuracy and concentrated blast radius of the missile can reduce civilian casualties, but in Gaza, Israel's targeting choices led to the loss of many civilian lives."[114] A joint study by B'Tselem, the Palestinian Centre for Human Rights and the Al-Mezan Center for Human Rights described evidence of 87 civilian deaths in 42 drone strikes.[115] And Amnesty International reported 58 civilians killed in Israeli drone strikes during the Israeli operation.[116]

Three years later, similar issues were reported during Operation Pillar of Defense. While the Israel Defense Force insisted it took significant measures to minimize harm to civilians (which it said included phoning and texting residents and dropping leaflets warning of impending attacks), as many as 103 Palestinian civilians died. The United Nations High Commissioner for Human Rights later criticized Israel and Palestinian armed groups for at times failing to respect international law during fighting. The report also questioned "whether the IDF took all feasible measures to verify that their targets were military objectives, in line with the principle of distinction under international humanitarian law, which requires that the parties to a conflict must at all times distinguish between civilians and combatants. Under international human rights law these cases may constitute violations of the right to life."[117] International NGOs raised similar concerns: "Human Rights Watch field investigations found 14 strikes by aerial drones or other aircraft for which there was no indication of a legitimate military target at the site at the time of the attack. In four other cases, attacks may have targeted Palestinian fighters, but appeared to use indiscriminate means or caused disproportionate harm to civilians."[118] More infamously, in 2014 Israel drew rare criticism from the United States after a ferocious bombing campaign on Gaza—including by drones—led to more than 2,000 Palestinian deaths. The IDF itself admitted that as many as half of those killed were civilians, while others placed the proportion far higher.[119]

Uniquely among nations, only Israel and the United States had claimed the right to carry out targeted or extrajudicial killings by drone away from the hot battlefield. A decade after the first such operations, President Obama's chief counterterrorism adviser had fretted that "If we want other nations to use these technologies responsibly, we must use them responsibly. If we want other nations to adhere to high and rigorous standards for their use, then we must do so as well."[120] Critics would argue that Washington had already helped establish a dangerous precedent, which other countries might yet follow.

4

THE CAULDRON
Iraq, 2003–2011

In December 2011, the last of more than 1.5 million American military personnel to have served in Iraq finally departed the country, four years after Barack Obama had promised to pull the United States from a war "that never should have been waged."[1] Iraq itself had shattered in the wake of invasion, occupation, insurgency, and civil war. More than 125,000 civilians were conservatively reported dead along with almost 5,000 US and allied military personnel and many more thousands of insurgents.[2] The war had cost the United States much of its global reputation, and the taxpayers back home at least $800 billion.[3] As the final convoy of 125 US military vehicles crossed into Kuwait, a solitary aircraft loitered behind for a few hours longer—an Air Force MQ-1 Predator. Most of the remotely piloted aircraft fleet had already been diverted to the recent conflict in Libya, or to Obama's secret wars in Pakistan, Yemen, and Somalia. The chances of any remaining drone firing a Hellfire missile had been next to zero since Obama had taken office. "We could not loose weapons, towards the end of our occupation in Iraq we were weapons-tight," former Predator pilot Bruce Black has recalled. "It took an act of a President to say 'Yes, that's somebody we need to strike.'"[4] That order rarely came, with just five recorded drone strikes in Iraq between 2009 and 2011.[5] Yet it had been in Iraq that the United States and its British allies had finally learned how best to exploit the Predator. The remote aircraft's intelligence-gathering capabilities—and its unique competence as an assassin's tool—would over a short time change profoundly how both nations fought their wars.

In the opening days of the 2003 invasion, attacks by Predators had still been rare enough to warrant a place in the Pentagon's official history: "March 22nd: A Predator unmanned aerial vehicle (UAV) destroys a ZSU 23-4 radar-guided anti-aircraft artillery vehicle outside the town of Al Amarah. This is the first armed UAV kill in Iraq."[6] That drone still "belonged" to the CIA, one of only seven armed Predators in the region which were barely enough to provide two Combat Air Patrols. Less capable Air Force Predators were put to creative use by planners. Baghdad was classed as a "Super-MEZ," or missile engagement zone, where a complex grid of Iraqi anti-aircraft guns and missiles could, in theory, still shoot down Coalition aircraft. "The Iraqi air defense network was in a state of near collapse, they couldn't fight their way out of a paper bag," recalls former USAF Major General Jim Poss. "But we couldn't prove beyond a shadow of a doubt that they weren't going to get their act together for 30 minutes and shoot someone down." In an operation dubbed Viking Funeral, a pair of worn-out, unarmed Predators which had first seen service in the Balkans were stripped of most technologies, then sent prowling slowly back and forth above Baghdad to invite attack. The Iraqis failed to take the bait, and eventually both aircraft ran out of fuel, with one falling into the Shatt-al Arab waterway. Fished out by locals, Iraqi TV claimed the drone had been "shot down."[7] Still visible on the Predator's airframe were the anti-Saddam obscenities daubed there by its US maintenance crew.

George W. Bush had famously proclaimed from the deck of the USS *Abraham Lincoln* in May 2003 that, "in the battle of Iraq, the United States and our allies have prevailed."[8] For a while it seemed this might hold true. The Sunni Baathists had been defeated, with Saddam Hussein on the run and soon to be captured. And despite the anarchy unleashed by the invasion, security was not yet in freefall. In early 2004, for example, the author was able to travel through much of central Iraq for the BBC in beaten-up taxis. Our single bodyguard, a former British Royal Marine, was not even armed.[9] Within months such actions became unthinkable as the insurgency took form, fueled by events in Fallujah and Abu Ghraib. Exploiting that chaos was an Al Qaeda-linked terrorist group which would soon represent the most significant threat to an already-weakened Iraq.

AL QAEDA IN IRAQ

The Bush administration had claimed prior to the invasion that Al Qaeda had a strong presence in Iraq; that the terror network had held regular meetings with Saddam's regime; and by direct implication, that Baghdad was involved in the September 2001 atrocities. None of this was true, with former Agency director George Tenet later bluntly insisting that the "CIA found absolutely no linkage between Saddam and 9/11."[10] A small Al Qaeda-linked presence certainly did exist in early 2003, in the Northern No Fly Zone policed from the air by the United States and Britain. As a key US Senate report would later dryly note, the group operated "in a mountainous no-man's land Baghdad has not controlled since 1991." One of those sheltering there, after recently fighting in Afghanistan against the United States in 2001, was Ahmad al-Khalayleh—better known to the world by his *nom de guerre* of Abu Musab al-Zarqawi. Even Iraq's dictator had spotted the danger this Jordanian represented: "Postwar reports indicate that Saddam Hussein attempted, unsuccessfully, to locate and capture al-Zarqawi and that the regime did not have a relationship, harbour or turn a blind eye towards Zarqawi," the US Senate would later conclude.[11]

Washington's postwar intelligence effort had at first focused on rolling up Baathist remnants. Yet al-Zarqawi's group Jama'at al-Tawhid wa'l Jihad represented a far more potent threat. Best translated as "Monotheism and Jihad," it was responsible for the deadly bombing of the UN headquarters in Iraq in August 2003. That same month, the group killed 83 people when it targeted the Imam Ali shrine in the city of Najaf, a holy site for the country's majority Shia Muslim population. Al-Zarqawi's aims were straightforward and vicious: to drive out the international community and to provoke a civil war between Shia and Sunni. In early 2004 a courier was intercepted carrying a letter from the Jordanian to Osama bin Laden. Swearing loyalty to Al Qaeda, al-Zarqawi outlined his plan to drag Iraq deeper into chaos: "Targeting and hitting them [the Shia community] in religious, political, and military depth will provoke them to show the Sunnis their rabies . . . and bare the teeth of the hidden rancour working in their breasts. If we succeed in dragging them into the arena of sectarian war, it will become possible to awaken the inattentive Sunnis as they feel imminent danger."[12] When later that year al-Zarqawi changed his group's name to Al Qaeda in Iraq (AQI), President Bush's claims of an active presence for the terror group had become a chilling reality. While the Predator would ultimately play a crucial role in dismantling the upper levels of AQI, Coalition delays in effectively targeting its leadership helped buy al-Zarqawi the time he needed to drag the nation into sectarian war. As the US General tasked with bringing down Al Qaeda in Iraq would later concede, "We had killed Zarqawi too late."[13]

While tens of thousands of regular Coalition troops were the public face of the Iraq conflict (and the main focus for militant attacks), much of the counterinsurgency was fought by elite Special Operations Forces (SOF). Chief among these was Joint Special Operations Command, better known as JSOC. Set up in 1980 following a shambolic US hostage-rescue raid into Iran, JSOC had evolved into an elite command comprising the US Navy's SEALS, the Army's Delta Force, and other highly skilled elements. Operating outside the normal US military chain of command, JSOC was led by its own three-star General or equivalent and was, in effect, answerable only to the President and to the Secretary of Defense. The unit would eventually quadruple in size during the War on Terror to around 4,000 front-line troops.[14] When Saddam Hussein was captured in December 2003, it was the work of JSOC and Kurdish troops. It was now tasked with bringing down Abu Musab al Zarqawi. JSOC embarked on a slew of operations to locate, capture, or kill key extremists in Iraq, supported by the CIA and British and Australian Special Forces. During five years of operations in Iraq, BBC correspondent Mark Urban has estimated that JSOC seized some 9,000 alleged militants and killed a further 3,000, in what senior British officers termed "industrial counter-terrorism."[15] For comparison, the entire covert US drone bombing campaign reached a similar lethal tally only after ten years of bombing across three nations. In the words of President Bush, "JSOC is awesome."[16]

The man responsible for "awesome" was General Stanley McChrystal, who commanded JSOC for five grueling years from September 2003 until taking command of international forces in Afghanistan. Described by former US Defense Secretary Bob Gates as "perhaps the finest warrior and leader of men in combat I had ever met,"[17] McChrystal was also a highly controversial figure. As he admits in his memoirs, JSOC was using "carefully controlled 'enhanced' interrogation techniques"—torture—on prisoners. Even after the Abu Ghraib scandal broke in April 2004, two JSOC interrogators "mistreated [a] detainee by electrically shocking him several times with a Taser," the retired General noted.[18] A blistering report from Human Rights Watch, based on first-hand testimony from US military personnel, catalogues systematic abuses. These included severe beatings, and on one occasion forcing a prisoner to drink urine.[19] By mid-2006, some 34 members of JSOC's task force had been reprimanded and 11 removed from the unit for mistreating prisoners.[20]

McChrystal himself was never disciplined, viewed instead by the Pentagon and White House as the right man to deal with the emerging Al Qaeda threat. With some humility, McChrystal later described the group's early terrorist successes: "Al Qaeda in Iraq's lieutenants did not wait for memos from their superiors, much less orders from bin Laden. Decisions were not centralized, but were made quickly and communicated laterally across the organization.... Money, propaganda, and information flowed at alarming rates, allowing for powerful, nimble coordination." What JSOC needed was high-quality information on this new and adaptive enemy. Yet traditional US military structures were too slow and bureaucratic to succeed, in McChrystal's view. In the end the General paid al-Zarqawi the compliment of remodeling JSOC on Al Qaeda's own structures:

> Although we got our message out differently than did our enemies, both organizations increasingly shared basic attributes that define an effective network. Decisions were decentralized and cut laterally across the organization. Traditional institutional boundaries fell away and diverse cultures meshed.[21]

From his new frontline headquarters at Balad airbase in central Iraq, McChrystal began fusing together JSOC teams with CIA analysts and National Security Agency (NSA) intercept specialists, creating units that could rapidly exploit fresh intelligence. That intel came from many sources—from ISR platforms, from human intelligence, and via material seized in the latest raid. For those more used to traditional military methods the impact could be startling, as one former analyst later recalled for the author: "When I was introduced to JSOC and that world, one of the things they really emphasized was that this was a flat organization. That your typical military structure is that of a modern feudal system, and the world of JSOC they are attempting to break the barriers, to share the information with as many people as possible, and basically to give each individual person who is involved directly with things like CT [counterterrorism] a voice or a platform to express their opinion on a matter," recalls the former intelligence operative. "Me, for instance, I could approach a colonel who is leading this whole apparatus and tell them, 'Hey, I don't feel comfortable about this or that,' or 'I think that you would do better if you tried this.' Not that that ever happened but that was there."[22] This flattening-out of hierarchical structures, heresy to some in the US military, would help lead to Al Qaeda's defeat in Iraq.

By mid-2004, Sunni-dominated Fallujah had become the epicenter of Iraq's growing insurgency. Marine Corps Sergeant Matthew Mardan was assigned with his scout-sniper platoon to the southern edges of the city: "Our job was to probe what's going on in Fallujah. Because the city was completely off-limits at that point, there was no friendly military inside the city at all," he recalls. The risks to personnel on the ground were extreme, with a number of Iraqi army operatives captured and executed that summer. With a fresh assault on Fallujah planned for November, JSOC was drafted in to help target key insurgents—among them al-Zarqawi. Armed drones began playing a key role. Mardan recalls one night watching a Predator precision strike on the city, something few had so far witnessed from the ground:

A call came in on the radio that there's going to be a Predator attack. I remember another guy in our team started freaking out. "What's a Predator attack? What's going on?" thinking there was going to be incoming fire. And we were like, "No no, a Predator, a drone! So let's sit here and watch!" So we just sat for ten minutes [using night vision]. We could hear a buzzing about a kilometer up in the air, you could hear the thing but you couldn't see it. A Hellfire missile hit a target. It didn't make a huge explosion but it definitely made an impact. You could tell it was a very specific precision attack. Our platoon commander who was with us at the time goes, "That's the future gents. That's what's probably going to replace all of us."[23]

That precision strike was almost certainly JSOC's handiwork. As McChrystal later recalled, JSOC aggressively targeted leaders, trainers, and key command and control centers in the city.[24] When the brutal US assault on Fallujah finally came in late 2006, Predators joined other aircraft above the city to help direct punishing fire onto insurgents.

Although JSOC could make limited use of the CIA's few armed drones in Iraq, it was still dependent on the conventional Air Force for most resources. By 2004 USAF had finally obtained its own small fleet of armed Predators, operated by the Nevada-based 15th Reconnaissance Squadron (15th RS). There was a major clash between JSOC and conventional forces on what role those few drones should play. "The first days of the war you could fairly well tell who the bad guys were because they were the ones trying the mass assaults and stuff," says Colonel Pete Forrest, who helped pioneer the Special Forces use of the Predator. "But as it became more of a counterinsurgency type of operation, they start to blend in, and it becomes much more difficult now to figure out who the enemy is versus who the friendlies are." For JSOC, the Predator's persistence and surveillance technologies were its main value, not its weaponry. As Forrest notes, "I'd be the first to say, if I needed the tactic for how to put a Hellfire down onto the target within 2 seconds? The 15th RS was a hell of a lot better at that than we were. But that wasn't our job. . . . Frequently we would take the Hellfires off of the airplane simply so we could get a little bit more endurance."[25]

In contrast, the conventional Air Force tended to gauge the success of each Predator mission by how many targets it had observed—and how many were hit. "At the very early stages we were very kinetic. We'd come in every day, we'd be, 'How many shots did you take that night?'" recalls Bruce Black, a former pilot with the 15th RS. "It was a new toy, it was the Wild West and we were a bunch of cowboys trying to figure out how to make this thing work."[26] Retired sensor operator Michael Haas agrees: "I think it started becoming a preferred weapon. We were shooting so damned many of them we were actually running out of missiles at one point. They weren't expecting JTACs [forward air controllers] to use it so readily. But they liked it because it could take out a building, it could take out a moving car, and there wasn't a big potential to frag any innocents. I think they went a little overboard with it."[27]

In an effort to bypass his dependence on conventional USAF, McChrystal oversaw the creation of the "Federal Air Force," a cobbled-together fleet of manned intelligence and surveillance assets. Yet none had the 24-hour persistence of a Predator. A meeting in January 2005 between General Bryan Brown (who headed JSOC's parent command USSOCOM) and Air Force Chief of Staff General John Jumper led to a significant decision. Brown's elite airmen from Air Force Special Operations Command would create an independent drone force, soon designated the 3rd Special Operations Squadron. It was a close-run thing whether General Atomics' Predators would even be used. On McChrystal's recommendation, Brown had at first proposed buying in Heron or Hermes drones from Israel, both of them advanced systems on a par with the Predator, and by then capable of being armed.[28] "We really didn't care what the air thing was, it was really the product at the end of the day, of 'OK can I get the video on here and can I get it fast?'" recalls one of those with knowledge of the discussions. "Then Jumper recommended, 'Hey I can give Predator to you,' and the quote was 'Faster cheaper better if you team with us.' And we basically started building the [AFSOC] MQ-1 fleet."[29] No longer would Special Forces need to be dependent on their colleagues in "Big Blue"—or see their drone assets rationed.

PATTERN OF LIFE

Officially "stood up" in October 2005, the new 3rd Special Operations Squadron was based at first alongside the 15th RS at Nellis Air Force Base in Las Vegas. Pete Forrest was a colonel with Air Force Special Operations Command (AFSOC), whose combat career already had taken him from the Balkans to Afghanistan. Now he was tasked with setting up the new Special Forces Predator squadron. There was an immediate culture clash, some of it petty. "They wouldn't allow me to rent any trailers to create an office so we could start up our guys. I couldn't get a desk. I couldn't get computers. There were a lot of things that were being resented," recalls Forrest. Initially the 3rd SOS ran its single Predator line, or mission, alongside those of the regular Air Force's Predators. Again there were problems: "There was no continuity on how the 15th's crews actually flew the line. They would come in, fly one line for an hour or two and take a break. Then it would be, 'I need to replace Joe on another line.' So they'd go off on that one, so they were bouncing around. . . . It was completely inefficient in that the guy had zero understanding of his target when he looked at it. And that was the debrief from my customer, 'Why after every couple of hours do I have to re-explain to the pilot and sensor operator,' This is what you're looking for. This is what's going on. Yes that's normal' "?

Although Forrest still refuses to discuss "the J-word," that customer was most likely JSOC. As its pool of skilled personnel grew, so did JSOC's ability to exploit the extraordinary ISR potential of the Predator. Operators and analysts in both Iraq and Nevada began to note down everything that took place on missions: "As minor as it sounds, that wasn't going on before. So we would begin keeping a log of activities, a log of what did you see. Red truck, blue truck, where did the truck go?" recalls Forrest. "That log then started creating a history of our target and then we'd start to realize things like: every day at X time he goes to get lunch; every day at Y time he goes to what we assume to be home because that's where he spends the night. You start seeing things." What was emerging became known as Pattern of Life Analysis, one of the critical US intelligence breakthroughs of the war. While Predators and Reapers played a key part in this, data could be built up over many months by multiple ISR assets, by agents on the ground, and by signals and electronics intelligence. The National Geospatial Agency also began uniquely GPS-mapping every building in some troubled Iraqi towns (just as it later did across much of Waziristan for the CIA). The term "Pattern of Life" was later conflated with the signature strikes of the CIA's drone targeted killing program. Yet according to former USAF intelligence chief Jim Poss, the two should have had little in common: "It's mainly an expression of how ultra-careful we are in collateral damage and positive ID of the target. We're not really there making sure for the 50th time that this really is the bad guy. We're making sure there's no civilians in the area, and that if we do drop a bomb on it, exactly what will happen if the SOF guys are going to go in?"[30]

There was a further tension between USAF and McChrystal's people which needed resolving. JSOC was initially dependent for its drone intelligence analysis on Langley Air Force Base in Virginia. DGS-1, as it was known, had originally been set up to analyze feeds from U2 spy planes, and now handled most ISR data from the war in Iraq. Forrest recalls a 2005 visit to the temporary hangar in which the hundreds of DGS-1 analysts were then housed. "It was very disheartening. I'd been over to Afghanistan, I'd been flying operations on the helos. To this date I've had 21 funerals I've had to go to from the Combat side of the house. So then I come in and I go to the DGS and you can immediately tell, you've got a very young crowd, but they're so detached from the war, from understanding what it is that they're seeing on the end of the video." Two Special Forces operations were being displayed live on the screens at the time of Forrest's visit. Yet the analysts barely seemed interested: "I'm looking at these kids supporting the line. And I've got one who's got a radio on and he's sitting on a table with a guy next to him. And I'm seeing a lot of movement on the video in the background to him. Then I see this other kid on the second line and he's one guy by himself, he's sitting there, and there's a raid going on at the time. And there's nobody else supporting him." Forrest ended up chewing out the young analysts:

I took the first one and said "Turn off the darned radio, get your butt turned around and look at the screen!" And then I tried to get them to see, "OK do you see, that guy is getting ready to walk into a building? Your job is to make sure he comes out of that building alive. You gotta understand that you are this guardian angel looking at these guys and trying to make sure you've given them everything that you could before they walk into that building." Trying to give them a personal vested interest in what was happening on the screen.[31]

The Predators were transmitting live, full-motion video. Yet most specialists back in the United States at the time were only trained to analyze stills photographs. Special Forces units began bringing in their own human intelligence experts, who could better understand what was taking place: "You're not looking at stills, you're actually watching people. Which door are they coming in? Which way are they walking? How are they greeting and talking to each other? Where's the bathroom at? Believe it or not that was a fairly important issue. Last thing you want to do on a raid is walk in on a path where folks regularly use to get to the bathroom." Frustrated, Special Operations Command (USSOCOM) eventually decided to split off its entire drone intelligence operation, standing up the 11th Intelligence Squadron (11th IS) at Hurlburt Field in Florida in August 2006 to create DGS: Special Ops. Ultimately made up of around 500 Air Force personnel and civilian contractors, within two years the 11th IS was analyzing half of all the full-motion video being collected by Predators and Reapers in

Iraq and Afghanistan—an indication of just how intensive Special Forces operations had become.[32] As the Pentagon boasted, "Having the 11th IS provide dedicated intelligence support to our warfighters will make us better able to find, fix and finish our adversaries."[33] One adversary in particular—Ayman al-Zarqawi—would require every new trick to finish.

Death of a Terrorist

Just before 7.00 a.m. on February 22, 2006, a dozen men in Iraqi army uniforms tricked their way into the al-Askari religious shrine in Samarra. Tying up the guards, the men then used explosives to destroy the famous golden dome of the mosque. Perhaps uniquely for an assault by AQI, nobody appears to have died.[34] Yet strategically the bombing would prove more devastating than hundreds of lethal AQI attacks. One of the holiest sites in Shia Islam now lay in ruins. Four hundred miles south in Basra that morning, I happened to be filming with the BBC at a British forward operating base. As the streets around us began filling with thousands of furious Shia clutching home-made banners and posters, it soon became clear that their wrath was aimed at Sunnis. Trails of smoke began appearing across the skyline, as one by one Basra's Sunni mosques were attacked. Towns and cities across the country experienced similar scenes. Abu Musab al-Zarqawi had told Osama bin Laden two years earlier that he aimed to provoke a sectarian war, yet Shia Iraqis had remained Stoic despite dozens of atrocities. The al-Askari attack proved the final straw, as al-Zarqawi finally forced Iraq's majority population to "bare their teeth." The ensuing violence drew Sunni and Shia into ethnic cleansing and civil war. Tens of thousands died, with some two million Iraqis eventually fleeing the horror.

The Americans had already missed a number of opportunities to kill or capture al-Zarqawi, a man whose early removal from the battlefield might have changed Iraq's bloody history. McChrystal describes in his memoirs unknowingly standing less than a block away from the terrorist leader in Fallujah in February 2004: "I did not know he and I were that close, nor did the Army special operators who . . . were nearer to him than I was."[35] That night al-Zarqawi appears to have escaped his would-be captors by jumping from a second-floor window. As AQI's atrocities mounted, including the beheading of two American captives on video, so the political pressure on JSOC to deliver grew. "The

President is going to want to have a meeting on Zarqawi and what is being done to get him—how many people are working on it, what the focus is, how it is operating, who is involved, what the coordination is, and the like," Defense Secretary Donald Rumsfeld flagged up to his commanders in May 2005.[36] Weeks earlier, JSOC had again failed to kill or capture the Jordanian. Traveling by road between Ramadi and Fallujah, al-Zarqawi was unaware he was being tracked by an AFSOC Predator high above—or of the JSOC ambush on the highway up ahead. Running the roadblock al-Zarqawi sought to escape, and the Predator was given the order to strike. But at a crucial moment the RPA's camera gyroscope malfunctioned.[37] "They lost him for a few seconds in video. And in that few seconds he'd actually gotten out of the car. And when they did the strike on the car they later found out he wasn't in it," recalls a former AFSOC pilot with knowledge of the operation. "So everybody was like, 'Wait a second! We know he got in the car!' and they go back and look and say, 'Oh yep, we lost him here.' "[38]

Tracking cars with Predators presented a significant challenge for operators and analysts. In Afghanistan with its sparse population centers, barren landscape and poor roads, moving targets could fairly easily be followed. Iraq's urban sprawl and fast roads were something else: one former drone operator admitted to the author losing "at least 20 vehicles" during surveillance operations there.[39] "The hardest job we had in Iraq was trying to find a vehicle. As simple as that sounds, the issue is you have buildings," says retired AFSOC drone commander Pete Forrest. "You basically have a line of sight from the airplane down to the ground, and buildings get in the way. So you'd have to understand the building height so that when hey, I'm coming up to an area that has tall buildings, alright push the aircraft closer so that I cannot lose him if he goes around the corner. Because a lot of times you don't know if he's going to make a left or a right."[40]

Al Qaeda began adapting to this new intensive surveillance. "They would do a lot of counter-tactics to us, sometimes swapping cars, sometimes going under bridges and stopping—then coming back in a different direction," says Forrest. Analysts back in the United States could play a key role in countering this, recalls USAF's former Director of Intelligence Jim Poss: "The guys in the Predator crew cannot take their eye off of that car. They have to follow it. They'll make a quick call to the DGS guys and say 'OK, what did that guy do under the bridge?' So they'll go back through and look at every frame and look at every angle and pull it up and enhance it, there's special software we've got, and then they might be able to make a call, 'Well he looks like he dumped something out of the back of the truck.' "[41] Another challenge was that multiple targets were often the subject of surveillance. At first operators thrashed out crude rules: "What do you do? Do you stay with the house or follow the car? Because waiting for five minutes to hear from somebody, you've lost the car." Eventually JSOC developed "Massed ISR," in which multiple drones or other aerial platforms worked a single mission. "Now you'd mass maybe three or four different [aerial] vehicles watching an area. OK, number 2's going to follow the car; number 1's gonna stay on the target."[42]

On May 19, 2006, JSOC finally got the breakthrough that would lead to al-Zarqawi's death. A captured Al Qaeda operative gave up the name of Sheikh Abd al-Rahman, the Jordanian's spiritual adviser who met with al-Zarqawi every ten days or so at an unknown location. Within hours, al-Rahman's home in Baghdad was under permanent observation by AFSOC Predators. The operation was a gamble. As McChrystal later noted, "the [Baghdad] squadron's intelligence staff and 70 per cent of its ISR assets were focused full time on Abd al-Rahman. The wait was grating. Every day that we watched Abd al-Rahman other targets went undisturbed."[43] There were daily debates on whether simply to arrest and interrogate al-Rahman, although the team held its nerve. Finally on the morning of June 7, 2006, the sheikh left Baghdad in a silver sedan and started heading north. Employing classic countersurveillance tactics, he soon swapped to a blue truck. But JSOC had learned its lessons. Three ISR assets were already above al-Rahman, and would soon be joined by five more as the spiritual leader used different buildings and vehicles in an effort to evade trackers. At last, al-Rahman led his unsuspected pursuers to a small house in a palm grove outside the village of Hibhib—just 25 miles from JSOC's own Balad headquarters. As a man moved forward to greet the arriving vehicle, live images from a Predator enabled analysts to positively identify the host as Abu Musab al-Zarqawi. With McChrystal unwilling to risk the terrorist leader escaping, an F-16 was ordered to drop two 500-lb precision bombs on the house. "We knew that if Zarqawi was there, he was not alone. His family—including perhaps both of his wives and their children—often stayed with him and would be killed in the strike," McChrystal later noted.[44] Nevertheless, the risk to civilians was judged proportionate given the threat the terrorist represented. Al-Rahman died instantly, along with the Jordanian terrorist's two wives and a child. Al-Zarqawi, seriously injured, survived only for a short while.

The death of al-Zarqawi in June 2006 was a major success for JSOC, which President Bush described as the single bright spot in Iraq that year.[45] The mission also highlighted the novel form of warfare the Predator was helping to mold in Iraq: "It took hundreds of hours of Predator time; and thousands of hours of analysts' time; and about six minutes of F-16 time to dispatch Zarqawi to the nether regions. So where's the level of effort here?" notes General Dave Deptula, who by 2006 was Air Force Deputy Chief of Staff at the Pentagon. "It's not just about the tightening of the Kill Chain, it's also about the expansion of the knowledge that accrues from the capability of these things to watch and persist." Yet even as JSOC celebrated, there was an awareness that the Al Qaeda leader's killing had come too late for Iraq. Noting that 3,149 Iraqis died in June alone in the sectarian violence now engulfing the country, McChrystal has admitted that "Zarqawi's focused sectarian killing helped inaugurate a system of violence that was, by the time he died, a self-propelling cycle."

Within 24 hours of al-Zarqawi's death, JSOC launched an additional 36 raids which killed or captured many of the leaders and mid-rankers of AQI. "We had done such a cripple there that we were able to immediately shift over and say 'Hey, what's our next series of targets?' Because really at that point Iraq became a sit-back-and-watch-again for a while," recalls Pete Forrest. With Al Qaeda in disarray, the hope was that AFSOC's Predators could swiftly be moved across to support JSOC operations in Afghanistan, where a major Taliban offensive in 2006 had put at risk any gains there since 2001: "As we said, it was time for Afghanistan to get some lovin'—we had to start building up our capability there."[46] The plan was for conventional drone units like the 15th RS to step up and support ongoing Special Forces operations in Iraq. But there was a problem. "The customers in Iraq went nuts. Because none of the tactics, none of the continuity pieces, none of that stuff continued with the 15th," says Forrest. "Getting them to change their spots really was a difficult thing. So the complete difference in how the squadrons worked and acted with each other really came to a head at that point. We had a four star [General] ask, 'Why is the performance so different between two squadrons here?'" In part this was because some conventional operators could see little benefit to JSOC's less kinetic aerial tactics. "To be fair they sometimes scored big-time in capturing wanted subjects. Nevertheless it seemed to make little difference in the overall scheme of things," complained Colonel Matt Martin in his memoirs. "If Predator took the 80 per cent of our time currently directed to Special Forces and turned it to tactical support of patrols and convoys that were IED'd and getting shot up every day, we could save a lot more lives and make more noticeable progress."[47]

The Air Force and its fast-expanding drone fleet had to serve every customer in the field. As a former SOF pilot notes, the conventional Air Force "had the issue of trying to support SOF most of the time, then go support the Marines or the Army and then come back. So their ability to provide the level of support was just degraded compared to what we were able to do."[48] With AFSOC's Predators now needed in two wars at once, the solution was a shotgun marriage between two drone units with very different philosophies. The conventional 15th RS was effectively swallowed up, with almost its entire personnel "rebadged" to the 3rd Special Operations Squadron. For some, teaming up with Special Forces was a welcome change: "It was a lot more ISR, the missions were a little bit more in-depth, they would take longer because they were collecting more information. With the 15th it was quickie little things here, quickie little things there," recalls former mission controller Janet Atkins, who was rebadged to AFSOC with more than 100 others. "We were now able to build more rapport with our operators, operationally they were more organized. We knew who we belonged to: it was like a little family."[49]

For those operators still flying conventional Predator missions, a revolution was now taking place on the Iraq battlefield. Although persistent surveillance missions continued, the drones also proved well-suited to providing topcover and close air support to regular troops below. "The ground troops when we first got there were very leery of letting us shoot. It took not only the ground controller saying he wanted to shoot but it took him trusting us to be able to do it," recalls retired Nevada Air National Guard Colonel Bruce Black. "It's not an exact parallel. But you know the black fighter pilots in World War Two, that squadron? I kind of likened us to them: we were the bastard children. Nobody really wanted us and nobody really trusted us, until they could figure out what we could do. And then oh my God all of a sudden, just like that they were the most requested fighter squadron for escort because they were really good. But it took a while for us to develop that trust. Not necessarily the technology but the trust."[50] USMC Sergeant Matthew Mardan, who had witnessed a JSOC strike from a "robot in the sky" back in 2004, left the service just as armed drones became prevalent. Like many servicemen and women at the time, he was still reluctant to put his life in the hands of an operator thousands of miles away:

> Everything happened so fast on the battlefield that I think we would have not trusted the idiot, especially if he's Air Force, sitting somewhere in an office running this. So much easier for us to just call in exactly what we need from a pilot or a gunship or an Apache or Cobra. That's what we were used to doing.[51]

Over time, ground troops would become more convinced. It was the versatility of the system which made it so valuable. During the intense battles of Fallujah and Najaf, Predators helped direct in precision fire from other combat aircraft and would sometimes attack themselves. In August 2004, US Marines found themselves pinned down near a shrine in Najaf: "You see crosshairs near a window of a building where a sniper has Marines pinned down. Some of the Marines are wounded from the sniper. Missile hits and blows the face off the building," reads a CNN description of the incident.[52] It was not just US troops who benefited from this fast-expanding fleet of Predators. Former sensor operator Michael Haas recalls helping a British Special Forces night raid make its way out of Sadr City: "They had just conducted one of their missions, and on their route out apparently there was bad communication between US and Brit forces. God, imagine that. The route they were going to take was blocked. They're trying to figure out how in the Hell they can do it and I came up with the bright idea to use the LTM [laser targeting marker] spotlight that we could shine down on the road. So every intersection on approach I'd shine it, either take a left or a right or go straight, and we guided them out of there."[53]

Back at the Pentagon incoming US Defense Secretary Bob Gates made it a priority to get more Predators and other ISR assets above the battle-field, later berating "a lack of enthusiasm and urgency in the Air Force, my old service ... When I turned my attention to the ISR problem in mid-2007 the Air Force was providing eight Predator CAPs and had no plans to increase that number." Told that his proposal for 92 CAPS would "eclipse the sun," Gates was nevertheless able to achieve almost 60 simultaneous Predator and Reaper combat air patrols by the time he retired in July 2011 (a figure which included both the AFSOC and CIA fleets).[54] One way this was achieved was to seize control of the intelligence, surveillance, and reconnaissance aspect of armed drones from the top guns at Air Combat Command. A new Air Force ISR Agency was created, headed up by three-star General Dave Deptula, who championed a more sophisticated use of RPAs on the battlefield. "We were dealing with a military culture that traditionally has segregated operations and intelligence. And what my goal was as I came onboard was to change this culture into one that realized the benefits of integrating both," he recalls. Under constant pressure from Gates, Deptula "rode herd" on colleagues across the Air Force to quickly deliver more armed drones to the battlefield. This also meant hundreds more operators, analysts, and support personnel back home, and the bandwidth and equipment needed to handle all the data. Yet the creation of the ISR Agency also split control of armed drones between two wings of the Air Force, with the operators and actual drones still "owned" by Air Combat Command. It was "an unfinished revolution" says Deptula, who believes that in a world where ISR is operations, "we were still faced with a set of organizations and people who grew up in the last century, the industrial age of warfare."[55]

In a grinding, deeply unpopular war with few US victories, images from successful Predator drones strikes in Iraq were filling a niche with embattled troops on the ground. In early 2007 General David Petraeus began rolling out his "troop surge," the massive US counterinsurgency program aimed at extinguishing Iraq's sectarian civil war. A key architect of that plan was David Kilcullen, who believes clips of successful drone strikes—"Predator porn"—played a part in boosting morale:

> In a counterinsurgency environment, you almost never see the enemy, you certainly never see them doing anything that's bad. Whenever you do encounter them, they're trying to hide amongst the population. That's incredibly frustrating for people. So when people can see a bad guy carrying a weapon, acting like a bad guy, getting blown up, it's enormously satisfying for some Humvee guy who goes out and spends all day driving around Baghdad getting shot at. He comes back and he fires up

some gun camera footage from an Apache or drone strike footage and says, "Well at least we got some guys today."[56]

Such material was not popular with everyone. "Unless it is absolutely necessary there was no point in sharing the act of killing, because to me it was counterproductive, it de-sensitized people to it and it created the wrong impression," one senior British airman who served regularly in Afghanistan told the author. Yet whatever commanders might have thought, many in the ranks appeared to have an insatiable appetite for videos of drones and other aircraft carrying out successful strikes. Digitized clips were passed between units, with some making their way onto new websites like LiveTV and YouTube.[57] When grisly footage of a US Apache helicopter gunning down civilians was passed to Wikileaks in 2010 by Bradley (later Chelsea) Manning, it was simply an extension of this process says Kilcullen: "The reason that Bradley Manning was able to leak such a vast amount including the Warriors attack footage, it's because people pass this shit around. . . . There are whole websites and channels that are devoted to this stuff. But there's also a lot of samizdat stuff that gets passed around within there, and that's the stuff that Manning picked up."[58]

The media too had a strong appetite for "Pred porn." Quick to hype the role of the CIA's Predators in the invasions of Afghanistan and Iraq, news organizations were still denied access to highly classified footage of actual strikes. USAF's own armed drones had fewer restrictions. In early 2005 the Air Force released ten short video clips of Predators in action over Iraq. Despite the historic nature of that footage, it can no longer be located by USAF. Thankfully CNN archived four of the short films, and the broadcaster's descriptions remain evocative: "Samarra—High Value Target house. Army called in a Predator to hit this house after a HVT ran into it. Air Force did not know who the target was or if the person had been killed by the strike."[59] Another clip, unfortunately not in CNN's collection, revealed alleged militants gathered near trucks just before a missile was launched.[60] As one report breathlessly noted back in 2005: "Vehicles lined up in a row are there one minute, and incinerated the next. Floors of building are wiped out. Walls collapse. And city corners go up in flames—all because of these killer drones."[61]

The British too were later happy to release material depicting "bad guys" killed by their new drone fleet in Afghanistan. "RAF Reaper strikes insurgent IED team" was posted on YouTube by the Ministry of Defence in late 2010 and shows a UK operation to kill an alleged insurgent.[62] Another clip depicts the destruction of a reported Taliban bomb factory. "They're constantly releasing videos of certain strikes to the media where they moved the weapon away and it's hit somewhere else, or strikes which are in their interests—and so there's already a selective release," says Chris Cole of campaigning group Drone Wars UK, who argues that those deploying armed drones should make all videos of drone strikes publicly available.[63] UN special rapporteurs Ben Emmerson and Christof Heyns noted during their investigation that "a detailed video and computerized record of all sorties is maintained, providing a solid audit trail of operations."[64] On occasion anonymous US intelligence officials have even cited such archived drone surveillance materials in their own defense—while at the same time refusing to make them publicly available for others to scrutinize.[65]

THE BRITISH DRONE PROGRAM

Stanley McChrystal's window-shopping for Israeli drones in 2005 had made sense, given the delivery pressures General Atomics was by then under for its Predators. Israel had long been a pioneer of unmanned aerial vehicles. During its 1982 invasion of Lebanon, for example, early UAVs had helped flush out Syrian surface-to-air missile batteries in the Bekaa Valley.[66] With their later strategic duopoly, neither the United States nor Israel was keen to share with other nations their weaponized systems. However, Israel in particular had strongly pursued commercial exports of unarmed drones, with an estimated $4.6 billion of sales between 2005 and 2013.[67] State-owned Israel Aerospace Industries (IAI) had exported remotely piloted aircraft to around 50 countries by 2014, for example.[68] As IAI's Danny Bichman told Al Jazeera: "People hear about it and they want this wonderful technology too. The Lebanon War, Operation Cast Lead, targeted killings, whatever drone use is publicised, it increases demand."[69] Chief rival Elbit Systems had also benefited, with its large unarmed Hermes drones bought or hired by a number of NATO countries to provide surveillance in Afghanistan. More than £180 million (around $300 million) was spent by the British Army leasing a score of Elbit's Hermes-450s from 2007 onward.[70] Remotely flown by the Royal

Artillery, the Hermes had a limited range of around 60 miles—still more over-the-hill than over-the-horizon. These Army drones were known as "organic assets," an independent ISR tool reserved solely for a particular service's use. In collaboration with Elbit and Thales, the British Army also developed the Watchkeeper, a variant of the Hermes which was supposed to enter service in 2010. Despite development costs of more than £1 billion,[71] the Watchkeeper began regular operations in Afghanistan just weeks before Britain's withdrawal in late 2014.[72]

With similarly problematic results, the US Army had pursued its own organic RPA asset, spending $4.75 billion developing the Gray Eagle—an armed variant of General Atomics' late-model Predator. Though planned to enter service in 2009, four years later the US Government Accountability Office was still warning that "the Gray Eagle program is undergoing design changes and has yet to demonstrate the maturity of its production processes. Until hardware and software design changes have been incorporated and production processes proven stable and mature, the program's cost and schedule remain at risk."[73] Supporters of organic assets pointed to the Army's use of attack helicopters over many decades as evidence that the approach could work well. Yet some former senior Air Force commanders are scathing: "The Army will reserve the right to use that as an organic asset, which means if the Army has got the remotest use for it, they're going to use it. And they're not going to give it up for centralized management by the Air Force," complains retired USAF Major General Jim Poss.[74]

While the British Army doggedly pursued its independent Watchkeeper program, the Royal Air Force took a very different approach. Uniquely among America's allies its personnel had been allowed access to USAF's secretive armed drones program almost from the beginning. British parliamentarians learned in 2013 that embedded RAF personnel had remotely flown thousands of missions on US-badged drones. Long after Britain became the first nation allowed to operate its own armed Reaper fleet, these dual-badging operations had continued.[75] "The benefit to the UK government? The RAF got in on the ground floor of distributed operations and was very familiar with how it goes," says Poss, a self-confessed Anglophile. "People forget the US Air Force and the Royal Air Force essentially grew up together: decades of every major operation with the RAF being there. We know how to operate with them . . . and they pretty much speak English too, so that helps."[76]

The British saw significant benefits to observing the Predator up-close, a weapon system which had the potential to radically impact aerial warfare: "Here was a capability that could be disruptive, but I think even ten years ago we couldn't have predicted how disruptive," notes a senior RAF commander. "The opportunity of insight into that, at a time when the US were short of manpower anyway, was going to be invaluable to us to help us make our own investment decisions four, five years later."[77]

Beginning in 2004 just as the regular USAF was receiving its first armed drones, a steady flow of British pilots and navigators was assigned to the 15th RS at Nellis AFB, where they were known as "1115 Flight." Other personnel were co-opted as real-time remote intelligence analysts; as lawyers at the CAOC in Qatar; and as launch and recovery ground teams in Iraq and later Afghanistan. By 2006 some 45 RAF personnel were at Nellis, remotely flying as many as one in seven of all USAF Predator missions.[78] They were generally popular with their American colleagues: "We did a lot with the Brits," recalls sensor operator Michael Haas. "They were invaluable, especially when they were working with JTACs [ground air controllers] speaking with those real thick Scottish accents. You know Americans: no one knows the Hell what the Scots are saying if you haven't grown up with them." Colonel Pete Forrest, by then establishing AFSOC's first drone squadron, was impressed by the British mindset:

> Because of the MQ-1 [Predator] crew mix, you had a lot of guys who kept wanting to talk about the weapons side. The weapon was a secondary effect, it was only there for when we saw the mole pop his head out of the hole and you had to take him out because it was the only chance you had to go get him. The weapon was really just a minor thing that we had to have on the platform. And the MQ-1 obviously only had the one to two Hellfires, so not a whole lot of punch with that. Reconnaissance was the mission. And the UK team embraced that.[79]

Although dual-badged drone missions would often support SOF on the ground, Britain was careful to keep itself firewalled from the AFSOC and CIA drone campaigns now emerging in Nevada and New Mexico. Limited to conventional missions on the regular battlefields of Iraq, Afghanistan, and later Libya, the British also operated under stricter Rules of Engagement (ROEs), a situation which could sometimes generate tensions.[80] As one senior British military officer jokingly characterized it to the author, "British RPAs are operating on a peacetime trigger, while US military ones are on a wartime trigger. And the CIA has no trigger guard."[81]

In his memoirs, American Colonel Matt Martin recalls an incident when a British drone crew had refused to fire on a reported Taliban patrol in Afghanistan, as a result of their stricter ROEs: "As far as I was concerned those four men down there had painted bull's-eyes on their own butts by shooting at our guys. I dispatched an American crew to take over Skybird's controls, and settle the refined British conscience. We Americans weren't quite so finicky over what we shot at."[82] This was likely an extreme example. Brian, a serving Air Force Colonel, describes a more measured process: "It wasn't ever blown off: if there was an issue you had to work through it and you still have to work through it. It did make it interesting at times, but I think we managed to get through everything respecting the national priorities as well as the battlefield priorities."[83] Richard Mason, an RAF combat helicopter commander in Afghanistan who sometimes had to finesse these differing rules of engagement, sees it as the manageable by-product of a working relationship between two close allies:

> It just gives greater strength and consistency to when we're engaged and conducting dual-badge operations that the US recognize, acknowledge, and respect that the UK view may be different, and certainly my experience says that the US have never failed to. They have been cross at times but there's never been a sense of coercion, never a sense of "Whose side are you on?"[84]

In 2007 Britain's own armed drone fleet was finally stood up, featuring the most advanced RPA in the US arsenal.[85] These Reapers of XIII and 39 Squadrons—initially remotely flown from Creech in Nevada and later from RAF Waddington in England—might find themselves supporting troops of over a dozen Coalition nationalities on the ground in Afghanistan. In a mark of the trust in which Washington held its close ally, seven years later the UK still remained the only nation with access to US armed drone technology.

The invasion and occupation of Iraq had proved highly damaging for both Britain and the United States. By focusing on the "wrong war" as Barack Obama later termed it, the Taliban in Afghanistan had been given vital breathing space to regroup, allowing the insurgency to rekindle in 2006. The allies had also lost much of their international influence and had further destabilized the Middle East—both of which would have significant consequences as the Arab Spring later unfolded. Ultimately that would lead to American drones and manned aircraft having to return to Iraq's skies in summer 2014, to confront Al Qaeda successor Islamic State—which by then had overrun more than half of the country. From this debacle there were few "good news" stories. Yet the rolling out of remotely piloted armed Predators during the Iraq conflict had not led to the "rampaging robots" or PlayStation killings which some had predicted. Instead, there had been a glimpse of a future in which smaller, more agile weapon systems with precision warheads might—if coupled with heightened battlefield intelligence—lead to fewer risks to civilians. For this to happen, the technological capabilities of the Predator and Reaper needed to be harnessed to a political will to reduce noncombatant deaths. As events were now showing in the CIA's secret drone war in Pakistan—and in the conventional Afghan war alike—this was not a given.

THE OCCASIONAL ASSASSIN
Bush in Pakistan

Pakistan among all nations came to symbolize the front line in the US covert drone war. By late 2014, some 400 airstrikes by CIA Predators and Reapers had killed more than 2,400 people there, in the longest sustained covert bombing campaign in US history. Almost every attack was aimed at the tribal region of Waziristan, with a land mass barely bigger than the Bahamas and a population of 800,000—the great majority of whom were civilians.[1] For many in the US military and intelligence worlds, the campaign was a logical and necessary extension of the war against Al Qaeda which began in 2001: "There are people out there saying 'Hold on, this isn't right to use an application of force outside the defined battle area!' Well that's an anachronistic construct that harkens back to the Clausewitzian days where people defined conflict as a result of lines on a map," says General Dave Deptula, architect of the Afghan air war which had routed the Taliban and Al Qaeda within months of 9/11. "Our adversary isn't limited to lines on a map? Then what is the most viable effective way to fight against that adversary?"[2]

The United States has insisted that no more than 60 noncombatants had died in Pakistan in a decade of covert bombings. Yet in a single reported drone strike in 2006, the CIA killed up to 80 civilians according to public records, most of these children. The continued refusal by Washington to officially confirm or deny any role in that attack—which may represent the highest civilian casualty toll of the entire covert drone war—perfectly illustrates the problems associated with a secret civilian intelligence service having been given command of a war. As UN investigator Ben Emmerson QC would later complain, this "created immediately a situation of huge lethality whilst at the same time an impossibility to achieve accountability."[3]

Maulvi Liaqat was headmaster of a seminary for boys in the village of Chenegai, in the Bajaur tribal agency. He was also a leader of the TNSM, an Islamist organization founded in 1992 and banned for extremism a decade later by Pervez Musharraf's military government. That move led to armed conflict with the state, though by autumn 2006 Islamabad was offering a peace deal to the TNSM in Bajaur. Similar agreements in Waziristan—requiring only that militants no longer target Pakistani troops—had freed up thousands of fighters to join the fast-growing insurgency in Afghanistan. With the deal scheduled for October 30. Mushtaq Yusufzai, now a local correspondent for NBC News, was one of a select group of journalists invited to Bajaur to witness the signing. On the day beforehand he had visited Liaqat's madrassa: "I couldn't really see many men, though two or three were teachers," he recalls. "Most of them were students aged 12 to 17." In the early hours of the next morning he was woken by a massive explosion. Rushing to the scene Yusufzai found that a direct hit on the school had caused immense damage: "I couldn't believe my eyes—there were many human body pieces, not a single complete body. Everything at the madrassa was shattered." Survivors and villagers helped gather up body parts, and by dawn the death toll stood at 81—most of them reportedly children aged 17 or under. The only militant confirmed dead by locals was Maulvi Liaqat himself, who had been expected to take part in the signing ceremony.

British barrister Shazadi Beg was staying at the time at the official residence of the Governor of North Western Frontier Province.[4] She recalls "utter pandemonium" the morning after the attack. "Governor Orukzai just looked shocked out of his head," she recalls. Based on intelligence received by the governor and his staff "he was 100% clear that this was the Americans from the moment it happened" says Beg.[5] That the precision night-time strike was the work of a US drone was supported by a number of credible sources. Yet in keeping with a secret 2004 accord with Washington, the Pakistan Army at first claimed responsibility for the attack: "The operation was launched after confirmed intelligence reports that a number of miscreants were getting terrorist training in a madrasah," a spokesman told reporters in Islamabad.[6] To add to the confusion, eyewitnesses report that Pakistan Army helicopter gunships turned up shortly after the bombing, to strafe hills close to the ruins. Video surveillance footage was also handed to the media purportedly showing militants receiving training at the school. Yet Islamabad was unable to contain the story. Although Bajaur's borders were immediately blocked, a few reporters including Mushtaq Yusufzai were already present. Shocking images revealed dozens of bodies laid out on crude cots under blankets. Those killed were almost all reported to be students—one as young as 7 years old. A member of the National Assembly produced a list of the dead, detailing names and ages of victims:

> It was claimed that one of the deceased was only seven-year old, three were 8, three 9, one was 10, four were 11, four were 12, eight were 13, six were 14, nine were 15, nineteen were 16, twelve were 17, three were 18, three were 19 and only two were 21-years-old.[7]

While other sources contested how many of the students were young children, most were in agreement that apart from Liaqat, only "innocents" had died. The FATA Secretariat, for example, in its secret internal reporting, described the casualties as "80 children 01 man all civilian," presumably classifying all students including those over 17 as children.[8] Shops and offices closed in protest throughout Bajaur, and the proposed peace agreement lay in tatters. For a time the Army aggressively challenged claims of civilian deaths, suggesting instead that while the names of those listed killed were correct, their IDs had been faked to hide their true adult status.[9] The Pakistan military's insistence that it had carried out the airstrike led to swift retaliation. A week later, 42 Pakistani soldiers died in a suicide bombing in the town of Dargai.[10] The attack, the worst single loss of military life so far in Pakistan's growing insurgency, was in revenge for Chenegai according to militants. Local sources told the author that the suicide bomber's brother and two of his cousins had earlier been killed in the school attack.

With the crisis showing no sign of abating, by late November a key aide to President Musharraf told the *Sunday Times* that the Chenegai attack had in fact been the work of the United States: "We thought it would be less damaging if we said we did it rather than the US. But there was a lot of collateral damage and we've requested the Americans not to do it again."[11] Musharraf himself later denied the deaths of "civilian children," telling the *New Statesman* while in exile: "I know for 100% sure, it's all bullshit, sorry for that word: this was a cover that there were civilian children studying the Koran. . . . They were all militants doing training inside."[12] Yet back in Pakistan the Army had by now dropped any such claim. Reuters correspondent Myra MacDonald was one of a small number of Western journalists allowed into Bajaur in 2010. There she was briefed by a military official who "was very clear that that bombing on the madrassa had inflamed the whole thing in Bajaur," she recalls. "I am very sure he talked about a large number of children being killed."[13]

Did the CIA carry out the bombing at Chenegai, as past and present officials in Pakistan now insist? If so, it would have been the first covert drone strike under new Director Michael Hayden, who had taken over the Agency weeks earlier in June 2006. While admitting that the Chenegai attack "could have been us," a former senior US intelligence official told the author he had "no recollection of that whatsoever. I would have remembered pictures, the narrative, just the whole thing. And I've got nothing on this in my memory." Asked to explain who might therefore be responsible, the former official would only say that "maybe it was them [the Pakistanis] and they just decided to toss someone else under the bus."[14] This view was dismissed in Islamabad. Former head of Pakistan's spy service the Inter-Services Intelligence (ISI), General Asad Durrani has said he is "as sure as I can be" that the Americans carried out the attack, once describing Chenegai as "a very clear message" from the CIA to Pakistan not to enter into further agreements with the Taliban.[15] He told this author that it was "foolish" of Pakistan ever to say it was a part of the operation.[16] Washington's continued refusal officially to confirm or deny a role in the Chenegai strike—or indeed in any of hundreds of covert bombings carried out by the CIA in Pakistan's tribal areas—lay at the heart of a decade-long struggle between those believing such actions required an element of accountability and transparency, and those insisting they remained in the shadows.

INDEPENDENCE AND REBELLION

After the United States and its Northern Alliance allies crushed the Afghan Taliban in late 2001—and with former Soviet states and even Iran cooperating for a time in the new War on Terror—the main escape route for Al Qaeda had been via Pakistan's poorly governed western fringes. There they entered the Federally Administered Tribal Area (FATA), the seven agencies including North and South Waziristan which were originally created as a buffer zone between colonial India and Afghanistan. For more than two centuries the fiercely independent Pashtuns of western Pakistan had been lauded and feared by the West. Winston Churchill, who in 1897 "embedded" with British forces in the region, complained that superstition among the Pashtun tribes "exposes them to the rapacity and tyranny of a numerous priesthood . . . and a host of wandering Talib-ul-ilms"—a reminder that the modern-day Talibs of Afghanistan and Pakistan drew on strong historical precedent.[17] The British had fought a series of rebellions in Waziristan, the last just prior to World War II. With access limited by geography and supply lines, London instead used aircraft to strike at rebellious villages. In 1928 alone, 182 bombs were dropped on Waziristan's settlements, more than half of which missed their target.[18] The RAF hierarchy spoke approvingly of this "inexpensive and effective means to observe and punish rebellious tribal behaviour."[19] Others feared the tactic risked "the permanent embitterment and alienation of the frontier tribes."[20] When CIA drone strikes began almost a century later, they stirred strong folk memories for some: "It was never something that was taught in the schools," recalls Waziristan resident Kareem Khan of his own childhood. "But anger at those earlier British airstrikes was certainly a part of our oral tradition."[21]

Poverty and illiteracy were endemic in Waziristan, a mountainous region where only a fraction of the land was arable; where one in three homes still drew water from a well; and where paved roads were poor or nonexistent. Even in 2014 female literacy was just 3%, with mobile phones and the Internet mostly absent.[22] Islamabad and Washington had few qualms about exploiting this potent mix of poverty and militancy when need be. In the 1980s a *jihad* was encouraged against the Russian occupation of Afghanistan: the tribal areas became a Western-funded laboratory, in which radical Islam was channeled into violent action. The CIA would ultimately pump over $3 billion into the campaign, even printing Holy Qurans in local languages.[23] Yet control was always tenuous, and as the anti-Soviet insurgency wound down, Osama bin Laden and others began discussing how Islamic *jihad* might be exported globally. Al Qaeda's operations had reached their zenith with the atrocities of 9/11, though the group was not destroyed by the Afghan war that followed in late 2001. As former senior CIA analyst Paul Pillar puts it, "I don't think anyone believed that rousting Al Qaeda from what had been its home in Afghanistan under the Taliban was the beginning of the end of the group."[24]

Islamabad came under immediate pressure after 9/11 to deal with Al Qaeda on its own soil, with President Musharraf later claiming Washington threatened to "bomb Pakistan back to the Stone Age" if it did not do everything required of it.[25] Despite the attribution of those words to Deputy Secretary of State Richard Armitage, he denies ever speaking them: "I had a whole career of 26 years in government, and several in the military, and I would have loved to tell somebody that sometime, but I've never been authorized to" he now says. As Armitage remembers it, Pakistan's spy chief General Mahmud Ahmed happened to be in Washington on 9/11. "He came into my office to see me, and I told him, he arrived in one country, he was now in another, and I was very desirous of getting him, that is Pakistan, on side with us, and explained to him pretty carefully what we were going to be demanding of Pakistan." The former US diplomat admits that it was "a tough discussion." When Ahmed started flanneling, "I cut him off which I normally wouldn't do to a guest, and said 'History starts today General, I am aware of the past history. History starts today.'"

Ahmed barely lasted another month as ISI chief before being sacked, now deemed to be too close to the Taliban. Responding swiftly to other US demands, dictator Pervez Musharraf secretly gave Washington access to half a dozen military sites from which to conduct its War on Terror. Although unarmed Air Force Predators arrived almost immediately, it would be three more years before the CIA began carrying out drone targeted killings on Pakistan's territory. This did not mean the drones were idle. By 2002, according to a former senior ISI official, Predators were already monitoring houses in the tribal areas used by commanders of the Haqqani Network, a group which would play a key role in the Afghan Taliban.[26] There was no pressure at first for kinetic operations. A weak nation torn between liberal and military elites, there was also widespread support for Al Qaeda across much of Pakistan immediately after 9/11. As the author observed first-hand, the markets of Quetta and Peshawar were awash with hagiographic prints of Osama bin Laden: one best-seller depicted him as Salah al-Din on a white charger, liberating Jerusalem.

Memoirs, private records, and government cables from the post-9/11 period show Washington attempting to balance the US's strategic and military interests with Pakistan's own unstable realities—a policy continued almost to the end of Bush's eight-year term.[27] As former CIA chief lawyer John Rizzo notes in his memoirs, "From the earliest days after 9/11, the Agency's priority was to capture Al Qaeda leaders, not kill them."[28] Brigadier Asad Munir was the ISI's head of operations in the FATA tribal areas between 1999 and 2003. He recalls the CIA's initial worry at working with a partner which just weeks earlier had been a primary supporter of the Taliban. He claims this soon dissipated, as the two spy agencies began breaking apart Al Qaeda's infrastructure:

> It was a relationship of complete trust which lasted for over two years. There was no double game, I would have known. We met almost every day: it was a routine, an exchange of information. Technically they were better equipped than us but they shared things, and we had a very effective humint [human intelligence] system in place in FATA, from before 9/11. So we would get information, share it, and conduct raids together with the CIA.[29]

Agency operative John Kiriakou ran counterterrorism operations in Pakistan from early 2002.[30] In March that year, Kiriakou's team got word that Al Qaeda's operational chief Abu Zubaydah was in the city of Faisalabad.[31] A combined action involving the FBI, the CIA, and Pakistan's Special Branch caught him in one of fourteen simultaneous raids, a mark of the huge US resources then involved in capture operations.[32] In all, Musharraf would later boast, Pakistan seized 689 "Al Qaeda operatives" during his presidency, 369 of whom were handed over to the United States in exchange for millions of dollars in reward money. Even with subsequent revelations that some were innocent, it was clear that these early, joint US-Pakistani law and order operations had a significant impact on the effectiveness of Al Qaeda, with operations continuing even after the CIA's drone campaign began in 2004. Many years later some senior Pakistani officials hoped that a revival of aggressive joint law enforcement actions against Al Qaeda after 2014 might even enable Washington to end its drone bombings.[33]

Yet as a former senior US intelligence official points out, Pakistan's cities were rarely the problem: "We did have great success rolling up Al Qaeda with the Pakistanis. But if you note, practically every one that was rolled up with the Pakistanis was done in the settled areas. And nothing was done in the tribal region in that regard."[34] Musharraf's support for the US campaign against Al Qaeda was not without consequence, alienating many religiously conservative Pakistanis. An influx of thousands of militants into FATA had also significantly changed the balance of power there. By 2004, home-grown Taliban groups were declaring local Islamic emirates, executing tribal leaders and attempting to impose a stricter form of Islam. They had also marked Pervez Musharraf and his leadership circle for assassination. As the threats against his government escalated, the dictator was willing to consider new tactics.

First Kill

Fourteen-year-old Irfan Wazir and his 8-year-old brother Zaman were the first civilian victims of the CIA's long-running secret drone war in Pakistan. The two lived and died in a village just outside Wana, the tiny provincial capital of South Waziristan which, by the summer of 2004, was also home to an array of militant and terrorist groups. The boys' misfortune was to be sitting near Nek Mohammad, a charismatic 29-year-old militant leader visiting their father. Like hundreds of other Waziris, Nek Mohammad had cut his teeth fighting with the Taliban in Afghanistan where he had regular contact with foreign forces allied to the former regime, including the Islamic Movement of Uzbekistan (IMU).[35] Numbering thousands of radical Islamist fighters in exile from the former Soviet state, the IMU had nowhere to go after the US invasion. Mohammad facilitated the group's move into South Waziristan, acquiring some powerful armed muscle in the process. According to a former Pakistani intelligence official, Nek Mohammad and his Uzbek allies had since coordinated a series of raids on a US military outpost just across the border at Shkin. "They would place these missiles on bricks and attach a timer device and fire it," he recalls "though I'm not sure there were any casualties at the post."[36] Secret US military cables from Afghanistan confirm half a dozen such attacks in the first half of 2004.[37]

Furious at recent attempts to assassinate him—and under continuing pressure from the Americans to act against rising militancy—Pervez Musharraf ordered the local Frontier Corps (FC) to seize the head of the IMU, Tahir Yuldashev, in spring 2004.[38] The operation failed spectacularly. In response, Pakistan broke with all precedent by ordering an assault on South Waziristan by its regular troops. Two weeks of intense air and artillery strikes did nothing to dislodge Mohammad and his allies, and turned the local population further against Islamabad. As the academic and former *London Times* correspondent Professor Anatol Lieven has noted, "In fierce battles, several villages were destroyed and hundreds of local people killed, including women and children. The army too suffered hundreds of casualties and, most worryingly of all, there were instances of units refusing to fight."[39] The Army was finally forced into signing a humiliating "peace deal" with Nek Mohammad in April, a document which even referred to him as a holy warrior or mujahid.[40] Promptly ignoring the agreement, Islamists began killing those maliks who had supported the government assault.

Six weeks later on the night of June 17, 2004, an explosion ripped through Sher Zaman Asrafkhel's house as half a dozen men and the two boys ate their supper in an outside courtyard. The homeowner and his sons died instantly, along with two Uzbeks. Nek Mohammed survived long enough to be rushed to Wana's hospital, where his last words were reportedly: "Why aren't you putting a bandage on my arm?"[41] Pakistan lacked the technical capability to carry out night-time precision airstrikes. Yet the ISPR, the Army's public relations wing, immediately claimed responsibility for the death of Mohammad, telling reporters that its "night-vision helicopters" had struck. "We will eliminate every miscreant who does not surrender or denounce terrorism or militancy," the Army's spokesman boasted.[42] Within two days the *New York Times* was reporting the truth: the CIA's Predator drones had struck lethally inside Pakistan for the first time. Despite a later willingness to claim the deaths of senior militants, US intelligence officials stayed silent in 2004, allowing the ISPR spokesman to reject as "absolutely absurd" any possible involvement by Washington.[43]

Similar untruths would be repeated half a dozen times over the next 28 months as Musharraf's government sought to cover up a growing US targeted killing campaign. This was part of a broader secret agreement allowing for drone strikes in the tribal areas, which according to *New York Times* correspondent Mark Mazzetti, was forged between the CIA's station chief in Islamabad and the new head of the ISI, General Ehsan ul Haq: "Pakistani intelligence officials insisted that they be allowed to approve each drone strike, giving them tight control over the list of targets. And they insisted that drones fly only in narrow parts of the tribal areas."[44]

That deal was never formally written down according to Musharraf, though evidence for its existence can be found elsewhere. A NATO air corridor already existed high above FATA, codenamed the Boulevard and used daily by Coalition aircraft to ferry troops and supplies to and from Afghanistan.[45] With the risk of collision, Pakistani aircraft also now had to know where the CIA's armed Predator drones might be. The nations agreed to two secret Restricted Operating Zones within FATA, which mapped out a three-dimensional space inside which the CIA's drones could freely operate at specified heights. Their existence was revealed in 2011, when secret US diplomatic cables obtained by Wikileaks showed Washington had been pushing for approval for a third zone.[46]

It would also emerge that the CIA's drone strikes were being launched from deep inside Pakistan's own territory. There was a precedent. In the 1960s U2 spy planes penetrating deep into Soviet airspace and "owned" by the CIA had secretly flown from Peshawar.[47] Forty years on and the remote Shamsi airfield in Balochisatan, and Shahbaz near the city of Jacobabad, provided new homes for the Agency's Predators. Offering some cover, Shamsi was officially leased to the United Arab Emirates for "royal game-hunting," and the UAE in turn "sublet" Shamsi to the United States. A grainy commercial satellite photograph taken in 2006 clearly shows three Predators on the airfield's concrete apron.[48] Right up to December 2011, the CIA continued to fly armed drones from the base, despite deteriorating US-Pakistani relations.

Former Bush administration officials have remained tight-lipped regarding the early years of the drone campaign. It is still unclear, for example, why Nek Mohammad was chosen as the CIA's first target in Pakistan. The United States insisted that any authority for its drone strikes beyond the regular battlefield was based on whether a target was part of Al Qaeda or an associated group; and whether they represented an imminent threat to US interests. Retired Pakistani General Talat Massoud is one who argues that Mohammad was killed for his links with terrorists: "He was a great facilitator for Al Qaeda, he was also helping them in many ways."[49] Others like former senior ISI official Asad Munir disagree, describing Nek Mohammad only as "a very very local leader, confined to a small area."[50] It seems most likely, as others have also argued, that this first targeted killing was an act of CIA "clientism"—where the assassination of Musharraf's enemies was used as leverage to secure further CIA strikes.[51] The impact of the young militant leader's death was certainly significant. Considered a hero by many in South Waziristan, Nek Mohammad had nevertheless been killed with apparent ease. As a local tribal elder noted at the time, "Nek's followers are in deep shock because a new dimension—the use of guided missiles—was added to the operation."[52] The military actions which preceded Mohammad's death would also prove to be the opening shots in Pakistan's own insurgency, one which would ultimately claim tens of thousands of lives.

It was almost a year before the CIA's drones struck again, killing alleged Al Qaeda explosives expert Haitham al-Yemeni in his car in North Waziristan. Despite Pakistani claims that al-Yemeni accidentally blew himself up, US intelligence officials were unable to contain their pleasure, and five days after the attack the role of a Predator was anonymously leaked to ABC News.[53] Amnesty International immediately protested the killing, claiming that "the USA has carried out an extra-judicial execution, in violation of international law" and calling upon Washington "to end immediately all operations aimed at killing suspects instead of arresting them."[54] Amnesty's protests appeared to carry more weight when it emerged that al-Yemeni had been under ground surveillance by US operatives in FATA, and yet no attempt had been made to seize him.[55] In December 2004, UN expert Philip Alston warned the General Assembly that any targeted killing policy carried the risk of abuse and illegality:

> Empowering Governments to identify and kill "known terrorists" places no verifiable obligation upon them to demonstrate in any way that those against whom lethal force is used are indeed terrorists, or to demonstrate that every other alternative had been exhausted. While it

is portrayed as a limited "exception" to international norms, it actually creates the potential for an endless expansion of the relevant category to include any enemies of the State, social misfits, political opponents, or others.[56]

Now Alston approached Washington and Islamabad directly, seeking answers to four questions: "What rules of international law does your Excellency's Government consider to govern this incident? What procedural safeguards, if any, were employed to ensure that this killing complied with international law? On what basis was it decided to kill, rather than capture, Haitham al-Yemeni? Did [your] government consent to the killing of Haitham al-Yemeni?"[57] Islamabad responded vaguely, noting only that "a car blew up," and that al-Yemeni's death could not be verified.[58] Washington's more fulsome reply when it came stunned Alston. As he later noted, the United States "took the opportunity to challenge the entire international human rights system," arguing "that international human rights law did not apply to the incident; that the laws that did apply could not be addressed by the Special Rapporteur or, implicitly, by the Human Rights Council; and that each State could determine for itself whether any particular incident could be addressed by the Council."[59] This growing war of words with the United Nations made clear Bush's unwillingness to allow any international oversight of his government's targeted killing project.

SHOOTING THE MESSENGERS

From the outset, officials in the United States, Pakistan, and Yemen had sought to hide any problematic evidence of the covert drone campaign. Journalists, in particular, tried to address this information vacuum, though not without risk. In early December 2005, the United States killed two men allegedly involved in Al Qaeda's deadly Madrid train bombings, who were now living in Pakistan's tribal areas. A Spanish woman married to one of the suspects, and two children, also died in the CIA attack (for more on this incident see chapter 6).[60] Islamabad put it about that the deaths were caused by a "mystery explosion," though locals were adamant that missiles had been fired at the house in the early hours of the morning.

Hayatullah Khan, a freelance journalist and photographer who had worked with the American PBS network, sensed a good story. Khan's previous assignments had already caused friction with the Pakistani authorities, the Taliban, and US forces in eastern Afghanistan.[61] Undeterred, he visited Asori village in North Waziristan just hours after the bombing. One of Khan's photographs shows a bearded tribal elder inspecting missile casing fragments. The words "GUIDED MISSILE, SURFACE ATTACK, AGM-114" are clearly visible. This was the US military designation for the Hellfire missile, carried by the Predator though not by any Pakistani aircraft. For the first time, Khan had obtained direct proof of the US covert air war in FATA. His photographs were published locally, and then widely distributed by the European Pressphoto Agency. Yet professional success for Khan would soon bring catastrophe.

Immediately after the photos were published, the photographer began receiving threats from unnamed tribal officials. He was given three options: "Leave North Waziristan, stop reporting or take a government job."[62] On December 5, 2005, Hayatullah Khan was kidnapped at gunpoint. He was never seen alive again. According to concerns later raised by the United Nations, "An official at the Governor's House in Peshawar . . . is reported to have recently told journalists who were protesting in favor of Hayatullah Khan's release: 'The more noise you make, the more you prolong Hayatullah's captivity.' "[63] Family members too were told that Khan was safely in ISI hands, and that they should stay silent. Yet in June 2006 Hayatullah Khan's corpse was found dumped in the Waziristan hills, with a bullet to the back of the head. An official Pakistan Army inquiry blamed his death on the Taliban, though Khan's widow continued to insist the ISI was responsible. In November 2007, a powerful bomb planted just outside her home killed her as she slept. The couple were survived by their five young children. The assassination of Khan's wife prompted Reporters Without Borders to note that "Hayatullah Khan's murderers, whom the authorities never tried to identify, may have felt the need to eliminate an irritating witness."[64]

Despite significant evidence pointing to the role of Pakistani intelligence in Khan's death, Washington's ambassador to Pakistan seemed minded to believe the ISI's own version of events. A secret cable from Ryan Crocker, dated June 20, 2006, describes his private conversation with a senior Pakistani security official who makes the implausible suggestion that Khan was killed by Al Qaeda for providing "information on the identities and locations of Islamic militants to Pakistani and American security forces." In an attached comment, the embassy notes rather credulously: "Assuming the security official's version is accurate . . . the ability of militants to kidnap, hold and execute Hayatullah and then dump his body in a public place is a graphic, but no longer surprising, illustration of their capacity to operate with impunity."[65]

Hayatullah Khan was not the only reporter caught up in the violence. A study in 2013 found that "at least 42 journalists have been killed—23 of them murdered—in direct relation to their work in Pakistan in the past decade. . . . Not one murder since 2003 has been solved, not a single conviction won."[66] Some reporters were killed by militant groups, some by criminal gangs or unknown assailants. Others were murdered by the security services. Syed Saleem Shahzad was a tenacious journalist for the *Asia Times*, who had built up a network of high-ranking contacts within militant and terrorist groups. Shahzad had been under direct observation for many months both by Pakistani Military Intelligence and by the ISI, according to a former senior Pakistani intelligence official with close knowledge of the case.[67] Indeed, in late 2010 Shahzad had been summoned to ISI Headquarters, where he was warned his reporting was making too many waves. Afterwards he complained to his editor of an implicit "murder threat" made at the meeting.[68] On May 30, 2011, Syed Saleem Shahzad's body was found inside his car, less than a day after he had disappeared from the streets of central Islamabad. Just as in Khan's case, officials suggested Shahzad had been killed by Al Qaeda. Instead according to the former Pakistan official, who has requested anonymity here, he was accidentally beaten to death by the ISI during interrogation. The Americans too believed they knew who had killed Shahzad, with the Chairman of the Joint Chiefs of Staff breaking with protocol to tell reporters that "It [the killing of Shahzad] was sanctioned by the [Pakistan] government, yeah."[69]

In early 2014, journalist and anti-drone campaigner Kareem Khan was picked up from his Rawalpindi home by a group of uniformed and plain-clothes men and "disappeared" for nine days. With fears that Pakistan's intelligence services might kill him, significant international pressure was brought to bear—aided by the fact that Khan was shortly due to address elected politicians in Europe. Upon his eventual release, Khan complained of having been tortured: "They abused me using vulgar expletives. Hung me upside down and sat on me while one other person beat my feet," he told CNN, though he said he was unable to identify his captors.[70] Little wonder then that Pakistan featured in the top five most dangerous nations for journalists in all but one year between 2005 and 2013. Deaths, beatings and threats were used as leverage by various parties to ensure reporters toed the line.[71] Mushtaq Yusufzai is a respected Pashtun journalist and a regular contributor for NBC News. His work covering the tribal areas meant he had extensive contacts with government and military officials as well as with the Taliban: "Sometimes it becomes very dangerous, and the Taliban suspect it is possible you are working for spy agencies, for the government," Yusufzai told the author. "Media people are already suspected [of being] spies by the militants. If you're working for the media and you ask someone about who was killed, then you are no more."[72] During field work in 2011 for a Bureau of Investigative Journalism study in Waziristan, its researchers were warned by militants that there would be violent consequences if they revealed the names of any Taliban killed in certain drone strikes. Local negotiations won a small concession, with militants permitting researchers to pass on the numbers, if not the names, of those Taliban killed.[73]

The United States too was not averse to pressuring journalists. Popular Pakistan TV presenter Hamid Mir (who survived a second assassination attempt in 2014, possibly by the ISI[74]) has described being banned by the US Embassy after raising the issue of CIA drone strikes during a visit by US Secretary of State Hillary Clinton. And when this author received leaked emails proving that the CIA had been secretly briefing against my investigations, I was told by one US intelligence official that I would find myself in "*a darker corner*" if I published the story.[75] On another occasion, after I had published evidence of possible US war crimes in Pakistan relating to the CIA's deliberate targeting of first responders (findings later independently supported by Amnesty International and by Stanford and New York University law schools), the *New York Times* reported a "senior American counter terrorism official" as saying:

> One must wonder why an effort that has so carefully gone after terrorists who plot to kill civilians has been subjected to so much misinformation. Let's be under no illusions—there are a number of elements who

would like nothing more than to malign these efforts and help Al Qaeda succeed.[76]

A key challenge for journalists and researchers was bypassing such aggressive pressures from state and non-state actors, as the US targeted killing program accelerated.

PLAYING BOTH SIDES

In January 2006, CIA Predators loitered high over Damadola village, six miles inside Pakistan in Bajaur Agency. Below, senior Al Qaeda and Taliban leaders had reportedly gathered to discuss their forthcoming spring offensive in Afghanistan. Among them, intelligence officials believed, was Al Qaeda's Ayman al-Zawahiri, second only to Osama bin Laden. The imminent US attack offered the best opportunity in years to strike at Al Qaeda's heart. While the CIA and ISI had captured or killed a seemingly endless supply of Al Qaeda's "number threes," the terror group's leadership had disappeared after the Battle of Tora Bora in December 2001. Osama bin Laden was by now already living in the fortified Abbottabad house in which he would later be killed. Al-Zawahiri was supposedly moving around the Federally Administered Tribal Area (FATA) while protected by the local Taliban. With a $25 million reward on his head, he was always at risk of exposure. Hellfire missiles now flattened three houses in Damadola. Between 13 and 22 people died, among them a crop of middle-ranking Al Qaeda and Taliban commanders. Or that, at least, was the story put out to the media. Marwan al-Suri, the head of Al Qaeda operations in Waziristan, actually died four months later in a gunfight for example,[77] while Abu Ubeidah al-Masri died of natural causes in December 2007.[78]

Many victims were soon identified by local officials as civilians, most of them from one family. Journalist Pir Zubair Shah visited graves at the site, seven of which held women and children, though locals refused to identify the dead men to him. His understanding was that other bodies, most likely those of militants, had been removed from the location. This was becoming common practice for FATA's various militant groups—a way of denying intelligence to the enemy while making it easier for spokesmen to claim on occasion that only civilians had died.[79] Others too were recording casualties that day. Pakistan's tribal authorities secretly tallied those killed in the CIA bombing as "05 children, 05 women and 6 men, all civilians," in what proved to be the first entry in an ongoing project by the FATA Secretariat to gather detailed information on US drone strikes. Years later, it would emerge that at least 200 civilian deaths caused by CIA drones had been recorded in this manner by the Pakistani authorities.[80]

The 2006 Damadola attack proved a major challenge for the United States when, for the first time since 9/11, Pakistan publicly expressed anger at American operations on its territory. Ambassador Ryan Crocker was called in for a "dressing down."[81] An ISI official even complained that "All those killed in the airstrike are innocent civilians. They [the US] are now trying to cover this up by leaking faulty information to the media."[82] There was a lesson here if the CIA was prepared to listen: even with the tacit support of the Pakistan military, killing large numbers of civilians risked significant blowback. The more noncombatants Washington killed, the greater the risk its secret drone strike deal might collapse.

Of greater concern to Washington was that even as the CIA was stepping up operations against Al Qaeda and associated militants in the tribal areas, Islamabad's military government had begun to waver. A series of local peace deals with so-called "Good Taliban" groups (those friendly toward Islamabad) were aimed at reducing violence on Pakistan's own soil. Inevitably this had led to a major upswing in attacks on US and allied forces in Afghanistan. Dr. Antonio Giustozzi has noted that following one such local deal in 2006, "according to US intelligence sources, cross-border attacks in Khost and Paktika rose from 42 in the two months preceding the agreement to 140 in the two months following it."[83] Both Pakistan and the United States had focused on common enemies in the immediate years after 9/11, namely Al Qaeda and those Pakistan-based militant groups which represented a threat to Musharraf's government.

Yet over time Islamabad's position had shifted, with a nagging fear that the United States would "betray" them by quitting the region once again following an Afghan withdrawal. Throughout the 1980s the CIA and ISI had worked closely with Saudi and British intelligence to defeat the Russians. Yet with the collapse of the Soviet Union, the Americans had literally walked away, locking the doors on their Kabul embassy in 1989 and only returning 12 years later after 9/11.[84] In the interim, the United States had effectively abandoned its 40-year alliance with Islamabad in favor of a long-term strategic partnership with Delhi, Pakistan's mortal foe.[85] Former President Pervez Musharraf remained bitter:

> Al Qaeda came into being, the Taliban came into being, four million refugees came into Pakistan between 1989 and 2001. For twelve years Pakistan was alone, fending for itself with whatever was happening in Afghanistan. All this blame was to the United States. We'd fought for you for ten years, helped you win the Cold War![86]

By 2006 the "Good Taliban" was seen by Islamabad as key to a post-US Afghanistan—a Pashtun counterbalance to any Indian influence. These factions enjoyed Islamabad's secret protection even as they used FATA as a base from which to assault US and Afghan forces. At first the United States believed Pakistan was only tolerating such raids. It soon became clear that elements of the ISI were actively fomenting and aiding Taliban attacks. Secret US military intelligence files, obtained by Wikileaks, describe Pakistan's ISI agents operating on both sides of the border, and even directing attacks against US and Coalition forces. These raw intelligence reports often reflect hearsay and rumor. Even so, beginning in 2004, hundreds of cables feature claims of the ISI's alleged role in anti-US operations:

> An operation of AL QAIDA has been started with the aim to infiltrate with 200 terrorists in order to conduct attacks against foreigners in Afghanistan. The operation plan is reported to have been issued on the 17th August 2004 during a secret meeting between TALIBAN, AL QAIDA and representative of ISI (PAK Intelligence).[87]

In late June 2007, US Lt. Col. Chris Nash was commanding an embedded training team in the Tora Bora Mountains when his unit was caught up in a "significant fight" with the Taliban. At a critical point in the battle, and to the American's astonishment, helicopters were reported by villagers and Afghan intelligence officials to have flown several resupply missions to the Taliban's base 20 kilometers inside Afghanistan. Nash believed those helicopters belonged to the ISI, he told the *Army Times*.[88] Later that same year, US interrogators at Guantanamo Bay were issued with classified *Threat Indicators for Enemy Combatants*, in which Pakistan's intelligence service the ISI was grouped along with 66 other global outfits including Al Qaeda,

Hamas, and Hezbollah, as a "terrorist or terrorist support entity."[89] Major General Asad Durrani, former head of the ISI, believes that any distrust cut both ways. "We're talking about cooperation and coordination between two countries whose interests do not coincide, indeed sometimes are even at times at cross purposes with each other," he told the author.

An opportunity for the CIA to loosen its uneasy alliance with the ISI came with an imminent transfer of power. Authority had begun slipping away from dictator Pervez Musharraf even before the election of Prime Minister Yousuf Raza Gillani in March 2008. Nowhere was this more visible than with the General's inability to influence the fast-escalating US drone bombing campaign. Furious at militant attacks being launched daily from Pakistani soil against US forces in Afghanistan—and under pressure from Barack Obama on the campaign trail—the Bush administration now decided to tear up the 2004 secret agreement on FATA drone strikes. US Director of National Intelligence Mike McConnell and CIA Director Michael Hayden confronted Musharraf and his army chief General Kayani in Islamabad on January 9, 2008. One former senior US official, with close knowledge of the meeting, recalls Hayden reading the riot act to Musharraf: " 'Mr. President we've had great success rolling up Al Qaeda. But our success has largely been limited to the settled areas, because you view Al Qaeda in the settled areas to be as much a threat to you as it is to us. But Mr. President, that's not how you view Al Qaeda in the tribal region. You essentially view that to be our problem, not yours. That calculus, if it was ever correct Mr. President, is now wrong.' "[90]

Under pressure, Pakistan agreed to significant changes. From now on, the CIA's drones would strike harder and more frequently. The Agency also took it that it could attack without Musharraf's direct prior permission. On January 29, 2008, it did just that, killing Abu Laith al-Libi ("The Libyan") and at least three other senior Al Qaeda figures along with four civilians. While Pakistan may have been unhappy with this newly imposed arrangement, it had little choice but to cooperate.

The Red Mosque

Nestled beneath the heavily wooded Margalla Hills in northwestern Pakistan, Islamabad only became the young nation's capital in 1966. With its wide avenues and neat parks, it offered a strange contrast with

Pakistan's other chaotic cities. Here politicians, soldiers, and spies rubbed shoulders with diplomats and business executives. Non-Muslim guests at international hotels could, until the early 2000s, register as an "alcoholic" and receive a daily "prescription" of a couple of beers. Upmarket prostitution reportedly thrived in the city. For a nation dedicated to Islam, the capital represented to many Pakistanis a godless place. One place of sanctuary was the Lal Masjid, or Red Mosque, once one of Islamabad's most important places of worship, though run-down and bullet-scarred by 2012. Suspicious guards clutching AK-47s paced the dusty compound, protecting a man many viewed as the spiritual father of Pakistan's homegrown Taliban. Mullah Abdul Aziz talked genially to guests of the need for Sharia law, even as he played down the risks of radical Islam. "When the army and the rulers [of Pakistan] jointly enforce Islam, then I think the temperature in the tribal regions will cool down, since the Taliban are fighting for Islam," the cleric told the author over tea. "When Sharia is implemented, the Taliban movement will end automatically."[91]

Five years earlier, the desire of Aziz and others to see Sharia law implemented across Pakistan had helped precipitate a crisis which would lead to the deaths of thousands. Yet until his assassination in 1998, Aziz's father Maulana Abdullah had run Lal Masjid with the nation's blessing. With its large attached madrassas, the mosque had become a focus in the 1980s for anti-Soviet militancy, recruiting jihadists from among the thousands of students who passed through its doors. Maulana Aziz succeeded his father as prayer leader, and while the mosque retained its radicalism this was increasingly directed toward Pakistan's own government and military for their "complicity" in the US War on Terror. When the Pakistan Army launched its 2005 offensive against the Mehsuds, Aziz went so far as to issue an edict or *fatwa* forbidding people to pray for troops killed in South Waziristan.[92] A furious Musharraf stripped the mullah of his formal role as prayer leader, though made no move to force him out of the Red Mosque.

By 2007 Aziz was openly defying the government. Seminary students had begun threatening local shopkeepers to end their "unIslamic behavior." Other locals were beaten and at least one kidnapped—all just a mile from Parliament. At first the Pakistan Army blockaded the mosque, as a loaned US Predator provided intelligence from above.[93] With the failure of negotiations with Aziz, the Army's elite Special Services Group attacked.

A secret military intelligence report seen by the author chronicles in graphic detail the consequences. In some rooms, students had frantically sought cover behind heaps of blankets now stained with blood. More than one hundred people were killed in the battle, most of them students, with almost 250 injured. Among the dead were Abdul Aziz's brother, his mother, and son.[94] The assault sent deep shock waves throughout Pakistan, leading to a massive upsurge in terrorist incidents and the founding of a federated group known as Tehrik-e-Taliban Pakistan (TTP). Led by Baitullah Mehsud, the TTP brought together more than a dozen militant organizations from across the tribal areas and promised to bring Pakistan's weak government crashing down. Waves of suicide bombings swept the country, aimed not only at the military and foreign interests, but increasingly at ordinary civilians.

In July 2008, Pakistan's recently installed Prime Minister Yousuf Raza Gillani was in Washington, DC, to ask for help. The TTP by now represented an existential threat to the nation's survival, Gillani argued. Could the United States not place Baitullah Mehsud at the top of its drone hit list? The response from the CIA's leadership was reportedly dismissive, and the meeting became an attack on Islamabad for not delivering up intelligence on the Haqqani Network, "a far higher US priority."[95] One reason for that mood was a devastating bomb attack on the Indian Embassy in Kabul three weeks earlier, which according to former senior US intelligence officials fed into a complete reappraisal of the drone targeted killing program across the border. Suspicion had initially pointed to Al Qaeda, which had used similar tactics against diplomatic missions in Kenya and Iraq. Then, recalls a former senior Indian intelligence official, an Afghan militant group tried to take credit for the embassy attack: "They claimed the reward money on the telephone from some of their handlers in ISI. And the ISI told them, "Look you fools, you are lying, we haven't done it through you, we've done it through somebody else." They were told to bugger off." That "somebody else" was the Haqqani Network working to orders from the ISI, separate US intercepts also apparently indicated. "This was a very specific attack by Jalaluddin Haqqani's men, the Haqqani Network," insists the former RAW official. "They were told by the ISI to give this message to the Indians: look, if you don't get out of Afghanistan or if you don't behave—this is what we can do."[96] It was becoming hard to distinguish some of the ISI's actions from those of Al Qaeda itself.

SIGNATURE STRIKES

For more than six months, senior CIA officials had been pushing President Bush to permit a major expansion of drone strikes in FATA. A senior former US intelligence official summarizes the Agency pitch to Bush and Vice President Dick Cheney as follows: "Knowing what we know now, there is no explaining our inaction after the next attack."[97] The CIA's rules of engagement for Pakistan had reportedly blocked drone strikes unless there was a 90% probability of success. That threshold was now lowered to 50%, according to the London *Times*.[98] The United States also began unilaterally attacking militants at will. Drones bombed "good" and "bad" Taliban alike, as well as Al Qaeda remnants. CIA Director Michael Hayden also ramped up so-called "signature strikes," the targeting by drones of unknown individuals based on their patterns of behavior. The deliberate targeting of named individuals—the sole purpose of the CIA's targeted killing program for its first four years—was now re-classed as a "personality strike." The Agency had been trialing signature strikes in Pakistan since January 2008. General Mike Flynn, later head of the Defense Intelligence Agency, has summarized the intelligence process which fed them as follows:

> While the enemy moves from point to point, airborne ISR tracks and notes every location and person visited. . . . Nodal analysis has the effect of taking a shadowy foe and revealing his physical infrastructure for things such as funding, meetings, headquarters, media outlets, and weapons supply points. As a result, the network becomes more visible and vulnerable, thus negating the enemy's asymmetric advantage of denying a target.[99]

The effect of signature strikes on Pakistan's tribal areas was significant, often resulting in scores of deaths from a single bombing. As a senior US counterterrorism official later told the *Los Angeles Times*: "The enemy has lost not just operational leaders and facilitators [in Pakistan]—people whose names we know—but formations of fighters and other terrorists. We might not always have their names, but . . . these are people whose actions over time have made it obvious that they are a threat."[100] Signature strikes bore a close resemblance to the tactic of aircraft seeking out targets of opportunity in wartime. "Targets of opportunity is a very good way of putting it, because that's what you do if you've got a battlefield. But Khyber Pakhtunkhwa is not a battlefield, it is where people live," notes Mike Martin, a former British Army intelligence officer.[101] Under Barack Obama, in particular, the signature strike would come to dominate phases of the secret Pakistan drone war, leading to damaging criticism both from Islamabad and from the international community. Those consequences risked eventually outweighing any benefits being achieved by CIA drone strikes in FATA, one knowledgeable former senior US intelligence official believes. Yet for a time at least, any risk from the CIA's intensified bombing campaign was worth it: "When we're convincing the President he has to go more aggressively in the first half of 2008, we know there are second order effects and third order effects. The second-order effect is it alienates allies because no-one else agrees with our legal theory. The third-order effect? In some sense it helps Al Qaeda recruit, although I think that's a bit over-blown.... But the first-order effect was so needful in 2008 that we just lived with the second and third."[102]

Pervez Musharraf claimed to have been able to influence the tempo of US drone strikes during his presidency: "I could pick up the phone and speak to President Bush and Colin Powell. And I used to put a lot of pressure on them, "Why has this happened, why?" So they used to be on the back foot, maybe they liked me, and therefore they had to go a long way to calm me down, to explain to me why this and that."[103] His departure in mid-2008 now heralded an era in which the views of Pakistan's leaders carried far less weight. Secret cables show the United States obtained early oaths of fealty. Prime Minister Gillani privately told the Americans: "I don't care if they do it [drone strikes] as long as they get the right people. We'll protest in the National Assembly and then ignore it."[104] And in November President Zardari, the widower of Benazir Bhutto, reportedly drawled: "Kill the seniors. Collateral damage worries you Americans. It does not worry me."[105]

These views when exposed were heavily criticized. Yet Gillani's comments had been made when the CIA had carried out just 20 drone strikes in Pakistan. Within two years an additional 210 bombings would take place, a huge increase which provoked a major local backlash. Those same secret embassy cables also demonstrate that Gillani and other senior figures repeatedly called in private for Washington to rein in the escalating campaign, yet to no effect. In November 2008, a visiting US Senator was told by the Prime Minister that "US drone attacks were counterproductive in winning the public's support."[106] A week later the US ambassador was rebuked by Pakistan's foreign minister for carrying out an attack "with no prior intimation" which "undermined our efforts against terrorism."[107] And in April 2009, Senator John Kerry was warned by Gillani that the CIA was generating "public relations windfalls for the militants."[108] Even as General Stanley McChrystal began trying to bring down civilian casualties in Afghanistan (see chapter 7), US special envoy Richard Holbrooke roughly brushed aside any Pakistani suggestions of equivalence:

> The loss of civilian life through US military action in Afghanistan was on the top of Holbrooke's list, he said. The effects of such actions rippled through and across into Pakistan. [Foreign Minister] Qureshi tried to compare this problem to the loss of civilian life caused by drone attacks in Pakistan but Holbrooke rejected Qureshi's charge, saying the two could not be compared, as drones were more targeted than bombs.[109]

In his final months in office George W. Bush made little effort to mollify Islamabad. In September 2008 he ordered a US military ground incursion into Pakistan, breaking a seven-year agreement. As part of Operation Cottonmouth, two dozen Navy SEALs with Joint Special Operations Command (JSOC) struck a "militant compound" in the South Waziristan village of Angor Adda. Their target was Al Qaeda, and the SEALs did grab an alleged low-level militant whom it was later claimed revealed information about the terrorist group. Yet the cost was significant. Up to 18 people died in the raid according to Pakistani intelligence officials, including women and children. Even US officials privately conceded that a woman and her baby were among the dead.[110] With some understatement, the US Director of National Intelligence later admitted that "the raid had been poorly planned and co-ordinated."[111] If Bush was testing Islamabad's new government to see whether it would tolerate more unilateral raids, he soon got his answer. When US Special Forces attempted a second assault 12 days later they were reportedly fired on by Pakistani troops and had to turn back.[112] The Cottonmouth raid significantly damaged relations between the CIA, JSOC, and the Pakistan military, just as the new civilian government was bedding in—yet for almost no benefit. In his autobiography

Bush describes the failed assault only as a justification for more CIA drone strikes:

> When our forces encountered unexpected resistance, they got into a firefight and made international news. . . . I looked for other ways to reach into the tribal areas. I authorized the intelligence community to turn up the pressure on the extremists. Many of the details of our actions remained classified. But soon after I gave the order, the press started reporting more Predator strikes.[113]

Over the next four months, 29 further CIA bombings hit the tribal areas, killing more than 170 people. Some of these deaths Islamabad would have welcomed, including that of Al Qaeda's operational chief Usama al-Kini, killed in Bush's 51st and final drone attack on January 2, 2009. Other bombings were less appreciated—especially those aimed at "good Taliban" leaders. On November 19, US drones even attacked outside FATA for the first time, when Al Qaeda's Abdullah Azzam al Saudi was killed in Khyber Paktunkwa Province. A blunt and prophetic secret assessment from the US Ambassador in Islamabad noted the damage to Washington's broader strategic interests:

> Even politicians who have no love lost for a dead terrorist are concerned by strikes within what is considered mainland Pakistan. . . . As the gap between private GOP [Government of Pakistan] acquiescence and public condemnation for US action grows, Pakistani leaders who feel they look increasingly weak to their constituents could begin considering stronger action against the US, even though the response to date has focused largely on ritual denunciation.[114]

This steep increase in drone attacks also had implications for the incoming Obama administration. At least 48 noncombatants reportedly died in Pakistan drone strikes in the last few months of Bush's presidency, around one in three of all of those killed. Indeed overall, it was estimated that of 400 or more people who died in Predator strikes between June 2004 and January 2009, at least 160 were civilians—the majority of them children.[115] Much had been made of the accuracy of drone strikes over other weapon platforms. Yet any precision was only relevant if there was intent to keep collateral damage to a minimum. In Afghanistan and Iraq, elected governments could bring pressure to bear on regular US forces. The people of FATA had no such champion, since Washington and Islamabad collaborated extensively on the secret drone campaign from the start. In later years, the CIA was able to reduce civilian casualties from its drone strikes, more closely matching the ratios seen in conventional operations. That begged the question of why Washington chose not to place a higher value on civilian life far earlier on in Waziristan. Had it done so, much of the most damaging criticism of its campaign might have been avoided.

Bush's drone targeted killings had begun as a supplement to joint US-Pakistani policing operations—designed to capture, not kill, the enemy who had launched the 9/11 attacks. Only in rare circumstances would Washington kill suspects in remote areas, and always with the full consent and assistance of Pakistan. By the time Bush's administration ended, the secret drone war had morphed into an intensive, predominantly unilateral bombing campaign often employing so-called signature strikes. This shift was testimony both to the growing acrimony and distrust between Islamabad and Washington, and to the Afghan war now spiraling out of control. This, then, was the targeted killing campaign which Barack Obama would inherit, amplify, and make a central and very public plank of US foreign policy.

THE ENEMY WITHOUT
Western Citizens Killed by Drones

In early 2011, an elite squadron of Predators flying above Yemen was cleared by their "customer," Joint Special Operations Command (JSOC), to kill US citizen Anwar al-Awlaki. Should they find him, President Obama himself would personally give operators the lethal order. Preacher al-Awlaki had once been a favorite of some US officials, even leading lunchtime prayers at the Pentagon after 9/11.[1] Yet with the disastrous invasion of Iraq, his sermons had become ever-more anti-American. Now, it was alleged, he was a senior Al Qaeda operative, and "Most Wanted" posters featuring the gaunt American were plastered inside every Ground Control Station (GCS) at Cannon Air Force Base in New Mexico—home to the 3rd and 33rd Special Operations Squadrons. Previous JSOC efforts to kill al-Awlaki dated back to December 2009—before he was even officially classed as a terrorist by Washington.

The involvement of Special Forces drone squadrons in Yemen marked a fresh escalation in Barack Obama's secret war. Brandon Bryant, a long-serving sensor operator in the program, recalls his feelings at the time on hearing that Barack Obama himself would be personally involved: "We got direction from some higher-up that the President would call our GCS and would issue the order directly to us as a crew if we needed to shoot. That's a little bit thrilling: they wanted people that were responsible, people that would follow orders if the President came to call, and as far as I was concerned, these were bad guys." For Bryant and his colleagues, the involvement of the president was unique—the Air Force had gone to some lengths over the years to keep politicians out of the cockpit: "I guess Obama felt it important enough. This guy [Awlaki] was still an American citizen. The only thing that would've given more respect was if President Obama would've come down himself and pulled the trigger."[2] The clandestine manhunt for Anwar al-Awlaki now involved near-continuous coverage of Yemen by armed Predators.[3]

> The missions were flying from Djibouti . . . as soon as one was getting close to the end of its mission they'd launch another one to take over. Then they'd RTB [return to base] the first one so they had consistent coverage. No break.

Along with other operators, Bryant spent months remotely scouring Yemen for signs of the cleric and the senior leadership of Al Qaeda in the Arabian Peninsula, or AQAP. "There was nothing there. Like, absolutely nothing there. And all we were doing was just SIGINT [signals intelligence]. They weren't really telling us anything that was going on. Except leadership once in a while would be like, 'Oh, we're getting really close to getting this guy.' "[4]

Much has been written of the Obama administration's killing of Anwar al-Awlaki and his 16-year-old son in separate strikes. Both deaths certainly highlighted legal and constitutional issues within the United States. Yet dozens more Westerners—at least one of them a woman—had also been killed by US drones since 2005 including British, Spanish, Belgian, German, Canadian, and Australian citizens. Some of those deaths have raised significant concerns regarding secret and unlawful cooperation among intelligence agencies. While Washington had continued to assert the lawfulness of its targeted killing program beyond the hot battlefield, such actions were generally viewed as illegal even by its closest allies.[5] One senior member of the Bundestag intelligence oversight committee believed that any involvement by German intelligence services in covert US strikes would amount to "complicity in murder," for example.[6] Even so Britain, Germany, and other nations may have shared intelligence which then played a role in the targeted killing of their own citizens by the United States.

WHO THE UNITED STATES KILLED

Washington had always insisted that its secret War on Terror was aimed at global terrorist groups such as Al Qaeda, rather than at the peoples of individual nations caught up in the conflict. Evidence from the war's covert battlefields nevertheless indicates that the great majority of those targeted and killed were either nationals of the bombed country, or of its immediate neighbors. In collaboration with the author, the Bureau of Investigative Journalism (BIJ) examined thousands of media reports and other sources to determine, where possible, the nationalities or regional origins of those targeted. During five years of drone strikes in Pakistan by the Bush presidency, for example, some three-quarters of an estimated 410 people killed appear to have been Pakistanis, Afghans, or from neighboring countries. Arabs and North Africans—representing the core Al Qaeda targets of the Bush bombing campaign—account for only about 20% of these deaths.[7] "An awful lot of those killed were Pashtuns from the border region around FATA and into Afghanistan. This has been billed as a global war on Al-Qaeda, an international terrorist group. So it surprised me that so many of the people that the drones were killing were reportedly from the local area," says Jack Serle, who maintained the Bureau's extensive databases on the US targeted killing program.[8]

By Obama's time in office, the CIA's strikes in FATA had become more homogeneous. Of at least 2,000 people estimated killed in drone bombings between 2009 and 2013, some 85% were recorded as being Afghans, Pakistanis, Uzbeks, and others from the immediate region. A further 150 Arabs and North Africans died—less than one in ten. Overall, citizens of the United States, the United Kingdom, Australia, Switzerland, and Germany were among 29 nationalities targeted by the CIA during the Obama years.[9] The CIA's own internal analysis backed up the Bureau's findings. Of almost 500 deaths the Agency believed it was responsible for in Pakistan in a year-long period to September 2011, most were lower level, local Pashtun militants, with just six senior Al Qaeda figures reported killed, leaked documents have shown.[10]

The United States was fighting a very different war in Yemen, as the BIJ data also makes clear. The nationalities of just over half of at least 600 people killed in confirmed and likely US drone strikes could reasonably be determined. Of these, 84% were Yemenis, a further 7% were from the immediate Gulf region, and almost all others were Arabs and North Africans. Only 10 deaths were of people from beyond this area—four Americans, two Australians, a Russian, and three Pakistanis. Concerns expressed to the author by a former senior Pentagon official that in Yemen "we may be involved in a local conflict more than a global conflict" appear borne out by these findings.[11] "While there is certainly a transnational terrorist group in the country—we've seen that with attempts to blow up international aircraft and so on—from my reading, it seems there's more of a very complicated series of local conflicts and feuds, many extremely tribal," says the BIJ's Serle. "So it doesn't surprise me that a lot of the people being targeted by the US are actually from the country or the near-neighbouring region."

The deaths of Westerners in covert drone strikes, in particular those of Americans, had tended to garner significant media coverage. Yet across all three covert conflicts—Pakistan, Yemen, and Somalia—no more than 40 of those killed were known to be from Europe, North America, or Australasia, out of more than 2,800 fatalities (see Appendix A). What Washington depicted as a global war against an international terror network often had the appearance—on the ground—of a series of insurgencies against occupation or national governments. The targeting and killing of those few Westerners nevertheless raised fundamental concerns.

BRITISH BEST FRIENDS

Mohamed Sakr was 27 when he died in a drone strike in central Somalia. His identity remained publicly unknown for over a year. After all, media reports at the time of his death simply noted that "a very senior Egyptian" had been eliminated.[12] In reality, Mohamed Sakr was a British-born man. That had not stopped the UK government from stripping Sakr and his childhood best friend Bilal al-Berjawi of their nationalities in late 2010—a move which may in turn have cleared the way for the UK's intelligence services to share potentially lethal information with the United States without risk of legal consequence. The men were just two of as many as 15 Britons reported killed by the CIA and Pentagon during the War on

Terror. Indeed, more Britons had died in US covert drone strikes than any other Western nationality (see Appendix). Even so, three successive UK governments had chosen to remain publicly silent on the issue.

A year after their son's death, Gamal Sakr and his wife Eman sat with the author in the formal parlor of their comfortable west London home, the ornate décor a reminder of the couple's Egyptian origins. Thirty-five years earlier, they had uprooted to England in search of better times. "It was democratic," Mr. Sakr explained. "There was no dictator here, no bad laws like there were back home, so we decided to start a new life."[13] Their eldest son Mohamed was born in 1985. In his teens he was a rebellious party-goer. Family photographs show a happy young man, on school adventure trips or playing soccer with his friends. Everything changed following the US and UK invasion of Iraq according to his parents, with Sakr one of a substantial number of young second- and third-generation British Muslim men radicalized by the war. Mohamed's best friend was Bilal al-Berjawi: the pair had met as children when their families lived in adjacent London apartments. By 2006, al-Berjawi was already deeply involved in a resurgent militant movement in Somalia, which would ultimately draw in hundreds of young European radicals. After fighting with the Al Shabaab militant group, al-Berjawi was sent back to the United Kingdom to secretly recruit and raise funds, as his Al Qaeda-penned obituary later noted.[14]

Childhood friend Mohamed Sakr was one of those he won over. In February 2009, the pair visited Kenya for what they told their families was a safari. Both were picked up in Nairobi under suspicion of planning terror attacks on Israeli-linked targets. The two were eventually deported back to the United Kingdom, where al-Berjawi alleged they were met by operatives of MI5, the domestic security service: "They escorted us off the actual aeroplane and they explained themselves, 'We are MI5.' Took my fingerprints, took pictures. The way I was dealt with was not nice to be honest. It's like I felt I was a man with no rights."[15] Concerned at the attention the friends were now attracting from counterterrorism officials, Mohamed's mother Eman began checking out the mosques her son attended: "I wanted to hear what they're saying. I was always on top of this, always. I wanted to know why the police were after him, why?" recalls Mrs. Sakr. "So he used to take me to different mosques, and the sermons were normal, nothing unusual." After a run-in with police at an anti-Israeli protest, Sakr and al-Berjawi slipped out of Britain in October 2009. Months later, they emerged in Somalia, having joined Al Shabaab, the militant group which by now controlled much of the country. Videos from the time show the pair in military fatigues holding guns for the camera.

Under domestic law, the British Home Secretary had the power to remove a dual national's citizenship without any reference to the courts if they deemed it to be "conducive to the public good." Historically this power had been used rarely. Yet in response to fears of terrorist attacks on the homeland after 9/11, successive British governments had made it far easier to act. Almost 40 dual-nationals had their citizenships stripped by the UK from 2010 onward by the Cameron government, mostly for alleged terrorism links.[16] For Mohamed Sakr and Bilal al-Berjawi this process had fatal implications. Sakr was informed via a letter to his family in September 2010 that new Home Secretary Theresa May had "personally decided" that he be excluded from the United Kingdom since "Her Majesty's Government assesses you are involved in terrorism-related activities." He was also accused of having links to "a number of Islamist extremists," one of whom was his childhood friend al-Berjawi whose family received a similar letter.[17]

Despite the duo's killing in US drone strikes 16 months later, the terrorism allegations against them remain classified. Some could be inferred. In November 2009, for example, the pair were accused by Ugandan authorities of "sneaking into the country" to plot terrorist acts. British court documents would also later assert that both Sakr and al-Berjawi were in Somalia for "terrorist training and activity."[18] Yet neither man was ever charged with, or prosecuted for, a terrorist-related offence while alive. On June 23, 2011, ex-Briton al-Berjawi was directly targeted in the first known US drone strike in Somalia, which CNN claimed to be a joint CIA-JSOC operation.[19] Seriously wounded, he was nursed back to partial health by best friend Sakr, who by then was going by the *nom de guerre* of Abu Ahed al-Masri. Seven months later Bilal al-Berjawi was finally assassinated, days before Al Shabaab "pledged obedience" to Al Qaeda Central.[20] He was tracked down and killed in a Pentagon drone strike on the road between Merca and Eilish Beya. Hours earlier, his wife had given birth in London to the couple's first son, and Berjawi had broken radio silence to speak with her. In a later obituary Al Shabaab described its version of events:

> His traitorous driver planted a cellphone that helped British Intelligence in tracking the location of the car. The driver then left

alleging he had to go pray, and while Bilal was busy on the phone, he was bombed by a drone and the whole car exploded. Nothing was left from his body, except his liver.[21]

Back in London the birth certificate issued for al-Berjawi's new son gave his father's occupation as "electrical engineer (deceased)."[22] With al-Berjawi dead, Sakr must have feared he was in peril. In February 2012, news agencies reported that a "high-ranking Egyptian Al Qaida official" had been killed in a US drone strike in Somalia. It would be days before the family in London learned that those reports actually referred to their British-born son.

Bilal al-Berjawi's role as a liaison between Al Shabaab, the local Al Qaeda affiliate AQEA, and with radicalized Muslims back in London raised major concerns among Western intelligence agencies. Sakr too was a cause for worry, although little publicly available evidence has emerged linking him to Al Qaeda. Yet the decision to kill the pair remained a radical one, in part because of their British origins and also because of the rarity of such US targeted assassinations in East Africa. Unlike the developing conflict in Yemen, drone and other airstrikes had been used sparingly in Somalia, for fear of further destabilizing the fragile nation. Indeed, less than 24 hours before the killing of al-Berjawi, US Secretary of State Hillary Clinton had told a major international conference on Somalia that any such armed intervention would be a mistake: "We see a lot of progress on the ground. I am not a military strategist, but I think I know enough to say that airstrikes would not be a good idea. And we have absolutely no reason to believe anyone, certainly not the United States, anyone is considering that."[23] Clinton's comments—and their awkward timing—again illustrated the limited ability of the State Department to influence the secret targeted killing program, to the consternation of its diplomats.

In death, if not in life, Mohamed Sakr proved that the British had most likely acted unlawfully in originally stripping him of his UK nationality. Bilal al-Berjawi had held a Lebanese as well as a British passport. Yet Sakr had been born in the United Kingdom and had never taken up the Egyptian citizenship his parentage entitled him to. British law stated at the time that the removal of a person's citizenship could not render them stateless. Yet that is exactly what occurred in Sakr's case, his father contends. "It's like stripping somebody of their clothes really. Having taken all of your rights just like that [clicks fingers] in one minute and you find yourself stateless. And because he never had an Egyptian passport he was stateless, stuck there."[24] For the Sakr family, the pain continued long after the death of Mohamed. Despite two years of effort by the family to have him declared officially dead, neither Egypt nor Britain would accept he had been one of their own citizens at the time of death. By late 2014 Mohamed's status remained in legal limbo. Britain's Supreme Court had confirmed in another case that it was unlawful for the UK to render any citizen stateless. In response, the Cameron government changed the law to allow the stripping of citizenship from any dual-national regardless—despite warnings that this was in breach of international law.[25]

The main beneficiary of the Sakr and al-Berjawi killings was the United Kingdom itself, since both men conceivably represented a threat to the homeland. As an anonymous US official told the *Washington Post* after the first attempt to kill al-Berjawi, those targeted "were looking to conduct attacks in Europe . . . the specific target was Britain."[26] Extensive evidence had emerged in 2013, due to the Snowden NSA revelations, of quite how deeply interconnected US and UK intelligence-sharing had become.[27] This appears to have extended to the secret drone war itself. According to UN special rapporteur Ben Emmerson, the nature of that relationship "makes it inevitable that intelligence which is shared by the United Kingdom with the United States will be deployed for lethal operations. It is inevitable."[28] Britain had historically opposed targeted killings by others. In 2004, for example, both Tony Blair and his Foreign Secretary Jack Straw had condemned Israel's killing of Sheik Ahmed Yassin (though neither ever publicly condemned the US campaign).[29] Yet Emmerson has questioned whether such opposition extended to the UK coalition government which had taken office in 2010:

> One can take it that they're not sufficiently robustly opposed enough
> to the US position to come out publicly and criticize it. And so it might
> be possible to infer that they in fact regard the US position as a modern
> interpretation of International Humanitarian Law.[30]

Ian Macdonald QC, a leading expert on British immigration law, has speculated that the removal of Sakr and al-Berjawi's citizenships by the British government paved the way for its intelligence agencies to share potentially lethal information with little fear of repercussion: "It means that the British government can completely wash their hands if the security services give information to the Americans who use their drones to track someone and kill them."[31] Mohamed Sakr's father Gamal also believes this to be the case: "That's why the British did this. By stripping them of their nationalities before they decided to give [the US] the go-ahead, their hands were washed." The head of the Secret Intelligence Service (MI6) told British MPs in late 2013 that "We do what we can to disrupt terrorist attacks overseas. We foil a good number."[32] Yet what form such disruption had taken remained unclear. With MI6, GCHQ, and the Home Office all declining to comment on grounds of national security, the circumstances behind the killings of al-Berjawi and Sakr remain a state secret. Parliament's Intelligence and Security Committee also showed no interest in investigating the matter. The decision in March 2014 by UN investigators to refer the Sakr drone strike to the British and US governments for comment did at least raise the possibility of further light being shed on the deaths of the two ex-Britons. However, both governments later chose not to cooperate further with the UN enquiry.[33]

German Fears

Concerns over potentially lethal intelligence-sharing were not restricted to Britain. In early 2011, an urgent order was issued by Germany's Interior Ministry: intelligence agencies could no longer pass information to the United States if there was any risk this might be used to kill German citizens.[34] Berlin's ban was triggered by a CIA drone strike on October 4, 2010, which according to early reports had killed as many as eight German nationals (two had in fact died).[35] In the days prior to that bombing, there were claims of impending terror attacks against Berlin and other European cities: "Terrorists plotting to carry out a Mumbai-style massacre in Western Europe have a list of high-profile targets in their sights ranging from the Eiffel Tower to a hotel near Berlin's famed Brandenburg Gate," ran one of many such stories, with Fox News reporting that the source was "a German-Pakistani national interrogated at Bagram Air Base in Afghanistan."[36] Meanwhile, an anonymous US official told Reuters: "It shouldn't surprise anyone that links between plots and those who are orchestrating them lead to decisive American action. The terrorists who are involved are, as everyone should expect, going to be targets. That's the whole point of all of this."[37]

Binyamin Erdogan was talking in the courtyard of his rented home with fellow-German Shahab Dashti and three Pakistanis when a Hellfire missile detonated among them at around 7.00 p.m. local time. Erdogan's widow, his pregnant sister-in-law, and infant nephew were just meters away, though survived unscathed. His brother Emrah was in a nearby room: "My eyes were full of earth because the houses were made of mud," he later recalled. Staggering outside, he found Dashti mortally injured and his brother Binyamin dead.[38] Testimony from Emrah's wife has described how her 1-year-old son had been playing with his uncle in the courtyard only minutes before a US missile struck. She recalled the scene imme- diately after: "The bodies of the three strangers had been cut into pieces by the attack and we could hardly find anything of them. The body of my brother-in-law lay in the soil. He was already dead and the back of his head had been blown apart. . . . Although our friend's [Dashti's] hand was still trembling he was dead already as well. . . . The whole courtyard had been turned to rubble by the attack."[39] Scared that he still risked being killed, and now on the run, the surviving brother contacted Hans-Christian Ströbele, the German Green Party MP:

> Emrah contacted me via mail, apparently from Pakistan and at first anonymously. He told me what he'd experienced, that he was present during the drone strike and was indeed unbelievably lucky to survive. He also sent me photos of his dead brother and asked for my help.[40]

Ströbele helped arrange for the return of Emrah Erdogan and his wife to Germany, where the former was ultimately imprisoned for seven years on terrorism-related charges.[41]

It was widely assumed in media reports that those Germans bombed by the CIA in Waziristan had been involved in the "imminent terror plots" described just days beforehand. Yet Germany's interior minister Thomas de Maziere had insisted at the time that "there is no concrete imminent attack plan that we are aware of. . . . We are looking at every- thing but there is no fever thermometer of danger."[42] The strike on the Erdogan home again raised concerns about the extent to which Western intelligence agencies were colluding in lethal operations. Discomfort at the deaths of Germans—coupled with the later criminal trials of Emrah Erdogan and others—saw key aspects of the intelligence process exposed. It emerged, for example, that Germany's intelligence agencies had known of the Erdogans' presence in Mir Ali, North Waziristan, for many weeks prior to the attack. Indeed, all phone calls made by the men were being recorded and analyzed. In a prophetic conversation in August 2010, for example, Emrah described his life in "dangerous Waziristan" to his family in Germany. *Stern* magazine, which obtained transcripts of the conversations, described how Erdogan believed that "houses are marked so that airplanes can identify them and bomb them more accurately." Only an American air raid would ever be able to reach them, he said.[43] Other calls reportedly described a planned suicide mission in Afghanistan by Binyamin which was designed to kill "many dozens of people." With the Mir Ali house under direct surveillance by both US and German intelligence agencies, it is unclear why the United States had proceeded with a lethal strike when it did—particularly since women and children were in immediate proximity to the targets.

Questioned by the Bundestag's oversight committee, the German intelligence community admitted, according to Ströbele, that on occasion "they gave information to US [intelligence] services but explicitly not for killings or executions by Special Commando or drones, they would not do this. Then I asked, 'Can you exclude the possibility?' and they answered, 'No.'" A government minister later insisted that while the intelligence services did share cellphone data with "other foreign secret services," this was "not specific enough to pinpoint exact locations." Critics complained that such data could still lead the CIA's drones to the near vicinity of a German citizen, from where its own electronic eavesdropping technologies might easily locate them.[44] Under pressure from MPs, in January 2011, prosecutors opened a criminal investigation into whether Germany's intelligence agencies had been complicit in the killing of citizens.[45] Marc Lindemann, a former Military Intelligence officer who has made a study of the Erdogan case, believes it was "pretty likely" that Germany shared material with the Americans related to the strike: "The only question for me was whether Germany's intelligence services had the intention to kill Binyamin or others, or just gave the information and didn't ask any questions."[46] Yet almost three years later, the inquiry concluded that there were no charges to answer, since Binyamin Erdogan had been a "civilian combatant" and was therefore "lawfully killed." Questions relating to intelligence-sharing were sidestepped.

Even as federal investigators gathered their evidence, other Germans were still being killed by the CIA in Pakistan—regardless of any ban on intelligence sharing. On the tenth anniversary of 9/11, Mohammad al-Faateh, a 27-year-old Berliner and suspected militant, was killed by the Americans in North Waziristan along with an alleged local Haqqani Network official and a Saudi Al Qaeda operative. Seven months later, Samir Hatour also died. According to a martyrdom video obtained by SITE, a for-profit organization that tracks the online activity of various extremist groups, "on the morning of 9 March 2012, which was a Friday, Abu Laith [Hatour] went to his family, and on the way with three other mujahidin, the car he was in was fired upon by an American drone and the brothers died as martyrs."[47] In October 2012 Ahmad B. was also killed, a 24-year-old man of Moroccan origin who had been born in the town of Setterich in the German state of Aachen. Announcing his death, the Islamic Movement of Uzbekistan (which took in many European radicals), pronounced in a 13-minute German-language video: *Dear brothers and sisters, the King of Setterich is now a martyr.*"

As the longest-serving member of the Bundestag oversight committee for Germany's intelligence community, Ströbele was deeply concerned at the issues raised by the killing of Binyamin Erdogan and other nationals: "Our intelligence agencies always deny any involvement with surveillance and the use of drones, because they know that it is a very delicate issue here. First they would be liable to prosecution and second they would be violating the constitution." Sitting in a Berlin office stacked from floor to ceiling with box files of investigations he has conducted, Ströbele admitted to being disheartened at how little true oversight politicians in Germany, Britain, and the United States now had over their respective intelligence services: "Too often we are dependent on good investigative journalists to get hold of certain facts, which then give us the chance to follow up with the intelligence services. Without the work of *Spiegel*, *Süddeutsche Zeitung* and others, our work would be far less worthy or of no worth at all."[48] It was a disheartening admission from a politician whose role was to help hold to democratic account the intelligence world.

The Pakistan Connection

For more than three decades, Pakistan's tribal areas had drawn in foreigners attracted to the idea of a holy war against invaders. During the 1980s according to Wajid Shamsul Hasan, Islamabad's former High Commissioner to the UK, Pakistan "issued over 100,000 passports and identity cards to all these mujahideen. They became Pakistan nationals. And there were Chechens, Bosnians, they came from South Yemen, North Yemen, Somalia, Ethiopia, any Muslim country where there were radicals and who would listen to Osama [bin Laden] and others and join hands."[49] Many went on to settle permanently in FATA in the 1990s, becoming a part of local communities. "They learned the language and they became a part of that society, both in Afghanistan as well as in FATA. Yet the Americans think they're still mujahideen or Taliban, so they target them as well. They don't know if they are killing people who have converted themselves into peaceful citizens," complains Hasan.

Former US officials counter that the only foreigners they were interested in were either those affiliated with Al Qaeda; or a new wave of would-be militants who arrived from Europe, the Middle East, and the Americas after 9/11 and the Iraq invasion. "What we saw was a resurgence of training areas and this flow of Westerners, described broadly, into the training areas," recalls one former senior US intelligence official. "These were folks who would not have called attention to themselves if they were standing next to you in the passport line or at McDonald's. And our analysts began to tell us, 'We're getting graduating classes from these cohorts.'"[50] Some of these Westerners fought locally in the Afghan insurgency. Others sought out Al Qaeda itself, often with the aim of carrying out terrorist attacks back in their home countries. Two of the London suicide bombers of 2005 had received terror training in the FATA tribal areas, for example.[51]

In December of that same year, 30-year-old Spanish husband and wife Amer Azizi and Raquel Burgos Garcia became the first known Westerners to be killed in the CIA's Pakistan drone campaign. Raquel's journey from the suburbs of Madrid to the tribal lands of Pakistan had been a strange one, according to investigative reporters Manuel Marlasca and Luis Rendueles. In 1996, she had met Moroccan-born Amer Azizi not long after his return from fighting in Bosnia. The couple married after Raquel converted to Islam, with Amer obtaining Spanish citizenship in 1999. Known in jihadist circles by his nom de guerre of Othman el Espanol, he allegedly had close ties to Al Qaeda, and by August 2002 the couple and their children had made their way to Waziristan following unwelcome scrutiny from Spain's security services. The investigation into the 2004 Madrid train bombings, which killed 191 people, later implicated Azizi and others in the planning of the atrocity.[52] At a house in North Waziristan on December 1, 2005, US drones struck. Raquel Burgos Garcia and her husband both died along with Abu Hamza Rabia, reportedly a senior Al Qaeda operative and head of the terror group's "foreign operations," and with a $5 million US bounty on his head. Within hours Pakistan's military leader Pervez Musharraf was boasting to reporters that Rabia was "200%" dead.[53]

Also killed in the CIA's bombing were two children, perhaps the couple's own. News magazine *Interviu* learned from Madrid officials that while the State Department and CIA officially denied involvement, "they did recognize off the record and orally to Spanish civil servants that one of their pilotless Predators killed two terrorists. Moreover, they said that agents from the CIA and US Navy Intelligence went to the bombed scene to check in situ the victims of the Hellfire missile, which was launched over a house where a mass gathering was taking place."[54] When asked by their Spanish colleagues to obtain DNA samples of those women and children killed, "the US Navy's answer was a categorical 'No.'" According to a Spanish official, "If we officially confirm that their missile killed a Spanish woman and her children, they know they can have problems." The deaths illustrated key challenges in the identification of those killed in more than a decade of secret US bombings. While officials were generally quick to claim credit for the killing of senior militant and terrorist leaders, silence invariably surrounded the deaths of civilians. The more controversial the strike, the less likely the United States appeared willing to accept any public responsibility for its actions, anonymously or otherwise. And when Westerners died—even alleged militants—few official details ever emerged.

In 2007 the CIA struck a training school for suicide bombers in Pakistan's tribal areas, shortly after ABC News obtained a propaganda video featuring a boastful training school participant: "Let me say something about why we are going, along with my team, for a suicide attack in Britain," the man said in poor English. "Whether my colleagues, companions and Muslim brothers die today or tonight, every drop of our blood will invigorate the Muslim."[55] Any Britons at the camp were not alone, with a Taliban commander also claiming the presence of "Americans, Canadians and Germans."

Years later, former CIA Director Michael Hayden told a Canadian newspaper that "One of the big issues that I was briefing to George Bush as 2007 turned to 2008 was the number of Westerners—broadly defined—who were showing up in the tribal regions of Pakistan." He went on to tell President Bush: "This is a safe haven that's being used to prepare people to come attack us. And therefore we recommended—and this is the best I can give you on this—stronger courses of action."[56] A former US intelligence official confirms that both Bush and Dick Cheney were eventually won over to the idea of targeting and killing alleged Western jihadists. "At the heart of our discussion was that this now is the recreating of the threat to the homeland," the former official recalls. "And that's a pretty stark place for the intel guys to put a policy-maker in. But that's kind of an accurate description of the box we built for the President and the Vice President in the summer of 2008."[57] The Agency was given far greater freedom to hit targets across the tribal areas. As the former official notes, "What was going on in the last six months of 2008 was so different. And it was so free of any Pakistani chop on what we were doing, that it really caught them off-balance and we could cross off pictures in the Top 20 list with surprising regularity."

Westerners were now key targets. In August, two unnamed Canadians died in a drone attack in South Waziristan, Pakistani intelligence officials reported.[58] A leaked CIA summary of the mission makes no mention of their nationalities, noting only that the strike "killed Al Qaeda paramilitary operatives subordinate to Al Qaeda commander and East Africa Embassy bomber Usama Al Kini." Who the dead were remained a mystery six years later, at least publicly. Certainly there had been concerns that some Canadians were being drawn to militant groups. Counterterrorism officers from the Royal Canadian Mounted Police had earlier issued arrest warrants for two men named as Ferid Ahmed Imam and Maiwand Yar, for example, following "evidence that two Canadian citizens conspired to travel to Pakistan [in 2007] for terrorist training." However, there was no indication that either man had been killed by the United States, with the RCMP noting to the author in 2012 that "We have no information to suggest that either Imam or Yar are deceased."[59]

Remarkably, of up to 40 Westerners killed by the United States in targeted killings since 2002, the identities of almost half remain a public mystery.[60] In a 2010 CIA bombing in Pakistan's tribal areas, two white converts from the British Midlands were killed—identified only as "Stephen" and "Mr. Dearlove" in reports. Extensive efforts by human rights lawyers to trace UK-based families came to nothing. The following year, locals in Waziristan reported the death of an Australian man. On July 5, a CIA drone had struck a guest house killing the owner and his guests, which a secret FATA Secretariat report described as "A Foreigner including his wife and two children." The "foreigner" was a man in his late thirties known locally as Saifullah, "a white Australian convert who had grown a beard and who had come to North Waziristan four years ago," according to field researchers for the BIJ. They also learned that the man had traveled from Khost in Afghanistan two days prior to his death and was suspected of fighting in the insurgency. Yet, Canberra's Department of Foreign Affairs insisted that "there is no information to indicate an Australian was killed in the alleged attack."[61] The true identity of "Saifullah" remained unknown at the time of publication.

Two more Antipodeans were killed by US drones in Yemen in late November 2013, both allegedly Al Qaeda "foot soldiers." They were named as Christopher Harvard and New Zealand dual citizen Daryl Jones, after Australia's Federal Police assisted in DNA tests. Both nations confirmed in the wake of the killings that their intelligence services had aided drone operations in Afghanistan. Less clear was whether they had assisted in the targeted killing of their own citizens elsewhere. Canberra claimed, for example, that "there was no Australian involvement in, or prior awareness of, the [Yemen] operation."[62] Yet with echoes of the Sakr and al-Berjawi affair, the government had cancelled the passports of both Harvard and Jones a year before the Americans killed them. And details also emerged of extensive collaboration with the US drone project from Pine Gap, a secret facility near Alice Springs jointly run by Australia's ASIO intelligence service and the American National Security Agency. According to former Prime Minister Malcom Fraser, Pine Gap was "very much involved in the targeting [process] of drones."[63] Signals intelligence expert Professor Des Ball in turn alleged that the facility had played a role as far back as the CIA's first targeted killing in Yemen in 2002: "Information from Pine Gap, intercepts of phone conversations from Pine Gap, were utilised in that operation," he told reporters.[64] More recently, a former Australian operator at the base described how "we track them, we combine the signals intelligence with imagery, and once we've passed the geolocation intel on, our job is done. When drones do their job we don't need to track that target any more."[65]

With more than a million Britons of Pakistani origin living in the United Kingdom, it was perhaps inevitable that some would be drawn into the War on Terror. Rashid Rauf was the first UK citizen to be deliberately targeted and killed by the CIA in Pakistan, in the final weeks of the Bush presidency. Rauf had fled Britain in 2002 following the fatal stabbing of his uncle—a crime the West Midland police were still keen to question him about a decade later, given there has been no formal confirmation of his death.[66] Basing himself in Waziristan, Rauf had by his own apparent admission helped facilitate the 2005 London suicide bombings.[67] The following year he was implicated in the airport "liquid bomb" plot, the discovery of which affected air travel for years to come. Seized by Pakistani police with the assistance of the CIA, Rashid Rauf was imprisoned for six months. During this time he was "beaten and mistreated," according to British and Pakistani intelligence sources, something which played a crucial role in the decision by Pakistani authorities to drop all charges against Rauf in late 2006.[68] Rearrested and now facing extradition to Britain, the alleged terrorist evaded his captors in farcical circumstances a year later: "Police allowed Rauf's uncle to transport him from the courtroom to the jail following an extradition hearing in his personal van rather than in a police vehicle," a secret US embassy cable noted. "While en route to the prison, the uncle also convinced the constables to stop and eat at a fast-food restaurant, and later to pray at a mosque. Rauf and his uncle then escaped during the prayer service."[69] Rauf made once more for Waziristan. Yet this time he was unable to evade the CIA's Predators.

Just as with al-Berjawi and Sakr's deaths in Somalia, Rauf's killing has raised concerns regarding the possible involvement of British intelligence. The United States was well aware that Britain wanted Rauf to stand trial for his alleged role in the London bombings; and the two nations had worked closely together in smashing the liquid bomb plot. Did Washington seek London's approval for Rauf's killing? Did Britain supply intelligence which played a part in the attack? Certainly claims had emerged that Britain had been directly supplying intelligence to the US covert killing campaign. Just as with Australia's Pine Gap facility, Britain's powerful GCHQ was alleged to have provided geo-locational intelligence for use in drone strikes. According to the *Sunday Times*, "the top-secret communications agency has used telephone intercepts to provide the Americans with 'locational intelligence' on leading militants in Afghanistan and Pakistan, an official briefed on its operations said."[70]

In January 2012, the CIA killed Aslam Awan, a reputed Al Qaeda operative who "had spent time in London and had ties to British extremists," according to a Reuters investigation. Reporter Chris Allbritton was told by a knowledgeable Pakistani security source that in preparation for such drone strikes "we run joint monitoring operations with our US and UK friends," in addition to the monitoring of mobiles and satellite phones. The source described cooperation with British intelligence as "extensive."[71] A former senior US intelligence official nevertheless insisted to the author that there were limits to intelligence-sharing with potentially lethal implications from partner agencies:

> I know that we are the only country on Earth who thinks that we're in a global war with Al Qaeda and we have the right to take the fight to the enemy outside of internationally agreed theaters of conflict. And I know there isn't an intelligence service in Europe—particularly in Western Europe—that would have given me the information to go ahead and kill one of these guys unless he was in Iraq or Afghanistan.[72]

In October 2012 Rashid Rauf's Birmingham-based family announced they would seek to have Britain's courts declare unlawful any UK intelligence-sharing related to targeted killings beyond the battlefield.[73] It was the second case of its type to be announced within weeks after relatives for Noor Khan, a civilian killed in a March 2011 drone strike in Pakistan, sought a ruling from the London High Court. That case was funded by legal charity Reprieve, an implacable foe of the US targeted killing program. Judges of the Queen's Bench Division were invited to declare that "a person who passes to an agent of the United States Government intelligence on the location of an individual in Pakistan or elsewhere, foreseeing a serious risk that the information will be used by the Central Intelligence Agency to target or kill that individual . . . may be liable under domestic criminal law for soliciting, encouraging, persuading or proposing a murder."[74] The High Court refused leave for a judicial review, in part because judges did not want to be placed in the position of effectively ruling on the legality of the US targeted killing program: "The claimant cannot demonstrate that his application will avoid, during the course of the hearing and in the judgment, giving a clear impression that it is the United States' conduct in North Waziristan which is also on trial," noted Lord Justice Moses.[75]

The Americans

In May 2013, the US Attorney General informed Congress of four named Americans killed "outside of areas of active hostilities" in covert drone strikes. While three were known to have been targeted in Yemen—Anwar al-Awlaki, his teenage son Abd al Rahman, and Al Qaeda propagandist Samir Khan—a fourth name surprised many. Hailing from Raleigh, North Carolina, Jude Kenan Mohammad had died aged 23 in a CIA drone strike in November 2011. He had arrived in South Waziristan three years earlier, where he had "engaged in planning and perpetrating an act of international terrorism against an international organization or foreign government" according to a Federal indictment.[76] Although anonymous US officials told the *New York Times* that Mohammad's death was the result of a "signature strike" and that he had not been directly targeted, this claim should be treated with some caution. As the paper also noted, Mohammad "had come under increasing scrutiny by American counterterrorism officials, who said he was involved in recruiting militants for Al Qaeda and the Pakistani Taliban, as well as making videos on YouTube to incite violence against the United States."[77]

Six weeks earlier, the United States had targeted and killed Americans Anwar al-Awlaki and Samir Khan in Yemen, only hours after the pair had produced the latest issue of an online Al Qaeda magazine aimed squarely at English speakers. The "Special Edition" of *Inspire*, dedicated to "*that glorious event*" the 9/11 atrocities, carried a number of pieces by al-Awlaki along with an article by Samir Khan which described AQAP's media work as "half of the jihad."[78] The other American killed was al-Awlaki's 16-year-old son Abd al-Rahman, bombed as he ate with a group of young friends on October 14. All four Americans were killed by the Obama administration within a seven-week window, with three linked directly to anti-US propaganda efforts. The final victim, al-Awlaki's son, died in an attack which some reports said was aimed at local Al Qaeda media coordinator Ibrahim al-Banna. Yet only Anwar al-Awlaki among them was "specifically targeted," Attorney General Eric Holder had insisted.[79]

For some time prior to the four killings, the Obama administration had aggressively asserted the legality of its targeted assassination programme, including the right to kill US citizens. Both the Pentagon's JSOC and the CIA were by now keeping lists, which between them featured the names of Americans who could be "specifically targeted for killing or capture."[80] In June 2010, John Brennan, Obama's chief counterterrorism adviser, had spoken of "dozens of Americans [who] have joined terrorist groups and are posing a threat to the United States," adding that "if an American person or citizen is in a Yemen or in a Pakistan or in Somalia or another place, and they are trying to carry out attacks against US interests, they also will face the full brunt of a US response."[81] Three days later, CIA director Leon Panetta focused in on just one American: "Awlaki is a terrorist who has declared war on the United States. Everything he's doing now is to try to encourage others to attack this country. . . . Yes, he's a US citizen, but he is first and foremost a terrorist and we're going to treat him like a terrorist. We don't have an assassination list, but I can tell you this. We have a terrorist list and he's on it."[82] The Denver-born preacher's sermons had gained wide popularity on the web, even as they grew more militant in the wake of the 2003 Iraq invasion. After a short period in London, al-Awlaki had returned to his ancestral country of Yemen, where according to a UN report:

> Mr. al-Awlaki was arrested and imprisoned by the Yemeni authorities for 18 months from 2006-2007 at the request of the United States Government after he sought to mediate a tribal dispute. During his imprisonment, he was reportedly repeatedly questioned by FBI agents. As subsequently reportedly admitted by United States Government officials, John Negroponte, then Director of National Intelligence, told Yemeni authorities that the United States did not object to Mr. al-Awlaki's continued detention.[83]

That "continued detention" was unlawful. By the end of 2007 Yemen's government secretly told the US embassy "that they do not have sufficient evidence to charge him and can no longer hold him illegally."[84]

On his release, Anwar al-Awlaki was increasingly drawn to Al Qaeda's local offshoot, which had by now rebranded as Al Qaeda in the Arabian Peninsula, or AQAP, though his precise role has never been properly clarified. When Barack Obama announced the eventual killing of the cleric in September 2011 he insisted that al-Awlaki was the "leader of external operations" for AQAP. A draft Department of Justice memo on the legality of targeting a US citizen had also required that any strike target a "senior operational leader of Al Qaeda or an associated force."[85] Yet as investigative blogger Marcy Wheeler has reported, no evidence of al-Awlaki's relations with Al Qaeda beyond his propaganda writings has ever publicly emerged.[86]

On December 24, 2009, the United States made its first attempt to kill the cleric, a month before the State Department officially designated AQAP a Foreign Terrorist Organization[87] Even then, al-Awlaki was not among the senior Al Qaeda leaders named.[88] And US officials had told the *Washington Post* at the time of that first attack he was "less an operational leader than an inspirational one."[89] Even so, cruise missiles struck the village of Rafdh in Shabwa province, killing at least four alleged militants. US officials claimed within hours that the "decapitating strike" had "probably" killed the preacher. Weeks later, Yemen's president would secretly confirm his survival to CENTCOM commander David Petraeus: "Extremist cleric Anwar al-Awlaki may still be alive, Saleh said, but the December strikes had already caused al-Qaeda operatives to turn themselves in to authorities and residents in affected areas to deny refuge to al-Qaeda."[90]

The oft-cited trigger for that first attempted US assassination of al-Awlaki had been the fatal shooting of 13 soldiers at Fort Hood a month earlier, after which investigators had found an email exchange between the killer, Maj. Nidal Malik Hasan, and the cleric. The media made much of this contact. Yet a somewhat different picture emerged when the FBI finally released the full email exchange in the summer of 2012—nine months after Anwar al-Awlaki's killing. Although Hasan had written 15 times over a year, al-Awlaki had responded only twice, on both occasions briefly and with vague platitudes. Despite claims of an email association with four other "known homegrown US radicals who took or attempted violent acts or training," a major Bureau report concluded that "The FBI is not aware of any evidence that Aulaqi [al-Awlaki] instructed any of these individuals to engage in violent acts."[91]

Brandon Bryant never did get the personal order from President Obama to kill al-Awlaki, retiring from AFSOC's elite drone squadron after almost six years on the job in spring 2011. A few weeks later he heard in the news of another botched attempt by JSOC to kill the cleric. That failure led to the CIA being given control of the project. Almost five months later, they finally succeeded when Anwar al-Awlaki and fellow American Samir Khan were incinerated in their truck with two other alleged AQAP members. In October 2013, Bryant told a UN panel in New York that he had been "party to the violation of the constitutional rights of a US citizen" during classified drone missions, an apparent reference to Yemen operations. Later, he described to the author a world in which it was repeatedly reinforced to AFSOC's drone crews that Anwar al-Awlaki needed to be killed:

> They were giving us so much propaganda: "He's a traitor to the American people and the American way of life; he's an American citizen that has joined Al Qaeda. He deserves to die. We need to hunt him down and kill him." That's what they were telling us. And I believed it for a while.

Bryant now views that world differently. "It wasn't until after I got out that I realized I was violating the Constitution. Everyone in the military needs to know the Constitution since they swear an oath to protect it."[92] For the Obama administration, al-Awlaki's killing was instead viewed as a significant victory against Al Qaeda, with officials asserting that any due process protections he may have had under the Constitution "must be balanced against the United States' interest in forestalling the threat of violence and death to other Americans that arises from an individual who is a senior operational leader of Al Qaeda."[93] That comment only emerged with the leaking of a draft Department of Justice memo, after Obama officials had aggressively resisted attempts to force full disclosure of any internal documents outlining the claimed legal basis for the targeted killing of American citizens. A heavily redacted version was finally published in mid-2014, on the orders of a federal court.[94]

"Judge, Jury and Executioner"

Controversial as the death of Anwar al-Awlaki remained, the targeted killing of his teenage son Abd al-Rahman by Special Forces Predators on behalf of JSOC did more than any other act of the US covert war to alienate ordinary Yemenis, claims London *Times* reporter Iona Craig. She recalls seeing for the first time the American flag being burned on the streets of Sana'a in late 2011, in an outpouring of popular anger: "It was a huge defining moment here. Of people really thinking enough is enough. Because Abd al-Rahman was a middle-class educated kid. A lot of the revolutionary youth knew him, and he was very much seen as one of them. It was 'If he's Al-Qaeda we're all Al Qaeda.' "[95] Although US intelligence sources would claim the intended target of the attack was AQAP's media coordinator Ibrahim al-Banna, early press reports citing Yemeni officials focused heavily on the young al-Awlaki's death, claiming variously that he was 21 years old, an Al Qaeda affiliate, and had been "hiding in the mountains of Shabwa for more than eight months."[96] The truth was very different. The 16-year-old had left the capital only a month earlier in September 2011, his family told investigative reporter Jeremy Scahill. Slipping away at dawn he had left his mother a note: "I am sorry for leaving in this kind of way. I miss my father and want to see if I can go and talk to him."[97]

Following the killing of Anwar on September 30th, his son was planning on returning to the capital. He never had the chance: "On October 14th, 2011 Abdulrahman, along with some of his tribe's youth have gone barbecuing under the moonlight. A drone missile hit their congregation killing Abdulrahman and several other teenagers," the family later said.[98] It was also doubtful whether Ibrahim al-Banna was present at the strike. Scahill cited a former senior Obama administration official as saying that chief counterterrorism adviser John Brennan "suspected that the kid had been killed intentionally and ordered a review. I don't know what happened with the review."[99] The targeted killing of four Americans within 48 days of each other—with each incident connected in some way to reported propaganda efforts against the United States—raised fundamental questions about claims by the Obama administration only to have "specifically" targeted Anwar al-Awlaki.

The Holder letter—the first formal acknowledgment of any named individuals killed in more than 400 covert and clandestine US drone strikes—chose only to reveal those Americans killed since Obama had come to office in 2009. Missing was any mention of at least three other US citizens killed by drones during George W. Bush's presidency. One name was well known, that of Kamel Derwish, who had died in the first ever US covert drone strike in Yemen back in 2002 (see chapter 3). Yet at least two other Americans appear to have been killed by the CIA. On November 7, 2008, the Agency bombed a militant training camp in North Waziristan. At the time it was only reported that "foreigners" were among the dead. Five days later according to veteran reporter Bob Woodward (who was present), CIA director Michael Hayden met with Pakistan's President, where Asif Ali Zardari was informed that "many Westerners, including some US passport holders, had been killed" in the Pakistan strike. Hayden refused to elaborate further "due to the implications under American law." As of early 2015, no details of any Americans killed in that strike had been released by Washington.[100] Nevertheless, former officials insist that any American deaths during Bush administration drone strikes were never deliberate. "I know of none that were intentionally targeted while I was in government," a former senior US intelligence official told the author. "We always had it in our mind that if we knew Americans were going to be involved, then that would require additional discussion. But we never had to do that."[101]

Any hope by critics of the deliberate targeting of Americans that Anwar al-Awlaki's death was a one-off appeared dashed in February 2014 when intelligence officials began leaking details of another US citizen in the Reaper's cross-hairs. Named by the *New York Times* as Abdullah al-Shami—and described as being "senior" in Al Qaeda's remnant Pakistan organization—according to one administration official "We have clear and convincing evidence that he's involved in the production and distribution of IED's [improvised explosive devices]."[102] If accurate, this implied that al-Shami was involved in counterinsurgency operations against US and allied forces in Afghanistan, rather than in any international terrorism plots. That in turn appeared to indicate a lowering of any internal threshold needed for the US government to target and kill its own citizens without reference to the courts. Accusing Barack Obama of acting as "judge, jury and executioner," Hina Shamsi of the American Civil Liberties Union complained that "there are some powers people should never concede to their government. That's why the Founders included due process in our Bill of Rights. Extraordinary powers consolidated in one office inevitably will be abused. That's true no matter who's behind the desk."[103]

The deaths of at least seven Americans in secret US drone strikes raised significant legal and political concerns for those back home. Yet these were a tiny element of a larger covert and clandestine bombing campaign by both the Pentagon and CIA, which had between them killed nationals of at least 34 countries by 2014.[104] If, as some insisted, the government had no authority to target and kill US citizens without reference to the courts, why was it any more at liberty to kill the citizens of other nations—including those of close allies—away from the hot battlefield? As Amnesty International had argued, "International human rights law explicitly prohibits discrimination on grounds of national origin when it comes to respect for human rights. The U.S. government is not allowed to treat the right to life of a non-U.S. citizen as less worthy of protection than the right to life of a U.S. citizen, just because the person is a foreign national."[105]

As even the CIA's own leaked data had shown, the clear majority of those killed in covert US drone strikes were Pakistanis, Afghans, or Yemenis involved in local or regional insurgent activities. Would-be militants and terrorists were nevertheless drawn from many other nations. The intelligence world had responded in kind, with allies sharing information on suspects which might have lethal implications. Oversight of this complex intelligence process, with its troubling potential for transnational abuse, had nevertheless remained stubbornly parochial. Parliamentary oversight committees in Germany, Britain, and elsewhere either had too little power—or had shown too little interest—in examining whether domestic intelligence agencies might be colluding with a targeted killing project which at least beyond America's shores, was generally viewed as unlawful.

OBAMA'S OBSESSION
"AfPak"

In July 2008, a month after beating Hillary Clinton to the Democratic Party presidential nomination, Barack Obama embarked on a major tour aimed at establishing his foreign policy credentials.[1] First, he traveled to the front line: "We're in Afghanistan because this is the central front in the war on terrorism. Those who actually attacked us on September 11 reside in the badlands between Afghanistan and Pakistan," Obama told US forces in Jalalabad—now under major pressure from a resurgent Taliban.[2] Over the next few days, the candidate visited Iraq, Israel, Jordan, and the Palestinian Territories. In Berlin he spoke to an adoring crowd of more than 200,000. In Paris and London, he was treated as if he were already President-Elect. At the end of the tour, NBC's Tom Brokaw asked Obama how he might respond "When you get home and Michelle says to you, "Barack, what did you learn that surprised you?" The Senator's reply was startling for its singular focus:

Well, I didn't see a huge shift in the strategic policies that I've laid out throughout this campaign. It was clear to me that Afghanistan is the central front on terror, that the Taliban and al-Qaeda have reconstituted themselves. They have safe havens along the Afghan-Pakistan border.[3]

The Afghan war—and Pakistan's role in it—had already become an obsessive focus for Barack Obama. A few months into his presidential bid in 2007, he made a speech titled "The War We Need to Win." Making clear he intended to withdraw US forces from the Iraq debacle, Obama shifted focus to events in South Asia: "We will not repeat the mistake of the past, when we turned our back on Afghanistan following Soviet withdrawal," the junior Senator from Illinois intoned. "As 9/11 showed us, the security of Afghanistan and America is shared. And today, that security is most threatened by the Al Qaeda and Taliban sanctuary in the tribal regions of northwest Pakistan." A planned unilateral US Special Forces operation within Pakistan in 2005 had been aborted, in part because of fears of alienating Islamabad.[4] Obama insisted he would not entertain such concerns: "Let me make this clear. There are terrorists holed up in those mountains who murdered 3,000 Americans. They are plotting to strike again. It was a terrible mistake to fail to act when we had a chance to take out an Al Qaeda leadership meeting in 2005. If we have actionable intelligence about high-value terrorist targets and President Musharraf won't act, we will."[5]

That tough speech was in response, aides said, to a secret 2007 US National Intelligence Estimate that had identified Pakistan as a vital base for Al Qaeda and Taliban militants. A declassified version refers to Al Qaeda as having "protected or regenerated key elements of its Homeland attack capability, including: a safehaven in the Pakistan Federally Administered Tribal Areas (FATA), operational lieutenants, and its top leadership."[6] While this was partially true, the real challenge from 2007 onward was the rising Taliban presence and the threat this represented to Afghanistan. "That's when you start seeing the [FATA] safe haven beginning to develop, and within a short period of time really beginning to affect events in Afghanistan. Which had really been quite quiet prior to that," recalls a former senior US intelligence official from the time.[7]

At this point in the election campaign, Obama was still the outsider, mocked for his naivety. Chief rival Hillary Clinton (later his Secretary of State) clashed in a live 2007 TV debate over Obama's intention to take the war to Pakistan. "I think it is a very big mistake to telegraph that and to destabilize the Musharraf regime, which is fighting for its life against the Islamic extremists who are in bed with Al-Qaeda and Taliban," she told the audience before adding scathingly: "You can think big but remember you shouldn't always say everything you think when you're running for President because it could have consequences across the world."[8] Republican rival John McCain even accused Obama of wanting to "invade Pakistan." Both Clinton and McCain regularly attacked Obama's "AfPak" policy during the primaries. Yet over the course of the election campaign, Obama would return to the subject of Pakistan on at least 30 occasions in stump speeches and interviews. Breaking a major taboo, he even referenced a US covert drone strike, telling a live audience that in Pakistan "just several days ago this [Bush] Administration . . . took out the third-ranking Al Qaida official"—an apparent reference to the killing of Abu Laith al-Libi and eleven others a month earlier.[9]

Among Obama's aides, the term "AfPak" was increasingly heard. "This is not just an effort to save eight syllables," remarked Richard Holbrooke, who coined the term and would go on to be special envoy for the region. "It is an attempt to indicate and imprint in our DNA the fact that there is one theater of war, straddling an ill-defined border."[10] Obama's advisers had seen the potential the Predator offered in this conflict. What few could then have anticipated was that as president, he would come to authorize eight times more targeted killing operations in Pakistan than his predecessor—and would expand the secret drone war to new fronts.

THE NEGLECTED WAR

The US's quick victory over the Taliban and its Al Qaeda allies back in 2001 had led some in Washington to conclude that the war there was done. Few military or intelligence assets were left behind in Afghanistan as Bush shifted his sights to conquering Iraq. Remotely piloted aircraft were no exception. General John Vines, who commanded US forces in Afghanistan in 2003, has recalled an incident in which a chance to once again track a man suspected of being Osama bin Laden had failed because there were so few Predators available. With the target vehicle able to take any of three possible routes, Vines's forces had to take a guess. "A UAV was positioned on the route that was most likely, but he didn't go that way," Vines told the Washington Post. "We believed that we were within a half-hour of possibly getting him, but nothing materialized."[11] Even had analysts chosen the "right" target, any tasked drone would have been unable to strike. Former drone operators told the author that only unarmed Predators were present at the time in Afghanistan. As Matthew Aid has noted, "In effect Iraq was sucking the life out of the US intelligence effort in Afghanistan by starving it of desperately needed resources."[12] By 2006, having rebuilt its strength over the border in Pakistan's tribal areas, the Taliban was ready to exploit the security vacuum. A major ground offensive caught the United States and its allies off guard, just as America's Middle East war was entering its most murderous phase. With so many US troops already committed to the Iraq surge, all the Pentagon could offer was increased airpower to help contain the Taliban. In 2005, the USAF dropped 176 bombs and missiles in Afghanistan. By the next year this had risen fifteenfold to 2,644 weapons released. And that number would double again in 2007.

Both conventional USAF and Special Forces drone squadrons were drawn into that campaign. "The missions I remember most were the ones where we either had some sort of intelligence that they were setting up camps in there, or Taliban [were] moving through an area we might just be scanning and then finding them, and then we'd fix them. Those we would eliminate," recalls former Air Force Special Operations Command (AFSOC) pilot Chad Bruton.[13] Yet as clashes with the Taliban grew in intensity, so alarm bells began ringing at the United Nations. More than 2,100 civilians were killed in the Afghan conflict in 2008 alone. Although the majority of these fatalities were the work of the Taliban, almost 40 per cent were attributed to the United States, its Coalition allies, and less often, to Afghan troops. Attacks from the air were the chief culprit. As the UN bluntly noted, "Air-strikes remain responsible for the largest percentage of civilian deaths attributed to pro-government forces."[14] Most of these strikes were still being carried out by manned aircraft such as the F-15 and F-16. Some caused terrible casualties. In August 2008, 92 civilians died in a single airstrike in Herat, 62 of them children. Two wedding parties were also bombed that year, killing 84 people. Although almost all munitions dropped in Afghanistan were by now precision-guided, manned aircraft were not necessarily the best tool for the job. "An F-16 is going very very fast. He'll be rushing from mission to mission to mission, so he'll get called to do a strike, will probably be in the area for a very short time, he'll have to rely heavily on intelligence provided by other sources that that's the appropriate place to make the strike," says Charles Blanchard, the Air Force's chief lawyer until 2013.

In contrast, Predators and Reapers could loiter for hours: "As a result, if it's a strike mission, there's a lot more awareness of what's around—and they can watch for opportunities for the target. So it's more likely to maximize opportunities not to affect civilians." Coalition lawyers treated drones little differently from any other aircraft above the regular battlefield, since all were covered by the same laws of armed conflict. That said, "your legal obligation is to use the weapon least likely at a given time to cause civilian casualties. And oftentimes that would be a Hellfire missile from an RPA," says Blanchard.[15] Despite the potential that drones offered for lower collateral damage, there was little comfort so far for civilians in Afghanistan. Of 1,923 airstrikes carried out in 2008, less than 7% were by drones. Most Predators and Reapers were still in Iraq.

Pakistan's government, keen as it was to play down the CIA's drone strikes given its own complicity in the covert program, had little incentive to protest mounting civilian casualties in the tribal areas. Afghan President Hamid Karzai was under no such obligation, loudly criticizing the United States and the International Security Assistance Force, or ISAF, when noncombatants were killed. "Our demand is that there will be no civilian casualties in Afghanistan. We cannot win the fight against terrorism with airstrikes," Karzai complained just days after Barack Obama had won the US presidential elections—and hours after US warplanes had killed another 47 civilians. "This is my first demand of the new President of the United States—to put an end to civilian casualties."[16] Yet as the incoming commander of US and NATO forces in Afghanistan would later note, any protests by Karzai to Coalition forces regarding the high number of civilian deaths "appeared largely discounted" at the time. General Stanley McChrystal planned to change that.[17]

The man given the job of winning Obama the war in Afghanistan was an unlikely choice to some. "Stanley McChrystal came out of five years as JSOC commander, and extensive efforts to do these raids and airstrikes, like the one that got Zarqawi in Iraq. So I don't think that he was pre-disposed to adopt a particularly touchy-feely approach to counterinsurgency ops," recalls one of the General's Afghanistan aides.[18] Yet McChrystal had also resisted the urge to use the Predator as a kinetic weapon in Iraq, instead focusing on its intelligence-gathering potential and on capturing the enemy where possible for intelligence-gathering purposes (see chapter 4). Whatever his prior reputation, McChrystal's Afghan counterinsurgency or COIN policy would now place a premium on civilian lives. In early July 2009, just two weeks after arriving in Kabul, the newly promoted four-star General issued a Tactical Directive stating that airstrikes would now take place only in "very limited and prescribed conditions." The reason was simple: "We must avoid the trap of winning tactical victories—but suffering strategic defeats—by causing civilian casualties . . . and thus alienating the people."[19] McChrystal put it more bluntly in private to his ISAF commanders: "We're going to lose the fucking war if we don't stop killing civilians."[20] He was supported in this by his head of intelligence Major General Michael Flynn, who noted in an influential report that "merely killing insurgents usually serves to multiply enemies rather than subtract them. This counterintuitive dynamic is common in many guerrilla conflicts and is especially relevant in the revenge-prone Pashtun communities."[21]

Although the tempo of ground offensives and Special Operations Forces activity controversially rose under McChrystal, airstrikes fell by a quarter during his time in Afghanistan. With support from the Pentagon, he was also able to obtain far more assets, including Predators and Reapers, to spy on an elusive enemy. Intelligence, surveillance, and reconnaissance (ISR) missions jumped by 50% to 28,000 in 2010. "Afghanistan is really not that big of a country, if you overlay it on the United States it's not overly large. You do get to know your backyard," recalls Jim, a serving Air Force colonel whose F-15 missions were now as much about gathering intelligence as providing air support.[22] On the remotely piloted side, crews more used to flying over busy urban Iraq found their new war theater more of a challenge. "Afghanistan was always in the mountains, almost all my missions were over in the north-east corner of Afghanistan or in that border along with Pakistan," says Chad Bruton. "I was always having to fight clouds and weather and stuff like that. And then the populations we saw were all farmers, sheep herders or goat herders. They all lived in these little compounds with mud walls. Very seldom saw any vehicles."[23]

On those occasions when drones did strike, it was usually either a pre-determined attack or in support of troops under fire. "This is not a strategic bombing campaign like World War II, this is not industrial-scale violence. The value of the system is that it combines the capability to conduct aerial intelligence with the capability to strike," says a senior Air Force officer who served with McChrystal in Afghanistan. "You can follow a particular target for hours, you can determine if in fact they're up to something; you can develop patterns of life, and when it may be an opportune or inopportune time to strike. So when you're talking about RPAs in the context of a large theater operation like Afghanistan those [kinetic] numbers are never going to be significant."[24]

Armed Predators and Reapers were now making use of new modeling software which could help avoid civilian deaths. The term "Bugsplat" has gained notoriety as a slang word reportedly used by Air Force operators to describe the aftermath of a drone strike on people below. Yet its origins lay in data modeling carried out by drone crews and analysts, seeking to mitigate civilian casualties. A former senior US intelligence official described the process to the author:

> You say something like "Show me the Bugsplat." That's what we call the probability of kill estimate when we were doing this final math before the "Go go go" decision. You would actually get a picture of a compound, and there will be something on it that looks like a bugsplat actually with red, yellow, and green: with red being anybody in that spot is dead, yellow stands a chance of being wounded; green we expect no harm to come to individuals where there is green. "I don't like that bugsplat, we're not going to use it. What direction are you coming in on?" "I am coming in from the North." "No, try from the South. Get me a bugsplat from the South. I don't like that, show me in the East." And you maneuver to get the highest probability of a kill against the target, and the lowest probability that you will do harm to somebody that you're not mad at. And then when all those conditions have been met, you may give the order to go ahead and spend the money.[25]

McChrystal's restrictions on the use of airpower in Afghanistan made him deeply unpopular with many Coalition troops on the ground, who feared they were losing their best source of protection in an escalating war.[26] Yet for Afghan civilians there was some relief. Although the number of Coalition bombings rose slightly in 2009, reported civilian casualties from airstrikes actually fell by a third to 359 deaths.[27] Over the border in Pakistan was another matter entirely.

THE SAME ENEMY?

Eleven days before Barack Obama's first inauguration, Vice President-elect Joe Biden arrived in Islamabad. Officially he was there to talk with Yousuf Raza Gillani's civilian government. Yet Biden also met secretly with Pakistan's army and spy chiefs (respectively Generals Kayani and Pasha), to help lay the blueprint for what would become the most success-ful US-Pakistani cooperation since the local roll-up of Al Qaeda in the months after 9/11. The 90-minute exchange was blunt: "Senator Biden said he needed to know that the situation had changed. . . . It was important to know if we had the same enemy."[28] Tellingly, there is no mention of Al Qaeda in a leaked US record of the meeting. This was about taking the war to those Taliban groups directly engaged in the Afghan insurgency:

> Senator Biden asked Kayani if he had the capacity and could obtain sufficient resources, would he then move against Taliban leaders like Baitullah Mehsud, Commander Nazir, and the Haqqanis? Senator Biden asked Kayani if he were prepared to move into the Waziristans.

In response, secret notes of the meeting obtained by Wikileaks report Kayani as saying that he was "painfully aware that the army had to retake South Waziristan since ninety percent of the suicide bombers came from Baitullah Mehsud. 'He has to be cut down to size.'" Crucially, Kayani added that "the Pakistani military could not fight everyone at once. They would have to go after Mehsud and Nazir sequentially (a point Pasha confirmed)."[29]

Mullah Nazir was a Pakistani Taliban leader the CIA had wounded in a drone strike just ten weeks previously.[30] Despite only being in his mid-thirties, Nazir had risen to become a *de facto* leader of the Ahmadzai Wazir tribe, which with the Mehsuds made up most of South Waziristan's peoples. Nazir was educated at the Central Madrassa in Wana, one of hundreds of hardline religious schools founded in the tribal areas in the 1980s. He had fought with the Afghan Taliban until 2001 and was close to its leader Mullah Omar. Now the self-styled "Emir of the Taliban Mujahidin in South Waziristan," Nazir was using his homeland as a base from which his 4,000-strong force could attack US and Coalition troops in eastern Afghanistan. He was also running militant training camps; was allegedly providing safe houses for Al Qaeda; and he sat on the Taliban's ruling council the Quetta Shura. The United States was keen to kill Nazir for his role in the Afghan insurgency. Yet for Pakistan's government and the Inter-Services Intelligence (ISI), he remained a "good" Taliban leader and a valuable ally. Nazir's militant group had recently fought as a proxy for Islamabad, defeating Uzbek Islamists in South Waziristan; and he was seen as a useful counterweight to other Taliban leaders who directly threatened Pakistan's interests. Captured by the Army in 2004, he was released almost immediately, and no Pakistani intelligence ever seemed to reach the United States on Nazir's whereabouts. Hearing Kayani and Pasha confirm that they intended to go after Nazir and others was an apparent breakthrough for the new administration.[31]

The first fruits of this improved relationship came on the second day of Obama's presidency, with rare reports of US drones being used inside Pakistan's borders for non-lethal purposes. Alleged Al Qaeda operative Zabu ul-Taifi, who had been linked to the 2005 London bombings, was arrested in Khyber Agency in a joint operation. Local papers claimed that CIA agents took part in the raid: "The Americans seemed quite excited after capturing the Saudi national and immediately bundled him into their vehicle," one military official recalled.[32] Meanwhile, according to the *Wall Street Journal*, "Predator drones hovered overhead and would have attacked if Mr. Taifi or other suspects had tried to escape."[33] The arrest had been planned for many weeks—yet the decision to publicize a joint raid so soon into Obama's presidency was carefully taken. Even so, any public relations benefit risked turning to dust just 24 hours later.

The semi-fertile Wana valley, running from the Afghan border to the administrative town of South Waziristan bearing its name, had seen dozens of fatal drone attacks during America's secret war. Pakistan covered 300,000 square miles, yet this tiny valley along with a few other locations in Waziristan—the towns of Miran Shah and Mir Ali, for example—had borne the brunt of bombings, testimony to a concentration of US foes. According to data provided by the BIJ, at least 154 people had died in 33 Wana Valley drone strikes between 2004 and 2013. Among the dead were at least 19 civilians and 30 named militant leaders. Both Bush and Obama launched their first covert drone strikes here—and both operations killed civilians.

Gulistan Khan had risen to become head of his family and a tribal elder, or malik, of the Ahmadzai Wazir. His village of Gangi Khel was a cluster of mud-brick farms tucked close to Wana itself. Like most families in the region, the Khans lived in a large fortified compound built by successive generations—in this case eight rooms built around a central courtyard, where the extended family shared their lives. One of those rooms was the *hujra*, a place for hospitality where male visitors were formally entertained. On the evening of January 23, 2009, the men and boys of the family were in the *hujra*, the women and girls nearby in the house.

Six thousand miles away in a windowless room near Las Vegas, two US Air Force operators with the 17th Reconnaissance Squadron sat watching satellite-relayed video images from a Predator high above the Khans' home. Their "customer" was the CIA, whose own analysts were directing the mission. Despite the physical distance, the time delay was no more than a second. Since it was now dark in Pakistan, the operators were using the drone's infra-red camera. They should have known, after hours of observation, how many people were present and where they were. A call was made to strike at an alleged High Value Target thought to be sitting in Khan's *hujra*. As with all covert US targeted killings, the attack had the personal authorization of the CIA's Director—then Michael Hayden, a former Air Force General and chief of the National Security Agency. Just three weeks from retirement, this would be Hayden's 46th and final Pakistan drone strike. Barack Obama had already been consulted on the attack earlier that day. According to national security correspondent Daniel Klaidman, Hayden had briefed the new president on "the geometry of the operation, the intelligence it was based on, and the risk of collateral damage."[34]

From Creech Air Force Base, the pilot used a joystick and keypad to expertly maneuver the 27-foot long Predator far above Khan's home. The sensor operator prepared the drone's weapon—an AGM-114 Hellfire missile slung beneath a wing—and then "lit" the target with the drone's laser designator. With the missile cleared for launch the pilot fired. Traveling at 950 miles per hour, the Hellfire hit the *hujra* almost instantly. Most of Malik Gulistan Khan's prized home was destroyed and the tribal elder killed. Dead alongside him were three of his sons (Habib Noor, Mohamad Ghulam, and Mohammad ullah, the last aged 3) and one of their young cousins Loi Khan.

Yet Malik Gulistan Khan was no militant. According to surviving family members and tribal elders from the village, Khan was pro-government and a member of the local peace committee: "We did nothing, have no connection to militants at all. Our family supported the government . . . no one has accepted responsibility for this incident so far," Khan's brother would tell researchers for the US-based NGO Civic.[35] At a special *jirga* convened in the village shortly after the attack, Islamabad's agent for South Waziristan was told by elders that all of those who died had been innocent. Keen to see surviving family members cared for, the *jirga* valued the damage done to Khan's family home at 18 Lakh rupees (around $18,000) adding: "The *Jirga* requested [that] early payment of blood money and property damages may kindly be paid."[36]

Three hours earlier in neighboring North Waziristan, another CIA drone strike had also gone badly wrong. In the village of Zeriki, 18-year-old student Faheem Qureshi was sitting with two cousins and half a dozen guests outside their own *hujra*. They had noticed drones flying above "but we did not expect them to attack because we are not terrorists, why should they attack us? But suddenly, while we were having tea and chatting the drones attacked," the teenager later recalled. At least nine people died in the attack including his cousins and guests. Faheem himself lost an eye and suffered a fractured skull.[37]

President Barack Obama's presidency was just 72 hours old, and at least 14 civilians were reported dead in secret actions he had personally authorized. Yet despite the killing of so many noncombatants, administration officials and the intelligence community remained silent. After all, the narrative for public consumption at the time was that no more than 20 civilians had been killed, in almost five years of secret bombings in Pakistan. Journalist Bob Woodward, granted exclusive access to Obama's inner team, would later report that Hayden told the president neither strike had actually killed the intended HVT but that "five Al Qaeda militants" had died. "Good," Obama allegedly responded, apparently adding that he "fully endorsed the covert action program, and made it clear he wanted more."[38] Woodward's account may have painted the CIA in a good light, but it was missing a crucial detail: the deaths of those civilians. Daniel Klaidman later offered a different version of events. After being briefed on the civilian fatalities, Obama had then attended the first meeting of his National Security Council (NSC):

Obama was understandably disturbed. How could this have happened? The president had vowed to change America's message to the Muslim world, and to forge a "new partnership based on mutual respect and mutual interest." Yet here he was, during his first week in the White House, presiding over the accidental killing of innocent Muslims.[39]

Yet instead of pausing the campaign, Obama reportedly used that same NSC meeting to approve a CIA plan to further expand strikes on Pakistan.[40] Within weeks, the president would also oversee the introduction of some of the most disturbing tactics employed by the United States during the War on Terror—the deliberate targeting of first-responders and funeral-goers in Pakistan, which would eventually lead to a UN team investigating his administration for possible war crimes. While preserving civilian life had become the core priority in Afghanistan, there was scant evidence of a similar policy on the Pakistan side of the same war. As for the *jirga*'s request for compensation, in line with all other drone strikes which had killed civilians in Pakistan, no US recompense was ever received by Khan's family.

The Pakistan Taliban

If Washington wanted Islamabad's help in smashing the Taliban's safe havens in the Waziristan tribal areas, it needed to give something in return. From its inception in December 2007, the Tehrik-e-Taliban Pakistan (TTP) had emerged as one of the greatest threats in the nation's short history. Suicide bombings—once confined to military and diplomatic targets—were now aimed heavily at civilian populations across Pakistan, after the TTP shipped in Al Qaeda instructors from Iraq. Suicide bomber "schools," some for children, sprang up in Waziristan.[41] During Obama's first term in office, an estimated 3,200 civilians died in 222 separate suicide attacks across Pakistan, according to the country's Human Rights Commission. Pakistan was in crisis. Although the TTP was a federation of Taliban groups, chief among them was the South Waziristan faction led by Baitullah Mehsud. At the time concentrated around the town of Sara Rhoga, Mehsud's forces had humiliated the Pakistan Army in early 2008, leading to yet another meaningless "peace" agreement. Emboldened, other TTP groups began pushing hard against the new civilian government. In the Swat Valley 120 miles north of Islamabad the TNSM, Pakistan's oldest Taliban faction, now seized control. A panicked government attempted appeasement, with a "permanent ceasefire" signed in February 2009.[42] For the new administration in Washington there were fears of Pakistan simply collapsing—a giant prize for Al Qaeda and its allies. As Secretary of State Hillary Clinton told Congress: "I think that the Pakistani government is basically abdicating to the Taliban and to the extremists," adding that terrorists were now "within hours of Islamabad . . . which is as we all know a nuclear-armed state."[43] Under intense pressure to act from the Obama administration, the Pakistan Army successfully assaulted the Swat Valley in May 2009. The operation smashed the TNSM, whose remnants now limped across the border into Afghanistan. Hundreds of thousands of civilians were internally displaced for a time, amid claims of atrocities by both sides.[44]

While Pakistan's military engaged the TTP in Swat, the CIA launched a major drone assault against Baitullah Mehsud's command and control systems in South Waziristan. Eight months earlier, Pakistan's new Prime Minister had been rebuffed when he sought Bush's help against Mehsud. Now, multiple drone strikes targeted the TTP between February and August 2009, aimed at training facilities, underground bunkers, and militia convoys. The Taliban responded by jerry-rigging anti-aircraft trucks to take on the Predators, but these too were destroyed. The attacks killed at least 184 people, among them an estimated two dozen civilians. *New York Times* journalist David Rohde was lucky not to be one of those casualties, held captive by the Taliban close to the site of a CIA bombing. He later recalled his brush with a Predator: "The missiles had struck two cars, killing a total of seven Arab militants and local Taliban fighters. I felt a small measure of relief that no civilians had been killed."[45]

The primary target of this CIA campaign was TTP leader Baitullah Mehsud, whose life was finally ended on August 5, 2009. He had risen to prominence after Bush's targeted assassination of Nek Mohammed back in 2004. Following the *Lal Masjid* or Red Mosque assault and aged just 33, Mehsud was elected head of the newly federated TTP. He proved a vicious foe for Pakistan's military and an adept manipulator of the media. Although he always denied it, Mehsud was also accused by both Pakistan and the United States of responsibility for the murder of politician Benazir Bhutto. The Bush administration would eventually place a $5 million "kill or capture" bounty on his head.[46] The diabetic militant leader was receiving a leg massage from his wife on the roof of a family home when a CIA Predator finally struck, killing them both along with other family members and bodyguards. A senior security official later told the *New York Times* that "He [Mehsud] was clearly visible with his wife. . . . His torso remained, while half of the body was blown up."[47] Clearly pleased with the killing, President Obama broke with protocol to boast in his weekly radio address that "We took out Mehsud."[48]

Two months after Baitullah Mehsud's death, some 30,000 Pakistan Army troops crossed into South Waziristan to confront the TTP in Operation Rah-e-Nijat—the Road to Salvation. The TTP's leadership was already in disarray after months of secret, mostly precision US drone strikes. The Pakistan Army's own assault was anything but precise. Tanks, artillery, and manned aircraft were all deployed against the Taliban in their home villages and towns, while more than 350,000 civilians of the Mehsud tribe were ordered to quit the region. In the ensuing fight, whole areas of South Waziristan were simply flattened. The campaign was secretly backed by US satellite and drone feeds and intelligence intercepts, while Pakistan's F-16 pilots were given US training to improve their precision. As a secret US cable had noted, "Kayani remains leery of too large a USG [US Government] military footprint in Pakistan, but to win he must be able to fight without creating the level of civilian casualties his forces' blind artillery and F-16 bombardments are now producing."[49] After weeks of bitter struggle the Taliban eventually fled.

Mehsud's death—and the subsequent routing of the TTP from South Waziristan—represented the high-water mark for the Obama administration's relations with Islamabad. Even three years later, the Taliban had not returned in any number, though nor too had most of the local population. Visiting the area with local commander Col. Mohammed Husayn, the author passed village after village devoid of life. As another senior officer joked, "we're presently in the safest place in Pakistan." Only when we arrived at an exposed mountain outpost was there a need to don body-armor, given the risk of Taliban snipers. Missing entirely from the scene was sight or sound of an armed US drone—the Predators and Reapers which had become synonymous with this part of south Asia. According to Husayn it had been years since the CIA's remotely piloted aircraft (RPA) had bombed here. Earlier in the day, the few returned men of Sara Rhoga, once the TTP's local headquarters, had confirmed his story. Back in 2009 three US drone strikes had hit the village, killing mainly TTP militants but also five civilians named by the locals. Then the CIA's drones had vanished. The reason for that absence was simple: the area was now under effective occupation by the Army, at huge cost to Pakistan and its US benefactor. Asked where the Taliban had moved on to, Colonel Hussayn was circumspect: "Some of them we killed, and some of them were thrown out. Where they have gone is very difficult to say, but they left this area."[50] Where they had gone was North Waziristan—and Islamabad's unwillingness to follow them there would eventually prove the undoing of its relationship with Washington.

Alleged War Crimes

Soon after succeeding Mike Hayden as CIA Director, Leon Panetta had said of drone targeted killings in Pakistan that "in terms of that particular area, it is very precise and it is very limited in terms of collateral damage and, very frankly, it's the only game in town in terms of confronting or trying to disrupt the Al Qaeda leadership."[51] Yet the intensive anti-TTP bombing campaign of 2009 had appeared to lie well outside US claims of domestic lawfulness for its covert bombings, which required an Al Qaeda-linked imminent threat to the United States. Mehsud, unlike "good" Taliban leaders, had focused mainly on Pakistani targets since 2007. Although the United States at the time insisted that Mehsud posed "a clear threat to American persons and interests in the region," this appeared to have been more prophesy than reality.[52] In early 2009, Afghan Taliban leader Mullah Omar had directly pressured the TTP to abandon its focus on Pakistan and instead fight foreign forces in Afghanistan. Yet despite a few proclamations to the contrary, the group's attention had remained on the home front.[53]

The *Washington Post*'s national security correspondent Joby Warrick, citing US intelligence sources, has claimed that the CIA pursued Mehsud after uncovering a "dirty bomb" plot aimed at the US homeland.[54] As he told the author: "It came up in their eavesdropping a couple of times, in a way that confirmed this was something the Taliban was very intent on using. And so the US administration took it very seriously, right up to the highest levels of the NSC [National Security Council]."[55] Such a plot would certainly have given the United States, in its view, the "imminent threat" needed to hit the TTP. Yet former senior Pakistani intelligence officials say they recall no knowledge of any such scheme. It appears more likely that the targeting of Mehsud was part of a broader US strategy to win over Islamabad by smashing its greatest enemy—even if that meant temporarily slackening off drone attacks on the Afghan Taliban or Al Qaeda. In turn, that could see the Taliban routed in Waziristan by the Pakistan Army, a key goal if the insurgency in Afghanistan was to be defeated.

One sequence of drone strikes in the CIA's campaign against the TTP in the summer of 2009 would help lead to allegations of war crimes against the Obama administration. In one of the Agency's worst mass casualty attacks, a funeral was bombed in June in the hunt for Baitullah Mehsud. As a UN investigation later summarized:

> Eyewitnesses have confirmed that whilst the mourners included active members of the Tehrik-e-Taliban, there were significant numbers of civilians present. Reports suggest that up to 83 people were killed. The estimated number of non-combatant fatalities varies between 18 and 50. However, credible reports indicate that 10 children and four tribal elders were reportedly among the dead. In addition, 27 people, including a number of children, were reportedly treated for injuries at a local hospital in Miranshah.[56]

Citing a number of US intelligence sources, Joby Warrick has described the CIA's funeral attack as deliberate. Having killed a mid-level Taliban commander earlier in the day, the Agency hoped that Baitullah Mehsud would show at the burial site, now staked out by armed Predator drones: "Initially they did think he was coming and they thought a number of his lieutenants were coming as well," says Warrick. Yet many hundreds, perhaps thousands of mourners had also gathered for the funeral, making the likelihood of civilian deaths high if the drones attacked. They struck anyway, although Baitullah Mehsud was most likely never present. Reflecting on the CIA's actions, Warrick offered these thoughts based on his conversations with US officials: "I don't think there's a whole lot of thinking or calculating of the moral cost of going after these individuals, other than the fact that they want to try to limit deaths of women and children. But they don't think twice about going after those they think are bad guys."[57]

Too often during its drone bombings in Pakistan the Agency had appeared to treat noncombatant deaths cavalierly. "Far and away the most troubling period of civilian casualties from this technology occurred, really, between 2005 and 2011 in Waziristan when the technology, this weapons-delivery system, was under the control of a CIA that perhaps wasn't entirely under the control of the Presidency at the time," as UN investigator Ben Emmerson has put it.[58] Certainly there seemed little awareness of McChrystal's point that in modern warfare there was a need to avoid the "trap" of killing civilians, which might offer tactical victories yet strategic defeats. "You killed the mid-level Taliban leader in a village in Afghanistan, and that counts for military advantage. But the one civilian that you killed has now turned an entire village against you and therefore, that has to be part of the calculus if your military or strategic goal is to win hearts and minds," notes law professor Greg McNeal, who had made a study of US targeting policies. "If you jump over the border into Pakistan, nobody's military or strategic goal, or at least nobody who matters, is to win hearts and minds."[59]

In the first few years of the Obama administration, apparent indifference to collateral damage in Pakistan or Yemen's secret wars only seemed to worsen. Credible reports began emerging that the Agency's Predators were now deliberately targeting rescuers at the scene of earlier drone strikes. In the first confirmed case on May 16, 2009, Taliban militants had gathered in the village of Khaisor in readiness for an attack on US forces across the border. The CIA struck first when a drone fired into the Taliban group. Villagers then joined survivors as they tried to retrieve the dead and injured. But as the rescuers clambered through the rubble the drones struck again, killing many more. At least 29 people died in total. For the United States, this novel tactic doubtless appeared successful. As a Taliban leader told local reporters, "We lost very trained and sincere friends. Some of them were very senior Taliban commanders and had taken part in successful actions in Afghanistan."[60]

Yet at least half a dozen of those slain were found by field investigators to be civilian noncombatants, villagers who had come forward to help retrieve the dead and injured. The deliberate targeting of overtly identified medics (for example, Red Crescent or Red Cross workers in marked bibs) is a serious violation of the laws of war. Yet in FATA with its poor health-care facilities, first aid tended to come from those immediately at hand, especially since drone strikes often focused on remote villages. Once it was known that rescuers were being targeted by the CIA, some healthcare workers also delayed visiting the site of drone attacks for up to six hours.[61] With neither the Taliban nor local civilian rescuers wearing uniforms, distinguishing between the two was near-impossible.

An investigation by the author for the London *Sunday Times* examined CIA drone attacks between May 2009 and July 2011 where news media including CNN, the *New York Times,* and Associated Press had described the killing of rescuers. Working with veteran Pakistani correspondent Rahimullah Yusufzai and field researchers in North and South Waziristan, we were able to confirm ten incidents in which first responders had been deliberately targeted. On almost every occasion Taliban militants died. Yet so too did civilian noncombatants. Of at least 74 people killed in the CIA's follow-up strikes, only 26 could be confirmed by researchers as Taliban members. Most were instead named as villagers who had offered assistance.[62] The findings demonstrated that it was impossible for the CIA deliberately to target rescuers without a high probability of their also killing noncombatants. As UN special rapporteur Christof Heyns later concluded:

> Where one drone attack is followed up by another in order to target those who are wounded and hors de combat [combatants unable to fight] or medical personnel, it constitutes a war crime in armed conflict and a violation of the right to life, whether or not in armed conflict.[63]

Those concerns helped prompt Heyns and fellow rapporteur Ben Emmerson QC into announcing an 18-month UN investigation into the role of armed drones on the modern battlefield.[64] By summer 2014, the duo was still awaiting clarification from the United States on its reported targeting of first responders and funeral-goers in Pakistan. Obama officials had remained tight-lipped about the CIA's tactics in Pakistan. There were two exceptions. An anonymous intelligence official had dismissed as "misinformation" the author's investigation for the *Sunday Times* into the targeting of rescuers, despite later corroborative findings by Amnesty International[65] and Stanford and New York University law schools.[66] In the only other known comment, the acting US Ambassador to Pakistan told a delegation of US peace activists in October 2012 that "For at least the last several years that I have been here in Pakistan and more intimately associated with the knowledge of this [drone campaign], there was never any deliberate strikes against civilian rescuers."[67]

Across the border in Afghanistan, a No-Strike policy instead expressly forbade the attacking of civilian and religious structures by US forces, in all but the most exceptional circumstances:

> Civilian structures, especially cultural and historic buildings, non-military structures, civilian population centers, mosques and other religious places, hospitals and facilities displaying the red crescent or red cross, are protected structures and will not be attacked except when they are being used for military purposes.[68]

Charles Blanchard, former General Counsel to the Department of the Air Force, recalls a visit to the Combined Air Operations Center in Qatar which oversaw the air war in Afghanistan: "They showed me the map that they were using, and there were mosques marked off including a little area around it as well. So that their software would alert them if they were getting close. It probably has varied over time but my sense is there's great sensitivity to these areas."

Yet in Pakistan, according to research by Forensic Architecture and the Bureau of Investigative Journalism, eight or more CIA strikes had targeted mosques or religious schools during a decade of bombings: "At least 99 civilians have been reportedly killed in these strikes," the study concluded.[69] Radically different tactics were now being pursued on either side of the "AfPak" border, and the continued unwillingness of US officials publicly to address the CIA's most problematic actions in Waziristan—some of which appeared in breach of the laws of war—was particularly troubling. Despite heavy damage being inflicted on the leaderships of Al Qaeda and the Taliban, Washington's contrary approach to civilian deaths during this period would eventually carry a heavy strategic price.

Even as Stanley McChrystal was cutting back on airstrikes in Afghanistan, the CIA was escalating its secret air war in Pakistan's tribal areas. As many Predator bombings were carried out in 2009 as in the previous five years combined. Richard Armitage, Deputy Secretary of State during the Bush years, had been a keen supporter of the early targeted killing program. Yet visiting Pakistan in 2009, he recalls being "quite surprised to see the alacrity with which this equipment was being used. . . . This program had to be judiciously used because of the possibility of collateral damage, which would have been inhumane first of all, and second bad policy because it just makes more enemies."[70] Although the escalation in bombings had so far barely registered in the United States, it was beginning to raise concerns closer to home. "For years and years there was this feeling amongst the ordinary, mainstream city-living population in Pakistan that FATA was the Wild West where they do things differently," says British barrister Shazadi Beg, a regular visitor. "Although it was widely known that drone strikes were happening, this didn't cause the kind of ripples you'd expect. But as the strikes increased people started to ask questions."[71]

The leap from one or two US targeted killings a year to weekly, even daily strikes had other consequences. As suicide bombings spread to major cities including Lahore, Karachi, Peshawar, and Islamabad, the Taliban would often directly blame their murderous attacks on previous US drone strikes, adding to Washington's unpopularity. In an October 2009 trip to Pakistan, Hillary Clinton found herself confronted by a hostile female audience. One described drone strikes as "executions without trial," Associated Press reported. Another asked whether Clinton believed drone attacks and suicide bombings were both acts of terror? To audience applause, a TV anchor told the Secretary of State: "It is not our war, it is your war. You had one 9/11. We are having daily 9/11s in Pakistan."[72] A few weeks earlier, Ambassador Ann Patterson had sent a blunt cable to Washington spelling out the risks of an escalating US drone war:

> Unilateral targeting of al-Qaeda operatives and assets in these regions is an important component of dealing with the overall threat. It is not/not, however, sufficient in and of itself to force al-Qaeda out of the FATA, so long as the territory remains largely ungoverned space. Increased unilateral operations in these areas risk destabilizing the Pakistani state, alienating both the civilian government and military leadership, and provoking a broader governance crisis in Pakistan without finally achieving the goal.[73]

The ambassador's cable fed into a major policy debate in Washington, DC, though the answer turned out to be yet more drone strikes. With

Obama still weeks from confirming his final plans for Afghanistan, in October 2009 CIA director Leon Panetta proposed another major expansion of counterinsurgency and counterterrorism actions inside Pakistan. Among ten suggestions put forward were an increase in the number of Predator and Reaper strikes; a larger "target box" for those strikes; a greatly expanded ground presence for the CIA and JSOC; and the embedding of more US military advisers with Pakistani units. "Let's do it," Obama reportedly said, approving all of the actions.[74] One result was that three secret "fusion centers" staffed by JSOC and CIA teams and their Pakistani partners were set up on the fringes of the tribal areas, which could share US intelligence directly with Pakistani forces. Army chief General Kayani also granted permission for half a dozen JSOC personnel to be posted deep inside Waziristan in Wana and Miran Shah, "to provide intelligence, surveillance, and reconnaissance (ISR) support and general operational advice." As Patterson secretly noted, the decision to allow JSOC back into FATA after a six-year absence "appears to represent a sea change in Pakistani thinking."[75] North Waziristan now stood as the last major sanctuary for Al Qaeda, the Taliban, and other militant groups in the tribal areas.

BLOWBACK

A curt US military cable in the final days of 2009 heralded the worst CIA loss of life in almost 30 years: "Chapman took suicide bomber, reporting mass casualties."[76] Four months after the Obama administration had killed Baitullah Mehsud, the Pakistan Taliban took its revenge when one of its agents carried out a suicide attack at a CIA base just inside Afghanistan. Humam Khalil Abu Mulal al-Balawi was a 32-year-old Jordanian doctor and father of two, who was angry with the US War on Terror. He made the mistake of posting those thoughts on local jihadist websites and was picked up in early 2009 by Jordan's efficient, pro-Western intelligence service. When the Jordanians finally believed they had "turned" the doctor following weeks of interrogation and possibly torture, they brought in the CIA. Al-Balawi was filtered into Pakistan's FATA region as a double agent.[77] Soon he was feeding back apparently high-quality information to handlers, particularly on the aftermath of drone strikes, and on Al Qaeda's elusive second-in-command Ayman al-Zawahiri.

Fatally, the Agency decided it wanted to meet its new hero face-to-face. Al-Balawi was slipped across the border into Afghanistan and driven to Forward Operating Base Chapman, a CIA and Special Forces outpost. Commercial satellite photos show a cluster of buildings with a long, dusty runway attached. The Jordanian was never searched as he entered the base. As his car pulled up outside the CIA's offices, a small crowd of analysts surged forward to meet their star spy. Instead, triple agent al-Balawi detonated a nail-packed suicide vest. Local commander Jennifer Matthews was killed instantly, along with five of her CIA agents. Also dead were al-Balawi's Jordanian handler; the camp's external security chief; and two security personnel from Blackwater—both former US Special Forces operatives. Eight other people were seriously wounded, among them the deputy chief of the CIA's Kabul Station. Agency director Leon Panetta would later admit there had been a "systemic breakdown with regard to the kind of judgment and scrutiny that should have been applied here."[78]

The ability of Washington's enemies to lay such an elaborately baited trap did not bode well. Blame was initially laid at the door of Al Qaeda, which had certainly played a part in feeding the CIA credible intelligence as bait. Yet it soon emerged the TTP had played the central role. The killing of so many operatives was a major blow, not just to morale but to the covert drones program. Determined to show it was still functioning, the Agency responded aggressively. In the words of one Obama administration security official, "in the aftermath of Khost, political sensitivities were no longer a reason not to do something. The shackles were unleashed."[79] In the two months after Chapman, the Agency launched more than 20 drone strikes across the tribal areas, an unprecedented tempo at that time. Two attacks came close to killing new head of the TTP Hakimullah Mehsud, with another targeted unsuccessfully at his chief bomb-maker Qari Hussain. On February 2, 2010, four bombings took place on one day.

Yet these CIA attacks often took place despite the presence of noncombatants, with young children among those killed. Three-year-old Ayeesha was slain, for example, when hit by shrapnel from a car which was destroyed near her family's home. The other victims of that strike were initially claimed to be militants. Yet papers filed with the UN's Human Rights Council by barrister Shahzad Akbar reported a different story, insisting that the five named adult victims, including a high school teacher, "have [never] participated in terrorist activities, nor have they been affiliated with terrorist organizations or people."[80] Six civilians were also reported killed in a single attack on February 24, including a 10-year-old girl named Naila. Local photographer Noor Behram, who visited the scene soon afterwards, claimed that "Naila was at home reciting the Quran when the strike hit the next-door building. A missile piece hit her and she died on the spot."[81] Such descriptions only added to a growing anger among tribal communities bearing the brunt of Obama's expanded drone campaign, as evidenced in mass protests, complaints to Islamabad, and promises of retribution.

The tit for tat war between the United States and the TTP continued. In February 2010, militants struck a rare blow against the secretive US military presence inside Pakistan. Sergeants David Hartman, Matthew Sluss-Tiller, and Mark Stets—all propaganda experts with Special Operations Forces—were killed by a suicide bomber as they attended an opening ceremony for a girls' school restored with US money. More than forty children were seriously injured after the college roof collapsed, and three girls also died in the attack, along with a Pakistani soldier.[82] In May, the TTP struck again—this time at the US homeland. In New York's Times Square, local street vendors spotted a parked car with its hazard lights on, the engine running, and with smoke drifting from the vents. Alerted police were able to disarm a homemade device. Packed with fertilizer and surrounded by propane gas cylinders, the bomb was designed to cause mass civilian casualties. At his later trial, naturalized US citizen and would-be bomber Faisal Shahzad admitted to having been trained in bomb-making by the Pakistan Taliban. Just as with al-Balawi a video later emerged showing TTP leader Hakimullah Mehsud with the would-be terrorist, the two men clasping hands under a jihadist banner.[83] Shahzad's motive was to see an end to drone strikes, as he later told the court:

> I want to plead guilty and I'm going to plead guilty 100 times over because until the hour the US pulls it forces from Iraq and Afghanistan and stops the drone strikes in Somalia and Yemen and in Pakistan and stops the occupation of Muslim lands and stops killing the Muslims and stops reporting the Muslims to its government, we will be attacking [the] US, and I plead guilty to that.[84]

Armed drones were in fact still a year away from operating in Yemen or Somalia (see chapter 9). Shahzad's insistence otherwise was an indication of how the term "drone strike" was now becoming a recruiting tool and motivator for jihadists. Yet if the TTP's Times Square attack had sought to halt US drone strikes in Pakistan's tribal areas, it achieved precisely the opposite. Just as with the bombing of the CIA's base in Khost six months earlier, the US unleashed a barrage of retaliatory strikes across FATA. Hillary Clinton used a TV interview to read the riot act. Conceding that there had been a "sea change" in Pakistan's assistance to US counterterrorism efforts, she nevertheless added: "We want more, we expect more. We've made it very clear that if—heaven-forbid—an attack like this that we can trace back to Pakistan were to have been successful, there would be very severe consequences."[85] Clinton's harsh comments made little concession to the fact that Pakistan was already locked in a bitter struggle with the TTP. In 2010 alone, more than 1,000 civilians would die in Pakistan Taliban attacks. The Secretary of State's public words also disguised an uncomfortable question. Would the TTP ever have struck at Khost or Manhattan had Obama not targeted the organization's leadership in 2009 on behalf of Pakistan's government? With the militant group now regarding American civilians and even the US homeland as legitimate targets, Washington appeared to adopt a *de facto* ceasefire with the TTP. For three years, the United States rarely targeted Hakimullah Mehsud's "bad" Taliban faction with drone strikes—the only exception being those, like chief bomb-maker Qari Hussain, who had played a key role in the Khost suicide bombing.[86]

Blowback aside, by 2010 Barack Obama might have assumed he had a valuable counterterrorism weapon in the Predator drone. Domestically, there was heavy support for operations, and despite private protestations Pakistan's civilian government was still cooperating with the program. Yet even among some of the staunchest early supporters of Washington's targeted assassination program, there was a growing unease: "I saw an element of drone strikes that I didn't like," says former Deputy US Secretary of State Richard Armitage. "Mr. Obama was popping up with these drones left, right and down the middle, and I would read these accounts, '12 insurgents killed.' '15!' You don't know that. You don't know that. They could be insurgents, they could be cooks."[87] Bush's occasional killing program had given way to a large-scale project under Obama which would soon spread far beyond Pakistan. In an interview for the film *The Gatekeepers*, former Shin Bet chief Ami Ayalon frankly discussed his concerns about Israel's own scaled-up targeted killing program: "When you start doing it en masse, 200, 300 people die because of the idea of targeted assassinations, suddenly the processes become a kind of conveyor belt. You ask yourself less and less where to stop."[88] The coming challenge for Obama would be how—or even if—he could turn off Washington's own conveyor belt.

GAME FACE ON
The Intimacy of Remote Killing

Like many of those operating armed drones above Iraq and Afghanistan, mission controller Janet Atkins had seen her share of disturbing sights, even at a distance of 7,000 miles. On one mission over the city of Mosul, Atkins and her 3rd Special Operations Squadron (3rd SOS) "line" had spotted a suspect running from a building during a raid. The man had slowed to a walk in a nearby street, oblivious to the unseen Predator now directing a Coalition helicopter onto his location. The mission's customer (most likely Joint Special Operations Command in Balad) had concluded that the fleeing man was the High Value Target it was seeking. The helicopter was ordered to kill him:

> He was running, we were staying Eyes On, able to tell them where the guy was at, and he hid underneath a van from my memory. Anyway the helicopter comes in and starts shooting at him. This guy, you can tell he got shot in the leg or something, but he just kept running, trying to run, and we're following him obviously. He jumped into peoples' yards, it was just like an episode of *Cops*. We're chasing him down, we're

watching him. Then before we knew it they were shooting him down, and I just remember me and the pilot going like "Ohhh!" because we weren't expecting it.[1]

Why no attempt was made to capture the alleged insurgent on this occasion was unclear—certainly that was JSOC's stated preference in Iraq. One issue may have been the possible risk to ground forces. Atkins recalls watching on another occasion, as a canine member of a Special Forces team died: "During a raid, one of the suspects went out the back door and we were told to follow them. All of a sudden we see one of the Blue Forces K9s [dogs] going after them, and the man had a suicide bomb on and blew up with one of the dogs on him." For the first time on the job, Atkins cried that day. "Part of me was like, the dog was on our side, our team, and I just couldn't believe it happened. That was the first time that I ever saw one of our own die. And I think too just because it was a dog, it's not like he knew what was happening. I know that it's their job but it hit me. I was like, 'Oh my God that could have been one of our guys!'"

Although Janet Atkins never left the drone bases of Nevada and New Mexico while fighting her War on Terror, she remotely logged over 2,100 drone combat hours above Iraq and Afghanistan. Physically remote as operators and analysts were, there was no doubting their frontline role—or their emotional connection to the fighting: "People have a real misconception about what happens in the Predator world. It's not like video games where we just get to shoot people and chase them down. Most of the time, it was so boring. And it takes a lot, a whole lot of coordination and a whole lot of approval for a Predator to shoot," says Atkins, who left the Air Force in 2011 to raise a family. "We're not killing people for the fun of it. It would be the same if we were the guys on the ground. You have to get to them [the enemy] somehow or all of you will die."[2]

MORAL CONCERNS

Despite routine assertions by US defense officials that no tallies were kept of casualties on the battlefield, someone at least was counting.[3] Every October, individual aircrew in a drone squadron—both conventional and Special Forces—received a summary of their actions over the previous year. Between September 2008 and August 2009, for example, mission controller Atkins learned from her Enlisted Performance Report that she remotely flew 730 hours with AFSOC's 3rd SOS. The Predator missions she participated in during that time, however briefly, had helped secure the detention of 194 detainees and the deaths of 73 enemy combatants. Among these were "40 high value Afghan Taliban leaders." Others report being shown similar data. When Brandon Bryant left the 3rd SOS in April 2011, he was told that over the preceding two years alone, his actions had helped contribute to the deaths of 1,626 enemy combatants. The numbers were startling if misleading. According to an AFSOC spokeswoman, such data "does not distinguish between the crew that actually fired the missile and all of the crews that supported the objective over its lifetime. It also does not distinguish between ground force actions on the objective that may have resulted in Enemy Killed in Action."[4] Indeed, the reality for most drone operators working with Special Forces units was that missions directly leading to a kill were a rarity—at least until 2011, when Barack Obama ordered AFSOC to begin using its drone fleet to carry out targeted killings in Yemen and Somalia.

Major Chad Bruton was a pilot with 3rd SOS who never directly killed anyone in over two years of Special Forces Predator operations: "We were there to gather intelligence so that we could capture bad guys. We were always after High Value Targets, almost never fired a missile. I never fired one."[5] Yet even as indirect participants, operators could still be deeply affected. Bruton is still troubled, some years after helping set up the killing of alleged Taliban fighters in Afghanistan by other aircraft:

> Even though I didn't drop the bomb and I wasn't lasering it at the time, I found them and I saw them blown apart by a 2,000 pound bomb. If you weren't told any different you would think it was just five to a dozen guys sitting around a camp fire. You have to take it on faith that these guys were tracked to this point, that they know these guys are Taliban.

Not knowing their combat status for sure still concerns Bruton: "It's grim, that's one of those recurring things that comes back to me every now and then. I don't know if you call that PTSD or not, but I certainly remember from time to time for no apparent reason seeing these guys," he told the author. "Maybe on one of them I saw a weapon, but there are lots of reasons to have a weapon. I know how fallible humans are. So if there is a judgment after this life, hopefully I will be exonerated." Others wondered if their own actions were in some ways reminiscent of those they were fighting. "The major way of fighting the war for our enemy is for them to use asymmetrical guerrilla tactics. There is a strange juxtaposition between that and the way you operate an RPA mission," says former US intelligence analyst Daniel Hale, comparing drones to roadside bombs or IEDs, a common insurgent weapon. "You are monitoring somebody for a long time and you're waiting for them to be in just the right spot and then you blow them up. The technology couldn't be any more night and day different, but when it comes down to it they're the same thing."[6]

Some found it challenging to understand where their own moral responsibility might lie with this new form of warfare. Drone sensor operator Michael Haas recalls guiding in an A-10 attack aircraft in Iraq: "That was my first real experience and it opened my eyes: this was real. I know it's on a screen and people say it's a video game, but there's no damn reset button. You gotta get it right, just that once, or you've failed. It stuck with me for a bit. Did I kill them technically? Was I the one who did it? Or was I just assisting? I never knew quite how much guilt to feel about that. So for the next few weeks I just blocked it out of my mind." Having a strong sense of a lethal mission's purpose could play a crucial role in calming moral concerns, anecdotes suggest. Haas only took part directly in one killing, though says he has no qualms about his actions in Afghanistan that day: "I feel lucky about that one shot, because it was a no-doubter, two guys in the middle of a wadi carrying a directly fired mortar tube that the JTAC [forward air support controller] on the ground had seen them fire. There was no question or not of whether they were innocent. Nobody uses a mortar for self-defense."[7]

Other incidents proved more traumatic for personnel, often made worse by operators having to passively observe: "This is a memory that is absolutely burned in my brain because that was the first time that I had ever seen somebody on our side get gunned down," former pilot Chad Bruton says of a Special Forces raid he was supporting. "They opened a door and there was a guy with an AK-47 on the other side waiting for them to come through and he just mowed them down and I was watching right behind them. I mean my view was just a slight offset from directly behind, so I saw every bit of it. I saw the muzzle flash, saw the splatter and them fall down and that was bad. I was told later on that they evac'd back and were still alive so hopefully they made it. But I have no idea. That's one other thing; you never get closure on any of that kind of stuff."[8] On another occasion, a young lieutenant on her first ever remote Special Forces mission was observing a Taliban car in Afghanistan that held a captured local leader in the trunk. "They brought him to a discreet location, they dug a hole about waist deep, put him there, shot him in the head with a pistol. He was still alive, they shot him again and then chopped his head off with a machete," recalls one former operator with knowledge of the mission. The new lieutenant broke down and needed immediate counseling. She never remotely flew with the squadron again. Another operator remembers being angry with her at the time:

You join the military knowing what you're getting into. It's war. You're there to support the military. You're not there to go to work, play some basketball at the gym and then go home. That's not how it happens. And so even at 20 years old, and I still believe it today, when you voluntarily sign up for the military you should be prepared to see something like that. But I understood why she cried. I cried when I went home. I didn't have the heart to cry at work, in my mind I'm in uniform, this is my job, I can cry about it at home with my family. When I go to work, it's Game Face On.[9]

The Air Force rushed to expand its armed drone fleet following huge battlefield demand. Yet there was little understanding at first of the strains this would place on thousands of personnel fighting from the home front. Steve, a former USAF major who flew armed Predators after 9/11, likens remote operators back in the United States to their local emergency responders: "People reference the police force, the fire department and the kind of work they do. It's very similar. The only difference is, when they get into part of a shooting incident, they have downtime. When we become part of a shooting incident, that's just one of several that day. And we'll do it again tomorrow and the next day."[10] A significant challenge for the USAF had been understanding how this novel form of warfare was affecting—and sometimes damaging—its men and women.

REMOTE KILLING

Much has been made of the remoteness of drone operators and intelligence analysts from the battlefield and the perceived risk that this divorces them from their actions. In 2010, special rapporteur Philip Alston warned the UN General Assembly that "because operators are based thousands of miles away from the battlefield, and undertake operations entirely through computer screens and remote audio feed, there is a risk of developing a 'PlayStation' mentality to killing."[11] Extended conversations between the author and many former and current Air Force drone operators and intelligence analysts indicated a very different picture. "This suggestion that people become gung ho or blasé and port their *Call of Duty* experience into the real world is frankly not tenable," as Wing Commander Richard Mason of the RAF puts it. "You would not want people who would, dare I say it, reduce the act of killing to a blip on a screen."[12]

The US's armed drone squadrons were nevertheless keen to encourage a war-fighting mentality. "We would walk into work and look at the pictures of bin Laden and all these leaders. And it would be 'Which one of these motherfuckers is gonna die today?' It's easy to get wrapped up in that attitude, because that approach was really pushed in to you," says Michael Haas, a sensor operator on both conventional and Special Forces drone missions. Personnel serving in Afghanistan were offered similar motivation at the Bagram command center from which numerous JSOC missions were controlled: "Immediately behind the entrance was an unexplained flat-screen TV displaying a repeating slideshow of pictures from the Twin Towers attack and George Bush looking somber in front of an American flag," says former intelligence analyst Daniel Hale. "It always seemed oddly placed to me, but I suppose it was just a half-hearted attempt to remind everyone why they were there."[13]

All drone operators were asked early on in their training whether they would be willing and able to take a life. At least one captain who refused to kill on conscientious grounds was placed in a "paper-pushing office job" for the rest of his Air Force career, say former colleagues. Haas, who also carried out operational training at Creech AFB for a time, was disturbed by the attitude of some students: "They all wanted to shoot. 'I wanna shoot, I wanna kill these guys!' I would say [to them] it's more important to spare the innocent than to kill the guilty. I would really try to push that home;

I think I got through to one or two of them. But they just had this mentality that they want to kill. They all want to shoot." Brandon Bryant, another imagery analyst who served with Haas, reports encountering similar views among some operators: "There was a lot of hooraying, a lot of tough, 'We're badasses!' I never once, never ever once thought any of us were badasses. There was one guy, I remember, he was a mission coordinator, never really part of the crew, he just gave the crew the intel. And every crew that he was a part of that fired a missile, he got a Hellfire missile tattoo on the side of his chest, under the word in Arabic for 'infidel.' He thought he was the biggest badass on the planet."[14]

In his memoirs, former Predator pilot Lt. Colonel Matt Martin comes across as gung ho at times, for example, when he complains of media reporting during the Iraq war: "If we caught a bunch of Muslim-killing foreign fighters in a safe house miraculously they morphed into innocent cobblers and goat farmers and loving fathers by the time the world's media were finished with it." Yet as other former operators point out, having an aptitude for killing was not the same as being bloodthirsty, or lacking empathy for those targeted. Martin's book also describes in frank terms how an elderly man and two children were accidentally killed during his missions—and the continuing psychological effect their deaths exerted upon him.[15] Physical absence from the battlefield, it was clear, was not the same as emotional remoteness. Perhaps snipers alone shared the ability of drone operators to build empathy with potential victims, after hours of hidden observation.[16] "I'd argue there's not many places in modern warfare where you get more intimately connected with the target than you do with unmanned aerial vehicle warfare," retired USAF Major General Jim Poss notes. "Figuring out which guys, in which building, which ways the doors open, whether they're screen or glass. Does he have a dog? What kind of dog is it, is it in the yard or chained up? How many kids? Does the target have family there? That's all from those RPA crews and the intel guys, and it can take weeks to do all that."[17] Sensor operator Brandon Bryant, who never owned a passport until after he quit the Air Force, still found himself learning plenty about Iraqi life:

> I remember watching a wedding and these people are all in a circle
> and they're doing like the cancan: they're kicking back and forth and
> they're moving in one direction, and switch directions, and then they

move further in the other direction. And I was fascinated because these were people enjoying themselves. Someone in that wedding was a bad person. But at that moment they probably weren't thinking about someone they wanted to kill.[18]

Bryant has likened some of his actions to those of a voyeur: "We're the ultimate peeping toms. No one's gonna catch us. No one's going to hear or see a Predator drone flying at the distance and height that we flew at."[19] Operators might later feel emotionally challenged if required to kill people they had spent time observing, though USAF clinical psychologist Wayne Chappelle describes this as a normal response: "I would think that's a very healthy and normal reaction and a reaction that would indicate a well-adjusted person, because if somebody doesn't have that experience, if somebody doesn't feel to some degree some level of discomfort, then what does that mean?"

FAMILY LIFE

The opportunity for remote drone operators and analysts to live and work from US soil—to be "on-station" as it was known—was routinely portrayed by the Air Force as a positive. For some it had certainly led to more fulfilling careers. Chad Bruton joined the Air Force hoping to fly PaveLow helicopters with Special Forces, though a training crash in 2005 almost cost him his life: "I took some terrible shrapnel to my femoral vein in my left leg, bled out half my blood," Bruton recalls. "For maybe a year or so I was recuperating and working in an office job. I attempted to get back in the cockpit but my injuries were too severe for me to be able to continue flying." In the days before remotely piloted aircraft, he would have been washed up before his flying career had ever begun. Now though (with echoes of the paraplegic hero of the futuristic movie *Avatar*) Bruton's injury had little impact on his ability to fly a Predator from a concrete box in Nevada, and he was able to join the 3rd SOS as a pilot.

That new lease on professional life carried other costs however. American crews of manned aircraft might serve six months on the front line, before returning home for major leave and retraining. In contrast, remote operators and analysts back home found themselves perpetually at war, as short-staffed squadrons placed grueling demands on personnel.

Assignments could last as long as three years. Former sensor operator Bryant complains of being on near-permanent duty during his time with Air Force Special Operations Command: "I'd fly on my weekends, they'd call me in. I never got leave for the first few years, and I accumulated over 120 days. When I went in to ask for leave they didn't believe me, I had to print off a sheet of paper that showed I had reached my maximum limit and it freaked everyone out. 'Why didn't you take leave, why didn't you do this?' And I was like, I would request it but they would deny it all the time." Bryant viewed his home at Cannon Air Force base only as somewhere to crash, "a place I could just go home and sleep, go to work. I had no girlfriend, no prospects of inviting people over for fancy dinners." A single man, he also found it tough to build and maintain relationships. He recalls one girl he was keen on while living in Nevada:

> She was gorgeous. She was pretty smart too. There's a lot of pretty girls in Vegas but there are very few pretty and smart girls in Vegas. But I couldn't ever give someone like that the attention that she deserved. What am I going to do? "Sorry I can't hang out with you, I've got a war to go to." Cheerio you know, hip hip.

Those already in relationships also faced major challenges. Chad Bruton found himself working six days a week, 12 to 13 hours a day, usually on the 3.00 p.m. to 3.00 a.m. shift. He barely saw his wife and young child. "I would come home and go to sleep and I would spend, well I guess in total I was spending about three hours a week with my wife and kid, that's not much of a life." Eventually he had to quit: "The people at Assignment were very upfront with me that because of my injuries I was gonna fly that front line for the rest of my career. And I knew if I did that I would not have a family." Other crew members tried to help out where they could. Janet Atkins flew most of her missions at night: "I volunteered for it. I was single. I felt that parents should be with their families. I was 20 years old, what's the night shift to me?"

For aircrews serving in manned aircraft, there was always a risk of death or injury. Yet there was still sympathy for remote-operators back home. "When you're flying a manned aircraft out of an airfield in Afghanistan you are living the war every day," says Jim, a serving USAF colonel who flew F-15E fighters. "But I will tell you, it's equally bad but different that you fly out of an airfield in the United States and then you've got to leave your cockpit and go to the grocery store, and then you gotta go home. And you want to protect your family, and so you internalize everything. In the combat theater you can relieve stress because you can talk to your buddies, everyone's under the same thing. Whereas these guys it's just different, and some would say much harder."[20] When Royal Air Force drone operators relocated to their new base in rural England, some missed the decompression time their daily commutes through the Nevada desert had previously offered. "The one hour drive to and from work was beneficial to them in keeping work distinct from home life. That commute was not a feature of operating from RAF Waddington," British MPs were told.[21]

Those with partners often found themselves unable to talk about the bad things at work. "Even though you just watched somebody bleed out, you gotta be nice for the three hours that you spend with the wife and kids," says Chad Bruton. "I didn't really know what I could or couldn't talk about. It was just better not to talk about any of it. If while I was on shift we made a major capture I might come home and say: 'We got somebody big today. It was a good day.' But I never gave her anything bad. I didn't tell her when I watched our guys get shot." Bruce Black, who served as a pilot with a conventional drone squadron, admits that he sometimes found it easier to cope at work than at home: "When you're in combat you can stay in that box and everybody's in that box with you. And it's easy to relate to everybody's stresses, everybody's heightened anxiety," he says. But going home at the end of his shift, Black could find it hard to relate to his partner's everyday concerns. "Probably one of the big problems that my wife had was that things that were important to her—and they were, they were important to her—just didn't get important to me. The urgency wasn't there for me. I was worried about, God could I have taken that shot sooner? Could I have saved that guy I was talking to on the radio? Did he make it out alive?"[22]

NOT JUST AN OFFICE JOB

Armed Predators and Reapers gave the United States what it had long sought on the battlefield: the ability to observe its enemies in real time, unseen, and to act instantly and with precision when necessary. "It had been a goal from World War II to reliably put a bomb in a pickle barrel from 30,000 feet. We've arguably been able to do that since 1971 when we first had laser guided weapons," says retired USAF intelligence commander Jim Poss. "But when you can do that, the enemy starts to move the barrels. What we'd forgotten was that we needed that real-time intel capability to match up with that real-time targeting capability. And we've got that now. And you've seen the effect that's had on world history. We've wiped the floor with Al Qaeda, we deposed Gaddafi in just a few weeks."[23] Once that capability was properly understood, the US arsenal of armed drones grew so rapidly that the Air Force struggled to keep up. Back in October 2001, the United States had been able to field just one armed Predator above Kandahar. By 2014, it could fly 63 simultaneous combat air patrols 24 hours a day in the skies of half a dozen countries. While more than 3,000 aircrew were needed in-theater to launch, recover, and maintain those drones, they were greatly outnumbered by personnel back home. Some 3,000 operators in the United States remotely flew the Reapers and Predators, while another 5,000 analysts provided real-time intelligence support.[24] Filling those posts presented a huge challenge. Many would-be pilots remained wary of flying remotely piloted aircraft, for example. A Brookings study found that in 2012, the Air Force was unable to fill a fifth of 150 Reaper training slots voluntarily—in contrast to a 100% volunteer rate for "traditional" piloting.[25] There was a sense for some that a drone operator's job held less value. As USAF spokeswoman Jennifer Cassidy bluntly told ABC News:

> People in this generation didn't grow up and say, "I want to fly an RPA." They were the ones that watched re-runs of "Top Gun" and said, "I want to be a fighter pilot.". . . So in fact the people that were lower ranking [in flight school], I guess you could say, are the folks that went to RPAs. It doesn't mean they were bad pilots, or bad officers, it just meant you got to have some at the top and some at the bottom. That's how that worked.[26]

Negative views were widely held throughout USAF, even after more than a decade of drone combat operations. "I've encountered hostility from other military personnel towards what are sometimes viewed as desk jockeys," reports Air Force psychologist Dr. Chappelle. Some operators report encountering similar feelings from conventional pilots stationed alongside them back in the United States: "While I was flying Predators I got grief from fighter guys all the time, because they didn't have any clue," says one. "I was like, 'You think my job is boring? At least I'm dealing with people on the ground. You're just wasting gas and driving my gas prices higher!' "[27]

It was this physical remoteness from the battlefield which appeared to lie at the root of tensions, to the chagrin of some. "The warrior approach has changed: in the evolution of warfare where do you draw the line? If you were in World War II and were the artillery guy, are you less of a combatant because you're back here and a rifleman's up front? How about a battleship two miles off?" asks Don Hudson, a senior military intelligence official.[28] Once trained, commanders also worried that their airmen were often rushed into remote battle: "It's frustrating at times, because you feel like 'Just give us a minute here to go ahead and properly train these folks. Prepare them to do the job, and you'll see a 10-fold increase in what they're able to do!' rather than just throw another camera airborne and hope for the best," says James, a serving colonel with Air Combat Command. "There might be a perception among some [leadership] that it's calming down and normalizing but I tell you, it's just as much a scramble today with what we're going to put on the airplane next, who's going to fly that, how's that going to affect what we're doing in the future. That has not stopped, it's constant."[29]

Those pilots flying Predator or Reaper missions also faced worse promotion prospects than their colleagues flying manned combat aircraft. As a damning US government report noted in 2014, drone pilots came at or near the bottom on 21 of 24 officer promotion boards.[30] Any official recognition for operator or analyst achievements was also poor. "For the enlisted, a ribbon [medal] is points towards your promotion. So if you didn't start taking care of the guys they were not going to get promoted," says retired colonel Pete Forrest, who pioneered the use of armed drones in Special Forces operations in Iraq and Afghanistan—yet found it difficult to win recognition for his aircrews: "If you don't have anything to show a pilot who's been here for three years, something's wrong. And [yet] CENTAF did not recognize UAS as an award platform. So we were not allowed to do air medals. And that was weird. Here I am part of the mission taking down Zarqawi, and we're not allowed a medal?"[31] When the Defense Department finally did suggest the Distinguished Warfare Medal for remote-warfare operators and intelligence analysts, there was such uproar in the media and among veterans that the plan was quickly booted into the long grass where it still remained in early 2015.[32] "When I think of valor, I think of bravery and actually being there, and you weren't actually there," one US Navy veteran complained of drone operators who might qualify for the suggested new medal.[33] The British too treated their Reaper operators differently. Personnel were given their own flying badge or "wings"—but were not entitled to combat medals. An unprecedented number of Distinguished Flying Crosses were awarded to UK helicopter pilots after combat missions in Afghanistan, notes Wing Commander Richard Mason: "If we hold that up and celebrate that as being what the Royal Air Force is all about, and yet we have another part of the organization where we give a different color set of wings, not even a campaign medal to say they were there or in any way involved, you can see there is potentially a conflict there."[34] These contradictory positions by the leaderships of both USAF and the RAF—that drone operators were vital to the war effort, while somehow being separate from it—did little to encourage those seeking a career in remotely piloted operations.

REALITY TV

Just a three-hour drive from Washington, DC, on the scenic Virginia coast, Langley Air Force Base is home to one of the most crucial components of the US armed drone program. Alongside a couple of squadrons of the F-22 stealth fighter, the inhabitants of a large, nondescript brick building deep within the base had been on a permanent war footing for more than a decade. Those like the author who lacked the necessary security clearance needed to be escorted front and rear by chaperones waving red glow sticks, a warning to any intelligence analysts who might walk by not to discuss classified operations within earshot. These men and women were part of Distributed Ground System One (DGS-1), a unit which traced its mission back to the 1990s and the earliest days of the Predator program. A sound-proofed viewing window revealed hundreds of intelligence experts working away in a cavernous darkened room, each small cluster of screens indicating an ongoing mission. Their job was to process vast quantities of data from the many aerial platforms (among them Predators and Reapers) now operating above conventional US battlefields. "When you come on-shift you go up to your

IMS, your Imagery Mission Supervisor, and he will task you out to what bird you're assigned to," explained Airman Ray, a young enlisted geospatial analyst. Some days Ray might pore over feeds from a U2 or an MC-12 Liberty, both manned surveillance aircraft. Other times, he could find himself assigned to a team analyzing images from an armed drone. Like everyone else here, Airman Ray was waging war—though in a few hours he would return home. "It's not something a lot of folk necessarily understand, that our airmen that you're seeing downtown really are doing a very important national security mission day to day. But they're kind of incognito in terms of blending in,"[35] says Colonel Lourdes Duvall, vice commander of the 480th Intelligence, Surveillance, and Reconnaissance Wing—home to most of the conventional Air Force's 3,500 analysts.

When Pete Forrest had visited Langley AFB in 2005, he had been disappointed to find intelligence analysts were emotionally distanced from the battlefield images they were seeing (see chapter 4). There were historical reasons for this. Even in the late 1990s, it might take days for stills photographs from a U2 mission to be processed and analyzed. "We were used to looking at photographs, listening in to enemy transmissions which, you know—abstractly lives are on the line and you never handle it cavalierly, but you didn't get that intimate contact," says another former senior Air Force commander. Now, intelligence analysts were being remotely exposed to combat on the front line all the time and were expected to deliver real-time assistance. Airman Ray described for the author a recent counter-narcotics mission in Afghanistan he had participated in, already in progress when he took over. As pro-government troops on the ground destroyed 1,500 lbs of drugs, from his desk in Virginia, Ray had spotted a group of armed men approaching the location: "They set up and started firing—AK-47s, RPGs, the whole works. Watching this live on a feed is pretty hairy. Luckily none of our guys got injured or killed or anything." An airstrike was then called in on the attackers: "The threat to our forces on the ground was too great. So the airstrike was conducted, it was a success, the insurgents were eliminated, and we provided BDA [Battle Damage Assessment] to determine the success of the strike." Ray's team continued to watch over the mission in preparation for a helicopter extraction. But then disaster struck:

We pan back to the helicopter that was supposed to land and we see it in pieces on the ground, it had crashed. It's one thing to go through training and looking at virtual scenarios of helicopter crashes. But seeing it live from thousands of miles away knowing those are our guys on the ground injured, it's an indescribable feeling.

Despite being remote from the scene, analysts at DGS-1 then helped guide in medevac teams to rescue injured personnel on the ground. Weeks after the event, Airman Ray was still clearly affected by what he had seen.[36] Langley was just one of more than a dozen hubs which made up the Distributed Common Ground System, or DCGS, the inelegant name for the US Air Force's intelligence network which provided real-time remote support to drones and manned aircraft.[37] Most hubs were in the United States, with other key sites found in Germany and South Korea. From 2011 Britain too had shared battlefield intelligence, through its own Crossbow facility at RAF Marham.[38] The CIA and Air Force Special Operations Command each ran independent teams of intelligence analysts whose job was to assess data coming in from their own Predator and Reaper missions in Afghanistan, Pakistan, Yemen, or Somalia—and if necessary to assist in a targeted killing. Indeed, so important to the war effort had these analysis networks become, that they were now classed as weapon systems in their own right. When an armed drone destroyed a target on the battlefield, it was in effect two weapon systems working in harmony—the drone itself, and the intelligence "tail" which sought to make sense of what was being observed. For Predator pilots like Bruce Black, this ability of analysts to pore over frontline intelligence in real-time was the true revolution behind remotely piloted aircraft, since it "slows the battle down so much and provides so much more situational awareness for the guys that have to make the decision."[39] With the Air Force needing thousands more analysts, there were challenges here too in training and retaining enough personnel. "The stress, particularly on the Air Force and Army intelligence communities from 2001 until really now has been horrific," says Jim Poss. "Our nations produce only so many people who'll join the military and are of high enough capability to work in intelligence. And we're constantly running out of those folks." The addition of so many Predator and Reaper combat air patrols (CAPs) on top of other intelligence, surveillance and reconnaissance (ISR) platforms meant that at its 2011 peak, the Coalition flew more than 38,000 individual intelligence-gathering missions over Afghanistan alone—with thousands more ISR operations that year in Iraq and Libya.

The introduction of ever-more sophisticated intelligence-gathering pods onto platforms—and the huge increase in data this entailed—increased the burden yet further on already-stretched analysts.

Boredom, Sleep and Viruses

With so much emphasis on the surveillance conducted by armed drones and the data they acquired, pilots and sensor operators often describe being relegated to monotonous secondary roles. One recalls an incident where a Predator had been circling a house in Iraq for hours, waiting for something to happen. Suddenly the suspect emerged, jumped into his car and began to move off. Sitting in their darkened Ground Control Station the remote crew should have known the drill: follow the vehicle. Yet nothing happened. From her desk in the Operations Cell, mission controller Janet Atkins knew something was wrong:

> I see the vehicle leave and I'm "Why isn't the tracker ball moving? Hello sensor? The vehicle is moving?" I said it the second the vehicle moved. The imagery analyst is texting "The vehicle has left! The vehicle has left!" The customer is like, "What the Hell is going on?" And I got on my headset and I'm screaming, "Sensor!!" I turn around, I'm talking to my senior mission coordinator and senior pilot. "Someone needs to go and wake them up! We're losing our vehicle!" Then finally the sensor operator wakes up, zooms out [on the camera] and the vehicle has gone. There's no way to even find it. We searched and we searched but we lost it. Oh my God, was there the biggest deal ever.[40]

On that occasion, both the pilot and operator had fallen asleep on the job. An Air Force recruitment video from 2010 portrayed an action-packed world for drone crews as their Reapers hurtled over the modern battle-field, gathering intelligence and dealing death. The mundane reality was "hours and days of boredom punctuated by a few moments of stark terror," according to former pilot Bruce Black.[41] With Predators cruising at speeds no greater than 100mph, long periods were often spent just getting to and from a location. Afghanistan, with its sparse landscape, was particularly challenging. Once on-target and particularly during pure ISR missions, the aircraft might spend many more hours slowly circling a single location.

If the drone had a special intelligence-gathering pod on-board, operators might not even be allowed to use their own instruments. "I knew a controller said he once went four months without touching the control stick [of the camera]. That's not an exaggeration because I did similar. I got paid for that!" says Michael Haas, a sensor operator with both Special Forces and the regular Air Force. "It got to the point that it was no longer about the ISR that the Predator could provide. It was, the Predator is now a vehicle that carries this equipment. We're just using the wings and engine."

Coping with the crushing boredom became a job in itself. A nap by at least one remote crew member was sometimes an option with Predators locked on autopilot, admits former sensor operator Brandon Bryant. "Sometimes the pilot would be like, 'I was up with my family all day, I'm tired.' I'd be like: 'Hey, just go ahead, take an hour nap or something and I'll wake you if something happens.'" Some other former operators also describe taking turns to grab sleep when they could. With their job of liaising with the outside world mission controllers had it tougher, sharing an open-plan room with the shift commander. Says one former napper, "They [mission controllers] couldn't fall asleep and so would often be our check. 'Hey guys wake up, shift commander is coming out to your GCS!' By the time they got to us we'd look busy." At least with unmanned aircraft, only the Predators or Reapers themselves were at risk. One NATO airman described to the author an incident in which the flight crew of a combat helicopter in Afghanistan fell asleep toward the end of a lengthy, high-stress mission. They were only awoken when proximity alarms began ringing as the aircraft strayed towards nearby Pakistan's airspace.

For those remote operators unable or unwilling to nap, there were other possibilities for distraction or stimulation. Some describe taking reading material into work: "I would always have a book with me, if I was in the bathroom I'd sit down maybe for five minutes and read a page," says one former airman. "Only if nothing was going on if we're just doing circles in the sky. I would never read if there was something going on." Others whiled away the hours talking with comrades. Michael Haas (who also spent hours learning to draw caricatures of fellow operators) recalls getting into a text conversation with a British mission controller:

> He explained to me what the Hell was actually going on in the game
> of cricket. He was sending me these really long explanations of wickets

and bowling. That's how bored you are! As an American, when are you even going to see a game of cricket happening? I didn't care—it was something other than that mission, so it was interesting. It killed three hours, I can't complain.

Not everyone would indulge. A former operator describes one pilot who refused to be drawn into casual conversation: "He would not let you have any off-mission conversation, not even "How is your day?" He'd pick up that DASH-1, the big information operating manual for the Predator in the GCS, and he would start asking trivia questions about the plane, about the sensor ball—and do that for eight hours! Oh God."

Most controversially, operators have for the first time described to the author how simple digital games were smuggled onto the operating systems at work. The software for Predators and Reapers was supposed to run on closed military systems—but at some point, it was realized that games created using Microsoft Excel could be imported. "One of my friends, he was brilliant when it came to breaking the rules. He created Battleship games, Chess games which you could play with another crew," one former airman told the author. "You'd pull them up on your headset and you'd be playing against one member of the other crew while the other would typically be the referee." Another recalls playing Pinball and Solitaire during their time flying missions. But the fun ended in 2011, when it was discovered the games had most likely enabled a minor virus to be imported into the armed drones' operating systems. "We keep wiping it off, and it keeps coming back. . . . We think it's benign. But we just don't know," an Air Force source told *Wired*. At the time, the magazine reported that "military network security specialists are unsure whether the keylogging was intentionally introduced into the system or if it is, in fact, from an outside attacker."[42] The Air Force later put out a statement insisting that "The malware in question is a credential stealer, not a keylogger, found routinely on computer networks and is considered more of a nuisance than an operational threat."[43] There was never malice involved, with the operators themselves most likely responsible for the security breach following the loading of Excel games onto the system. "That was probably how the virus got in," a former airman told the author. "That virus was essentially a result of absolute boredom."

"Prolonged Virtual Combat Stress"

Despite expectations to the contrary, for many remote operators and analysts serving in the drone wars there was a personal cost to their work—though it took the Air Force some time to understand this. "It was essentially taking on a task and trying to achieve certain objectives, but not having adequate manpower strength to achieve those objectives. And, as a result, folks have to work longer hours and more rapid shifts, and you can carry on something like that for a short period of time. But if you have to carry it on for several weeks to several months, eventually it's going to wear you down," says senior USAF psychologist Dr. Wayne Chappelle. "Because you're not geographically separated from family or other sorts of social connections, there's also oftentimes the expectation that you would continue to function and meet those demands and obligations in your personal life. And I think that then creates a bit of a double whammy for folks." For decades the medical world had known of the acute mental health risks posed to combat personnel. Significant resources were invested by the US military in guarding against post-traumatic stress disorder (PTSD), and treating those it might affect: "The PTSD rates for troops returning from Iraq and Afghanistan . . . have varied a bit based upon the mission that you're performing on the battlefield, but they range anywhere between 13% to 18%. In some cases I've seen it as high as 21%," says Chappelle. In contrast, PTSD indicators among the drone community were far lower. "It ranges anywhere between 2% and 5%, so significantly less. The average rate of PTSD in the US population is about 5%. So it's either at or less than what you would expect in the general population."

Of increasing concern to psychologists was whether traditional markers for measuring combat stress like PTSD were the most reliable way to gauge the very real problems among remote warriors. Chappelle wonders whether a new term might be needed: "It could be that in reality, we just haven't identified what the most appropriate label would be for the condition. It could be something like 'Prolonged Virtual Combat Stress,' and not necessarily fall into the same sort of arena as battlefield combat stress. So it could be that we see something starting to surface." Others agree. "Specific combat-related stress is not the crux of the issue, it's more characterized as this chronicness of, over a large period of time there isn't the detachment from the job," says Colonel Lourdes Duvall, responsible for the well-being of thousands of US-based intelligence analysts. "When you're matching being in a combat mind-set with then having to compartmentalize that and deal with your financial, your personal, your relationship and all of those other issues, the kids' homework—it's a uniqueness."

Research confirmed that many of these stresses were being amplified by poor working environments—even more so perhaps than by remote combat itself.[44] Air Force ergonomic specialists, more used to working on F-16 designs, were brought in to look at how the layout of Ground Control Stations and analysts' desks might be improved. Personnel were given advice on how to manage their home lives, and even on the risk of over-caffeinating. Perhaps the biggest challenge was in ensuring operators and analysts had somebody to talk to. Former sensor operator Brandon Bryant, ultimately diagnosed with PTSD when he left the Air Force, says there were few options available to him as his stress levels mounted: "If you wanted to go talk to a therapist about it they would say, 'Well if you do, your security clearance is gonna be taken away.' And that scared a lot of people, because security clearance is sacred. We could go see a chaplain but we can't tell the chaplain anything that we've been doing. We can just tell him how we feel about things, like I feel bad about my job. And the general response that we would get was, 'It's part of God's plan.' And then no one decided to ever go see the chaplain again, especially me."[45]

Similar levels of stress and PTSD indicators were found among intelligence analysts. "I may not have been on the ground in Afghanistan, but I watched parts of the conflict in great detail on a screen for days on end. I know the feeling you experience when you see someone die. Horrifying barely covers it," former DGS-1 analyst Heather Linebaugh wrote in the *Guardian*. "When you are exposed to it over and over again it becomes like a small video, embedded in your head, forever on repeat, causing psychological pain and suffering that many people will hopefully never experience." Linebaugh also described how two friends and former colleagues committed suicide within a year of leaving the service.[46] In an unexplained twist, the RAF reported that its own medical personnel "have not detected any adverse psychological and physical trends for RAF pilots of RPAS."[47] Any variance might perhaps have been related to the all-volunteer nature of the British crews, or to an enhanced sense of camaraderie due to their posting abroad to Creech AFB. However, at the time of publishing, the British Ministry of Defence was unable to identify for the author any primary research which supported its claim of lower stressors for UK crews.

By 2013, USAF was so concerned about stress among drone operators and analysts that its ISR Agency was trialing the full-time presence of psychologists on the operations floor: "The chaplain and the psychologist in this unit try to do preventative programs, they call it 'Getting left of the bang,' to be less reactive and more pro-active about building that resiliency among our members," a senior intelligence commander at Langley AFB told the author. "They're very much into education, prevention and pro-active outreach, so that they can minimize the chance of problems developing."[48] Airman Ray, the young enlisted analyst with DGS-1—who had described for the author his harrowing remote mission in Afghanistan—confirmed that he and others did have access to a mental health team if needed: "They are fully cleared so you can speak if you have anything mission-related that affects you, you can go up and speak freely."

Air Force Special Operations Command had also begun to confront stress among its drone operators: "There is a Military Family Life consultant and chaplain in each of the RPA squadrons," a spokesman told the author. "There are also two psychologists who visit the units and talk to the personnel."[49] Whether such preventive measures would be enough to help mitigate "prolonged virtual combat stress"—or whatever this novel condition among remote-combatants would come to be known as—remained unclear: "Our individuals are facing very similar types of stressors: they are in a no-fail business. They are virtually engaged in combat operations, making decisions that have life or death impact. So the information they're putting forward has a battlefield effect, and we always want them to be the positive battlefield effect: but that's not war," says Colonel Duvall. Despite the apparent attraction of being based back on US soil, even in 2014 many drone operators still wished for the physical battlefield. When the Government Accountability Office asked ten focus groups of Predator and Reaper pilots what they thought of their working lives, the majority reported that "being deployed on-station negatively affected their quality of life" with many asking instead to be deployed into theater, and to be "separated from their family and friends."[50]

Despite the US's aggressive transition to remotely piloted combat, too little was still known about the long-term effects not only on those personnel now fighting thousands of miles from the front, but on the conduct of warfare itself. Politicians rarely shared these qualms. Announcing that armed drones (and manned US combat aircraft) would be returning to Iraq's skies in summer 2014 to confront resurgent Islamists, President Obama cited his five-year long, secret air war against Al Qaeda in Yemen as evidence of what could be achieved "without putting large numbers of U.S. troops on the ground. . . . Looking at how we can create more of those models is going to be part of the solution in dealing with both Syria and Iraq," he told reporters.[51] Yet it was still far from clear whether Obama's major expansion of the secret drone wars into Yemen and Somalia had actually lessened terrorist activity—or instead had achieved the opposite.

The last Predator, tailfin number 268, at its handover ceremony in March 2010.
SOURCE: NEWS RELEASE IMAGE ORIGINALLY PROVIDED BY GENERAL ATOMICS

Washington Redskins cheerleaders are given a tour of a Predator.
Ali Air Base, Iraq, November 2007.
SOURCE: US AIR FORCE/ A1C JONATHAN SNYDER

Neal and Linden Blue with a map of South America, 1957.
SOURCE: TIME LIFE/ GETTY IMAGES

A photograph by Pakistani journalist Hayatullah Khan—of a Hellfire missile fragment from a 2005 CIA strike—which led to his murder.
SOURCE: EUROPEAN PRESS AGENCY

Predator tailfin 3034, now hanging in the Smithsonian Air and Space Museum, Washington, DC.
SOURCE: AUTHOR'S PHOTOGRAPH

Maulana Aziz, a spiritual leader of the Pakistan Taliban, at the Lal Masjid (Red Mosque), Islamabad, December 2012.
SOURCE: AUTHOR'S PHOTOGRAPH

Cruise missile fragment from JSOC's disastrous first attack in Yemen on December 17, 2009, which killed more than 40 civilians.
SOURCE: AMNESTY INTERNATIONAL

NO. 180 /APA(K)R, DATED WANA THE 3 /FEBY:2009.

From:- .. The Assistant Political Agent,
South Waziristan Agency Wana.

To:- .. The Political Agent,
South Waziristan Agency, Tank.

SUBJECT :- COLLETRAL DAMAGES

Memorandum It is submitted that today on 2.9.2009, a jirga
of Gangi Khel Wazir called on me wherein I offered condolence
on sad demise of Malik Din Faraz and his family members due to
Dron attack on 23.1.2009.

In the jirga, the enclosed application duly
supported by all the Gangi Khel elders, was presented to me
wherein it has been stated that the following family members
were died in the Drone attack :-

1. Malik Din Faraz S/O Zakim Khan,Alikhonai.
2. Habib Noor S/O M.Din Faraz - -do-.
3. Muhammad Ghulam S/O Din Faraz -do-
4. Mohammadullah S/O Din Faraz -do-
5. Loi Khan, Cousin of M.Din Faraz -do-

In addition to above, the residential house
containing 8 rooms & Drawing Room full of luggages are completely damaged. As per rough assessment, the property damages come
to Rs.18,00,000/- (Rs.Eighteen Lacs).

The jirga requested for early payment of blood
money & property damages to the affectees may kindly be made.

The payment of above being genuine is recommended with the request to please take up the case with authority
concerned for early release of compensation so that greivences
of aggreived family are redressed.

Assistant Political Agent
South Waziristan Agency Wana

ATTESTED

A.P.A, Wana, S.W.A.

A complaint from South Waziristan villagers at the death of civilians in President Obama's first covert drone strike, January 2009.
SOURCE: AUTHOR'S ARCHIVE

Bilal al-Berjawi, the ex-Briton assassinated January 21, 2012, by JSOC, hours after the birth of his son.
SOURCE: SCREEN GRAB FROM AL SHABAAB PROPAGANDA—AUTHOR'S ARCHIVE

Mohamed Sakr, the British-born man also killed by JSOC in Somalia, February 24, 2012.
SOURCE: SCREEN GRAB FROM AL SHABAAB PROPAGANDA—AUTHOR'S ARCHIVE

Abdullah Mabkhut al-Amri, the bridegroom whose wedding convoy was bombed by a JSOC Reaper drone in December 2013, killing his son and up to a dozen other civilians.
SOURCE: VIVIAN SALAMA

Oum Salim and her daughter, with a photo of her late son Salim Hussein Ahmed Jamil, killed in a US drone strike January 2013.
SOURCE: VIVIAN SALAMA

President Barack Obama with his first choice to win the war in Afghanistan, General Stanley McChrystal, May 2009.
SOURCE: WHITE HOUSE/PETE SOUZA

The author (far right) with villagers in Sara Rhoga, South Waziristan, November 2012—scene of CIA drone strikes three years earlier.
SOURCE: ISPR

The author (center) with cameraman and Pakistan Army's Colonel Mohammed Husayn, overlooking North Waziristan, November 2012.
SOURCE: ISPR

A Pakistan Army soldier looks down onto North Waziristan from a fortified hilltop, November 2012.
SOURCE: AUTHOR'S PHOTOGRAPH

Young Waziri army cadets, part of Pakistan's de-radicalization scheme, South Waziristan.
SOURCE: AUTHOR'S PHOTOGRAPH

Pakistani barrister Mirza Shahzad Akhbar, campaigner for civilian drone strike victims and according to the CIA an ISI agent seeking to harm Americans.
SOURCE: AUTHOR'S PHOTOGRAPH

An early Reaper drone in Afghanistan, December 2007.
SOURCE: USAF MEDIA

A Royal Air Force Reaper in Afghanistan, March 2011.
SOURCE: RAF/ CORPORAL STEVE FOLLOWS

AN ABSENCE OF TRANSPARENCY
Yemen and Somalia

For Abdullah Mabkhut al-Amri and Warda al-Sorimi—each widowed and marrying for the second time—December 12, 2013, should have been one of the happier days of their lives. The 60-strong wedding party had already gathered for a communal lunch of roasted lamb at the bride's house. By late afternoon, eleven vehicles full of guests were heading to the nearby village of al-Abusereema, where the couple would make their new home. Yet among them were a small number of tribesmen allegedly affiliated with the local Al Qaeda franchise. As the wedding convoy made its way along a stony dirt road, US drones attacked. Up to four Hellfire missiles targeted a number of cars, and at least a dozen men died including Saleh—the groom's 25-year-old son by his first marriage.[1] Most if not all of those killed were civilians. Dozens more were injured. According to reports, "shrapnel grazed the bride under one eye, and blew her trousseau to pieces." As Warda's new husband later noted, "We were in a wedding but all of a sudden it became a funeral . . . Why did the United States do this to us?"[2] London *Times* correspondent Iona Craig visited the bride and groom's village in al-Bayda province in the immediate aftermath of the

US bombing. She describes a complex local scenario, in which tribal and regional disputes had become deeply bound up with anti-government protests, and with groups such as Ansar al-Sharia, a proxy of Al Qaeda in the Arabian Peninsula:

> You've got a civilian population that feels neglected by the government, a lack of basic services, emboldened by a tribal dispute. When you have all that and then you have US strikes that are killing civilians, it's stoking that anti-government sentiment. . . . This completely plays into the hands of those who are trying to boost the position of Ansar al-Sharia in al-Bayda, which is very strong.[3]

Initial claims by Yemen's security apparatus that only "terrorists" had died in the attack were replaced within hours by a fulsome apology.[4] A joint letter from the military commander and governor of al-Bayda offered "the condolences of the political leadership [in Sana'a] and we come to you in solidarity with the victims of the strike." The government also offered "100 Kalashnikov rifles and 32 million Yemeni riyals [$150,000] in total compensation for the dead and injured."[5] Photojournalist Vivian Salama, shown the letter while on assignment for *Rolling Stone* magazine, views this as a clear indication of targeting errors in the US drone strike: "For a letter like this to exist, that's basically the [Yemen] government indirectly conceding that it was a total mess-up. Otherwise there would be nothing."[6]

Field investigations by NGOs and journalists reached similar conclusions: "The attack may have violated the laws of war by failing to discriminate between combatants and civilians, or by causing civilian loss disproportionate to the expected military advantage," Human Rights Watch stated.[7] Two UN experts added their voices to a growing chorus of international concern, noting that "Yemen cannot consent to violations of the right to life of people in its territory."[8] Finally, in Sana'a the national parliament voted for an end to all US drone strikes, echoing similar (and equally impotent) moves by Pakistan's parliament almost two years earlier.[9] As one local official noted, "the Yemeni public is angered by the drone strikes. The people's representatives [have] reflected on the tone of the streets."[10] Whatever the intended consequences of the drone strike, its impact on Washington's strategic interests had been severe.

General Stanley McChrystal later complained that when he took command of international forces in Afghanistan in 2009, he inherited a situation where "over time, as Coalition airstrikes continued to hit misidentified targets like wedding celebrations, Afghan tolerance grew brittle." Worse, "Americans frequently responded defensively to charges of misguided strikes."[11] As a consequence, McChrystal had made the preservation of civilian life—and the open admission of errors—a cornerstone of his Afghan warfighting policy. Four years on, it seemed Washington had not learned those lessons elsewhere. Noncombatant deaths from confirmed US drone strikes in Yemen had almost tripled in 2013, with upwards of 33 civilians killed.[12] As a consequence, Obama risked alienating the very mainstream population the United States needed to win over if it was to defeat Al Qaeda locally. The drone which bombed the wedding party was remotely flown by operators from Cannon Air Force Base, on behalf of Joint Special Operations Command (JSOC). One former JSOC analyst argues that civilian casualties caused by Yemen strikes were most likely a result of local conditions. There were limits to the numbers of armed drones available, and only a small number of suspects were being sought over a large geographical area: "In order to eliminate the threat, or in more literal terms assassinate this person . . . commanders and decision-makers are more likely to go through with a strike, even if it means that other innocent people are involved, because of the limited opportunities to strike," the former analyst believes.[13]

In the face of all public evidence relating to the wedding party strike, anonymous Pentagon officials nevertheless told the Associated Press that "the US government did investigate the strike against al-Badani—twice—and concluded that only members of Al-Qaida were killed in the three vehicles that were hit."[14] Yet prior to that attack, JSOC was reportedly warned that the CIA "did not have confidence in the underlying intelligence." And afterwards, "CIA analysts assessed that some of the victims may have been villagers, not militants," according to the Los Angeles Times. The Pentagon and White House subsequently blocked publication of two internal reports into the bombing.[15] Some questioned how thorough they might anyway be: "If these two internal investigations do involve research on the ground I see no evidence of it. They are doing a pretty good job of keeping it secret, because not one person I've interviewed has been interviewed by anyone from the US government about these strikes," complained Letta Tayler, who had coordinated Human Rights Watch's own field investigation into the attack. In her view, Obama's secret war in Yemen represented "an accountability black hole."[16]

THE AL QAEDA FRANCHISE

Paul Wolfowitz's boast back in 2002, of America's first Predator assassination beyond the hot battlefield, had helped see Sana'a lock the CIA's armed drones out of its airspace for nine long years (see chapter 3). For a while at least, their presence would have made little difference. That drone killing of local Al Qaeda leader Qa'id Salim Sinan al-Harithi, coupled with ongoing arrests by Yemen's security forces, had all but broken the terrorist group in southern Arabia. As former US ambassador to Sana'a Barbara Bodine has written, "I think the general assessment all the way up our government is that by about 2004, we and the Yemenis had the conventional Al Qaeda problem reasonably under control."[17] As the US military focus shifted first to Iraq and then once again to Afghanistan, better uses could be found for the Predator. Back in Yemen and Somalia, the United States was playing a low-key waiting game. The expectation was that under pressure from drone strikes and other counterterrorism operations, the leadership of "Al Qaeda Central" would flee Pakistan's tribal areas and instead take control of local offshoots. No one anticipated that a new, homegrown terror leadership cadre would instead emerge in places like Yemen. "It was certainly the expectation the Agency had that if we punished Al Qaeda Main enough in the tribal region, they would move. And it was the movement of the leadership that we anticipated. Rather than their just staying there and dying," one former senior official now admits. " 'Somewhere else' for us always was Yemen and Somalia. And so we were kind of making preparations, because you know, an organization like that in movement is more vulnerable than when it's stationary. And so we were trying to anticipate how we would deal with that. And frankly they never moved."[18]

Instead, Al Qaeda's regional revival had its origins just beyond Yemen's northern border, with a wave of attacks against Saudi and western targets which were in part a response to the US invasion of Iraq. Nine Americans were among 36 people killed in a May 2003 terrorist strike on a housing compound in Riyadh, for example. When the group responsible was finally smashed by Saudi security forces, the remnants slipped into Yemen.[19] There, they joined up with local Al Qaeda leaders who had recently escaped in a mass prison breakout, instigating a wave of terror attacks against Yemeni military and security officials and non-Arab targets. Twice in 2008, for example, terrorists struck at the US embassy in Sana'a killing 18 people. One victim was newlywed Susan Elbaneh, an 18-year-old American from Lackawanna, New York (coincidentally the home town of the first US citizen killed in a covert CIA drone strike six years earlier) who was slain with her husband as they waited in line for the embassy to open. One of Elbaneh's own distant cousins was an affiliate of the local Al Qaeda group which had killed her.[20]

The Yemen and Saudi terror franchises ultimately merged under the banner Al Qaeda in the Arabian Peninsula (AQAP), announcing the move just days before the inauguration of Barack Obama.[21] In response, the US president began contemplating a new front in the covert War on Terror. His chief adviser in this was John Brennan, the CIA's former station chief in Riyadh. Meeting the Saudi king on Obama's behalf in March 2009, a leaked US diplomatic cable reveals "Brennan warned that the US feared Yemen could become another Waziristan, and urged that the US and Saudi Arabia needed to work together to keep Al-Qaeda in Yemen from growing even more dangerous."[22] Six months later, and Brennan was back in the region to meet with Yemen's authoritarian leader Ali Abdullah Saleh—now in his 20th year in power. "Saleh pledged unfettered access to Yemen's national territory for US counterterrorism operations," a secret embassy cable noted. In an aside, Yemen's president made clear that success or failure now lay with Obama: "Highlighting the potential for a future AQAP attack on the US Embassy or other Western targets, Saleh said, 'I have given you an open door on terrorism, so I am not responsible.'"[23] Later still, a palace photographer captured JSOC's new commander Admiral William McRaven sitting starchily next to Saleh in early October 2009, as the pair discussed "areas of cooperation between Yemen and the United States in the military sphere and the fight against terrorism."[24]

Ten weeks after that meeting, on December 17, JSOC launched its first airborne strike in Yemen. The attack on the small tented hamlet of al-Majala was a disaster, almost derailing Obama's new offensive in the War on Terror. With AFSOC's armed Predators and Reapers all re-deployed to Afghanistan, JSOC had to depend on whatever assets it could acquire from regular forces. Instead of using 100-lb precision Hellfires, the United States had instead fired a 2,800-lb cruise missile, packed with cluster munitions—the use of which was banned by many other nations. As Amnesty International noted:

> This type of missile, launched from a warship or submarine, is designed to carry 166 cluster sub-munitions (bomblets) which each explode into over 200 sharp steel fragments that can cause injuries up to 150m away.[25]

JSOC's target was Saleh Mohammed al-Anbouri, also known as al-Kazimi, who it was alleged was about to launch an attack on the British embassy in Sana'a.[26] Yet instead of the supposed "terror training camp" at al-Majala, only a few of those present in the Bedouin tented village were alleged militants. Of the 58 people killed, 44 were confirmed by a later Yemen parliamentary inquiry to have been noncombatant civilians. Among the dead were 12 women (five of them pregnant) and 22 children. Entire families were annihilated. Ahmed Mokbel Salem Louqye died with his wife, son and three young daughters. His brother Ali's seven-strong family was also wiped out. The intended victim also died, though as the parliamentary inquiry complained: "The main target of the strike, Mohammed Al-Kazimi, moved between different towns and villages and could easily have been targeted in a different location, using a different method. The air strike that targeted Al-Kazimi was not based on accurate information, which led to a greater loss of civilian lives."[27]

Just as in Pakistan earlier that year, Obama's first intervention in Yemen was a tactical and strategic failure, which thanks to its propaganda value had significantly strengthened Al Qaeda's hand. A cover-up of America's role in the attack only compounded this. US officials certainly knew almost immediately of civilian deaths. Yemen's deputy Prime Minister Rashad al-Alimi told US Ambassador Stephen Seche three days afterwards "that the civilians who died were largely nomadic, Bedouin families who lived in tents near the AQAP training camp and were assisting AQAP with logistical support."[28] Yet when CENTCOM's commander later conspired with Yemen's President and Prime Minister to hide any US involvement in the al-Majala bombing, General David Petraeus denied any large-scale noncombatant deaths—despite Saleh himself expressing significant worries.

"The General responded [to Saleh] that the only civilians killed were the wife and two children of an AQAP operative at the site," a secret US embassy cable reported.[29]

Despite the disastrous outcome of that first JSOC operation, the terrorist threat from Yemen remained very real. On Christmas Day 2009, a young Nigerian named Umar Farouk Abdulmutallab attempted to blow up Northwest Airlines Flight 253 as it landed in Detroit, with 290 passengers and crew onboard. The plot was the work of AQAP, its first direct attack on the US homeland. Washington was unprepared. As the Senate Intelligence Committee later noted: "Prior to the 12/25 plot, counterterrorism analysts at NCTC [National Counter Terrorism Center], CIA, and NSA were focused on the threat of terrorist attacks in Yemen, but were not focused on the possibility of AQAP attacks against the US homeland."[30]

The US counterterrorism focus now shifted heavily toward southern Arabia. JSOC had built a fearsome reputation for kill/capture operations in Iraq and Afghanistan, yet this had been based on high-quality ISR missions by Predators and other aircraft above, and on fast-moving Special Forces units on the ground. In Yemen, JSOC had access to neither. Instead, strikes by aircraft from the US Gulf fleet achieved some success in early 2010, killing a number of mid-ranking Al Qaeda operatives. In return, AQAP threatened revenge for al-Majala, with radical American cleric Anwar al-Awlaki himself noting that "We cannot stand idly in the face of such aggression, and we will fight back and incite others to do the same."[31] Yet before the United States could build any momentum to its campaign, targeting errors once again led to the banning of US airstrikes on Yemen's soil, after JSOC accidentally killed a deputy provincial governor in May 2010.[32] It would be another year before Washington could take advantage of the chaos of the Arab Spring—and President Saleh's slow fall from power—to return to the offensive. In its absence, Al Qaeda had been busy.

INSPIRE

When JSOC's strike team left Osama bin Laden's compound in May 2011 after killing the Al Qaeda leader, it took with it a vast digital trove of documents. Details soon emerged of an exchange between AQAP's own commander and bin Laden himself. Nasir al-Wihayshi had trained with Al Qaeda in Afghanistan, rising to become a key lieutenant. Yet despite having led the terror group in Yemen for four years, in 2010 he had written to bin Laden apparently suggesting that he step down in favor of the media-savvy American Anwar al-Awlaki. Appointing him would be a propaganda coup, al-Wihayshi claimed, and would boost Al Qaeda's popularity. Bin Laden was not convinced. He had recently expressed dissatisfaction at one of AQAP's pet projects, the English-language Al Qaeda web magazine *Inspire*, to which al-Awlaki was a regular contributor. With glossy features on "My life in Jihad" and "How to build a bomb for $4,000," the online magazine was a hit with younger radical readers. But bin Laden—a man responsible for the deaths of thousands of innocents—was apparently offended by an article advocating the use of sports utility trucks as "the ultimate mowing machine" among crowds of civilians. Bin Laden told al-Wihayshi to stay put as leader.[33]

From its earliest incarnation, Al Qaeda had focused on mass spectacle as a means of conveying its twisted agenda. The simultaneous African embassy bombings of 1998; the 9/11 attacks on the United States; the Madrid train bombings of 2004; and the London suicide attacks of the following year were all atrocities designed not only to sow terror locally but also to utilize the world's media as a propaganda vehicle. The emergence of the World Wide Web in the late 1990s also allowed Al Qaeda and other terror groups to communicate more directly with sympathizers. Jihadist chat rooms proliferated, while sophisticated media wings of Al Qaeda franchises pumped out propaganda which could reach mass audiences on sites such as YouTube. In Yemen, Al Qaeda's efforts were at first only locally focused (plans to exploit the lethal bombing of the USS *Cole* in 2000 were botched when the cameraman overslept, Johnsen notes).[34] In early 2008, the south Arabian group began publishing the Arabic-language online newsletter *Sada al-Malahem* (Echo of Battles). Crude but popular, articles ranged from polemics on the "Crusader" wars and advice on committing terror attacks, to more homely features on how to overcome coughs and colds on the battlefield.

Of more immediate concern to Washington was a publication once dubbed "the most dangerous download on Earth."[35] In mid-2010, AQAP also began producing the high-quality English-language magazine *Inspire*, aimed at the "millions of Muslims whose first or second language is English." Clearly written by native English speakers, the glossy online publication had a penchant for vicious humor. An article in the first issue, written by "the AQ Chef," was titled "Make a Bomb in the Kitchen of Your Mom." Prominent early features were attributed to Osama bin Laden and his lieutenant Ayman al-Zawahiri. Also peppered throughout were inspirational comments from Anwar al-Awlaki, along with two articles penned by the US-born cleric himself. Whatever the truth of al-Awlaki's exact relationship with the group, there was now no doubting his allegiance to Al Qaeda's cause. Calling directly for the assassination of a US cartoonist, Awlaki wrote in *Inspire*'s first issue in June 2010:

> I specifically invite the youth to either fight in the West or join their brothers in the fronts of jihad: Afghanistan, Iraq, and Somalia. I invite them to join the new front, Yemen, the base from which the great *jihad* of the Arabian Peninsula will begin, the base from which the greatest army of Islam will march forth.[36]

Anwar al-Awlaki's preachings and emails had earlier been linked peripherally to a number of US terror plots. Now he was directly exhorting Muslims in the West to carry out "lone wolf" terror acts. With the death of Osama bin Laden, Barack Obama reportedly viewed the cleric as "threat number 1."[37] It appears likely that *Inspire* also played a key role in al-Awlaki's downfall. Just three days before his death, the latest magazine had appeared online: a "special edition" glorifying 9/11 on its tenth anniversary. This time there were no articles by the American cleric (though there was the promise of a later piece from him on "Targeting the populations of countries that are at war with the Muslims.") Instead there was a lengthy feature by Samir Khan, another US citizen who had joined AQAP and who would be killed along with Al-Awlaki: "If Awlaki was the professor, Samir Khan, the editor-in-chief, was the geek," James Bamford has written. "On the pages of the magazine, Khan was a thoughtful but accessible voice, his language stripped of the Koranic references and stiff didactic pronouncements common to Awlaki's prose."[38] Khan's piece in the final issue before his death, "The Media Conflict," laid out the importance of an online war in which "media work is half of the jihad."[39]

Khan and al-Awlaki had been under observation for almost two weeks before their killing, US intelligence officials later told *Newsweek*.[40] That timeframe indicated that the production processes involved with *Inspire* may themselves have led the CIA to the two American citizens. A year earlier in "Operation Cupcake," British intelligence had hacked the second edition of the magazine, substituting jihadist propaganda for baking recipes.[41] Since then, a decision had been taken to leave the magazine alone in the hope that it would lead counter-terrorism forces to al-Awlaki and other leaders. That gamble appeared to have paid off. Yet Obama's insistence that Al Qaeda in Yemen was now "weakened" would prove wide of the mark, as the terrorist group continued to grow in strength.

HUNTER-KILLERS

During the Iraq conflict, JSOC had helped hone the Predator into an effective counter-insurgency tool which rarely needed to fire its missiles in anger. As former Special Forces drone commander Pete Forrest recalls, "We did not want to have to shoot the Hellfire. That meant something went wrong. We did not want to have shots fired on the target."[42] Instead, Predators on JSOC missions had focused on gathering vital intelligence on insurgents who could then, with luck, be captured by other Special Forces units on the ground. Although this pure intelligence, surveillance, and reconnaissance (ISR) role remained key, in 2011 the Obama administration had given Air Force Special Operations Command (AFSOC) a new task. After two years of bombings in Yemen using manned aircraft and cruise missiles, AFSOC's armed Predator and Reaper squadrons would now take the strain. Any hope that the presence of drones might reduce the risk to non-combatants was misplaced. In September 2012, for example, an airstrike on the town of Rada'a killed a dozen civilians as they returned by minibus from the local market. Three children and a pregnant woman were among the dead. When one young man arrived at the scene he saw the corpses of a woman and girl still inside the burnt-out Toyota land cruiser and "clutched in a lifeless embrace," as Human Rights Watch would later describe it:

> "The bodies were charred like coal. I could not recognize the faces," said Ahmad al-Sabooli, a 23-year-old farmer. Moving in closer, al-Sabooli realized that the woman and girl were his mother and 10-year-old sister. He also saw his father among the dead.[43]

It would be the quietest news day of the year—December 25, 2012—when it was revealed that a US official had anonymously admitted a Pentagon aircraft, most likely a drone, had mistakenly killed the shoppers in Rada'a.[44] Some months earlier, there had been hopes of improved accountability for such errors, after Obama partially declassified US operations in Yemen.[45] Yet for civilians on the ground, this had no effect. Department of Defense (DoD) officials contacted by the author at the time still refused to discuss any such bombings for reasons of "operational security."

Complicating matters further, in late 2011 the CIA had begun its own lethal drone operations over Yemen from a separate airbase at Umm al-Melh in Saudi Arabia. The Agency was brought in, not in response to high civilian deaths but because of the continued JSOC failure to kill Anwar al-Awlaki. A fresh assassination attempt in May 2011 had seen US Marine Corps Harrier jets, Predator drones, and other aircraft pursue the American preacher in his pick-up truck. Surprisingly al-Awlaki had escaped: "It looks as if someone was a bit angry with us this evening," he later taunted from the pages of *Inspire* magazine.[46] That failure led to a shake-up in US operations: "I hear it just pissed off a lot of people and I think they brought in OGA [Other Government Agencies—generally a reference to the CIA] to fly those missions and get the job done," recalls a former Special Forces operator. From now on, the CIA had the lead in targeting al-Awlaki and other senior Al Qaeda figures, although both the CIA and JSOC operations continued to maintain separate kill lists.[47] Accountability had become even more problematic. As US officials tortuously explained to Associated Press: "By statute, the military strikes can be acknowledged, but the CIA operations cannot. The officials said if they explain one strike but not another, they are revealing by default which ones are being carried out by the CIA. The officials spoke on condition of anonymity because they were not authorized to discuss the drone operations publicly."[48]

By September 2014, the CIA and JSOC had between them killed anywhere from 500 to 1,400 people in Yemen, mostly in covert drone strikes. Of those fatalities, at least 120 were civilian noncombatants.[49] According to former NSA analyst Edward Snowden, the US lethal targeting program in Yemen had grown to such an extent that it became a trigger for his later whistleblowing:

The stuff I saw really began to disturb me. I could watch drones in real time as they surveilled the people they might kill. You could watch entire villages and see what everyone was doing. I watched NSA tracking people's Internet activities as they typed. I became aware of just how invasive US surveillance had become.[50]

Snowden's subsequent release of top secret documents raised key questions about the accuracy of intelligence behind lethal targeting.[51] Yet still there appeared little appetite among those US politicians tasked with overseeing the campaigns to investigate further.

Poor Oversight

While Obama, like Bush before him, had refused to make either JSOC or the CIA publicly accountable for their targeted killings, he did appear to place some faith in secret congressional oversight. As he had noted:

To say a military tactic is legal, or even effective, is not to say it is wise or moral in every instance. For the same human progress that gives us the technology to strike half a world away also demands the discipline to constrain that power—or risk abusing it. And that's why, over the last four years, my administration has worked vigorously to establish a framework that governs our use of force against terrorists—insisting upon clear guidelines, oversight and accountability.[52]

The Senate Select Committee on Intelligence (SSCI) and the House Permanent Select Committee on Intelligence (HPSCI) were between them supposed to watch over the CIA's activities, with all members cleared to view top secret materials. Bombings by JSOC were instead, in theory, the purview of the Armed Services committees. Yet while US targeted assassinations had begun with an attack in Yemen back in 2002, congressional oversight remained for years an ad hoc affair. A former senior intelligence official insisted to the author that "we were not hiding the football on this from anybody. Certainly not while I was there." The Agency's director would instead telephone the chair of the SSCI following any "significant intelligence activity," and outline a particular mission. At a time when Bush's government was under sustained congressional attack as a result of the CIA and Pentagon torture scandals, Agency officials were also careful to include senior Administration figures in the decision-making process around targeted killings, and to leave "a paperwork trail to follow," in the words of the former senior official.[53]

Worryingly, consistent oversight only began eight years into the US targeted killing program. In early 2010, key Obama ally Dianne Feinstein—the powerful Democratic Party senator from California and now chair of the Senate Intelligence Committee—introduced "monthly in-depth oversight meetings." In Feinstein's own words, the aim of these joint SSCI and HPSCI gatherings was "to review strike records and question every aspect of the [drone] program including legality, effectiveness, precision, foreign policy implications and the care taken to minimize noncombatant casualties."[54] Others were more skeptical. According to Lawrence Wilkerson, former chief of staff to US Secretary of State Colin Powell:

> The CIA supposedly has to tell each of the Select Committees in its testimony, or at least in its testimony in closed session to the few who are able to get it, what it's doing. It never does of course, and it lies consistently. But it at least it has to say something to somebody, and if they ask the right questions—which sometimes they do—it has to say even more.[55]

The Obama administration had hinted that it wished to see the Pentagon take over all drone strikes.[56] "I will increasingly turn to our military to take the lead," the President himself told West Point graduates in May 2014.[57] This was supported, in principle, at least, by John Brennan, who during his confirmation hearing as the CIA's new Director a year earlier had told Senators that some of the Agency's post-9/11 activities had been "a bit of an aberration from its traditional role," and that "the CIA should not be doing traditional military activities and operations."[58] In short, the administration wanted to see the CIA's drone programs in Yemen and Pakistan shifted to JSOC. Yet if supporters were hoping this might lead to greater accountability, oversight of JSOC's lethal actions was even weaker than for the CIA's operations, according to critics. Members of the House and Senate Armed Services committees were rarely told of Special Forces targeted killing operations, according to one knowledgeable former senior intelligence official: "Don't think that JSOC doing it is going to be more transparent than the current situation. Because JSOC doesn't talk much to the Armed Services guys, compared to what some other committees get."[59]

Perhaps the more pertinent question was whether any Congressional oversight might be effective. Senator Feinstein was certainly no neutral observer, having expressed strong support for targeted killings outside the hot battlefield. Discussing an alleged Al Qaeda terrorist in Yemen, she told Fox News: "I am hopeful that we will be able to, candidly, kill this bomb maker and kill some of these other associates."[60] Her opposite number, Mike Rogers, who chaired the HPSCI, was equally bullish. In 2014 he sharply criticized the Obama administration for, in his view, restricting the ability of US military and intelligence officials to target suspects: "Today, individuals who would have previously been removed from the battlefield by US counterterrorism operations for attacking or plotting against US interests remain free because of self-imposed red tape," he complained.[61]

When both committees did investigate problematic CIA drone strikes, the results when known were not encouraging. In June 2012, the Agency had killed Al Qaeda's new number two in Pakistan, Yahya al-Libi. Multiple sources, some based on survivor testimony, reported that at least a dozen people (half of them possibly civilians) had died alongside al-Libi in two linked missile strikes, which included the controversial tactic of targeting rescuers. As one major investigation noted: "Ten to 16 people were killed in total, including six local tribesmen who, as far as Amnesty International could determine, had come only to assist victims."[62] Yet according to a *Los Angeles Times* report, oversight committee staff members were only ever shown the video feed of Yahya al-Libi himself being killed, and not of any associated strikes, indicating that Congress may have been misinformed (though the CIA robustly denied to the author that this was the case).[63] A subsequent investigation found that oversight was also a highly insular affair. Since 2010, no congressional intelligence committee member or staffer had reached out to any academic body, NGO, or news organization which had uncovered compelling evidence of civilian casualties in Yemen or Pakistan. That had not prevented Feinstein from informing Congress that the Senate Intelligence Committee was doing its "utmost" to verify CIA claims of low civilian deaths from drone strikes.[64]

A War within a War

JSOC's lethal operations in Yemen were at first aimed squarely at Al Qaeda's senior leadership. The turmoil sweeping North Africa and the Middle East soon changed that equation. Yemen's own Arab Spring uprising against the authoritarian president Ali Abdullah Saleh, which began in January 2011, exposed deep fractures within the country. In Sana'a and elsewhere, protesters occupied the streets to demand a democratic and more inclusive future, even as police and army units began taking sides. Exploiting this weakened central control, AQAP and its proxy Ansar al-Sharia began seizing territory across the south of the country, including the cities of Jaar and Zanjubar—where the black flag of Al Qaeda soon flew.[65]

As the risk of AQAP permanently holding territory in southern Arabia grew, Saleh's collapsing regime was almost powerless to act. Yemen's counterterrorist troops—on which the United States had lavished millions of dollars—were instead used to protect the president. A frustrated Washington helped force Saleh out of office, and then coordinated a major offensive to take back the south. In the view of local journalist Saeed al-Batati, Washington's intervention played a crucial role: "Without that American support I think Al Qaeda would have stayed in Abyan and Shabwa provinces for a longer time. The Yemen military had the capability to remove them, but not within a month."[66] With Yemeni troops providing the muscle on the ground, US combat aircraft and drones pounded militant positions from above, guided by American Special Forces now stationed just 45 miles from the front line.[67] Many of those militant positions were inside cities and towns, and it was proving near-impossible to hold to account those responsible when civilians died. "You've got the involvement of the US, you've got Yemeni fighter jets up there as well. And at times certainly during 2011 and 2012 when the war was going on in Abyan [province] you had the Saudis too. Which makes it such a complicated mix. It can be very difficult to figure out who's carried out a strike," says Iona Craig of the London *Times*. This absence of transparency lay behind a wide variance in casualty estimates. While there was no doubt that hundreds of people were killed in airstrikes (the majority most likely militants), less clear was where responsibility lay. In one notorious 2012 incident, at least 14 civilians died when an unknown aircraft struck the site of an earlier attack—a tactic reminiscent of CIA actions in Pakistan. According to eyewitness evidence presented to the US Senate:

> The aircraft returned to bomb the people who had gathered to aid the wounded from the first strike. Rockets fell a few meters away from me. I was in my car and saw that it was on fire. I quickly got out of the car and saw a number of people in front of me lying on the ground. They were burning without any clothes. I saw at least seven or eight of them die at that moment.[68]

Two years later, it was still not known whether an American, a Yemeni, or even a Saudi aircraft had carried out the attack. That said, Yemen's new President Abd Rabbuh Mansur Hadi was far more open about US drone strikes than his predecessor had been. The nation's air force was poorly equipped with Russian MIGs, none of which had precision strike capabilities.[69] Hadi now confirmed publicly that many airstrikes in Yemen were the work of the Americans, who "helped with their drones because the Yemeni Air Force cannot carry out missions at night."[70] In a backhanded compliment, Hadi told reporters while on a Washington visit: "They pinpoint the target and have zero margin of error, if you know what target you're aiming at."[71] The Yemeni president's new openness was matched elsewhere in his government. Within hours of most US bombings, the names of those alleged militants killed would often be posted on the Ministry of Interior's website. Hadi also tolerated significant dissent within his administration. Hooria Mashhour, his human rights minister, was a particularly outspoken critic— once using an op-ed in the *Washington Post* to blast both governments:

> More often than not, US drone strikes leave families bereaved and villages terrified. Drones tear at the fabric of Yemeni society. Wronged and angry men are just the sort extreme groups like AQAP find easiest to recruit. Our president may reassure the United States of his support for drone strikes but the reality is that no leader can legitimately approve the extrajudicial killing of his own citizens.

The Minister also pointedly noted that "Yemen's National Dialogue Conference—which President Obama has praised—decided by a 90% majority that the use of drones in Yemen should be criminalised."[72] The

NDC's job was to decide Yemen's new constitutional framework moving forward. The fact that both it, and the national parliament, had now voted by significant margins for an end to US drone strikes was pointedly ignored by the Obama administration—just as it had closed its ears to long-running protests by Pakistani legislators.

A CONFLICT WITHOUT LIMITATIONS

Back in the United States, even some senior military and intelligence figures were unclear about what President Obama's secret air war was trying to achieve. "I am not convinced that what we are doing in Yemen makes sense either politically or even that we're striking the right people," says a recent former senior Department of Defense official. "You get more of a sense that we may be involved in a local conflict more than a global conflict."[73] In scale and ambition, the 2012 Yemen offensive had more in common with the recent Libyan conflict than with other counterterrorism campaigns. There, US and European aircraft had acted as a proxy air force for rebels on the ground trying to dislodge the Gaddafi government. To the anger of some, Obama had not sought congressional approval for that war. As a *New York Times* editorial complained, "the president must receive Congressional authorization or terminate the mission. No word games can get him off the hook."[74] The same could be said for Yemen. It was more than a decade since the Authorization for Use of Military Force Against Terrorists (AUMF) had been passed as emergency legislation by Congress. Yet US officials were still claiming it provided them the necessary domestic authority to strike where and when they wanted in the War on Terror—including in Yemen. "There is nothing in the AUMF that restricts the use of military force against al-Qa'ida to Afghanistan," John Brennan insisted.[75]

Some US legislators challenged these claims. In an epic 13-hour filibuster on the floor of the Senate against the appointment of Brennan as CIA Director, Rand Paul told fellow Congressmen that "the problem is as this war has dragged on, they take that authorization of use of force to mean pretty much anything. And so they have now said that the war has no geographic limitations, so it's really not a war in Afghanistan, it's a war in Yemen, Somalia, Mali. It's a war in unlimited places."[76] In turn, Obama officials insisted that the AUMF still provided the necessary domestic legal basis for covert drone strikes. Groups such as Al Shabaab and Al Qaeda in the Arabian Peninsula were "associated forces" it was argued, defined by Department of Defense General Counsel Jeh Johnson as: "An organized, armed group that has entered the fight alongside al Qaeda, and ... a co-belligerent with al Qaeda in hostilities against the United States or its coalition partners."[77]

Yet Somali group Al Shabaab had been founded in 2006 with no link to the 9/11 atrocities, while AQAP had been forged in Yemen only in 2009. Concerns that AUMF no longer provided a fit domestic legal basis for the secret drone wars were shared by some senior figures within the intelligence community itself. "The tether between some things in my mind that seem appropriate and lawful and due and necessary with the current threat—the tether from that action as justification back to the AUMF is getting very very taut," says former CIA Director Michael Hayden. "The logic sometimes gets very distant from those who participated in or supported the attacks of 9/11, which is roughly the line we took at the beginning."[78] Barack Obama appeared not to disagree:

> The AUMF is now nearly 12 years old. The Afghan war is coming to an end. Core al Qaeda is a shell of its former self. Groups like AQAP must be dealt with, but in the years to come, not every collection of thugs that labels themselves al Qaeda will pose a credible threat to the United States. Unless we discipline our thinking, our definitions, our actions, we may be drawn into more wars we don't need to fight, or continue to grant Presidents unbound powers more suited for traditional armed conflicts between nation states.

Obama's promise in the same speech that he would be "engaging Congress and the American people in efforts to refine, and ultimately repeal, the AUMF's mandate" had come to little as this book went to print.[79] The president had already blocked as "unnecessary" efforts by Congress to extend the scope of the AUMF.[80] Yet the administration showed little interest in actually repealing the authorization, which officials still insisted granted Obama those powers necessary to bomb Yemen, Somalia, and elsewhere without any reference to the legislature.

Whatever their domestic legal status, Washington's secret drone strikes in Yemen had continued. Following the routing of Al Qaeda and Ansar al-Sharia from Yemen's southern cities, militants had dispersed throughout the country in mid-2012. The drones had followed. With strikes now recorded in almost every province of Yemen, fear among the general population appeared to be growing. According to local reporter Saeed al-Batati, "everywhere now in Yemen there were victims, people had relatives who were killed by the American drone strikes." Clinical psychologist Dr. Peter Schaapveld presented a report to British MPs, based on a limited number of interviews with airstrike victims: "Entire communities—including young children who are the next generation of Yemenis—are being traumatised and re-traumatised by drones," Schaapveld claimed in a study which echoed similar findings in Waziristan.[81] This helped feed an increase in anti-US sentiment. "You will struggle to find anybody to say a good word about the Americans or American policy here in Yemen," London *Times* correspondent Iona Craig told the author.[82] Academic Gregory Johnsen notes that Al Qaeda in Yemen had, according to the US State Department's own estimates, grown from just a few hundred members to thousands since Washington had begun targeted killings in the country.[83]

Yet a growing dislike of Washington need not translate into anger at attacks on Al Qaeda. "You would think that everybody in Sana'a would be like, 'Yes, this is terrible, our sovereignty!' But no, there are so many people who are pro-drones in Sana'a," says reporter Vivian Salama. "Like crazy pro-drones. Because they feel like outside of Sana'a, it's the Wild West."[84] Just as in Pakistan, the drones had changed Al Qaeda's behavior in Yemen, suppressing its ability to openly organize. Yet it remained a potent and lethal force, often venting fury at remotely piloted US strikes by lashing out at locals. A suicide attack killed almost 100 troops in the capital in May 2012, for example, with Al Qaeda later stating that the intended targets were Yemen's Defense Minister and "the US advisers who operate the war against our families."[85] The question for Washington—as so often with its targeted killing program—was whether any tactical success against Al Qaeda might yet undermine longer term US goals in the region.

SOMALIA: A FREE-FOR-ALL

In March 2014, an investigator told the UN Human Rights Council that of 35 problematic drone strikes which his team was presently examining, only one related to the East African nation of Somalia: "That is not to be taken to imply that the level of civilian deaths in Somalia as the result of the use of remotely piloted aircraft is lower or higher than elsewhere," British barrister Ben Emmerson noted. "It merely confirms that there was very little reliable independent evidence of civilian casualties."[86] The presence of media and some local governance in even the most troubled parts of Yemen and Pakistan ensured that covert US drone strikes were reasonably well charted there, even if not fully understood. Much of Somalia had neither governance nor media, enabling the Pentagon and CIA to operate with near-freedom from scrutiny. Somalia was the original "failed state." To the north were the breakaway regions of Somaliland and Puntland. To the south was territory variously controlled by Islamist militants, by foreign occupying troops and a UN peacekeeping force, and even by pirates. "The Somali government is in no position whatsoever to question the soldier that is standing at the gate of the presidential palace defending him from the attack from Al Shabaab," Somali diplomat Omar Jamal told reporter Jack Serle in 2012. "Whoever comes trying to help them defeat Al Shabaab, they are more than welcome . . . they are given a licence to completely ignore any local or international law."[87]

In 2012, UN monitors had published photographs of CIA helicopters "reportedly used to deploy US Special forces from Djibouti to northeastern Somalia."[88] Investigative reporter Jeremy Scahill had also described not only a CIA counterterrorism center adjacent to Mogadishu airport but also how the Agency made use of a prison run by Somalia's own intelligence services to interrogate terror suspects. "While declaring an end to the secret prisons [of the Bush era] Obama and his counter-terrorism team found a backdoor way of continuing them," Scahill asserted.[89] The reason for this heavy US intelligence and Special Forces presence was made clear in a frank US national security assessment from 2006, later leaked by Chelsea (Bradley) Manning:

Somalia is the epicenter of terrorist activity in the region, an active safe haven qualitatively different from others in the world because it overlays a failed state. The al Qaida presence in Mogadishu is part of a larger network, Al Qaida East Africa (AQEA), which maintains operatives, facilitators and associates in Somalia, Kenya, Tanzania, Djibouti, Ethiopia and probably Sudan and Eritrea. AQEA has close ties to al Qaida core leadership in Pakistan and Afghanistan, and has links to the UAE, Saudi Arabia and Yemen and appears to be funded by sources in these countries as well as the Somali diaspora.[90]

When the United States assessed the global risk represented by Al Qaeda in the immediate wake of 9/11, most of Somalia's inwardly-directed militant activity was judged of little concern. The exception was Al Qaeda East Africa (AQEA), the terrorist group's regional cell, which in November 2002 targeted a hotel popular with Israeli tourists in Mombasa, Kenya, killing 13 people. Simultaneously, the group had tried to shoot down an Israeli-chartered passenger jet. George W. Bush had no intention of following his father's example by deploying conventional US forces to Somalia. Instead, the Pentagon and CIA at first sought to dismantle AQEA by working with proxy militia groups. Just as in Yemen and Pakistan, the early focus in what became known as the "Shadow War of Mogadishu" was often on seizing targets: "Operation Black Hawk's aim was to kill or capture the 20 or so main members of the al-Qaida cell in East Africa" noted *Army Times* reporter Sean Naylor, who interviewed a number of Special Forces and CIA operatives involved at the time. "Rather than use US forces to do this, the CIA's plan would have Somali warlords capture the al-Qaida personnel before turning them over to the US to send—or 'render'—them to an American ally or one of the agency's secret prisons."[91]

In an echo of the Musharraf regime's actions in Pakistan, "Somali militias attempted to sell innocent Arabs living in Mogadishu to Western intelligence services" according to academic Stig Jarle Hansen, who has chronicled the rise of Al Shabaab.[92] In 2003, for example, warlord Mohammed Dere grabbed supposed Al Qaeda member Suleiman Abdallah from a hospital bed in Mogadishu. A later UN investigation described his extraordinary rendition to Afghanistan, where Abdallah was held by the United States for five years without charge.[93] While there, he was abused as part of the CIA's torture program. A case study in the *Annals of Internal Medicine* describes a man with the pseudonym "Rashid" (understood to be Abdallah) as suffering "severe beatings, prolonged painful stress positions, prolonged solitary confinement, forced nakedness and humiliation, sleep deprivation, withholding of food, sexual assault (anal rape and sodomy), forced intravenous medication during interrogation that he thought might be a 'truth serum' and painful shackling." Author Dr. Sondra Crosby concluded: "Rashid was given a document upon his release that confirmed his confinement as well as his innocence. I have a high degree of medical certainty that he was tortured while in US custody."[94] As international and domestic outrage grew at Bush's torture program, the administration began exploring other methods of containing Al Qaeda and its alleged associates.

Proxy War

In the early 2000s, a loose coalition of moderate and radical factions in Somalia had come together to form the Islamic Courts Union. In some ways, the ICU resembled the Taliban in Afghanistan a decade earlier: an attempt by a religiously inspired bloc to wrest control of their nation away from warlordism. The ICU was a popular draw for many in the international Somali diaspora, keen to see their ancestral nation united under an Islamist banner. Like the Taliban too, some factions of the ICU were overtly influenced by Al Qaeda. One of these was Al Shabaab ("The Youth"), an extremist Somali element which numbered among its supporters former Afghanistan war veterans and remnants of Al Qaeda East Africa. Usman Ahmed had grown up in Sweden but now traveled home with his wife in the hope of building a new country, though he insists "I was never Al Qaeda, never Al Shabaab." Instead Ahmed, like many others, supported more moderate factions, he says today.[95] Within months of forming, the ICU had seized control of much of the south of the country along with the capital and had set about forming its own government. Washington was alarmed—viewing the ICU as a direct threat to regional stability. It eventually backed a proxy invasion of Somalia by 10,000 Ethiopian troops in December 2006, which soon saw the ICU abandon the capital.[96] For the first time since 9/11, the Pentagon ordered JSOC to carry out airstrikes in Somalia. On January 7, 2007, an AC-130 gunship attacked a bogged-down convoy near the Kenyan border which had been tracked by a Predator drone. The primary target was Al Shabaab leader Aden Hashi

Ayro. Though he survived, there were reports of multiple civilian deaths. As the *New York Times* noted at the time:

> According to Abdul Rashid Hidig, a member of Somalia's transitional parliament who represents the border area, the American air strikes in the area wiped out a long convoy of vehicles carrying Islamist leaders trying to flee deeper in the bush. "Their trucks got stuck in the mud, and they were easy targets," he said. Mr. Hidig said two civilians were also killed. But representatives of the Islamist forces said that the number of civilian deaths was much higher.[97]

Unusually for a clandestine action, US officials openly discussed the bombing—with a Pentagon spokesman telling CBS News that the strike was based on intelligence "that led us to believe we had principal al-Qaeda leaders in an area where we could identify them and take action against them."[98] Another US official later offered a different version: "Frankly, I don't think we know who we killed."[99] The AC-130 attack on Ayro was one of around 10 known US targeted killing operations in Somalia between 2007 and 2011, which also utilized helicopter gunships, cruise missile strikes, and even naval bombardments. In his memoirs, General Stanley McChrystal recalls being at JSOC's Iraq headquarters while waiting "for a missile impact two thousand miles away in a rural compound in Somalia."[100] The target was once again Ayro, who this time did not survive. McChrystal makes no mention of the terrorist leader's wife and children, who reportedly perished alongside him.[101] Ayro's death was certainly a blow to Al Shabaab, with the group vowing "to take revenge on Americans and American interests."[102] Yet any hope such killings might improve the security situation in Somalia itself were misplaced. "Ethiopia toppled a fairly popular regime in the ICU, and ran into the teeth of a broad-based Somali backlash against its presence," as a paper prepared for the US Joint Special Operations University noted.[103] When the Ethiopians finally retreated having crushed the Islamic Courts Union, they left behind a power vacuum which the more extremist Al Shabaab was well-placed to fill. The group was also drawing to its ranks a new wave of radicalized Westerners who, according to US government analysts, were motivated "by a sense of Somali nationalism, jihadist propaganda, and the presence of foreign troops in the country. . . . This includes North Americans, including at least 20 young men who were recruited from Minneapolis alone [home to a large Somali immigrant community], and recruits from European countries with large Somali diasporas."[104] By the time Barack Obama became President in 2009, radical militants were once again in control of Mogadishu, and much of the fractured nation.

INFORMATION VACUUM

In Yemen and Pakistan, armed drones had become the primary means by which the CIA and Pentagon targeted alleged militants and terrorists. Yet no more than ten US drone strikes had been confidently confirmed in Somalia by early 2015.[105] Always the work of JSOC, these took place with the active consent of the Transitional Federal Government in Somalia and its successor. This did not, however, guarantee that such operations were lawful. After decades of civil war, Somalia was the subject of an international arms embargo which forbade military activity by any other than Security Council-approved forces. A UN team attempted to track the unregulated and possibly illegal use of remotely piloted aircraft within Somalia in 2011: "The Monitoring Group currently considers UAVs to be of an exclusively military [purpose]; their importation to and use in Somalia therefore represents a potential violation of the arms embargo," its annual report noted. With drones beyond the control of local air traffic control, one had almost accidentally downed a charter aircraft with 112 African Union troops on board, according to the United Nations.[106] No nation ever publicly accepted responsibility for the incident.

AFSOC had begun flying regular Predator missions over Somalia in mid-2010, according to former operators. These flew from Camp Lemonnier, the same Djibouti airfield as the Yemen-bound flights.[107] Yet the operational tempo in Somalia was very different. "We had one aircraft flying in Somalia which would happen every week, once a week or so," recalls Brandon Bryant. "It wasn't very often because there was a bunch of stipulations." There was a lively debate in Washington about whether Al Shabaab should even be targeted, with reporter Daniel Klaidman describing a meeting in February 2010, at which the Pentagon's chief legal counsel Jeh Johnson had blocked plans to target the group: "Johnson said he would no longer approve the targeted killing of Al Shabaab members. There would be exceptions for the most senior operatives, those who had 'dual-hatted' status as sworn members of al-Qaeda, but it was no longer his view that the Shabaab was broadly covered under the AUMF." Though there are few public records of any US targeted killings in Somalia for this period, Klaidman describes them as dropping "precipitously" in the wake of Johnson's ruling.[108]

The first known JSOC drone strike in Somalia came with an attempt to kill Bilal al-Berjawi in June 2011. Stripped of his UK nationality nine months previously, he was according to his Al Shabaab obituary a key liaison between a re-emerging Al Qaeda East Africa and the Somali militant group, and so fitted neatly Johnson's "dual hatted" rule. Though badly injured al-Berjawi survived, only to be killed six months later by a JSOC Reaper (see chapter 6). Throughout 2011 and 2012, there were many dozens of reported airstrikes targeting Al Shabaab in southern Somalia. Some could be verified. An attack on militant training camps was confirmed by Somalia's deputy Defense Minister, for example, who while refusing to say who carried out the bombings noted that "the foreigners and senior officials of the terrorist group are afraid. They secretly hide amongst the civilians. The airstrikes will continue until we minimize the enemy from our country."[109] On another occasion, French and US officials each suggested that aircraft of the other nation had tried to kill Al Shabaab leader Ahmed Godane.[110]

With so many foreign military and intelligence operations taking place in Somalia—many of which the perpetrators were keen to deny—it was perhaps inevitable that this information vacuum would be exploited for propaganda purposes. More unexpected was the source. Between July 2011 and October 2012, more than 100 "US drone strikes" in Somalia were reported by Iranian news agency Press TV.[111] A bombing in Kismayo in September 2011 was said to have killed nine women and children, the first reported civilian deaths from drone operations in Somalia. On another occasion, "A US drone strike has killed at least 16 civilians and injured 50 others in southern Somalia near the border with Kenya," it was claimed. Between them, these Press TV reports listed hundreds of deaths, among them scores of civilians.

Yet almost every reported "drone strike" was a fabrication. Investigative reporter Emma Slater attempted to trace any record of more than 50 supposed incidents. Named "officials" cited in Press TV's reports turned out not to exist, while "no representatives from the

United Nations, Amisom (the African Union Mission in Somalia), non-government organisations, or journalists in Somalia were able to confirm the strikes." As a senior UN official told Slater, "Press TV is not a reliable source. It exaggerates and openly fabricates reports."[112] Quite why the Iranian broadcaster chose to fake these "drone strikes" was never made clear. State-funded, it may simply have been exploiting the information vacuum in Somalia as part of Tehran's broader, decades-long cold war with Washington. Slater's reporting on fabricated claims of drone strikes in Somalia would help win her a prestigious British Journalism Award.[113] With some irony, her employer the Bureau of Investigative Journalism had previously been accused by anonymous US intelligence officials of producing "wildly inaccurate" estimates of US drone strikes.[114] Yet it was Washington's ongoing refusal to publish details of any covert or clandestine attacks—or to confirm or deny civilian deaths when they occurred—which so often laid it open to attack. As Barack Obama himself would later admit of the drone targeted killing campaign:

> When we cannot explain our efforts clearly and publicly, we face terrorist propaganda and international suspicion, we erode legitimacy with our partners and our people, and we reduce accountability in our own government.[115]

Even so, Washington appeared unable to overcome its addiction to secrecy regarding details of the covert drone program—to the detriment of civilian victims and public accountability alike.

THE LONG ROAD HOME
Afghanistan and Pakistan

As Pakistan grappled with its worst floods in many years during the summer of 2010, the country's Health Minister made a startling claim: "Health relief operations are not possible in the flood-affected areas of Jacobabad because the airbase is with the United States," he told surprised members of the Senate's health committee. Khushnood Lashari's job was to ensure that vital aid reached those areas hardest hit by the devastating floods. With 18 million people affected and 2,000 so far killed, it was a major challenge. Yet there was a problem. The CIA had long secretly used the Shahbaz facility near Jacobabad for its drone campaign. Now, during one of Pakistan's worst-ever natural disasters, the Americans were allegedly refusing to allow the base's use for Pakistan's own humanitarian purposes, despite its being the largest facility in the region. As one Senator complained to *Dawn* newspaper, "It is very unfortunate that Americans can launch a drone attack from Shahbaz airbase but the government is helpless even in using the country's base for relief operations."[1] The US embassy in Islamabad was quick to rubbish the allegations as "completely false," insisting that Shahbaz "is a Pakistan Air Force base, commanded and operated by PAF forces."[2] This was only half-true. In reality, according to a former senior Pakistani military officer, the United States had for many years operated its own inner base hidden within Shahbaz.[3] If any block on relief aircraft using the airfield did exist it ended that same day, when transporter planes from the Pakistan Air Force began delivering aid to Jacobabad.[4]

The CIA's bombing campaign in FATA had seen a three weeks' pause from late July 2010, as American troops helped deliver vital relief supplies by helicopter and transporter plane across Pakistan's troubled regions. Yet there was significant pressure for airstrikes to resume, with the Agency's drones assigned a key role in a forthcoming anti-Taliban offensive. Simultaneous operations would take place on both sides of the "AfPak" border, with the expectation that this would herald the start of Pakistan's long-awaited assault on militants in North Waziristan. According to US defense officials, the plan was for the CIA's drones to hammer Haqqani Network elements fleeing into Pakistan. Floods or not, it was decided to proceed.[5] Between August and November 2010, the United States delivered more than 1,000 tons of aid to Pakistan's flood survivors and helped rescue more than 8,000 people.[6] At the same time, it conducted 59 drone strikes in the tribal areas, with at least 33 civilians among 360 or more reported killed. Forty-two homes were severely damaged or destroyed in the CIA's air campaign during this period.[7] There were few clearer examples of the complex and often contradictory nature of Washington's relationship with the troubled south Asian nation.

AFGHANISTAN: KILL NOT CAPTURE

Across the border, Stanley McChrystal's counterinsurgency strategy had been built in part around majorly reducing airstrikes. That policy had barely been road-tested before the "Runaway General" was dumped in the wake of the *Rolling Stone* scandal, after McChrystal and his close aides unwisely ridiculed senior Obama administration figures.[8] Replacing him in July 2010 as the third US commander in Afghanistan in just 13 months was David Petraeus, the charismatic General who had won plaudits for his role in the 2007 Iraq "surge" and had since risen to command CENTCOM. As part of Afghanistan's own "surge" of 30,000 extra US troops and an aggressive plan to defeat the Taliban militarily, Petraeus now oversaw a steep escalation in air attacks. Between August and November 2010, the allies released 3,064 bombs and missiles from the air—more than twice the number dropped in the same period in 2009.[9] A steep rise in bombings need not mean more civilian deaths. As UNAMA would note: "Although the number of air strikes increased exponentially, the number of civilian casualties from air strikes decreased in 2010." In fact they had more than halved to 171 killed, although numbers would slightly rise again in 2011.[10] Pressure on the United States and the International Security Assistance Force (ISAF) by the United Nations, by Afghanistan's government, and by others—coupled with an acceptance that civilian casualties could undermine the broader war effort—were proving effective. Greater precision from drone munitions might also have helped, with 1 in 10 Afghan airstrikes in 2010 now by remotely piloted aircraft.

Obama's Afghanistan surge carried a bloody price, with more than 1,600 US soldiers and almost 700 NATO allies killed during his first five years in office.[11] While regular troops bore the brunt of insurgent attacks, Special Operations Forces (most notably JSOC) stepped up a vicious "Kill/Capture" campaign against the Taliban's command structures. The number of JSOC strike teams in Afghanistan reportedly rose from 4 to 20 in less than a year, with waves of night raids across the country. These were heavily supported by armed Predator and Reaper drones, remotely flown by AFSOC out of Cannon AFB, New Mexico. "Usually at night time there was one raid at least over there, so you would be doing pre-raid stuff. If there was a village you'd be searching it, you'd be doing patterns-of-life on a house. You'd just be looking for dogs, animals, activity, and that was your job, to give these guys a clear picture of what they were going into," recalls former AFSOC sensor operator Brandon Bryant.[12] Yet what was happening below was now very different from Iraq, with far less focus on seizing the enemy.

The shift had its origins in Executive Order 13491 issued just two days into Barack Obama's presidency, which ended many of the abuses of the Bush era. Torture or "enhanced interrogation techniques" was banned, and everyone—the CIA and JSOC included—was now required to obey the same interrogation rulebook, the *US Army Field Manual*. The order also led to the shutting of all secret, permanent "ghost prisons" run by the CIA; it allowed full access for the Red Cross to US facilities and prisoners; and it restated Washington's commitment to the Geneva Conventions.[13] It was a bold move by Obama, sending a message that the United States hoped to reclaim some moral authority in its War on Terror (a term which was itself officially put out to pasture). Yet the strategy would eventually generate perverse effects. "We lack, as a nation, a place to put terrorists if we catch them," said US Senator Lindsey Graham in 2013, characterizing Obama's new approach. "I can tell you that the operators are in a bad spot out there. They know that if they capture a guy, it creates a nightmare. And it's just easier to kill 'em."[14] The *Washington Post* was reporting "dozens of targeted killings and no reports of high-value detentions" just a year into the president's first term.[15] The leaking of thousands of classified US military documents by Bradley (later Chelsea) Manning in 2010 led to revelations that the names of more than 2,000 alleged senior Taliban and Al Qaeda leaders featured on a "kill or capture list." According to the *Guardian*, some US Special Forces routinely killed suspects without attempting capture, and "also killed civilian men, women and children and even Afghan police officers who have strayed into its path."[16]

The CIA's aerial targeted killing program in Pakistan had become notorious. Yet in Afghanistan too, thousands were killed on the ground in a program whose conduct often lay starkly at odds with the professed values of those responsible. One former officer with ISAF later recounted for the author an incident in which an Afghan suspected insurgent was being held in custody. It was decided that, while there was not enough evidence to hold the man, there were suitable grounds to assassinate him. "There then followed this conversation. 'OK, so how long do we need to wait [after] he's been released from custody before it would be appropriate to kill him?' Obviously, the easiest place to kill him was as soon as we've let him out of the front gate, but that would have been a bit unsporting."[17]

Regular ISAF troops had little control over the actions of US Special Forces coming into their areas, yet were left to deal with the consequences. "You would get a phone call at half midnight and be given four grid references and told. . . . 'We're taking over your battle space for the next three hours, move all of your units out. We will give you the battle space back at the end.' And then you would say 'What are you going to do?' 'We can't tell you. You will find out later,'" complains former British Army intelligence officer Mike Martin. "Some of us called them cowboys," recalls Marc Lindemann, a captain with German Military Intelligence who later wrote a best-selling book about his country's war in Afghanistan: "There were problems in that the American Special

Forces didn't cooperate with us, for example, when entering our Area of Responsibility in Kunduz. We had a few examples where they just came in, carried out an operation, and left behind some killed people on the ground. Within the German military, the Americans were generally seen as not taking care in preventing civilian casualties."[18] Mike Martin shares that view:

> They were killing people and they didn't even know their name let alone their tribe. They just picked them up from signals intelligence. And so we repeatedly tried to say there's a wider context here. In the end they introduced something called a "No Strike List" . . . but getting people put on that was like turning wine into water, because the Special Forces were incredibly powerful and they could basically do whatever the fuck they wanted.[19]

These killings, well-targeted or otherwise, were not restricted to ground forces. AFSOC's drone operations (and also some by conventional American and British RPA squadrons) began more closely to resemble the CIA's actions across the border, albeit under tighter Rules of Engagement. As a senior Agency official told the *National Journal*: "It's a lot simpler and easier for a sniper to shoot or to use a Predator to launch a lawful attack than to detain and interrogate prisoners. . . . Once they're dead, then Human Rights Watch or Amnesty International doesn't bring a habeas [corpus] case for them. If we're not going to hold them, we're 'pure.' "[20] Whatever the legality of the CIA's operations, battlefield targeted killings did at least appear to conform to the laws of war. Yet some have since raised troubling questions: According to former British Military Intelligence officer Martin, "the Special Forces stuff that I used to see—they used to put together target packs that were meant to be legal and then classify them and they would go to a Judgement Board that was basically officers who all said, 'Yeah, that's fine you can kill him.' And they made it sound like it was some kind of legal process. It was complete bollocks. If they had gone to a court of law they would have laughed at it."[21]

Those supportive of the "Kill/Capture" program in Afghanistan instead believe it was an effective—and lawful—response to the escalating Taliban insurgency. One senior Air Force officer who served there believes each targeted killing had to be judged on its effects: "In terms of political-strategic impacts those can be as damaging as airstrikes or as help-ful, if we're removing somebody who needs to be removed. Zarqawi and bin Laden being the spectrum of guys that got taken out in different ways to similar effect."[22] Asked about Britain's own battlefield targeted killings, a senior RAF commander insisted to the author that any such operation could only take place within very tight parameters and with an expectation of zero civilian casualties: "I think we also have to recognize that warfare is not tidy. We want to make it as discreet as we can and I think precision weapons bring with them the ability to be clear in purpose that we've not had before."[23] Most of those targeted and killed by land or air were alleged insurgents. That said, as many as half of all civilian casualties caused by the United States in Afghanistan were inflicted by its own Special Forces troops, studies for ISAF had shown.[24] Afghanistan's President Hamid Karzai had pleaded for the Special Forces operations to be reined back, with even his own cousin shot dead in error during one night raid.[25] Those pleas were mostly ignored.

THE REAL ENEMY

Almost a decade on from the 2001 atrocities, Obama officials were still insisting that Al Qaeda remained the focus of the CIA's drone strikes in Pakistan. In 2010, for example, the State Department's chief legal adviser Harold Koh noted that "we continue to fight the perpetrators of 9/11."[26] Yet relentless pressure—not least by those same lethal drone strikes—had by now severely degraded the Al Qaeda network. As the head of Britain's domestic security service noted that same year, MI5 had seen a one-third drop in "priority plots and leads" emanating from Pakistan, which was "partly attributable to the pressure exerted on the Al Qaida leadership there."[27] Barack Obama made much the same point on the ninth anniver-sary of 9/11 when he told journalists: "One of the things that we've been very successful at over the last two years is to ramp up the pressure on Al Qaida and their key leaders. And as a consequence, they have been holed up in ways that have made it harder for them to operate."[28] With the death of Osama bin Laden, Al Qaeda Central was soon being described as "inef-fective" with just two senior figures remaining whose deaths "would mean the group's defeat."[29] Yet drone strikes in the tribal region had continued at a fierce tempo.

As already outlined in chapter 5, by 2008 the CIA's covert anti-Al Qaeda campaign was in truth providing cover for a border-straddling counterinsurgency against the Afghan Taliban. Reports by monitoring groups indicate that only on a few known occasions was Al Qaeda the intended target in the CIA's autumn 2010 bombing campaign, for example, as when the alleged head of its Pakistani operations Abdul Razzak was killed. Other strikes targeted an alleged European terror plot (see chapter 6). Yet almost all other CIA bombings were focused on the Haqqani Network and other Taliban groups fighting the Afghan insurgency. A leaked CIA briefing document obtained by McClatchy reporter Jonathan Landay supported this view. Analysis showed that of 95 Pakistan drone strikes recorded by the CIA between October 2010 and September 2011, at least 43 had no connection to Al Qaeda by the Agency's own admission. As Landay noted, "at least 265 of up to 482 people who the US intelligence reports estimated the CIA killed during a 12-month period . . . were not senior al Qaida leaders but instead were 'assessed' as Afghan, Pakistani and unknown extremists."[30] Only in 2013 would Barack Obama concede that many covert drone strikes were in fact linked to "force protection" for Coalition troops in Afghanistan.[31] This switch in US targeting within Pakistan's tribal areas from Al Qaeda to insurgent groups did much to drive a wedge between Washington and Islamabad believes analyst Talat Masood, a retired Pakistani three-star General:

> The American concept of a military operation within Pakistan, and a Pakistani military operation on its own territory, are very different. This they do not understand. We are killing our own people. Americans are killing their so-called enemies. So even if the people have risen against the [Pakistani] state and are threatening its existence, the fact is we can always win them over. We don't want to multiply the militancy. We want to minimize the militancy.[32]

The CIA had once focused heavily on smashing Baitullah Mehsud's Taliban faction as a prelude to the Pakistan Army's offensive in South Waziristan. Islamabad had embraced that drone campaign, since it damaged a potent enemy. Yet now Washington was blitzing the "good Taliban" in North Waziristan, groups which Islamabad still saw as valuable regional proxies. While both the United States and Pakistan wanted a secure and stable Afghanistan, neither could agree on what that might look like or how to get there. A secret cable from US ambassador Ann Patterson summed up Pakistan's expected position when Washington finally quit Afghanistan: "General Kayani [head of the Pakistan military] has been utterly frank about Pakistan's position on this. In such a scenario, the Pakistan establishment will dramatically increase support for Taliban groups in Pakistan and Afghanistan, which they see either as ultimately likely to take over the Afghan government or at least an important counter-weight to an Indian-controlled Northern Alliance."[33]

Islamabad's critical error was assuming that, as in the 1990s, it would be given a free hand in deciding the fate of its western neighbor. Yet with 100,000 US troops now on the ground in Afghanistan (and Obama's reputation on the line), the outcome there was just as vital to US domestic interests. As former CIA analyst Bruce Riedel, the author of Barack Obama's original "AfPak" policy, bluntly put it: "This strategy is focused on a concise goal, and I think the President made that very clear. And it's a goal that is about protecting American citizens and American interests."[34]

With Pakistan's military chief General Kayani now wavering on confronting the Taliban in North Waziristan, US media reports throughout autumn 2010 carried a series of thinly veiled threats from Washington. The CIA was demanding the right to fly drones directly over Pakistan's major cities, it was claimed. Meanwhile US commanders began calling for the right to unilaterally insert troops into Pakistan at will, to capture or kill militants.[35] When Kayani himself visited the United States in October 2010, Barack Obama added to the pressure. "Dropping in" on a meeting of Kayani with the US national security team, Obama reportedly told the General that Pakistan was expected to deliver on the North Waziristan campaign, which the Army and ISI chiefs had seemingly promised to US Vice President Joe Biden 18 months earlier.[36] Yet now Kayani demurred. According to one of those with knowledge of the meeting, he instead handed Obama a dossier with the words: "Mr. President, this is my analysis of where and why you're going wrong in Afghanistan. And this will also explain why I am afraid that I cannot meet your expectations in what you want me to do."[37]

Kayani was conscious of the high cost Pakistan had paid the previous year. The army had lost 800 troops in its South Waziristan and Swat Valley offensives—a 50 per cent rise in fatalities on 2008.[38] Taliban militants had also retaliated with suicide bombings across the country, and more than 2,600 Pakistani civilians were killed in terrorist attacks in 2009 alone.[39] With up to 20,000 battle-hardened militants from multiple factions still holed up in North Waziristan among almost half a million civilians, there were serious doubts within the highest ranks of Pakistan's military whether such an operation could even be successfully mounted. In the incongruous setting of a Chinese restaurant in Islamabad, a Taliban operative once boasted to the author of how the Pakistan Army was powerless to challenge militant activity in North Waziristan. I was shown high-quality images taken from a Taliban forward observation post in Miran Shah, revealing the Army bottled up in its local base. Government supply convoys were forced to negotiate access through militant checkpoints and on occasion, Army patrols were assaulted "to show the military who is in charge." Weeks prior to my meeting, nine soldiers had died and a dozen more were seriously injured in an ambush outside the town, after which militants had desecrated the corpses.[40]

Kayani's refusal to act on North Waziristan was a view not universally shared within the Pakistan military. As General Athar Abbas, at the time the Army's chief spokesman later told BBC Urdu: "The delay has strengthened the extremists . . . they have grown in numbers and they are more resourceful."[41] Months of improved US–Pakistani security cooperation were also now threatened. "Many of us hoped that the Pakistani Army would follow up on the success of the 2009 Swat campaign by "clearing out" North Waziristan. It didn't happen," notes Cameron Munter, sworn in as Ambassador to Islamabad just two weeks before the Pakistan Army chief's Washington visit. "I have two guesses why that was the case: first, because the militants in North Waziristan were very strong. Second, and perhaps more compelling, as US-Pakistani relations deteriorated the political task of getting the Pakistani people to support what would have been a tough and bloody campaign became more difficult, and coordination with ISAF [in Afghanistan] more politically charged as well."[42] Any hope that Kayani's refusal to strike North Waziristan was a temporary hiatus was soon dashed.

A PROBLEM ASSIGNMENT

The public naming of the CIA's Islamabad station chief in late 2010 has become a defining moment in the collapse of US-Pakistani relations. In the Hollywood movie *Zero Dark Thirty*, angry crowds are seen protesting drone strikes outside the US embassy, as they demand local CIA chief "Joseph Bradley" is jailed. At one point, the film's heroine turns to her outed boss to utter the words: "ISI fucked you." It was claimed by some that the revelation of Jonathan Banks's identity (his actual name) was a plot by Pakistan's own intelligence service, in revenge for a recent humiliation of their spy chief. The chosen conduit was supposedly local lawyer Mirza Shahzad Akbar, whom anonymous CIA sources would later claim planned "to put targets on the backs of Americans serving in Pakistan and Afghanistan."[43] In fact, the outing of Banks had its origins in a CIA bombing a year earlier, just a day after the killing of seven Agency operatives at Khost. One of the CIA's retaliatory strikes was aimed at Haji Omar Khan, a local Pakistan Taliban commander who appears to have died in the attack: certainly he was never reported alive subsequently. More clear was the fact that civilians had been killed, after the attack destroyed the home of Kareem Khan. His 17-year-old son Zahinullah, his schoolteacher brother Asif, and local stonemason Khaliq Dad all died. Khan later described seeing his son's corpse in the rubble: "Zahinullah had a wound on the side of his face and his body was crushed and charred," he recalled.[44] The attack that day was one of many in which the CIA had killed civilians in Pakistan, barely noticed by the outside world. But local journalist Khan ("linked to the Taliban," US officials would later anonymously brief inquiring journalists) wanted justice. He was also unafraid of any consequences: "My own life doesn't really matter. I'd be fearful if my family members were harmed yet that had already happened. There was nothing worse that could be done to me. And in any case I was on the moral high ground, the legal high ground," he later told the author.[45] Khan's subsequent actions would help lead to the naming of the local CIA station chief, in a lawsuit designed to grab the world's attention.

Recent Harvard law graduate Christopher Rogers moved to Islamabad in late 2009, hired by the American NGO CIVIC[46] to assess the impact on civilians of Pakistan's recent military operations. As Rogers now admits, so little was then known about casualties of US drone strikes that they barely featured in the planning stages of his report: "Civilian deaths from drone strikes just weren't on people's radars at the time. I remember getting the first calls from the *New York Times*: 'Guys, what's going on over there with this thing?' "[47] Washington-based think tank the New American Foundation was concerned enough to begin publishing casualty data on the CIA's strikes around the same time. As the project's director Peter Bergen recalls, "On the one hand the US government was either saying nothing on the record about the drone program, or making claims about no civilian casualties on background, while the Pakistanis were making claims about massive civilian casualties. Neither of these positions could both be true, and since drone attacks are public events I thought it would be useful to see what the public record was showing."[48] What that record indicated was that a significant number of those being killed by the CIA at the time were civilians.

By the time CIVIC's report was published in September 2010, Rogers had gathered enough evidence on drone deaths to dedicate a chapter to the subject. It represented the first major field examination of US drone strikes in Pakistan's tribal areas in more than six years of bombings. Nine drone strikes were analyzed, all of which took place during Obama's time in office. With access to Waziristan impossible because of the security situation, Rogers arranged for witnesses to travel to Peshawar and elsewhere for interview, and he also visited camps for internally displaced people on the edges of the tribal belt. His study flagged up major concerns: "It is almost certain that civilian casualties are higher than the US currently admits," he concluded. At the time, US officials were claiming that no more than 15 or 20 civilians had died since 2004, Rogers recalls. Yet as his report noted, "CIVIC uncovered more than 30 civilian deaths in only nine cases we investigated, including at least 14 women and children, all of which took place after January 2009."[49]

Rogers was keen to take further action, though feared US courts would be unwilling to engage on cases relating to national security: "I started asking, 'Why can't we file cases here domestically in Pakistan, going after US officials or even Pakistani officials who are complicit in these operations?' But I obviously needed a Pakistani lawyer who understood the law to see whether that was possible." Coincidentally, Rogers had met British-trained barrister Mirza Shahzad Akbar a few months earlier, and the two began discussing with the London-based legal charity Reprieve how such a case might be brought. What was needed was someone directly affected by a US drone strike. Kareem Khan, the journalist who had lost family members in December 2009, appeared the ideal candidate. Akbar issued legal papers in November 2010 which sought to sue the CIA for $500 million damages. The stunt might have warranted little notice but for one sentence:

> The undersigned believes that one person namely Jonathan Banks, an American national who is CIA's Islamabad Station Chief, is responsible for the murder of his son and brother.[50]

"When I filed against CIA, everyone even in Pakistan labelled us as crazies or mad people. Asking 'How could you sue the CIA? Nothing can come of it,'" Khan now recalls.[51] To this day, his lawyer Shahzad Akbar refuses to say who provided him with the name of Jonathan Banks. Some argued that it could only have been supplied by the ISI, since the CIA's station chief was supposedly in Pakistan under deep cover. The suggested motive for any ISI betrayal had occurred 10 days previously, with a lawsuit filed in the US District Court in Brooklyn, New York, on behalf of US victims of the Mumbai massacre. That suit claimed that "the ISI has long nurtured and used international terrorist groups, including Lashkar e-Taiba, to accomplish its goals," and cited ISI chief General Pasha in six of nine counts.[52] However, the Obama administration later filed papers with the court opposing on principle the naming of foreign government officials in such cases, and Pasha was able to visit Washington unimpeded on at least four occasions throughout 2011.[53] In fact, Jonathan Banks had been in Islamabad for over a year under his own name when he was "outed," with his identity known not only to top ranking Pakistani military, intelligence, and administration figures but also to senior diplomats of other nations.[54]

That did not stop US officials from pinning the blame directly on the ISI from the start. CIVIC's Christopher Rogers happened to be meeting with State Department officials at the Embassy on the day the CIA's man was outed: "I asked them, have you heard about this whole drones report? And they said 'You mean the ISI report?' I knew Shahzad and I knew where this really came from, and it wasn't ISI."[55]

With his cover now blown and cited for murder, Banks was forced to flee the country. The fast-escalating deterioration of relations "certainly affected our ability to coordinate with Pakistani intelligence on counter-terrorism," admits former Ambassador Cameron Munter, "in part because one of the elements of that deterioration was a serious decline in trust between the intelligence experts of both sides." That decline was nowhere near rock bottom. Islamabad had by now become a problem posting for the CIA's local commanders, and two more would be publicly named in relation to the secret drone war. In May 2011, a local TV station partially identified Banks's successor. And in November 2013, Imran Khan's political party named the new CIA station chief, accusing him and Agency director John Brennan of "committing murder and waging war against Pakistan." At the public press conference, lawyer Mirza Shahzad Akbar could clearly be seen on the PTI's podium almost three years to the day since he had first outed Banks, though he would decline to be drawn on whether he had played a role in this latest affair.[56]

BLOOD MONEY

Even before the outing of Banks, the United States was secretly complaining of obstruction by Pakistan's military and intelligence agencies, including "harassing [of] Embassy personnel."[57] Local media was in turn awash with stories of US "diplomats" stopped by police in Islamabad, Karachi, or Peshawar and allegedly found carrying unlicensed weapons or driving vehicles with fake plates.[58] The ISI was concerned that Washington had flooded Pakistan with dozens of undeclared spies, focused not only on the tribal areas but also on militants living in major cities. According to a European analyst with close knowledge of Pakistan's intelligence community, "there was a powerful view within ISI that it had lost control of chunks of its territory: with the US running shadow ops and even, ISI feared, responsible for terrorist attacks."[59] A former senior official with India's RAW intelligence service believes there were other concerns: "The drones were very successful in knocking down the militants, much more successful even than the wildest imagination of the ISI. In fact that is what surprised and soured their relationship. 'How the bloody hell are these Americans getting these people when we don't know about them?' "[60]

On January 27, 2011, the Pakistan Army began a fresh offensive against militants in the Mohmand tribal area of FATA. Helicopter gunships pounded "hideouts" while ground troops used mortars to dislodge Pakistan Taliban (TTP) cadres. More than 20,000 civilians would flee the fighting.[61] While this was not the North Waziristan assault the Americans wanted, Islamabad felt it was nevertheless demonstrating significant sacrifice, while bringing relief to NATO forces in eastern Afghanistan. Yet that same morning in Lahore, a burly American who had spent his adult life in the shadows was about to create a fresh crisis for the two nations. Raymond Davis was sitting at traffic lights when he noticed two young Pakistani men on a motorbike. Faizan Haider and Faheem Shamshad had been following Davis for some time. Now Faheem parted his clothing to reveal a gun. It was meant as an act of intimidation, say Pakistani intelligence sources. But Davis, believing the men represented a threat to his life, shot them both dead. Aggravating the affair, a "US consulate car" sent to rescue him ran over and killed a cyclist before itself fleeing.[62]

In different times, Davis might have been allowed to slip away and the matter glossed over. Three years later, when a JSOC commander and a CIA operative killed two alleged Al Qaeda kidnappers in a Sana'a barber shop, that was precisely what happened.[63] Yet relations between Islamabad and Washington were already too fraught, and Davis was placed in custody. Barack Obama used his weekly presidential address to emphasize the status of "our diplomat in Pakistan."[64] This was untrue, since Davis was in fact a CIA contractor who enjoyed no diplomatic protections. Neither were his victims ordinary robbers: instead they were small-time contractors either of Pakistan's ISI or of a local militant group.[65] Haider and Shamshad had monitored Davis for two hours that day, filming his movements on one of the five cellphones they carried. Both men also reportedly held licenses for their weapons, something no minor crook would bother with.[66] If the two were ISI contractors, their deaths would have been added to a toll of some 85 Pakistani intelligence operatives by then killed in the line of duty after 9/11.[67]

With his connections between the CIA, US Special Forces, and mercenary group Blackwater, Raymond Davis was a gift to Pakistan's conspiracy-obsessed media. Serving with the US 3rd Special Forces

Group in Afghanistan until 2003, Davis then worked for Blackwater in an unspecified role. Later taken on as a CIA contractor, Davis was part of an undercover combined Agency and JSOC "fusion" team based out of Lahore and Peshawar. Its reported role was to spy on militant and terrorist groups including Lashkar e-Taiba, responsible for the 2008 Mumbai massacre.[68] The "consulate car," which had so disastrously sped to Davis's aid, was most likely carrying colleagues. Now facing murder charges, Raymond Davis became a lightning rod for the simmering rage building between Washington and Islamabad. In order to maximize damage, every possible detail relating to the Davis case was leaked, from the contents of his cellphones to his wage slips. Unreported by Western media, the ISI even leaked the names of 55 alleged CIA and JSOC agents to a Pakistani paper. According to retired Brigadier Shauqat Qadir, "What they [ISI] did was pretty brilliant I thought, using this as an opportunity to get rid of all the rogue CIAs that were roaming around. They made that a precondition before anything else would happen."[69] Dozens of supposed US diplomats left the country, their visas abruptly cancelled. Despite Congress threatening to cut off billions of dollars in aid, the Lahore legal system continued to process Davis as a common criminal.[70]

By the hour the crisis deepened. Pakistan's Foreign Minister was sacked for challenging US claims.[71] The young widow of one of Davis's victims—convinced her husband's killer would escape justice—publicly committed suicide and demonstrations and riots swept the country.[72] On March 16, Davis was formally charged with two counts of murder after 48 days in custody. Yet within hours he was rushed out of Pakistan on a US military plane, after an estimated $2.3 million in blood money was paid on Washington's behalf to victims' relatives. Relations between the two countries were now at their lowest point since Pakistan's founding. As Cameron Munter, the US ambassador at the time notes with some understatement, "the immediacy of our counterterrorism difficulties made it hard for diplomats to balance the relationship between short-term and long-term interests." Even so, diplomats hoped they could salvage the relationship. Yet just a day after Davis's release—and seemingly oblivious to any crisis—the CIA unilaterally carried out the 202nd Pakistan drone strike of Barack Obama's presidency, in the process killing upwards of 40 civilians. It was, it was later claimed by a US official, an act of "retaliation" for the Davis affair.[73]

WHEN NO MEANS YES

The CIA had at first paused its drone campaign following the arrest of Raymond Davis. Yet three weeks later and with the contractor still sitting in a Lahore jail, the strikes resumed, once again hitting alleged militants in North and South Waziristan. Barely noticed by the media on March 16, 2010, the chaotic day of Davis's eventual release, the Agency had struck a car near the village of Datta Khel in North Waziristan, killing five alleged insurgents. It was that operation which perhaps alerted the CIA to a large gathering of men in the village itself, in an area with an apparent reputation as "a known hub of Taliban, Haqqani Network, and Al Qaeda activity."[74] Had Washington still had access to field intelligence from its erstwhile Pakistani allies, it would quickly have been able to ascertain that the 60 or so men below were not insurgents, but tribal elders gathered for an approved two-day *jirga*, or reconciliation meeting, to discuss a local mining dispute. "We in the Pakistan military knew about the meeting, we'd got the request 10 days earlier. It was held in broad daylight, people were sitting out in Nomada bus depot," the regional Army commander later revealed.[75] Along with the tribal elders were local Khassadar police and a small Taliban delegation. For the next 24 hours, the CIA kept Datta Khel under surveillance as it tried to assess the gathering. Denied accurate Pakistani intelligence from the ground, analysts decided they still had enough information to conduct a "signature strike," an attack based on perceived patterns of behavior below. After all, it was "a large group of heavily armed men, some of whom were clearly connected to Al Qaeda and all of whom acted in a manner consistent with A.Q.-linked militants," as an anonymous US official would later tell the *New York Times*.[76]

The US Ambassador to Islamabad tried to halt the planned strike when routinely consulted, saying it risked damaging US-Pakistani relations even further in the wake of the Davis affair. To this day, Cameron Munter believes his advice should have been heeded:

> I believe that, per the traditions of American foreign policy, the ambassador is the senior representative of the President in the country to which he's accredited, and should have final say over any US government initiatives (and personnel) in that country. All other agencies of

the US government should express their preferences, but the ambassador should decide.[77]

Instead, Munter was overruled by Agency Director Leon Panetta, and at 10.45 a.m. on March 17, the CIA's Predators again struck the village of Datta Khel. "It was in retaliation for Davis. The CIA was angry," one of Munter's aides told Associated Press.[78] Former ISI chief Asad Durrani also told this author that he believes the *jirga* strike was "clearly a show of [American] anger" in response to the Davis affair.[79] The result was carnage. Some 42 people died where they sat, most of them tribal elders. The most senior among them was Daud Khan, initially claimed by some to be a "senior Taliban figure." His son Noor told the author that this was "an absolute lie. My father was not a militant but an elder who was working day and night for his people." Hajji Babat was one of six local policemen killed, though he "was not an enemy of the United States of America or any other country" according to his son. The bus station and surrounding buildings were still burning six hours after the drone strike, eyewitnesses reported. Body parts were scattered for hundreds of yards, and had to be collected up in sacks. Fateh Khan, a former British Telecom worker, lost his 25-year-old nephew Din Mohammed. He later described how the body had to be buried in pieces, and that his nephew "left behind four children, all of whom now live in my house. His eldest child is currently only five years old."[80]

Anonymous US officials pushed back hard against news of significant civilian casualties:. "These people weren't gathering for a bake sale. They were terrorists," one told the *New York Times*. Pakistan was certainly clear about what had happened, with the FATA Secretariat secretly noting that "it is feared that all the [41] killed were local tribesmen."[81] While Prime Minister Gillani complained that the US's "irrational behaviour" made peace in the tribal areas less likely, President Zardari told a visiting US congressional delegation that the bombing was "intolerable."[82] Chief of the Army Staff General Kayani also "strongly condemned the Predator drone strike" in which "a jirga of peaceful citizens including elders of the area was carelessly and callously targeted with complete disregard to human life."[83] Kayani's deliberate referencing of a Predator was designed to send a clear message to Washington: Islamabad no longer felt itself bound by those long-standing secrecy arrangements which for seven years had protected the CIA's drone war.

While drone strikes halted for a month in the wake of the Datta Khel fiasco, their resumption in mid-April 2011 signaled that Washington now had little interest in Islamabad's cooperation or consent. The chosen target was linked to "good Taliban" leader Mullah Nazir, an ISI ally. As a senior Pakistani intelligence official complained to CNN, "It's unilateral action. What is this? A message [from the Americans] that it's business as usual, irrespective of what we ask of you? If it is, it's a crude way of getting your message across."[84] A US official retorted elsewhere that "this was about protecting Americans in the region. This is not about sending a signal to Pakistan."[85] Of longer term concern to Washington was the decision by Pakistan's Foreign Ministry to publicly condemn this latest strike. "Drone attacks have become a core irritant in the counter-terror campaign," a statement read. "Pakistan has taken up the matter with the US at all levels."[86] The Gillani government, concerned at the steep rise in drone strikes since Obama came to office, now sought to halt them. As the Foreign Ministry publicly protested almost every subsequent CIA bombing, its diplomats were ordered to bring international pressure to bear on the Americans. Pakistan was a signatory, for example, along with China and Russia, to a UN Human Rights Council motion successfully calling for an investigation into drone targeted killings.

From the beginning of the secret drone wars, maintaining at least the nominal consent of those nations on whose territories attacks took place had mattered to the United States. Bombings only occurred in Yemen and Somalia with the express permission of their governments—and had halted when consent was temporarily withdrawn. For seven years in Pakistan, similar permissions had been a given, even if informally. Now Washington was faced with a quandary. With the Afghan war still raging and no opportunity to put boots on the ground in Pakistan's tribal areas, drone strikes were still viewed as a necessity. "Consent" from Islamabad now became an interpretive affair. Once a month, the CIA faxed the ISI a general outline of where it was planning to bomb, the *Wall Street Journal* reported. The spy agency's failure to respond—along with the continued existence of the Restricted Operation Zones established years earlier to make sure that Pakistani aircraft didn't crash into the CIA's drones—was taken as "tacit consent to conduct strikes within the borders of a sovereign nation."[87]

Some pointed to Pakistan's not having shot down any US drones as a further measure of consent, though former President Pervez Musharraf dismissed this out of hand, believing that Washington would view any attack on its drones as a hostile act. "Then it's war and you will be beaten, and India will be very happy," he told the *New Statesman*.[88] There was still some policy ambivalence, however. Despite the cumulative crises of 2011—which would soon include the killing of Osama bin Laden by JSOC commandos deep inside Pakistan—the CIA's drones were allowed to keep operating from Shamsi airfield right up to the end of that year. What finally cost the Agency its decade-long loan of the strategically placed air-field was not even its fault. A NATO airstrike in November, which acciden-tally killed 28 Pakistani border troops, led in turn to a complete blocking of vital NATO supply lines through Pakistan; to a then-unprecedented 55-day halt to CIA drone strikes; and eventually, to the very public evic-tion of the Agency's drones from Shamsi airfield.[89]

The secret US drone campaign in Pakistan never fully recovered from the disastrous events of 2011, although the Agency still managed to launch 75 strikes that year. Over the following years, strike numbers would reduce to levels last seen under George W. Bush. That decline marked not only an adjustment to tensions with Pakistan, but to a shifting of priorities: the CIA now also operated from a new drone base in southern Saudi Arabia, and some of its Predators and Reapers were shifted there as the war against Yemen's Al Qaeda heated up. Back in Pakistan, the CIA also appeared to have changed its targeting practices. While strikes still focused on "good" and "bad" Taliban along with the remnant Al Qaeda and its proxies, non-combatant deaths were occurring far less frequently. In part, this was linked to the apparent phasing out of the controversial signature strikes. Of at least 220 people killed by the CIA in covert drone strikes in 2012, only 13 were confirmed by the Bureau of Investigative Journalism to be noncombatants. Over the next two years the Bureau flagged six further possible civilian deaths, none of which it was able to confirm.[90]

Barack Obama had a point—at least in recent times—when he claimed that "drones have not caused a huge number of civilian casualties, for the most part they have been very precise precision strikes against Al Qaeda and their affiliates."[91] Yet for Washington, this shift in strategy had come far too late. Pakistan was now loudly and aggressively opposing US policy. And internationally, the issue of covert drone strikes was proving almost

Table 10.1 CIA Directors and Pakistan drone targeted killings, 2004–2014

Director	Tenure	Strikes
George Tenet	July 11, 1997–July 11, 2004	1
Porter Goss	September 24, 2004–May 26, 2006	6
Mike Hayden	May 30, 2006–February 12, 2009	47
Leon Panetta	February 13, 2009–July 1, 2011	222
Mike Morrell	July 1, 2011–September 6, 2011	27
(acting Director)	November 9, 2012–March 8, 2013	
David Petraeus	September 6, 2011–November 9, 2012	58
John Brennan	March 8, 2013–December 31, 2014	43
(incumbent)		

as effective a stick with which to beat the United States as torture and rendition had been a decade earlier (table 10.1).

A NEW APPROACH IN PAKISTAN

The CIA had always known that the intended outcome of its targeted killing program (the removal of Washington's enemies) might one day be overwhelmed by other factors, most notably the role of drone strikes as a militant recruiting tool, and in the alienation of key allies. "I am totally open to the argument—indeed I would even make the argument now—that relatively speaking those second- and third-order effects have gained in importance in the overall basket of effects from the strikes," says one former senior US intelligence official. "And therefore it is at our peril that we treat those second- and third-order effects cavalierly or casually in this constant pursuit of the first-order effect that we just want to go make this guy dead."[92] Paul Pillar, former deputy director of the CIA's Counter Terrorism Center, makes a similar point:

> It cannot be denied that the direct kinetic effect on these groups has caused immediate damage to their operational capability. This may have come to be outweighed, however, by the broader, longer-term negative effect of incurring resentment and anger against the United States for the collateral damage and casualties.[93]

For a while, it looked as if a drone strike in Pakistan on Christmas Day, 2013, might have been the last in the CIA's nine-year secret program. With 27 recorded bombings that year—the lowest number of Agency strikes in the tribal areas since 2007—monitoring groups also for the first time could confirm no civilian casualties.[94] Among those who were killed were some of the most powerful leaders of the Taliban, including Hakimullah Mehsud, the leader of the Pakistan Taliban (TTP) who was blasted in his car in November. The CIA's targeted assassination of his predecessor four years earlier, an act of clientism for Islamabad, had brought no respite from terror. As US Secretary of State John Kerry noted on Hakimullah's death: "This is a man who absolutely is known to have targeted and killed many Americans, many Afghans and many Pakistanis. A huge number of Pakistanis have died at the hands of Mehsud and his terrorist organisation."[95] If Washington was expecting public thanks for killing Hakimullah Mehsud, it would be disappointed. Islamabad had been preparing for peace talks with the TTP and had begged the United States to hold off on its drone strikes until these concluded.

The United States finally agreed, and for almost six months the program was paused as Islamabad tried to carve out a peace deal. When those talks ultimately collapsed, Pakistan finally embarked on a military solution to the North Waziristan problem. After days of intense airstrikes—and the evacuation of 450,000 civilians from the area—thousands of Pakistani ground troops assaulted the tribal agency in late June 2014. Operation Zarb e Azb—the Prophet's Sword—may have come four years later than Washington had hoped for, yet it helped lead to a major rapprochement. When the CIA's drone strikes resumed on June 11, 2014, they once again had the tacit approval of Pakistan. As a senior Pakistani military source told the author, for the time being at least the strikes served Islamabad—though there was an acceptance that at some future point, US and Pakistani interests might once again diverge.

At the time of writing, the United States had conducted over 400 secret bombings in Pakistan since George W. Bush first approved the killing of Nek Mohammed back in June 2004. In those intervening years, an estimated 2,400 people had been killed by the CIA under seven different Directors. At least 400 of those killed were most likely civilians. What, then, had Washington actually achieved in South Asia? Many of the most powerful leaders of Al Qaeda and the Taliban had been assassinated, and those same groups had also been forced into making profound changes in the ways they operated. In an age of lightning-fast global connections, militants and terrorists in the tribal areas were often reduced to pre-industrial communication. "Al Qaeda Central" now barely existed, although its leader Ayman al-Zawahiri still eluded the vast US military-intelligence machine. The asymmetric advantages which the Agency's hunter-killer Predators and Reapers granted often appeared absolute. Yet still the Taliban's insurgency in Afghanistan had ground on. And regional groups bearing Al Qaeda's name were now wreaking havoc across North Africa and the Middle East. America's longer term regional goals had also suffered in the pursuit of short-term counterterrorism objectives, former US Ambassador Cameron Munter now believes:

> We struggled to maintain our common fight against the militants, we had less consensus to build the trust necessary for mutual efforts to reform the Pakistani economy, support good governance, and build the kind of stability in Pakistan that stood at the center of our post-Musharraf efforts to support Pakistan's success.[96]

There had also been a profound cost to Pakistan, both domestically and in its relations with the United States. The country experienced its own War on Terror after militants had turned on the state, the army and the people and an estimated 30,000 Pakistanis died in terrorist acts between 2001 and 2013. How many of those deaths represented displaced violence from the secret drone war is unclear, though time and again militants claimed to be motivated by revenge. Unable to strike at remote US operators, Pakistan's soldiers and civilians may instead have borne the consequences. Then there was the mistrust which often existed between the former allies. As a major opinion poll from Pew noted in 2012, "roughly three-in-four Pakistanis (74%) consider the US an enemy."[97] When the CIA's drone strikes resumed in summer 2014, Pakistan's politicians still could not resist exploiting this anti-American sentiment. Even as the military was once more secretly aiding US bombings, the government was publicly condemning every strike.

THE INCONSTANT VALUE OF A CIVILIAN LIFE

On December 10, 2009, an explosion in Spalaga, a hamlet on the Waziristan borders, killed four "foreigners" and two local tribesmen. Early reports attributed the incident to the CIA's drones, though in a rare public denial, the Pakistan military insisted that "No Predator drone strike has taken place today."[1] The army was deep into its bloody operation to clear South Waziristan of Hakimullah Mehsud's Taliban faction, which had already seen 600 alleged militants and 80 troops killed.[2] Any confirmed involvement by US drones might jeopardize local ceasefires, designed to keep the "good" Taliban out of the fight. US journalist Bill Roggio nevertheless directly challenged the ISPR's assertion: "US officials contacted by The Long War Journal confirmed the [drone] strike," he wrote, noting his sources' view that the Pakistanis "haven't achieved their goal: to kill or capture Hakeemullah Mehsud and Taliban's leadership, and they don't want to be one-upped by the US."[3] There were perhaps other reasons for sensitivities that day. Three thousand miles from Waziristan, Barack Obama was accepting the Nobel Peace Prize in Oslo's City Hall. In his speech, the president acknowledged he was accepting the award even as the United States remained in bloody conflict in

Afghanistan and Iraq: "The instruments of war do have a role to play in preserving the peace," he told assembled dignitaries. This was a leader struggling to reconcile global hopes for peace with a superpower almost permanently at war:

> Where force is necessary, we have a moral and strategic interest in binding ourselves to certain rules of conduct. And even as we confront a vicious adversary that abides by no rules, I believe the United States of America must remain a standard bearer in the conduct of war. That is what makes us different from those whom we fight.[4]

Perhaps uniquely, after less than a year in office Obama had been granted the Nobel Peace Prize in anticipation of what may yet come. Many hoped for an end to the US's eight-year-long "Global War on Terror." Yet just a week after receiving a gold medal inscribed with the Latin phrase *Pro pace et fraternitate gentium* ("For the peace and brotherhood of men"),[5] Obama would open a new front in that war when cruise missiles struck a Bedouin village in Yemen—in the process killing 44 civilians (see chapter 9). In the words of one US Senator, instead of bringing peace, Obama now risked trapping the United States in "a permanent global war on terrorism without any geographic limitations."[6] George W. Bush had gone to war in September 2001 to avenge the deaths of almost 3,000 civilians. Yet in the resulting battles, 18,000 or more civilians had been credibly reported killed by US and allied forces in Iraq, Afghanistan, and the covert drone wars.[7] Too often, operations by the US military and intelligence communities had placed an unacceptably low value on the lives of innocents—in turn risking American defeat in those same wars.

From War to COIN

On the eve of the invasion of Iraq by American and British forces in 2003, President Bush claimed that the fight was with Saddam Hussein's regime, and not with the Iraqi people: "I want Americans and all the world to know that coalition forces will make every effort to spare innocent civilians from harm," he insisted.[8] Yet during Washington's eight-year occupation of that country, an estimated 127,000 Iraqi civilians died as a direct result of war-related violence. Tens of thousands of those deaths were the work of insurgent groups such as Al Qaeda in Iraq, or a result of sectarian violence between Sunni and Shia Muslims. Yet 14,000 noncombatants were killed by Coalition troops, according to the respected monitoring group Iraq Body Count—most of these a result of US actions. Half died in the first few months of war, many of them victims of almost 20,000 Coalition airstrikes during the invasion.[9] As the war transitioned first into an uneasy occupation and later, into a full-blown counterinsurgency (COIN), civilians remained at risk from occupying forces. Professor Greg McNeal has made a comprehensive study of US military targeting procedures in modern warfare.[10] He identifies the noncombatant casualty value (NCV) as a crucial measure used by US military commanders in determining what levels of civilian casualties might be tolerated. For the Iraq invasion and its aftermath, this was set particularly high:

> If after mitigation a commander in Iraq expected a pre-planned operation would result in more than 30 noncombatant casualties [an NCV of 30], the strike would have to be briefed through the chain of command and authorised by the Secretary of Defense. If the collateral damage estimate was less than 30, the target was defined as a low collateral damage target, and, in most circumstances, required approval by either the Commander of Multinational Forces Iraq or a Division Commander.[11]

In short, as many as 30 Iraqi civilians could be killed in an operation without high-level approval being required. Even within a single conflict, the NCV assessment might rise or fall, depending on US political and strategic imperatives. According to McNeal, as the Pentagon's counterinsurgency in Iraq expanded, the NCV was lowered to 6, meaning that "only" half a dozen civilians might now be killed in pre-planned operations before commanders had to seek high-level approval. And in Afghanistan—where civilian deaths would become such a political concern—the NCV was eventually set at just one death. Such decisions could have profound implications for how non-combatants were then treated by US forces. Traveling incognito on Iraq's freeways in early 2004, the author saw first-hand how jumpy American troops could be, even before the insurgency had gained traction. On a number of occasions, our BBC team witnessed US soldiers firing above vehicles which in their view were getting too close to convoys. Such incidents could prove fatal. Data obtained by Bradley (later Chelsea) Manning and passed to Wikileaks revealed that hundreds of ordinary Iraqis were killed in such Escalation of Force (EOF) incidents, involving US military convoys and checkpoints. Secret military cables showed that by the Pentagon's own estimates, in their fear of attack by insurgents, occupying US troops were in reality far more likely to kill civilians: "681 cases of reported civilian deaths were caused by coalition Escalation of Force incidents. This is more than five times the number of insurgents killed in such incidents," one study of the leaked documents noted.[12]

As Iraq spiraled deeper into sectarian violence and insurgency, civilians paid an ever-greater price. Washington's troop surge in 2007 was aimed at creating a "fire break" in this bloodshed, explicitly placing US forces in harm's way in order to protect communities (900 American troops died in 2007 alone). "My interest in counter insurgency in Iraq was always about saving civilian lives" says David Kilcullen, an architect of the surge. "Because I thought the war was just stupid, and to me the only thing stopping us from getting out was the fact that so many civilians were being killed."[13] Coupled with an uprising against Al Qaeda by parts of the Sunni community, the surge enabled the national government in Baghdad to gain some control, while laying the groundwork for American forces to later quit Iraq in some semblance of order. Yet in the first year of a surge designed to protect civilians, more than 1,320 were reported killed by the Coalition—a rise of almost 50 per cent on the previous year.[14] One reason for this spike in casualties was an extraordinary rise in airstrikes, up from 229 munitions dropped the previous year to 1,708 bombs and missiles released in 2007.[15] In both Iraq and Afghanistan, it was US airstrikes which so often placed noncombatants at greatest risk of harm. According to those spoken to for this book, airmen and women nevertheless sought to prioritize the preservation of civilian life where possible. "We don't just show up, fire and leave. There's a lot of checks and balances through all that," as one former Predator pilot notes. Yet ambivalent battlefield terminology, an aggressive emphasis on preserving US lives above those of locals, and laxer rules of engagement (which could vary even between US military units) together helped contribute to a more permissive environment, one which ultimately placed civilians at greater risk of harm from American forces.

TROOPS IN CONTACT

Shortly after taking command of Coalition forces in Afghanistan in 2010, David Petraeus issued a Tactical Directive to all troops. Emphasizing it was still the case that "every Afghan civilian death diminishes our cause," the General also insisted on the following rule: "Prior to the use of fires [release of weapons], the commander approving the strike must determine that no civilians are present. If unable to assess the risk of civilian presence, fires are prohibited."[16] One exception related to Troops in Contact situations, or TICs, where Coalition troops were caught up in a firefight with insurgents and needed immediate close air support. Of all air operations in Iraq or Afghanistan, these represented the greatest threat to civilian life. Crucially, any "self-defense" situation bypassed the need for approval from the Secretary of Defense if high collateral damage was expected.[17] Armed drones had often proved helpful in battle because of their precision and low explosive-yield missiles. Yet in TIC situations, drones could be as much a hindrance as a help. Former Predator pilot Bruce Black recalls that, because of the very limited field of view provided by the drone's cameras, weapon releases were usually tightly controlled in combat: "I would never roll into, say, the Battle of Fallujah and just start picking things out and shooting them. We just didn't do that. And everybody understood we were looking through the straw. And that's why we always worked with a ground controller unless it was a self-defense situation: the guys screaming 'Shit! Shoot 'em!' Then we were allowed."[18]

Most TIC incidents in Afghanistan involved Special Forces, rather than conventional troops—a reflection of the former's intensive operational tempo. The response was then coordinated through the Joint Operations Center, or JOC, the Special Forces command center at Bagram. Research by Air Force psychologists found that any airmen dispatched to assist, whether remotely or in manned aircraft, identified powerfully with such events, particularly if Coalition forces were at serious risk of death or injury: "When you're engaged in a mission that allows you to protect troops on the ground and increase the likelihood that they return home safe and sound; that has in our experience . . . had a very strong and inspiring effect on the RPA operators," says USAF psychologist Dr. Wayne Chappelle. "Because what they often say is 'I know my job is making a difference, I helped save a life today,' or 'I helped protect somebody on the ground who I was personally speaking with.' And they can carry that home and have a sense of accomplishment."[19]

Former AFSOC mission controller Janet Atkins recalls her strong desire to help protect friendly forces, even while overseeing a mission from her desk thousands of miles away. "My mentality was, let's find these guys shooting at them. . . . It always felt intense. But at the same time that's what we're there for, it's one of those things where your emotions just have to go out the window." She recalls one particular TIC incident in Afghanistan in which some Coalition troops had already been killed:

> For a little while it felt like it was chaos. I remember that anxiety, we have to find these [bad] guys, oh my God. In my mind I was like, "Stay cool Janet, stay cool." Hearing the JTAC [forward air controller] over the radio, "Do you see them? Do you see them? They're coming at us from this side." It was just like a movie, really intense and you've got to find them within seconds or things are just gonna keep happening. And I remember we spotted three guys on top of a ridge, there they were going for our guys. That was it. We got the "OK," and we blew up the side of the mountain. I was with a Reaper, we used the GBU [a 500-lb munition] to make sure we got them.[20]

Unfortunately—and perhaps because of this strong desire to protect their own troops—there was also an increased risk of collateral damage in any TIC incident, particularly where US aircraft were involved. "High civilian loss of life during airstrikes has almost always occurred during the fluid, rapid-response strikes, often carried out in support of ground troops after they came under insurgent attack," a Human Rights Watch study concluded in 2008.[21] Many at the Pentagon would not disagree. "Troops in Contact is the one, in my experience, that tends to give us the biggest problems" says Charles Blanchard, who retired as the USAF's General Counsel in December 2013. "In a planned attack and in dynamic targeting, you have a lot more information. And almost by their very nature you don't have to hit that target that day. So you can choose your moment, usually when civilian casualties are not an issue. In Troops in Contact you have less information. You haven't been watching that house for 48 hours, all you know is that firing is coming from that area, and the Rules of Engagement are different because it's a self-defense arrangement."[22]

Yet this threat to civilians was not a constant, with a greater or lesser risk of injury in any TIC often dependent upon the nationalities of aircrews involved. One senior British airman with combat experience in Afghanistan believed there were key reasons for this: "I think you can have too much empathy. And certainly when your own nation's soldiers' lives are at risk, in my observation the US perhaps may be more inclined to interpret the Rules of Engagement in a way that suits the situation as they see it."[23] Former US military intelligence analyst Daniel Hale put it more bluntly to the author: "If you are of the mentality that American lives are more important than the lives of the people in the country that you're conducting a strike in, if the only people who have to die in a drone strike are Afghans or Yemenis or Pakistanis, who cares if a kid also gets killed in the strike? You still got the bastard that was gonna kill an American!"[24] Such variations in how the Americans and their allies were each defining and interpreting the rules of battle would have significant implications for civilians caught up in the War on Terror (table 11.1).

Table 11.1 UN estimates of Afghan civilian conflict-related deaths, 2008–2013

	All civilian noncombatant fatalities from conflict	Civilian deaths by pro-government forces only	Civilian deaths from Coalition airstrikes only (and as % of deaths caused by pro-government forces)
2008	2,118	828	552 (66%)
2009	2,412	573	359 (63%)
2010	2,792	429	171 (40%)
2011	3,133	519	235 (45%)
2012	2,768	323	125 (39%)
2013	2,959	341	118 (35%)

Source: Data from UNAMA Annual Reports on the Protection of Civilians, 2008-2013, and subsequent updates, available at http://unama.unmissions.org/Default.aspx?tabid=13941&language=en-US.

A More Transparent Approach

The targeted killing programs of the CIA and JSOC did much to cloud both British and American public opinion, even regarding the conventional battlefield use of drones. For the Royal Air Force, which had made a significant investment in the new remote weapon systems, there was increasing frustration at having to remain silent about a project senior officers were actually proud of. As one senior UK airman has described it, "We put a screen around our drone programme, only to find that everybody threw crap at it."[25] Yet British Reapers were being used only on the conventional battlefield, in strict adherence to the laws of war and with far tighter Rules of Engagement than their American colleagues employed, senior UK officers insist. Indeed, the British position in Afghanistan was "an expectation of zero civilian casualties" in any airstrike, according to a senior RAF commander:

> We do have different Rules of Engagement, we have a different approach to warfare. That doesn't mean it's not complementary, we think in the vast majority of cases it is. When it's not, the fact that we can have a really vigorous debate across a CAOC floor [Combined Air Operations Center in Qatar], which is where most of these things play out—and we would always reserve the right to do something which absolutely accords to our view rather than a US view—I think is one of the key strengths of the relationship.[26]

British officials were careful not to directly criticize the United States, noting only that their differing approach was a reflection of "sovereign intent." Yet the practical implications were significant. According to UN special rapporteur Ben Emmerson QC:

> The United Kingdom in Afghanistan is not adopting the full-back proportionality principle in international law, which says if we've got a high-value target we can kill that person even if it involves killing 30 civilians. The United Kingdom does not invoke that principle in its Rules of Engagement, or in analyzing the legality of its military operations in Afghanistan. Unsurprising then that there's a relatively lower number of civilian casualties.[27]

Under pressure from MPs, journalists, and campaigners—and with internal calls for more openness—the UK's Ministry of Defence began releasing some details of its own drone operations in Afghanistan. It had become necessary, according to one senior RAF officer, "to demonstrate that we have nothing to hide."[28] The data showed that Britain's two armed Reaper squadrons had been busy. In total, the Royal Air Force had fired more than 400 Hellfire missiles, and 50 of the more powerful GBU-12 bombs, from its armed drones to 2013.[29] Yet, in all of those operations, the RAF declared that it had accidentally killed just four civilians. An alleged insurgent commander had died in a British strike on two trucks, though "sadly, four Afghan civilians were also killed and a further two Afghan civilians were injured," according to a spokesman.[30]

There was some skepticism about this low civilian casualty figure, not least after the United Kingdom admitted it could not know how many insurgents it had killed in Afghanistan "because of the limited information available from imagery and immense difficulty and risks that would be involved in collecting robust data on the ground."[31] Civilian casualties of drone strikes, it emerged, also needed to be pro-actively reported at military bases by friends or families of those killed—a situation which led some to question the veracity of British claims. Peace campaigner Chris Cole, whose research had done much to reveal the UK drone program, summarized those concerns: "We know from data that there have been somewhere between 400 and 900 civilians killed in roughly the same number of strikes in Pakistan as there have been in Afghanistan. So it's incredible to believe that the UK would be 100 to 200 times better at drone warfare than the US. It's possible, but it's very hard to believe."[32]

Privately, senior British commanders claimed just that, noting that an insistence on a zero expectation of civilian deaths before any airstrike had had a major operational impact. This was not a philosophy generally shared by the two other nations then using armed drones. As Israel informed a UN Human Rights Council investigation in 2014, "a standard of zero anticipated civilian casualties goes beyond the mandatory requirements of international humanitarian law and would remain unattainable whilst legitimate military targets, particularly in Gaza, used civilian institutions as a base for military operations."[33] Israel's subsequent bombing campaign in Gaza, in which more than 1,000 Palestinian civilians died, made starkly clear its different stance on collateral damage. The United States also accepted the possibility of civilian deaths during missions, where allowed for under international humanitarian law (IHL), "as long as you try to minimize them and then do a proportionality analysis" according to former USAF General Counsel Charles Blanchard. That said, he believes this position changed significantly over time during the War on Terror:

> It quickly became apparent in Iraq that even if an action was permissible under IHL, the negative effects of a strike might be so huge that they became counterproductive. So I don't think the change was as much driven by a recalculation of the humanitarian value of human life, but based on a military decision about the adverse consequences of any civilian casualties.[34]

Washington was slow to grasp the corrosive impact of civilian deaths on its overall war strategy. Repeated assertions by officials at the highly precise nature of modern aerial warfare—particularly of drones—often did not help. "If we keep telling people that we're perfect and then we kill civilians, can we blame them if folk then think it's deliberate?" one former USAF commander noted to the author.[35] "I get disturbed by the oversell on 'surgical strikes,'" says Blanchard. "It's not perfect, no. The technology can make errors and people can make errors." Nevertheless he believes that "as our capabilities become greater for precision, I think that the expectation that we will avoid civilian casualties also rises." With echoes of the UK position, in response to mounting criticisms of civilian casualties from covert US drone strikes, President Obama began noting in 2013 that "before any strike is taken, there must be near-certainty that no civilians will be killed or injured—the highest standard we can set."[36]

Battlefield Errors

One frustration for researchers hoping to understand the impact of remotely piloted aircraft on the modern battlefield was Washington's unwillingness to share information. With hundreds of Predators and Reapers making up some 63 combat air patrols by 2014, the US armed drone project had evolved into a complex and heavily intertwined system. Regular USAF drone squadrons were carrying out strikes not only on the conventional battlefield but also—at the behest of the CIA—in Pakistan and Yemen.

Air Force Special Operations Command, too, was flying missions on and off the regular battlefield. The Pentagon was loathe even to release information relating to conventional battlefield drone operations—insisting that to do so might endanger "operational security." Yet greater British openness made this position less tenable, and in late 2012 CENTCOM finally produced figures on the use of armed drones in both Afghanistan and Iraq.

Although the Pentagon still refused to release associated casualty data, this improved transparency nevertheless meant researchers were able to measure the effect of drones across both conventional and secret conflicts for the first time.[37] The exercise was to prove short-lived. CENTCOM abruptly terminated the release of data early in 2013, and officials were ordered to erase all previously issued records from Pentagon websites. Claims by a spokesman that journalists and researchers would still "be able to lay hands on the monthly weapon release stats if they are willing to file a Freedom of Information Act request" proved wide of the mark.[38] Just such a request by the author was rejected by the Pentagon in March 2014, on the grounds that US conventional drone strike data was now "classified in the interest of national security"—a significant ratcheting-up of the secrecies protecting even regular US armed drone operations.[39] The British, meanwhile, continued routinely to issue their own Afghanistan drone data. This renewed US reluctance toward transparency—even on the regular battlefield—came at a crucial time. The United Nations reported a tripling of civilian fatalities from drones year-on-year in 2013.[40] According to a senior UN official, the reason for this jump was "the way that ISAF is now fighting the insurgency. They have less ground troops, way less ground troops. They're doing way less conventional air strikes, and they're using more drones."[41] Washington's refusal to release even basic information on its expanding drone use appeared to fly in the face of recent—and generally successful—civilian harm-reduction programs in Afghanistan.[42]

RPA operators insisted during a round table discussion with the author that internally, the reduction of civilian casualties was always a key priority. According to Steve, a major who flew Predators, "for the person sitting in the seat looking down at the people on the ground, everyone is either a friendly or a civilian. You don't look at it the other way around. You have to be talked into wanting to put a bomb on somebody, that's a different mindset." Jim, a serving colonel who flew F-15Es in Afghanistan, noted the broader frameworks which governed any strike decision: "The MQ1-9

[Predator-Reaper] is a platform. Our collateral damage concern does not rest on a platform, it rests on Rules of Engagement. And those are very clear. And if there's ever a question we are taught to upchannel the question, "Hey, is this within our rules or not?" before we ever hit the button to release any type of weapon. So regardless of the platform, we understand it takes that long [snaps fingers] to get on CNN. We understand that today bad information flows at the speed of light, good information goes a little slower."[43]

Yet errors did occur. In February 2010, three vehicles in Uruzgan province in Afghanistan were rocketed by US attack helicopters, after extensive surveillance by a Predator. Up to 23 men were killed and 12 people injured, among them three children and a woman. Survivor reports were harrowing: "There were people screaming and crying. One of the women lost a son and her husband was wounded. The women were crying that some other helicopters might show up and hit us again," as one later recalled. Despite civilians having been observed before and immediately after the strike, that information was at first withheld from US commander General Stanley McChrystal. Caught off guard when the Afghan government protested, he ordered a full inquiry. As Major General Tim McHale's team discovered, those in the vehicles had actually been farming families, who had the misfortune to be traveling in the vicinity of a US Special Forces raid. Shadowed by a conventional USAF Predator drone for almost three hours, all the obvious markers that civilians were present were ignored. McHale's report identified significant issues that day, including poorly trained personnel and unclear lines of command. He saved his most damning criticism for "the inaccurate and unprofessional reporting of the Predator crew operating out of Creech AFB Nevada which deprived the ground force commander of vital information," adding that there was "a desire to go kinetic." According to the drone crew's own safety observer: "Everyone around here [at Creech], it's like *Top Gun*, everyone has the desire to do our job; employ weapons against the enemy." There had been excitement among the Predator's crew at the chance of attacking so-called "squirters" in the aftermath of the attack—ugly slang among Air Force operators for those fleeing an initial airstrike. Even with women and children now clearly visible among the survivors, the drone's crew had instead "identified the women on the objective as men in women's clothes with earrings and jewelry," battlefield logs showed.

The McHale Report made clear that the Pentagon was capable of intervening aggressively on the issue of civilian deaths when it wished to, even when Special Forces were involved. Numerous personnel from command level down were disciplined, and $175,000 in total compensation paid out to affected families. Even following the deaths of civilians then, longer-term damage to strategic US and Coalition interests could—if properly managed—be mitigated. Just over the border in Pakistan, the CIA was to a significant degree fighting the same war. Yet here, the Agency placed a far lower value on civilian life for many years. Coupled with a complete absence of transparency or public accountability, its actions would have profound implications for the overall US war effort.

THE NUMBERS GAME

In Yemen, Somalia, and Pakistan, civilians were generally at greatest danger of death or injury, not from the US's secret drone strikes but from actions by insurgents, or from local pro-government forces. This was mainly a result of poor equipment, munitions, and training—or in the case of some militants the deliberate targeting of noncombatants. Pakistan Air Force pilots using "dumb" bombs frequently inflicted heavy civilian casualties during counterinsurgency operations in the tribal areas, often far in excess of any caused by relatively precise drone strikes. In 2010, the American NGO CIVIC described one such attack: "Pakistani jet fighters bombed targets in Sra Vela, a village in Khyber Agency, believing they were hitting a meeting attended by a high-level militant commander. Instead, they hit the home of a pro-government family. . . . A second bomb hit crowds of neighbors as they tried to help those injured in the first strike. At least 60 civilians were killed and 30 injured."[44] Yemen had experienced similar, as residents of one heavily-bombed town told *London Times* correspondent Iona Craig:

> For people in Jaar it became a dark joke. "We know the difference between a US drone strike and a Yemeni fighter jet attack because the latter will hit everything but the target."[45]

These proportionally lower noncombatant casualties by US drones were not just a result of the weapon systems themselves. Particularly after late 2010, both the CIA and JSOC were under pressure from the Obama administration to lower civilian death rates. The trigger for this shift in Pakistan, according to reports, was a particularly bloody strike in August that year on the village of Danda Darpakhel in North Waziristan, aimed at Afghan insurgent group the Haqqani Network.[46] Although a dozen alleged militants died, so too did as many as nine civilians—killed when missiles struck an adjacent house. Among the dead were Bismullah, his wife and two of their five young children. The bombing was one of a number of CIA attacks which killed civilians that year. Just days earlier, seven civilians including a 10-year-old boy had died in the nearby village of Asori, according to a field investigation by Associated Press.[47] Word came from the Oval Office that civilian deaths needed to be reined back. As Barack Obama's counterterrorism adviser John Brennan would later note, "One of the things President Obama has insisted on is that we're exceptionally precise and surgical in terms of addressing the terrorist threat. And by that I mean: if there are terrorists who are within an area where there are women and children or others, you know, we do not take such action that might put those innocent men, women and children in danger."[48]

In that same speech in June 2011, Brennan also made the extraordinary claim that "nearly for the past year there hasn't been a single collateral death because of the exceptional proficiency, precision of the capabilities that we've been able to develop." A US counterterrorism official confirmed to the author at the time that the CIA shared Brennan's analysis: the armed drone was "the most precise weapon in the history of warfare" and civilian deaths were no longer occurring in Agency drone strikes in Pakistan.[49]

This was a remarkable assertion, given that the Agency had carried out more than 130 bombings in the claimed period, killing over 1,000 people. Casualty trend data from observers monitoring CIA drone strikes in Pakistan certainly indicated that from late summer 2010 onward, noncombatant casualties in the tribal areas had fallen. Yet they had not halted—with Pakistan's own government recording many noncombatant deaths in a single incident just weeks prior to Brennan's controversial remarks.[50] Indeed, field research in Waziristan commissioned by the author in 2011 for the Bureau of Investigative Journalism found compelling evidence of numerous civilians killed:

> While we cannot always be categorical, in at least 10 of the 25 cases we have identified [during the Brennan window], we understand that civilians were killed. The evidence shows that at least 45 civilians died in these strikes. Six of them were children under 16 years old.[51]

Field researchers were able to name almost all of those killed, details of whom were passed to the CIA. Instead of engaging, the Agency dismissed the findings as "wildly inaccurate" and continued to insist for some months that it had killed no civilians in the stated period.[52] Yet leaked CIA briefing documents—most likely prepared for members of congressional oversight committees—later demonstrated that the Agency itself had internally admitted to at least one civilian death in a Pakistan drone strike during Brennan's "zero casualties" window.[53] Claims of no civilian deaths were patently false.

Weeks after Brennan's remarks, in summer 2011 the Bureau of Investigative Journalism first published its overall casualty estimates from CIA drone operations in Pakistan, reporting 390 civilian deaths to date.[54] Anonymous US officials responded with the Agency's own tally, noting that "about 2,000 militants have been killed and in the neighborhood of 50 noncombatants."[55] Subsequent leaks gave more detailed insights into the Agency's estimates during particular periods, with its internal counts often bearing an uncanny resemblance to the public estimates the CIA so often berated. As national security analyst Micah Zenko of the Council on Foreign Relations has noted:

> I've seen the CIA estimates, and it's very clear they don't know who they're killing. Some of the qualifiers they use are "Taliban," a few are "Al Qaeda," but a lot of them are just "Other." That's the term they use: "Other." And they say, "between three and seven people were killed." So they don't know exactly who was killed, or exactly how many people were killed.[56]

The CIA's overall casualty claims in fact closely matched low-end estimates, not only of the Bureau but of two other monitoring organizations—the Long War Journal and the New America Foundation.[57] At issue, then, was not the accuracy of total casualty numbers, but estimates of civilian noncombatants killed. The subsequent leaking of an internal FATA Secretariat report lent weight to claims of a far higher civilian death toll in Pakistan than the 50 to 60 fatalities the CIA was allowing for, with at least 147 civilians reported killed by tribal officials to 2009 alone.[58] And following a country visit in 2013, UN investigator Ben Emmerson reported:

> The [Pakistan] Government has been able to confirm that at least 400 civilians had been killed as a result of drone strikes, and that a further 200 individuals were regarded as probable non-combatants. Officials indicated that due to under-reporting and obstacles to effective investigation on the ground these figures were likely to be under-estimates of the number of civilian deaths.[59]

In Yemen too, incoming President Hadi had abandoned his predecessor's policy of publicly denying that US strikes were causing civilian deaths. Despite anonymous Pentagon officials aggressively insisting that no civilians had died in the December 2013 bombing of a wedding convoy, for example, Sana'a had not only apologized to affected families but had also paid out significant compensation (see chapter 9). Critics of higher civilian estimates caused by the CIA's campaigns had routinely depicted these as Taliban, ISI, or Al Qaeda propaganda—a position which became harder to entertain as reported civilian casualties steadily diminished after 2010.[60] Far more likely was that a significant gulf existed between the definition of a civilian noncombatant as widely understood by the governments of Pakistan and Yemen, by international NGOs and by monitoring groups on the one side—and that employed by the US government on the other.

Military-Aged Males

During General McHale's inquiry into the 2011 Uruzgan incident, it had emerged that for American military personnel, crucial terms used on the battlefield had no agreed meaning. This ambivalence could have lethal implications. As the inquiry noted, there was no shared understanding of the word "adolescent," for example. One intelligence screener thought the term referred to "a child, a non-hostile person" aged 9 to 14. Another believed an adolescent was 7 to 13 years old, adding that "in a war situation they're considered dangerous." And an unnamed Special Forces commander claimed adolescents should in part be considered "military-aged males" on the bizarre grounds that he was aware of a "midget guy . . . leading the insurgency out there." Although intelligence analysts had at first correctly identified children as being present in the vehicle convoy, as a result of this linguistic ambiguity they would later be re-classed first as "adolescents," then as "voluntary human shields," and finally as "military-aged males" in mission logs. The helicopter crew which was eventually ordered to destroy the vehicles was never told that children had been reported present.

International humanitarian law does not ban the killing of civilians in wartime. Instead it "allows the use of force that is necessary to wage war and gain a military advantage, as long as that force is not directed against and does not cause excessive incidental harm to the civilian population, [or] to persons who are not or no longer taking a direct part in hostilities."[61] Yet who in wartime was a civilian? Growing asymmetries on the battlefield—the huge technological and military advantages some nations now enjoyed over their opponents—coupled with a rise in non-state actors had, in the words of the International Committee of the Red Cross (ICRC), produced "a marked shift in the conduct of hostilities into civilian population centres, including cases of urban warfare, characterized by an unprecedented intermingling of civilians and armed actors." In Pakistan's tribal areas or the Gaza Strip, drone operators might have trouble distinguishing between an innocent civilian and someone participating in conflict—after all, both might be dressed the same, or live in the same building. New, non-binding guidance from the ICRC in 2009 stated that any civilians taking "a direct part in hostilities" could be considered combatants, no longer entitled to protection from attack.[62] When Germany dropped an investigation into its own intelligence services following the killing by the CIA of one of its citizens, it did so after determining that as a "civilian combatant" Binjamin Erdogan had been lawfully killed by a US drone.[63] Erdogan's situation appeared fairly straightforward, given his alleged participation in a militant group. Yet what of other civilians whose role in a conflict was less clear?

A former Afghanistan-based JSOC analyst told the author that concerns about casualties during US missions never appeared to focus on the potential for harm to civilian males. Instead, "over time they learned that people were complaining about their livestock being killed, so they try and avoid killing any animals along with women and children."[64] Much was made of a 2012 *New York Times* report, which asserted that US estimates of civilian deaths from drone strikes in Pakistan were particularly low because "Obama [had] embraced a disputed method for counting civilian casualties that did little to box him in. It in effect counts all military-age males in a strike zone as combatants, according to several administration officials, unless there is explicit intelligence posthumously proving them innocent."[65] The White House later denied this, insisting that "it is not the case that all military-aged males in the vicinity of a target are deemed to be combatants."[66] According to the former General Counsel of the Department of the Air Force, it would be absurd if the term were applied to every single adult male: "Especially in Iraq or Afghanistan where the military-aged population is huge it would have defeated the whole focus. Especially when given the kind of fight they were engaged in, which was a counterinsurgency. It would have been counterproductive."[67]

Yet in truth, the phrase "military-aged male" permeated both the conventional and unconventional US battlefield, a nebulous term often used as justification for an attack where the roles of some or all of those present were not known. Former USAF intelligence analyst Heather Linebaugh has complained, for example, that "I watched dozens of military-aged males die in Afghanistan, in empty fields, along riversides, and some right outside the compound where their family was waiting for them to return home from the mosque."[68] As McHale noted in his report:

> Use of the term military aged males or (MAMs) for adult males implies that all adult males are combatants and leads to a lack of discernment in target identification. Also, the term lacks a defined age. Based on the experiences of encountering young teenage insurgents, several officers identified MAMs as being as young as twelve or thirteen years old.[69]

In Iraq and Afghanistan no less than in Pakistan or Yemen, military-aged males of unknown identity were routinely targeted by US personnel, even though the Geneva Conventions state explicitly that "in case of doubt whether a person is a civilian, that person shall be considered to be a civilian."[70] Among former pilots, operators, and analysts interviewed for this book, the targeting of "unknowns" often proved the most troubling episodes of their careers (see also chapter 8). Daniel Hale is a former US military intelligence analyst, who served in Afghanistan until 2012. He complains that too often when targeting a "person of interest" in a lethal strike, Special Forces would kill unknown males in the near vicinity:

> Oftentimes as long as that individual is surrounded by persons who could be distinguished as military-aged males, they're assumed to be associates of the target, the person of interest. And basically if they're associating with, are willing to be around a person who is this bad in terms of how the military and intelligence community sees them, then they must also have ties to terrorist activity and insurgent activity. So they might as well kill two birds with one stone.

Hale's concern was that he and other analysts simply did not have enough information to make those kill decisions:

> I don't understand the cultural differences, the language, or even what goes on in Afghan peoples' day to day lives. . . . So when they would kill five people to get after one person—there is no evidence or intelligence that tells you that those other people are also actively trying to kill Americans and kill Afghans. There's nothing like that. You can't get that information. And then there's a press release that says "Five militants were killed in this area, we've suppressed this threat today."[71]

Across the border in Pakistan, the CIA behaved little differently. As an Agency informant from the tribal areas admitted to *Der Spiegel*: "When a target is selected and there are people in the immediate vicinity, they die as well. After all, a drone doesn't select a single person from a group. For instance, when a Taliban commander goes to a village, people are curious and come out to greet him. If a drone strikes at that moment, it also hits people who have nothing to do with the Taliban."[72] The Agency counted any such casualties not as civilians, but as legitimate targets according to the *New York Times*. And even women and children, it seemed, could be classed as combatants in the CIA's view.

Homes and Compounds

One issue of concern to the international legal community was the use of civilian populations to deter attack—and in particular what came to be termed as either involuntary or voluntary human shields. The former were civilians used against their will as deterrents, for example, with the placing of anti-aircraft defenses in proximity to a school. However, the ICRC also recognized human shields might be willing, "where civilians voluntarily and deliberately position themselves to create a physical obstacle to military operations of a party to the conflict." Could such civilians be targeted? As the 2009 Red Cross Guidance notes:

> While there was general agreement during the expert meetings that involuntary human shields could not be regarded as directly participating in hostilities, the experts were unable to agree on the circumstances in which acting as a voluntary human shield would, or would not, amount to direct participation in hostilities.[73]

In the Pentagon's view, any voluntary human shields were indeed "willing accomplices who support the belligerent nation [who] lose their protected status and are valid military targets."[74] Yet once again, there appeared significant ambivalence in the battlefield use of such a crucial term. As the McHale inquiry found, prior to the Uruzgan attack the Predator drone crew had assessed a "scuffle" in the vicinity of the monitored vehicles as meaning "the possible use of human shields. There was no basis for that determination [yet it] fed the impression that the vehicles were hostile." Use of the term as a designator for hostile intent appears to have been widespread among US forces, although former Air Force General Counsel Charles Blanchard says he never came across the term "voluntary human shield" being used as justification for a strike itself.[75] There was concern that nations might strip out from casualty mitigation efforts and post-strike assessments any such civilians classed as "voluntary shields": "The consensus, and certainly the line we take as a human rights organization, is that there is almost no situation in which voluntary human shielding would justify targeting civilians—or would justify stripping those voluntary shields of their civilian status and classifying them as anything but collateral damage," notes Letta Tayler of Human Rights Watch.[76] This was a legitimate worry. As the Pentagon's own 2009 guidelines noted, "Only involuntary human shields must be accounted for in casualty estimation."

Whatever misgivings critics might have had about US targeting policies in Afghanistan, they were at least clearly governed not only by international humanitarian law but also by specific Tactical Directives and Rules of Engagement. While the latter remained classified, there was still a significant element of transparency and accountability involved. In neighboring Pakistan, whatever Rules of Engagement were in place—and whatever interpretations of IHL were being followed—remained top secret. That transparency vacuum had major implications for civilians on the ground. In November 2005, the CIA attacked the North Waziristan home of Abu Hamza al-Rabia, a Syrian described as Al Qaeda's number three. Though wounded in the leg, the alleged terrorist escaped.[77] His sleeping family was not so lucky, and al-Rabia's wife and three young daughters were all reported killed. Local TV reporter Nasir Dawar lived nearby and rushed to the scene. As he later recalled, "There was nothing left but body parts, and a kid lying under some bricks."[78] Did the Agency know that night that al-Rabia's family was at home? It appears likely. The CIA would have had the property under extensive aerial and possibly human surveillance. Even so, the attack was carried out when the likelihood of immediate family members being present was at its highest, a common US tactic in Pakistan: "Houses are twice as likely to be attacked at night compared with in the afternoon. Strikes that took place in the evening, when families were likely to be at home and gathered together, were particularly deadly," a study by academic group Forensic Architecture and the Bureau of Investigative Journalism found.[79]

Another US bombing in September 2008, aimed at the home of Jalaluddin Haqqani, killed at least four alleged senior militants. Yet also among the dead were eight of Haqqani's young grandchildren, his wife, his elder sister, his sister-in-law, two nieces and other relatives. Even the CIA secretly conceded that "Members of the extended Haqqani family were killed."[80] The Haqqani Network, a Pashtun militant group which straddled the Afghan-Pakistan border and was involved in numerous attacks on US and Coalition forces, was not actually designated a terrorist organization by the State Department until four years later. The CIA had worked with and funded the group in the 1980s, and policymakers still hoped the Haqqanis might be won over.[81] It must be wondered what impact the killing of 13 members of Jalaluddin Haqqani's immediate family had on those prospects. So routinely were buildings targeted in which women and children were present in Pakistan—and so low had the CIA's own noncombatant estimates remained—that it appears likely the Agency was discounting many women and children from its tallies of noncombatants killed. As UN investigator Ben Emmerson QC has noted:

> It may be that there's an armed group who's being sheltered, it may be that they're going home to their family at night, it may be that they are forcing the community to look after them, it may be that [there's] sympathy. It's very difficult to draw these distinctions—and the US therefore says, really, anybody who forms part of that operation as a whole is legitimately targetable, and we will not accept the notion that what the US describes as voluntary human shields should be immune from attack. That's why you get women and children being killed who would not be categorized by the US as civilians.[82]

Conscious of the high risk of civilian casualties when bombing villages and houses, in Afghanistan both ISAF and Special Forces Rules of Engagement were changed, as far back as 2008, to forbid such attacks except in rare circumstances.[83] Royal Air Force squadrons even banned use of the loaded term "compound" in internal reporting: "We're trying to get it into the guys' heads that this is not compound number 28, it's 34 Acacia Drive—so you don't hit it," a senior commander told the *Daily Telegraph*. The newspaper also reported that RAF Reaper operators in Afghanistan were "forbidden to attack buildings if there are women and children in the area and they avoid targeting property."[84] In Yemen too, both the CIA and JSOC had mainly struck vehicles moving between towns, when targeting suspects. In doing so, they had apparently sought to limit noncombatant casualties, with fatalities generally confined either to when the wrong vehicle was attacked, or when a passing civilian vehicle strayed into the immediate kill zone. Even Al Qaeda was aware of the risk to civilians should houses be struck. When Osama bin Laden urged operatives to flee the CIA's drones over Waziristan in 2010, he warned them to stay away from homes where possible, since the Americans "will start focusing on houses and that would increase casualties among women and children."[85]

Yet despite the clear risk of higher civilian casualties, the CIA routinely targeted homes in the tribal areas. The Forensic Architecture/BIJ study found that of 383 US drone strikes in Pakistan to the end of 2013, as many as two-thirds were aimed at "militant compounds"—homes—although the BIJ also noted that "militant groups often rent or commandeered such buildings." As report author Alice Ross pointed out: "Despite a recognition over the border in Afghanistan that the bombing of domestic buildings represented a clear risk to civilians, the practice has continued up to the present day in Pakistan."[86]

FLAWED INTELLIGENCE

Shortly after being appointed Director of the Central Intelligence Agency in 2013, John Brennan was asked about widespread claims of historically high civilian deaths caused by the CIA's drones in Pakistan. In reply, he spoke of "The misunderstandings—or, what really bothers me are the intentional misrepresentations of the facts, which take place on a fairly regular basis."[87] Weeks earlier during his confirmation process, Brennan had also complained that people were "reacting to a lot of falsehoods that are out there."[88] The narrative which both the Agency and the Obama administration chose to construct was that few civilian noncombatants had ever died in the covert drone war—and that those claiming otherwise were mostly "propagandists."[89] One resolution to this tension would have been for the CIA to publish details of who it had killed: indeed Brennan himself had expressed the view that "the US Government should make public the overall numbers of civilian deaths resulting from U.S. strikes targeting al-Qa'ida." Yet this came to nothing.[90] And when a bipartisan measure was introduced into Congress requiring officials to publish annual tallies of civilians killed in targeted killing operations, it was withdrawn at the urging of the Director of National Intelligence. According to James Clapper, such information would instead "require context and [to] be drafted carefully so as to protect against the disclosure of intelligence sources and methods."[91]

One reason the Obama administration might have been so unwilling to release detailed casualty data for the secret drone wars was that it would allow researchers to measure the government's unfeasibly low estimates, not only against the public record but also against other recent US conflicts.

The United Nations found that around 5 percent of an estimated 400 drone strikes by Predators and Reapers in Afghanistan in 2013 had ended with civilian deaths.[92] These were drones operating under strict Rules of Engagement and within the clear boundaries of international humanitarian law. Such a casualty rate was actually far lower than that of most other weapon systems, senior Pentagon commanders insist: "If you just go to the history of warfare and you think through the number of civilian casualties that a force inflicts in a time of war, these [RPAs] are incredibly discriminate instruments of power," notes General Bob Otto, commander of the Air Force ISR Agency. "We do make mistakes. They get highly publicized. Occasionally you'll hear of a wedding that Hellfires hit through a mistake, and those are absolute tragedies. But statistically, they are a much smaller proportion of the total casualties than they have ever been."[93]

When civilian deaths did occur, error was often the cause. In Afghanistan, according to a Pentagon study, the majority of civilian deaths caused by the Coalition were not a result of their being caught up in the bombing of enemy forces, but through a misidentification of targets in the first place.[94] "A lot of people don't understand it's all intelligence. You can have the most precise Hellfire missile in the world, you can use Reapers, Predators whatever, but if your intelligence is flawed you're going to have fuckups," says former State Department official Lawrence Wilkerson:

> I don't know anybody . . . that I worked with at the CIA on the Iraqi WMD [weapons of mass destruction] for example, none of them would say that intelligence is any better than 60 percent accurate at any given time. So that's 40 percent that you're going to be killing innocent civilians. Women and children. And it doesn't matter how precise your missile is. In fact that very precision is operating against you if your intelligence is bad.[95]

That view was widely shared among former intelligence analysts spoken to by the author, who had served in Afghanistan: "If President Obama fully understood the technology as well as somebody who's dealt with it day to day, he might be reluctant to say it's surgical and precise," argues former military intelligence analyst Daniel Hale. He described how, even after extensive planning, Special Forces raids could still be based on major errors: "Sometimes it's because that person just wound up not being there when we thought they were, or because the individual might have gotten away, or the individual might be there but they [human intelligence sources] lied about who they were and we didn't figure it out until we questioned them. So a lot of those raids, it just turns up nothing." As Hale notes, this could apply just as equally to lethal operations: "Finding people isn't any different whether you're trying to capture or kill them. There is no guarantee that when you perform a kinetic strike that is supposed to eliminate a threat from the battlefield, that that person or indeed the people that surround them were actually terrorists."[96] The system was also highly vulnerable to manipulation, with local informants at times feeding false information to settle scores with rivals. "Even though it is 2014, the problem is that a lot of the intelligence comes from human intelligence and human intelligence hasn't changed for 10,000 years. It is appalling," says former British Army intelligence officer Mike Martin, who served multiple tours in Afghanistan. "We fail to realize that people will manipulate the labels that we're using—Taliban, Al Qaeda, whatever—they will manipulate those labels to wipe out their tribal enemies."[97]

In such an environment, it was perhaps a significant achievement by international forces to reduce civilian casualties to the levels they did by the end of the conflict. Across the border in Pakistan, for too long there was little incentive to do likewise. Indeed, for Obama's first few years in office, the CIA pursued aggressive tactics which would not have been tolerated on any regular US battlefield—tactics which included the frequent drone bombing of homes, of first responders, and even of funerals.[98] The majority of civilian deaths then appear to have been absented from the official record—at least for a period—by the simple expedient of reclassifying many noncombatants as "military-aged males" or as "human shields." As at least one former senior US intelligence official has noted: "I was surprised that John [Brennan] in essence was saying everybody is a military-age male therefore there is no collateral damage. I don't think that's an accurate way of judging."[99]

Claims by John Brennan and the CIA that drones on covert operations were miraculously able only to kill enemy combatants were always fanciful, placing as they did unrealistic expectations upon Air Force and Agency operators and analysts alike. Intelligence flaws, technical challenges, and human error all meant that noncombatant deaths were inevitable—even before the Agency's targeting policies were taken into account. As President Obama himself noted in 2013: "There's a wide gap between U.S. assessments of casualties and nongovernmental reports. Nevertheless, it is a hard fact that US strikes have resulted in civilian casualties, a risk that exists in every war."[100] Obama's administration had done much over time to reduce the risk of such deaths. Yet on both the conventional battlefield, and in America's secret drone wars, civilian noncombatants had too often been the victims of ambivalence or disinterest by US military and intelligence officials. It was unclear, for example, why it had taken until the eighth year of the Afghan conflict for commanders to state, in McChrystal's choice words, that "We're going to lose the fucking war if we don't stop killing civilians."[101]

In the complex struggles which characterized the War on Terror, the killing of civilians in a Pakistani village or by an Afghan road might undermine months of patient counterinsurgency work. Yet civilians were too often confronted with a treacherous hierarchy of risk whose rules they were never allowed to know. Innocent civilians on the Pakistan side of the border were at far greater risk of death or injury from a drone strike than those in Afghanistan, until late into the CIA's secret campaign. Even within Afghanistan, the risks faced by civilians could vary wildly depending on which forces were conducting an operation, and under which rules. Whether an air asset was operated by the United States or by Britain could mean the difference between life and death for civilians. And while most US troops in Afghanistan operated under ISAF's stricter Rules of Engagement, Special Forces followed their own rules—ones which even close allies say left them barely accountable for their actions. Civilian deaths inflicted by the Taliban, in both Afghanistan and Pakistan, far outstripped those caused by Coalition or CIA operations. Yet the prevention of noncombatant deaths would become a key Western war aim, one requiring constant vigilance. No military operation could reasonably place an absolute value upon civilian life. As the ICRC itself has noted, the laws of war are "a compromise based on a balance between military necessity, on the one hand, and the requirements of humanity."[102] Even so, it was possible for nations significantly to reduce the risk to any civilians caught up in fighting given the right political will—and a requirement of accountability and transparency from those forces involved.

COUNTERMEASURES AND CRITIQUES

When armed drones first debuted above the battlefield in 2001, those targeted at first had no idea how they were being hunted. General Chuck Wald, who commanded the air war in Afghanistan, recalls observing the feed from a Predator as it pursued a group of Taliban for almost four hours: "We'd track 'em, we'd bomb 'em, they'd get in a ditch. On those first couple of nights they didn't know what infra-red was, so weren't savvy enough to know that a ditch just doesn't hide you." The surviving Taliban talked a passing farmer into letting them escape on his hay trailer. The Predator then fired its remaining Hellfire missile: "They hit the trailer with the Hellfire, just blew the thing to smithereens." Even unarmed, the drone was still able to direct nearby F-18s onto the few survivors and "vaporize" the compound they were now hiding in.[1] "And you say, 'My God warfare has really changed, this is awesome,'" says Wald on the capability this new weapon brought to the battlefield.[2]

As hunter-killers, the Predator and Reaper each proved well-suited to the "post-conflict" environments where much of the War on Terror was fought. Unmolested by enemy aircraft or air defense systems, their effect on the Taliban and Al Qaeda was often devastating. Yet over time, these same groups began to adapt: "There was I'm sure a 'gotcha' point for them where they went, 'Wait a minute!'" says Don Hudson, a former deputy commander of Air Force remote-intelligence operations. "If every day I threw a rock at you at 12 o' clock when you came out of your house, you'd probably stop coming out of your house at 12 o' clock. So we realized that the adversary was going to start learning and evolving their own tactics to counter ours." Jim, a serving colonel with Air Combat Command, describes the Taliban's adaptability in Afghanistan:

> The enemy is misperceived. People think they're dumb, and being dumb and being illiterate are two different things. They may not be able to pick up a text book and quote chapter and verse or be able to do a chemistry equation. But they are anything but dumb. And they are very, very fast learners in how to survive. So while we have the technology, they have the know of the land. While we have however many troops, they have a resolve. It's their country and they know it much much better than I do.[3]

The evolution of enemy tactics, techniques, and procedures in response to US drone operations ranged from simple evasive maneuvers, to major counterintelligence operations leading to the deaths of dozens of alleged US spies. Feeding into this counter-strategy were the technical limitations of the drones themselves.

The Limits of Technology

To the Special Forces sensor operator sitting in New Mexico, what they had just witnessed appeared to be a clear violation of the laws of armed conflict. The drone's camera had shown a Navy SEAL shoot a captive during a mission: "They're sitting there and they see one of the SEALs takes a shot at a guy on the ground. And they decide to declare a LOAC [Laws of Armed Conflict] violation," reports another former operator with knowledge of the event. A subsequent military inquiry found that the SEAL had acted appropriately. The quality of the cameras on the RPA had simply been too poor to determine what was transpiring. "You're getting a comms eye view on a grainy video from afar, and you're going to second guess a guy on the ground who's watching him trying to pull a grenade out of his jacket? That's what the SEAL was doing, that's what was actually going on over there," says the colleague.[4] On another occasion in 2011, in the only known "friendly fire" incident involving a remotely piloted aircraft, two US Marines died in Afghanistan when they were mistaken by the drone's operators and intelligence analysts for militants. While a subsequent inquiry "placed much of the blame" on the Marine platoon's leader for not knowing where his men were, there were clearly faults elsewhere. The US troops had been targeted because they were thought to be firing on their own comrades. As a *Los Angeles Times* investigation noted: "Replaying the video and voice communications, [the Predator pilot] was stunned to see that the muzzle flashes were aimed away from the road. He was 'completely confused as to how I saw exactly the opposite sitting in the seat.'"[5]

Much had been made of the supposed high quality of surveillance imagery produced by the Predator and Reaper. Yet among pilots, sensor operators, and analysts there was often far less certainty: "You never knew who you're killing because you never actually see a face," says former operator Michael Haas. "What we're looking at are shadows and silhouettes. Just because some remote guy in a chair says 'Yep that's him'—I mean anybody who's in this Age of the Internet knows never to trust a screen-based pseudonym telling you to do something. There's no way to confirm that; he doesn't look any different from anyone else on that screen. How the Hell can you know?"[6] Heather Linebaugh was an intelligence analyst with the Air Force. She too has described serious challenges to interpreting images:

> The video provided by a drone is not usually clear enough to detect someone carrying a weapon, even on a crystal-clear day with limited cloud and perfect light. This makes it incredibly difficult for the best analysts to identify if someone has weapons for sure. One example comes to mind: "The feed is so pixelated, what if it's a shovel, and not a weapon?" I felt this confusion constantly, as did my fellow UAV analysts. We always wonder if we killed the right people, if we endangered the wrong people, if we destroyed an innocent civilian's life all because of a bad image or angle.[7]

Other factors could also affect quality. Typically in Iraq, Predator missions had flown at 10,000 feet. In Afghanistan, armed drones were required to fly at twice that height, leading to poorer imagery: "It really sucked because the picture wasn't as clear as it was over in Iraq," says former sensor operator Brandon Bryant. As the number of drone combat air patrols grew, so too did the amount of data generated by each mission, with a risk of information overload. Full-motion video was upgraded to high-definition, for example, while the Gorgon Stare system swapped the single "soda straw" view of a drone's camera for as many as 64 individual filming points across an area the size of a city.

So much information was now being harvested from the battlefield that the Distributed Common Ground System (DCGS)—the Air Force's huge remote intelligence program—was gathering in 100 terabytes of data every 80 hours.[8] In comparison, it had taken the Hubble Space Telescope 24 years to amass the same amount of data on the universe.[9] This vast trove of information did bring benefits, says General Bob Otto, commander of the Air Force ISR Agency: "Quality adds to certainty of judgment and quickness of judgment. So there are some things that make that an easier analytic problem than otherwise, even though it takes more bandwidth."[10] Yet there was also a risk that so much information might overwhelm. "We're going to find ourselves in the not too distant future swimming in sensors and drowning in data," as Otto's predecessor Dave Deptula warned.[11] Should it stick to conventional staffing quotas, "by 2015 the Air Force could, in theory, require up to 117,000 personnel dedicated to motion imagery exploitation alone," a study for the Pentagon noted. That same Rand report even turned to the world of reality TV for inspiration, looking at how popular shows were able to process and prioritize vast quantities of live material 24 hours a day, seven days a week.[12]

Despite the hype of manufacturers and defense officials, armed drones clearly had weaknesses—which those being pursued sought to exploit. As a result, US targeted killing operations had always needed to depend on a far wider array of intelligence sources than generally understood. Often most crucial of all was the information obtained by spies on the ground, at great risk to those involved.

CONFESSIONS OF A "SPY"

The final words of 22-year-old Isaac Omar Hassan were recorded for posterity in hi-definition video. Dressed in a plain white t-shirt and seated against a faded pink wall, the former jihadist sometimes forgets his imminent fate as he jokes with his unseen interrogators. Then fear returns to his eyes, as Hassan confesses to conspiring to enable the United States to kill two Al Shabaab operators in Somalia. In a grim echo of the military's own "drone porn," which celebrated strikes on alleged militants (see chapter 4), a thriving jihadist film industry had grown up featuring the last words of suspected "US drone spies."

Hassan's lengthy confession appears in a polished one-hour English-language film, released by Al Shabaab's media wing in late 2012. A cook who worked at a militant camp, Hassan claims he was "turned" by Somali intelligence shortly after being picked up and tortured. True or not, his decision to betray his own comrades was incentivized by two payments totaling $5,000. Hassan's first target was Bilal al-Berjawi, the reported liaison between Al Shabaab and Al Qaeda East Africa (see chapter 6). Hassan's Somali handlers (who he claimed worked for the CIA) handed him a modified cellphone, which would act as the locator device to lead JSOC's drones to their target. "Placing the device in the car was fairly easy for me because I was close to Bilal Berjawi," Hassan says matter-of-factly. "The difficult part was turning it on." To help him, he recruited his friend Yasin Osman Ahmed, who occasionally acted as al-Berjawi's driver. Short of money for a new business venture, Ahmed found it impossible to resist $2,000 in cash (around three times the average annual income for Somalis at the time).[13] The tracking device was first planted unseen in al-Berjawi's car as he shopped for a new gun. Days later, as the senior militant spoke to his wife back in London following the birth of their son, Ahmed quietly activated the device and slipped away before the Hellfire missiles struck.

The killing of Bilal al-Berjawi caused uproar within Al Shabaab, and its counterintelligence wing began a manhunt for possible betrayers. It was too slow. Within weeks, al-Berjawi's close friend Mohamed Sakr was also killed, along with two other militants and a local shepherd. This time Isaac Hassan's accomplice was Abdirahman Osman, a cousin of Sakr's driver, who was bribed for just $200. The tracker was "a very small device, similar to a flash drive but slightly smaller, with ON/OFF buttons," which Osman hid beneath the collar of a jacket before giving it to his cousin as a gift. With planning for a third betrayal already underway, Al Shabaab's counterintelligence team finally swept up the alleged spies.[14] Soon after the filming of their confessions, the three were executed by firing squad "in compliance with Islamic sharia."[15]

Portrayals of drone warfare tended to focus on the sophisticated onboard technologies used to pinpoint targets. Yet many senior terrorists and militants had abandoned electronic communications, once it became clear how easily they could be monitored and targeted. Osama bin Laden's home in Abbottabad had no Internet connections or phone lines, for example. The Al Qaeda leader was located after a decade-long hunt, only because his personal courier had been found.[16] Both on and off the hot battlefield, this behavioral shift instead required the use of people on the ground, prepared to risk their lives in order to identify high-value targets. In the words of Al Shabaab:

> All their technological advancement would amount to nothing and they would be shooting in the dark without a dedicated stream of human intelligence personnel to connect the dots and provide the exact co-ordinates for their targets. And as a result a large network of spies including both men and women have been deployed to the areas under the control of the mujahedin—not to engage in combat but rather to direct the strikes of the Predator drones.[17]

Some of those spying for the United States never knew their true employer. According to a former Agency officer who worked in Waziristan, the CIA recruited mainly poor local men to help identify targets. Some of these were "cut-outs," unwitting informers who may have believed they were working for Pakistani intelligence.[18] Others were happy to work for the Americans. In a lengthy interview with *Der Spiegel*, Pashtun tribesman "Mohammad Hassan" described receiving about $200 a month in return for spying for the CIA: "I provide information about everything I see and believe is worth reporting. Information about foreigners who turn up here, about places where meetings are held, things like that," he claimed. In Mohammad's case, an ideological opposition to the Taliban provided his primary motivation: "We are at war, and I am part of this war. When does a war make sense? To be honest, I think the US drone missions are the right thing to do. Believe me, no weapon is more effective in fighting extremists." Yet his actions meant he was in constant fear for his life:

> The Taliban know that someone has to be passing on information. There is a special unit whose job is to expose spies and punish them.

Even someone who is suspected of being an informant has a problem. When a spy is exposed, he is shot to death or blown up. The last few minutes before the execution are filmed. When they pull out the video camera, you know that it's the end. And then these people turn up as corpses along the side of the road, along with the DVD of the execution and a note stating that this is the fate all spies can expect.[19]

Terror proved the most common tool at countering this human intelligence. Jan Mohammad was the first known victim in Pakistan, killed in the wake of a 2006 attack on a school in Bajaur Agency (see chapter 5). The local farmer's fate appears to have been sealed after he arrived "too soon" at the scene of a bombing which killed up to 80 students and a senior militant commander. A sign was hung around the corpse's neck, accusing Mohammad of "spying for the US and Pakistan."[20] As CIA drone strikes intensified, so too did the Taliban's terror tactics against locals. Carrying out this campaign was a dedicated counterintelligence cell later known as Lashkar-e-Khorasan (LeKh). According to reports, suspects were taken before a secret Taliban court where "if proved guilty, the person is executed immediately."[21] More than 100 alleged spies had been killed in Pakistan's tribal areas by 2009 alone, with a further 250 executed on the Afghan side of the border. *New York Times* reporter David Rohde, imprisoned by the Taliban in FATA at the time, has described the paranoia and fear which gripped the region: "For months, our guards told us of civilians being rounded up, accused of working as American spies and hung in local markets."[22] In summer 2008 a crowd of 5,000 had watched the execution by beheading of two alleged US informants—with Taliban commander Wali ur-Rehman telling the crowd that "Whoever, for the sake of money, for the sake of America, harms the interest of the Islamic world will meet the same fate."[23] Rehman himself was slain in a drone strike five years later, betrayed by a CIA asset.

Such brutal counter-tactics were not confined to South Asia. In 2001, a Palestinian court sentenced four collaborators to death for their role in Israeli targeted killings, as thousands outside chanted "Execution!"[24] And in summer 2014, 18 alleged Palestinian collaborators were summarily executed by Hamas following their trial in a "revolutionary court" in the wake of Israel's devastating assault on the enclave. As human rights group B'Tselem complained, "International humanitarian law entirely prohibits any state or organization to carry out summary executions, regardless of the nature of the allegations."[25] In Yemen, the local Al Qaeda affiliate crucified alleged spies on at least two occasions. Amin Abdullah Mohammed al-Mu'alimi was killed in early 2014, for example, his body hung on a soccer goalpost with a sign around his neck reading "An American spy in the Arabian Peninsula." A linked statement threatened "any intruder who infiltrates among Muslims, places chips in their vehicles and their wedding convoys and gets them killed in return for a few dirhams."[26]

As AQAP's comment indicated, the primary means employed by spies to lead the drones to their targets were those same tiny tracking devices which had betrayed Sakr and al-Berjawi in Somalia. "The money was good so I started throwing the chips all over. I knew people were dying because of what I was doing, but I needed the money," claimed Habibur Rehman, a 19-year-old executed by the Pakistan Taliban in 2009. US officials dismissed his last words as "extremist propaganda."[27] Yet the chips—nicknamed *patrai* by local Pashtuns—were a reality.[28] In 2010, the Taliban discovered that the night vision setting on a home video camera could reveal the tiny, pulsing infra-red beacons used to direct in precision-guided missiles from drones.[29] So paranoid did militants become that LeKh even began executing car mechanics. A number were beheaded in 2011 "after they were blamed for placing chips in a Taliban Hilux car to make them a target for US drone strikes."[30]

Yemen expert Dr. Gregory Johnsen has described one disturbing case where an 8-year-old boy was used by the Yemen military to "plant tiny electronic chips" on AQAP bomb-maker Adnan al-Qadhi, which then led US drones to him. The boy's father received $230 for convincing his own child to carry out the mission. AQAP later issued a "confessional video" featuring father and son. "I climbed on the table where his [the drone target's] coat was and put [a tracking chip] in his pocket," the child claimed. According to Johnsen "The evidence strongly suggests that America's allies in Yemen recruited the boy, but there is nothing to indicate that US officials knew anything about Barq's role as a child spy." The father was executed, though the "innocent" child was spared, according to Al Qaeda.[31]

Targeted killings by drone were often described as bloodless affairs, with remote operators insulated from battlefield risks. Yet any precision to

these strikes was often bought at a high cost. Hundreds of alleged "spies"—
many of them doubtless innocent people caught up in counter-surveillance
hysteria—were killed by militant and terrorist groups seeking to minimize
the impact of remotely piloted aircraft.

DEFENSIVE MEASURES

When French forces overran militant positions in Timbuktu in northern Mali in 2013, accompanying Associated Press reporters came upon
a fascinating document.[32] Originating in Yemen and written in Arabic,
the slim paper offered practical solutions to militants hoping to foil the
secret US drone war. Some of the 22 measures were simply good battlefield
practice: the use of spies to detect the launching of drones from neighboring countries, for example. Others revealed a detailed—and doubtless
hard-won—knowledge of how armed drones had proved most effective,
and where any weaknesses might lie. Militants were urged to make use of
dense cloud cover, or "to hide under thick trees because they are the best
cover against the planes." Better still, they should meet in underground
shelters, since "the missiles fired by these planes are usually of the frag-
mented anti-personnel and not the anti-buildings type." Cars were viewed
as particularly problematic—a reflection of US drone operations in Yemen,
which generally targeted vehicles rather than buildings. "When discover-
ing that a drone is after a car, leave the car immediately. And everyone
should go in a different direction, because the planes are unable to go after
everyone," readers were urged. Even before some of the finer details of
NSA capabilities had been revealed by Edward Snowden, militants were
cautioning leaders not to use radio communications "because the enemy
usually keep a voice tag through which they can identify the speaking person and then locate him."

The most technically detailed suggestions related to electronic coun-
termeasures. Militants were urged to use military-grade transceivers
to interfere with the drones, a tactic it was claimed "the Mujahidin have
successfully experimented with." Finally, readers were told to buy a
Russian-made device which could "infiltrate the drone's waves and fre-
quencies." SkyGrabber had first made headlines in Iraq two years earlier,
when Shia militants discovered that Predator video feeds were being transmitted on unencrypted channels. The Russian-made software, described

as an "offline satellite internet downloader," retailed at the time for just $26. Hooked up to a satellite dish, SkyGrabber allowed insurgents to hack directly into drone video feeds. According to one former drone operator Brandon Bryant, only conventional US drones were vulnerable, since AFSOC had always encrypted its Special Forces feeds: "The reason why they [insurgents] were able to do that was because . . . we sometimes would send off a signal, an analogue signal to people on the ground so that they can get our ROVER feed."[33]

The Pentagon only became aware of this serious flaw in December 2008, when video of a Predator feed was found on a captured insurgent's laptop. Eight months later, "days and days and hours and hours of proof" of extensive hacking was obtained from another source, according to the *Wall Street Journal*.[34] Although the Pentagon played down the affair as it sought to plug the loophole, such vulnerabilities should not have come as a surprise. In 1997, Hezbollah had reportedly hacked into an Israeli Special Forces drone feed, enabling it to ambush a raid on the Lebanese village of Antsaria. "We succeeded in analyzing these pictures, and assumed Israel was planning on operating there,' Hezbollah's General Secretary later boasted. 'Our men waited there for a few weeks, and on one of the nights the commando soldiers walked into the ambush we prepared.'"[35] A dozen Israeli commandos died.

More radically, militant and terrorist groups had also attempted to take control of the drones themselves. An alleged Al Qaeda operative was arrested in Turkey in 2010 and charged with multiple terrorist offences, including attempting to hack the controls of unarmed Heron drones being used by British, German, and Canadian troops in Afghanistan.[36] This may have been part of a concerted effort by Al Qaeda to combat drones electronically. "The Defense Intelligence Agency (DIA) reported that al-Qaeda was sponsoring simultaneous research projects to develop jammers to interfere with GPS signals and infrared tags that drone operators rely on to pinpoint missile targets," the *Washington Post* noted, citing documents leaked by Snowden. According to the DIA, while the terrorist group lacked the technological capabilities at the time, should it achieve them, "such a system probably would be highly disruptive for US operations in Afghanistan and Pakistan."[37] Iran claimed to have done just that in December 2011, when it captured one of the CIA's top-secret RQ-170 stealth drones. Although US officials insisted that the remotely piloted aircraft had simply malfunctioned, its intact status on capture lent credence to Iranian claims to have "spoofed" the aircraft into landing.[38]

Terrorist and militant groups also sought to build their own drones. Hezbollah was an early pioneer, with a number of its presumed remote aircraft shot down by Israel. In 2013 alone, local law enforcement officials raided "drone workshops" in three nations. Hamas-aligned engineering students were arrested in the West Bank by the Palestinian Authority, after allegedly making a drone "designed to carry an explosive payload that could target an Israeli critical facility."[39] In Iraq, the Interior Ministry smashed "a drone manufacturing workshop" set up by Sunni extremists, seizing four small RPAs.[40] And Pakistani intelligence officials uncovered an "Al Qaeda drone laboratory" in Islamabad. Although the small aircraft only had a range of 1 km, "if made operational, [it] could carry a significant quantity of explosives to damage vital buildings and other sensitive installations," according to one police source. It was alleged that the man leading that Al Qaeda project was a professor of electronic engineering.[41]

The development focus of each of these operations was on small, tactical remotely piloted aircraft, each modified to carry lightweight explosives. Given the prohibitive technological and cost barriers involved in obtaining or hacking large strategic drones, this made sense. "Smaller systems could become the next IEDs," a Rand Corporation study noted in 2012. "One can imagine US forces fighting future insurgent movements that use large numbers of cheap UAVs operating with line-of-sight controls. Such UAVs could detonate near US forces, posing a constant threat."[42] While relatively harmless individually given their short range and limited payloads, particularly if operated in swarms, these represented a significant risk. In anticipation of such rogue drones, the Israel Air Force began conducting major exercises in 2014: "This threat is growing steadily, and the air force is not closing its eyes and ignoring it, but rather, it is preparing for the hour of need," as one officer told the *Jerusalem Post*.[43]

ON THE ATTACK

The devastating joint Al Qaeda and Pakistan Taliban (TTP) attack on the CIA's forward base in Khost, in the last days of 2009, showed that militants and terrorists were capable not only of generating a complex understanding of US drone operations but also of striking hard at them. Two videos were later released by the TTP, featuring the Jordanian suicide bomber Humam al-Balawi. The first showed him with Hakimullah Mehsud, the new leader of the Pakistan Taliban: "We say that we will never forget the blood of our Emir Baitullah Mehsud, God's mercy on him," al-Balawi says to camera—a reference to the former TTP leader killed in a US drone strike in August 2009. A second, less reported film showed the Jordanian seated in a car. In poor English, he directly references the US drone campaign: "We will beat you CIA team. . . . Don't think that [because] you are just pressing a button killing mujahedeen you are safe. Inshallah death will come to you in unexpected ways."[44] The triple agent had fed crucial details of the CIA's Waziristan drone strikes back to the Agency as proof of his ability to deliver. Some of those al-Balawi then killed were key players in the Agency's covert drone operations. Elizabeth Hanson, for example, was described as the Agency's chief targeter: "She had helped the CIA locate some of the biggest players in the jihadist world, from Osama al-Kini to Baitullah Mehsud," according to national security correspondent Joby Warrick.[45]

With Washington cooperating with host governments in Pakistan, Yemen, and Somalia, terrorists increasingly attacked local bases linked to the drone wars. A major Pakistan Taliban assault on the Mehran naval base in Karachi in May 2011 killed 16 people. "Their first targets were aircraft parked on the tarmac and equipment in nearby hangers," the BBC reported, with at least two US-supplied P3-C Orion surveillance aircraft set ablaze.[46] Across the border, the Afghan Taliban frequently targeted airfields crucial to the Coalition's air war. While most attacks failed, a complex assault on the British-run Camp Bastion in Helmand province in September 2012 proved far more devastating. Dressed in fake US military uniforms, the attackers were able to enter the base and destroy or disable an entire squadron of Marine Corps Harrier jets fitted with advanced surveillance pods. The squadron's commanding officer was also killed. The attack was described as "the worst loss of US airpower in a single incident since the Vietnam War," with the destruction cost at around $200 million.[47] The Taliban also routinely claimed to have shot down Predators and Reapers in Afghanistan and more occasionally in Pakistan. While Washington generally denied such claims, at least 30 of the remote aircraft were confirmed lost in the region, mainly attributed to pilot error, mechanical problems, or to adverse weather. Many more US armed drones were lost in Iraq, Yemen, and even in Mali.[48]

Al Qaeda in the Arabian Peninsula also frequently struck at what it believed to be command and control hubs, linked to US intelligence-gathering operations. Certainly such facilities existed, as President Hadi liked to boast: "You go to the operations center and see operations taking place step by step," he told the *Washington Post* in September 2012. Later the President told Human Rights Watch that a "joint operations room"—which he said was staffed by US and British personnel—"identifies in advance" individuals who are "going to be targeted."[49] In its first known assault aimed at drone command and control systems, AQAP destroyed an alleged facility in al-Mukalla in autumn 2013—proclaiming that "such joint security targets, which participate with the Americans in their war on the Muslim people, are a legitimate target for our operations, and we will puncture these eyes that the enemy uses." Yemeni officials insisted that the facility was only used in regional anti-piracy operations.[50] Similar assaults were launched at suspected control rooms in Aden, and even in the capital Sana'a, with an assault in 2013 killing 52 people at Yemen's Department of Defence, and at a next-door military hospital.[51]

The ferocity of these attacks was an indication of quite how damaging armed drones had become to Al Qaeda and its allies. Almost 500 secret bombings across three continents not only killed dozens of the most senior leaders but had also majorly degraded the ability of groups to operate effectively. Papers seized after the killing of Osama bin Laden indicated just how deeply Al Qaeda's leadership was affected. One undated missive complains that "our Waziristani brothers . . . were frankly exhausted from the enemy's air bombardments."[52] In another, written in 2010 during the most intense period of US drone strikes, bin Laden urged his supporters in the tribal areas to take extreme precautions, and even called on his own son to flee the area: "Make sure to tell Hamzah that I am of the opinion that he needs to get out of Waziristan."[53] A senior Pentagon official, well-versed in the drone targeted killing program, puts its impact bluntly: "We denied the enemy the ability to move. We denied him the ability to communicate. Prior to that they could do a thousand things. Now they could do one thing. Hide."[54]

LOWERING THE THRESHOLD FOR WAR

Despite the hostility toward armed drones from some quarters—particularly as a result of the targeted killing campaign—the great majority of former operators spoken to for this book felt they had contributed positively to the war effort. As one former Predator pilot, Chad Bruton, puts it:

> I am 100% certain that we would have lost a lot more lives in Iraq and in Afghanistan had we not been there, so I am very proud to have done that. That's not to say that I necessarily supported those campaigns—us being there at all. I have my own thoughts on that. But we were there; and I signed an oath basically that I was going to do what I was told when I was in service, and that's what I did.[55]

Other former operators were similarly positive: "I'm proud of that part of my military life. There is nothing I regret or anything I feel I should be ashamed of," says former mission controller Janet Atkins. "It's something that had to be done and it wouldn't be any different if I was on the ground shooting people. It's just what happens. It's war. Obviously I wish it didn't need to happen but it did."[56] Although armed drones above the conventional battlefield were increasingly involved in targeted killings, there remained fundamental differences with the covert campaigns elsewhere. "It is, I think, qualitatively different to strike at a declared enemy in a war zone at a time of war than it is to strike a civilian population in time of peace," as counterinsurgency expert David Kilcullen puts it. "And if we don't think that's a real distinction, what the fuck have we been doing since the Middle Ages?"[57] Some former operators would agree: "Drones can be used for good as far as protecting the troops, getting a strike that needs to happen in a warzone. But I think using them outside of a warzone as far as assassination goes is wrong," says former Special Forces sensor operator Brandon Bryant, now a harsh critic of many aspects of the US drone program.

Yet even before their impact on conflicts was fully understood, the use of armed drones both on and off the conventional battlefield was fast expanding—as the lines between such operations blurred. During NATO's Libya intervention in 2011, armed Predators and Reapers remotely flown by US and British crews carried out 145 strikes—still a fraction of actions which saw 7,600 weapons released by all aircraft.[58] Although NATO refused to give a detailed breakdown of how RPAs were deployed, the Vice Chairman of the US Joint Chiefs of Staff said of drones at the time that "what they will bring [to Libya] that is unique to the conflict is their ability to get down lower, therefore to be able to get better visibility on targets that have started to dig themselves into defensive positions. They are uniquely suited for urban areas."[59] This was a surprising comment to some—Israel had been criticized for carrying out drone strikes and other aerial attacks on densely populated areas, while Coalition forces in Afghanistan had, in the main, banned airstrikes on built-up areas.

At the end of the Libyan campaign, NATO's Secretary General would make a startling claim, reminiscent of John Brennan's "zero civilian casualties" assertion of five months earlier: "We conducted our operations in Libya in a very careful manner, so we have no confirmed civilian casualties caused by NATO."[60] Anders Fogh Rasmussen's boast was later shown by four separate investigations to be untrue.[61] The UN International Commission of Inquiry on Libya confirmed, for example, at least 60 civilian deaths in airstrikes, including an attack on first responders:

> The single largest case of civilian casualties from a NATO airstrike in Libya took place in the town of Majer on 8 August 2011 where the Commission found NATO bombs killed 34 civilians and injured 38. After the initial airstrike killed 16, a group of rescuers arrived and were hit by a subsequent attack, killing 18.[62]

The dogged refusal of NATO to investigate or follow up any claims of civilian casualties in Libya was as disturbing as its glib assertion that no noncombatants died. The proportion of those deaths caused by drones was unknown, since NATO refused to disaggregate its airstrike data. Specialists expressed particular concern that few of the recent, hard-won lessons on civilian casualties from Afghanistan had been brought to bear in Libya: "The difference in how NATO interacted with me in each place was striking," noted Marc Garlasco, a former Human Rights Watch and United Nations investigator. "I had a collegial, open relationship with officials in Afghanistan—and an adversarial and frosty one with those in Libya. . . . How can NATO uphold its mandate to protect civilians while denying civilian harm?"[63]

Of equal worry, to some, was the Obama administration's justification for not seeking congressional approval for the Libyan war—the first US conflict since 9/11 to fall squarely outside the scope of the Authorization for the Use of Military Force. Many in Congress argued that the War Powers Resolution should therefore have come into effect. This required that, within 60 days of the start of any military operation, the president had either to obtain congressional authorization, or to withdraw US forces.[64] Yet according to Obama officials, the War Powers Resolution did not apply, in part because there were only planes and drones above Libya, rather than troops on the ground: "US operations do not involve sustained fighting or active exchanges of fire with hostile forces, nor do they involve the presence of US ground troops, US casualties or a serious threat thereof."[65] For critics, this view amply demonstrated that armed drones, by the nature of their remote operation, carried a greater risk of involvement in conflicts. As Medea Benjamin of US peace campaigners Code Pink argues:

> Drones make these wars possible. From being able to wage them without even having to go to Congress, because according to the administration's definition of war, war is when you put your own soldiers' lives at risk. And since we're not doing that with drones, it's not war. It doesn't have to be agreed in Congress. It doesn't even have to be open to the American people. It can be carried out in total secrecy.[66]

There was certainly an increased willingness by the three early adopters of armed drones—the United States, Israel, and the United Kingdom—to expand their use. Washington's operations had spread far beyond Afghanistan and Iraq, with confirmed strikes in Pakistan, Yemen, Somalia, Libya, and Syria by late 2014, and with persistent talk of lethal US drone operations in the Philippines.[67] American Predators and Reapers were also supplying lethal targeting information to the Turkish military's anti-Kurdish operations,[68] and to French armed forces in Mali.[69] The temptation to reach for armed drones—especially in circumstances where there was no willingness to risk US forces on the ground—was ever-present. Speaking to the author in 2014—shortly before American drones resumed lethal operations in Iraq after a three year pause—one former senior US intelligence official, who until recently wanted to see targeted killings reined in, now had doubts:

I'd really have been for, you know "You need to start cranking this stuff back. You just don't want to get too used to it, you know?" But frankly the past 18 months have not been very pleasant. Al Qaeda in Yemen, Al Qaeda in Iraq, and God knows Al Qaeda in Syria. You've got this resurgence that pushes you back away from—I think law enforcement's going to be good enough for this for now, but you better keep those other tools in your kitbag because we've got a repeat of the FATA in 2007, 2008 in Syria now.[70]

Israel too had expanded its drone operations, with strikes credibly reported in Lebanon, Sudan,[71] and Egypt's Sinai desert.[72] Asked about alleged attacks inside Sudan in 2009, then-Prime Minister Ehud Olmert told reporters: "Those who need to know, know there is no place where Israel cannot operate. . . . We operate in many places near and far, and carry out strikes in a manner that strengthens our deterrence."[73]

The British, with their two squadrons of armed Reapers, were in a quandary given their expected 2014 withdrawal from Afghanistan. Keen to maintain "continuity of capability" with the US drone program, senior Ministry of Defence officials initially considered sending their Reapers to the Horn of Africa. This was controversial. Djibouti, the proposed new base, lay at the heart of US counterterrorism operations against Al Qaeda and Al Shabaab—conflicts which the British military (if not British intelligence) had so far avoided. Some MPs were concerned that the government might seek to avoid parliamentary scrutiny of any involvement by British drones in potentially unlawful US counterterrorism operations.[74] With doubtless some relief, defence officials instead redeployed the Reapers to Iraq in late 2014, as part of Britain's expanding anti-Islamic State operations.[75] Crucially, that conflict had the full support of parliament.

Keeping the Courts Out

While the proliferation of remotely piloted aircraft on the conventional battlefield was of concern, it was their role in targeted killings which continued to excite most controversy. Only late into George W. Bush's second term had the CIA used armed drones with any intensity. In contrast, the Obama administration majorly expanded the targeted killing program, had codified it, and was prepared to defend it publicly. In a Google "town hall debate" in early 2012, President Obama openly discussed how "a lot of these [drone] strikes have been in the FATA [Federally Administered Tribal Area]." In a break with the Bush era, other administration officials also now discussed the claims of legality for covert US targeted killings. "I do think it's fair to say that the administration inherited the program, and then set about an ex post facto legal rationalization to determine how it could fit within international humanitarian law," says UN investigator Ben Emmerson QC, who has met with many of Obama's key policy advisers on drones. "I think one of the reasons that it took them so long to break cover and to state authoritatively what their legal justification was, during the first term, was partly because they weren't themselves sure what their legal justification was."[76] Yet this openness did not extend to allowing federal courts to test those opinions. Court papers filed by the Pentagon, the CIA, and the Department of Justice (DoJ), five months after Obama directly referenced covert drone strikes in FATA in his Google event, have an absurdist ring to them:

> Plaintiffs speculate that the President must have been speaking about CIA involvement in drone strikes. They base this inference upon the President's reference to drone strikes in the Federally Administered Tribal Areas of Pakistan, and cite media reports stating that the Department of Defense does not conduct drone strikes in Pakistan. It is precisely this sort of unbridled speculation that is insufficient to support a claim of official disclosure.[77]

This was not a one-off. In October 2011, Obama appeared on the popular *Tonight Show*, describing for millions of Americans the killing of Anwar al-Awlaki: "This was probably the most important Al Qaeda threat that was out there after bin Laden was taken out, and it was important that working with the [Yemenis], we were able to remove him from the field." Once again deploying bizarre logic, the DoJ later insisted that "President Obama's statements did not identify what role the United States played in the events that led to Aulaki's death, and thus could not constitute an official acknowledgment that the US government was responsible."[78] As journalist Glenn Greenwald would note, "The Obama administration runs around telling journalists how great and precise and devastating the CIA's assassination program is, then tells courts that no disclosure is permissible because they cannot safely confirm in court that the program even exists."[79]

The Department of Justice (DoJ) saw its role as ensuring no US federal court ever got to rule on the legality of secret drone strikes. When Anwar al-Awlaki's father attempted to bring a lawsuit preventing the United States from assassinating his US-born son, the administration "declared that courts should play no role in overseeing the executive branch's wartime targeting decisions, argued that Mr. Awlaki's father had no legal standing to bring the case, and invoked the state secrets privilege," as the *New York Times* reported.[80] In December 2010, the judge threw out the suit. Nine months later, Mr. al-Awlaki's son and grandson were killed in Yemen without due process, on the basis of legal advice which to this day remains heavily censored.

Absurdly, despite the overt discussion of the targeted killing campaign by Barack Obama, by his Attorney General, and by many other senior administration officials, the official position of the CIA remained that it could "neither confirm nor deny the existence or non-existence" of any campaign. Judge Colleen McMahon, of the US District Court of Southern New York, complained when throwing out a request for more details on the Anwar al-Awlaki killing that "I can find no way around the thicket of laws and precedents that effectively allow the Executive Branch of our government to proclaim as perfectly lawful certain actions that seem on their face incompatible with our Constitution and laws, while keeping the reasons for their conclusion a secret."[81] Moreover, the Department of Justice insisted in its submissions that the judiciary should have no say whatsoever in "those controversies which revolve around policy choices and value determinations constitutionally committed for resolution to the halls of Congress or the confines of the Executive Branch." District Judge Rosemary Collyer was outraged at this suggestion:

> Your argument is that the court has no role in this—none, none none. I find that a little disconcerting. The scope of your argument concerns me. It gobbles up all the air in the room. . . . The most important part of the United States is that it is a nation of laws.[82]

Collyer ultimately ruled for the government when she decided that CIA and JSOC chiefs could not be held personally liable for the targeted killing of American citizens. Yet in doing so, she firmly asserted the right of federal courts to intervene: "The powers granted to the Executive and Congress to wage war and provide for national security does not give them carte blanche to deprive a US citizen of his life without due process and without any judicial review," the judge noted.[83]

Such obstruction and obfuscation was not restricted to the courts. Congressional committees given the job of overseeing the CIA found themselves in a four-year battle to see key Justice Department memos relating to the claimed lawfulness of the targeted killing campaign. Of eleven known Office of Legal Counsel (OLC) opinions, only five had been shown to members of the Senate and House intelligence committees at the time of publishing.[84] Some of the memos contained "secret protocols with the governments of Yemen and Pakistan on how targeted killings should be conducted," according to one US Senator.[85] While these might have provided reasonable grounds for withholding some of the OLC opinions, influential figures remained concerned. "Democracies do not make war on the basis of legal memos locked in a DoJ [Department of Justice] safe," former CIA director Michael Hayden fretted. "This program rests on the personal legitimacy of the president, and that's not sustainable."[86]

Since 2002, both George W. Bush and Barack Obama had aggressively asserted the lawfulness of targeted killings beyond the hot battlefield while preventing the courts and Congress from competently examining any basis for such claims. Only in spring 2014 was this somewhat challenged, when the US Court of Appeal overturned Judge McMahon's earlier ruling. Instructing the government to release a heavily redacted Office of Legal Counsel memo, which discussed the claimed legal basis for the al-Awlaki killing, the three judges noted: "Whatever protection the legal analysis might once have had has been lost by virtue of public statements of public officials at the highest levels."[87] The memo itself—or what could be read of it—asserted that Awlaki's status as a US citizen, and his subsequent right to due process, were overridden by the "continued and imminent threat of violence or death" he posed to US citizens, thanks to his alleged role as an operational commander of Al Qaeda.[88] The *New York Times* was among those blasting the memo, describing it as "a slapdash pastiche of legal theories—some based on obscure interpretations of British and Israeli law—that was clearly tailored to the desired result."[89]

INTERNAL CONCERNS

George W. Bush had kept America's secret drone wars in the shadows. His successor had dragged them half into the light, and now argued the case for targeted assassinations taking their regular place alongside other US foreign policy tools. As Barack Obama told an audience at the National Defense University in 2013, "Targeted action against terrorists, effective partnerships, diplomatic engagement and assistance—through such a comprehensive strategy we can significantly reduce the chances of large-scale attacks on the homeland and mitigate threats to Americans overseas." For the 44th President of the United States, the use of armed drones in targeted assassinations was win-win: "Dozens of highly skilled al Qaeda commanders, trainers, bomb makers and operatives have been taken off the battlefield. Plots have been disrupted that would have targeted international aviation, US transit systems, European cities and our troops in Afghanistan. Simply put, these strikes have saved lives."[90]

Yet at the very highest reaches of the US military, intelligence, and diplomatic communities, there were concerns at Washington's increased reliance on armed drones beyond the hot battlefield. General Jim Cartwright, former Vice-Chairman of the Joint Chiefs of Staff, had once been a key Obama adviser. Now he argued that the United States was experiencing "blowback" from its heavy use of drone strikes: "If you're trying to kill your way to a solution, no matter how precise you are, you're going to upset people even if they're not targeted," he noted.[91] Fellow General Stanley McChrystal also continued his attacks on any overreliance on drone warfare:

> Although to the United States, a drone strike seems to have very little risk and very little pain, at the receiving end, it feels like war. Americans have got to understand that. If we were to use our technological capabilities carelessly—I don't think we do, but there's always the danger that you will—then we should not be upset when someone responds with their equivalent, which is a suicide bomb in Central Park, because that's what they can respond with.[92]

David Kilcullen, a key counterinsurgency adviser to both the Bush and Obama administrations, was particularly scathing of the latter, which he believes used covert drone strikes as a form of political theater: "They see foreign policy issues, including the war, solely through the lens of their impact on US domestic politics. They really don't have a strategy as such and they don't really think about what they are trying to achieve in the region. They want to be seen to be doing things in order to generate certain political effects at home."[93]

Among some former senior US diplomats too, there was concern that any short-term tactical benefits of drone strikes were not being weighed against their strategic implications. "We've plunged into the tactical aspects of it, if you will, and we revel in the fact that we're killing people, bad people. We disregard the innocents we are killing, or we say if we do regard it, 'Oh, it's much smaller than if we dropped a whole load of 500 pound bombs on them, the collateral damage is really acceptable in this case.' So the strategic dimensions in my mind are adverse, the tactical dimensions notwithstanding," argues former State Department official Lawrence Wilkerson.

Strikes could also undermine US relations with those same countries whose cooperation was badly needed in the fight against Al Qaeda and its allies: "Our counter-terrorism efforts have had a very significant effect. There are militants who wish us harm, and we need to fight them, preferably with the firm cooperation of friends and allies," says the former US Ambassador to Pakistan Cameron Munter. Yet as he notes, "When events such as those in Pakistan from 2010-2012 erode trust, our counter-terrorism effectiveness declines as well. So we need to ask the strategic question: do our immediate counter-terrorism efforts help or hurt our longterm security, especially if the manner by which we carry out those efforts makes us less able to cooperate with others?"[94] Richard Armitage, former US Deputy Secretary of State, recalls his own discomfort on encountering the stepped-up US covert drone campaign in Pakistan in 2009: "It was so antiseptic and was so lacking in any oversight, of checks and balances. And since no Americans were being killed or even in danger of being killed, because of it I thought it could be very easy for the administration to get the US into big trouble."[95]

The intelligence community also had its doubters. Michael Leiter ran the US National Counter Terrorism Center for almost four years to 2011. As he later warned Congress, while he supported targeted killings in appropriate circumstances, "I do believe that our reliance on kinetic strikes has in some cases allowed other efforts to atrophy or at least pale in comparison. This is enormously dangerous, as we cannot strike everywhere nor can we lethally target an ideology. As we increase targeted killings we must double down on our soft power and ideological efforts—building capacity in civilian security forces, increasing the rule of law to diminish under-governed or ungoverned safe havens, and the like—lest we win a few battles and lose a global war."[96] Michael Hayden, the CIA Director who had done much to expand the targeted killing program, now expressed concern at the expanded nature of the project and its longer term effects. And Paul Pillar, former deputy at the CIA's own Counter Terrorism Center, warns that by enraging local populations, drone strikes risk creating perpetual violence. As he told the author:

> To some immeasurable but still significant degree, this anger and resentment has increased the pool of people willing to take the extraordinary step of becoming terrorists themselves. In this sense the killings may have passed a point not only of diminishing returns, but a point of becoming on balance counterproductive as far as counterterrorism, broadly defined, is concerned.[97]

International distaste at US targeted killings had also grown as the program expanded. As part of its long-running study into the global reputation of the United States, in 2013 the nonpartisan Pew Research Center asked citizens of 39 nations for their views on US covert drone strikes. In most, a clear majority disapproved, often by large margins. As Pew noted, more than three-quarters of citizens were against "in 15 countries from all corners of the world, including nations from the Middle East, Europe, Latin America and Asia." Only in Israel, Kenya, and the United States itself were majorities found to be in favor.[98]

The United Nations too continued its criticism of the program, routinely describing covert strikes as extrajudicial killings. For more than a decade, Washington had locked the UN out, insisting it had no jurisdiction. However, in a surprise move a special rapporteur was finally invited to Langley in 2013: "I was brought in—called in—by John Brennan, who is the Director of the CIA, who reaffirmed his view that that is not the job of an intelligence agency, to go around the world conducting assassinations," Ben Emmerson QC later told British MPs. Yet this may have been wishful thinking on Brennan's part. Almost two years after he first proposed the Agency's drone operations be transferred to the Pentagon, there had been no change. In part this was due to a turf battle between the CIA and the Pentagon. Prior to 9/11, neither wanted control of the newly armed Predators. Now both sought ownership of a vastly expanded program which employed tens of thousands of military and intelligence personnel—and commanded billions of dollars in budgets. The secrecy protections and deniability, which CIA operations offered, may also have proved too beguiling for politicians wary of public scrutiny. As the Agency's former Acting General Counsel noted in his memoirs: "I would respectfully predict that future presidents will not only continue to be in the business of killing, but will double down on it. And that the CIA will salute the commander in chief and be in the middle of it, without hesitation or resistance."[99]

Armed drones—remotely piloted aircraft—had amply demonstrated their value on the modern battlefield. A combined weapon platform and intelligence system, used wisely they could significantly reduce the risk faced by civilians caught up in war. Yet it was their role as an aerial sniper rifle which continued to generate most controversy. The United States targeted and killed more than 2,800 people in its secret conflicts in Pakistan and Yemen to the end of 2014. This was four times the number of executions carried out on US soil over the same period, as a consequence of due process.[100] And as many as one in five of those killed were civilians—whatever the CIA's claims to the contrary. President Bush once described America's newfound ability to bring "sudden justice" to its enemies below. For more than a decade, the United States had enjoyed a near-monopoly in remote targeting, revolutionizing modern warfare—and pushing hard at the boundaries of international law in the process. With dozens of countries—and even terrorist groups—likely to have access to their own armed drones in the near future, the challenge ahead lay in convincing others not to follow Washington's own recent rule book.

REPORTS OF WESTERNERS KILLED IN US TARGETED STRIKES, SEPTEMBER 2001 TO DECEMBER 2014

Date	Name	Nationality	Place of death
November 3, 2002	Kemal Darwish	American	Yemen
December 1, 2005	Raquel Burgos Garcia	Spanish	Pakistan
	Amer Azizi	Spanish	Pakistan
January 2007	4 unknowns	British	Somalia*
June 2007	1 unknown	British	Somalia*
	1 unknown	American	Somalia*
	1 unknown	Swedish	Somalia*
August 30, 2008	2	Canadian	Pakistan
November 7, 2008	2+	American	Pakistan
	2+	"Westerners"	Pakistan
November 22, 2008	Rashid Rauf	British	Pakistan
? 2010	"Abbas"	British?	Pakistan
? 2010	Inaam	American?	Pakistan
September 8, 2010	Abdul Jabbar?	British	Pakistan
October 4, 2010	Binyamin Erdogan	German	Pakistan

(*Continued*)

(Continued)

Date	Name	Nationality	Place of death
	Shahab Dashti	German	Pakistan
October 18, 2010?	Hayrettin Burhan	German	Pakistan
October 27, 2010	2 unknown	"Westerners"	Pakistan
December 10, 2010	"Mr. Dearsmith"	British	Pakistan
	"Mr. Stephen"	British	Pakistan
July 5, 2011	"Saifullah"	Australian	Pakistan
September 11, 2011	Mohammad al Faateh	German	Pakistan
September/ November 2011	Ibrahim Adam	British	Pakistan
	Mohammed Azir	British	Pakistan
	0–2 unknown	British	Pakistan
September 30, 2011	Anwar al-Awlaki	American	Yemen
	Samir Khan	American	Yemen
October 14, 2011	Abdel-Rahman al-Awlaki	American	Yemen
November 16, 2011	Jude Kenan Mohamed	American	Pakistan
January 21, 2012	Bilal al-Berjawi	British	Somalia
February 16, 2012	Patrick K	German	Pakistan
February 23, 2012	Mohamed Sakr	British	Somalia
March 9, 2012	Samir H	German	Pakistan
October 10, 2012	Ahmad B	German	Pakistan
	Moezzedine Garsalloui	Belgian/Swiss	Pakistan
November 19, 2013	Christopher Harvard	Australian	Yemen
	Daryl Jones	Australia/NZ	Yemen
	"Abu Salma al Russi"	Russian	Yemen

* Airstrike with other assets.

NOTES

INTRODUCTION

1. Barack Obama, "Remarks by the President on the Situation in Iraq," White House, June 19, 2014, at http://www.whitehouse.gov/the-press-office/2014/06/19/remarks-president-situation-iraq.
2. Ben Kiernan and Taylor Owen, "Bombs over Cambodia," The Walrus, October 2006, at http://www.yale.edu/cgp/Walrus_CambodiaBombing_OCT06.pdf.
3. This generously assumes 1,500 Hellfire missiles fired between 2002 and 2014 in Pakistan, Yemen, and Somalia, with each weighing around 50 kg (giving an estimated 100 tons total) and an additional 650 GBU-112 strikes, each weighing 230 kg (giving a further 150 tons). While no CIA munitions data has been released, figures from the Royal Air Force for its Afghanistan Reapers show that no more than two missiles on average were released in kinetic sorties over a four-year period. "UK Armed Reaper Activity in Afghanistan," via Drone Wars UK, archived at http://dronewars.net/uk-drone-strike-list-2/.
.4.. See for example "Hezbollah uses UAV to attack al-Qaeda backed rebels," YNet News, September 21, 2014, at http://www.ynetnews.com/articles/ 0,7340,L-4573625,00.html.

CHAPTER 1

1. Estimates provided by the Department of the Air Force.
2. Lawrence Spinetta, "The Rise of Unmanned Aircraft," *Aviation History* magazine, November 10, 2010, archived at http://www.historynet.com/the-rise-of-unmanned-aircraft.htm. Reuters reported that in 2011, USAF trained 350 RPA pilots against 250 bomber and fighter pilots: Tabassum Zakaria, "In New Mexico Desert, Drone Pilots Learn New Art of War," Reuters, April 23, 2013, at http://www.reuters.com/article/2013/04/23/us-usa-security-drones-idUSBRE93M04520130423.
3. Interview with the author, January 2014.
4. Interview with the author, September 2013.
5. According to the MoD, between March 2011 and June 2014, of 388 precision-guided munitions dropped by the United Kingdom in Afghanistan

317 (81%) were by drones. See Defence Minister Mark Francois, Written Answers, Hansard, July 7, 2014, at http://www.publications.parliament.uk/pa/cm201415/cmhansrd/cm140707/text/140707w0006.htm.

6. Chuck Blanchard, General Counsel, US Department of the Air Force, speaking at "Drones, Remote Targeting and the Promise of Law 2," New America Foundation, February 24, 2011, archived at http://www.ustream.tv/recorded/12909598.

7. Total US troop numbers at November 2013, via Report on Progress toward Security and Stability in Afghanistan, US Department of Defense, at http://www.defense.gov/pubs/October_1230_Report_Master_Nov7.pdf.

8. See, for example, "Hamid Karzai Refuses to Budge over Delay on Security Pact," Guardian, November 26, 2013, at http://www.theguardian.com/world/2013/nov/26/hamid-karzai-afghanistan-security-pact.

9. Michael R. Gordon and Eric Schmitt, "U.S. Sends Arms to Aid Iraq Fight with Extremists," New York Times, December 25, 2013, at http://www.nytimes.com/2013/12/26/world/middleeast/us-sends-arms-to-aid-iraq-fight-with-extremists.html.

10. Report on Progress toward Security and Stability in Afghanistan, US Department of Defense, November 2013, at http://www.defense.gov/pubs/October_1230_Report_Master_Nov7.pdf.

11. Interview with the author, May 2014.

12. Hamid Karzai, Statement from the Office of the President, November 30, 2013, author's copy.

13. Rod Nordland, "U.S. General Apologizes after Afghan Drone Strike," New York Times, November 29, 2013, at http://www.nytimes.com/2013/11/30/world/asia/drone-strike-in-afghanistan.html.

14. Declan Walsh, "Afghanistan and U.S. Sign Bilateral Security Agreement," New York Times, September 30, 2014, at http://www.nytimes.com/2014/10/01/world/asia/afghanistan-and-us-sign-bilateral-security-agreement.html.

15. Reliable casualty figures are not available prior to this time, though estimates indicate an additional 5,000 or more civilians died as a result of conflict 2001-2006. UN data is inclusive from 2007 to 2013. For all data sets, see http://unama.unmissions.org/Default.aspx?tabid=13941&language=en-US.

16. The remaining civilian deaths could not be attributed directly to either party or were the result of anti- and pro-government clashes. Afghanistan Annual Report 2013: Protection of Civilians in Armed Conflict, UNAMA, February 8, 2014, at http://unama.unmissions.org/Portals/UNAMA/human%20rights/Feb_8_2014_PoC-report_2013-Full-report-ENG.pdf.

17. UNAMA reported a total of 1,523 civilians killed in 2007. Some 700 deaths were attributed to anti-government elements, with 629 civilians reported killed by pro-government forces. Civilian Casualties during 2007, UNAMA, at http://unama.unmissions.org/Portals/UNAMA/human%20rights/PoC-Civilian-Casualties-report-2007.pdf.

18. "Unfortunately, some people are using allegations of civilian casualties for political purposes," an anonymous ISAF official claimed just days before the Nazir killing. Rod Nordland, "Karzai Insists U.S. Forces Killed Civilians in a Raid,"

New York Times, November 23, 2013, at http://www.nytimes.com/2013/11/24/world/asia/us-upset-by-karzais-claim-about-civilian-deaths.html.

19. Karzai first publicly protested civilian deaths in July 2005, with his spokesman noting that "the president is extremely saddened and distressed to hear the report that recent military operations in Konar by the coalition forces resulted in the death of civilians." "US Afghan Tactics 'Need Rethink,'" BBC News, July 5, 2005, at http://news.bbc.co.uk/1/hi/world/south_asia/4653481.stm.

20. Ruth Fowler, "The Kabul Diaries 5: Drones," August 13, 2013, at http://theworldbreakseveryone.com/the-kabul-diaries-5-drones/.

21. Interview with the author, background terms.

22. Larry Lewis, "Drone Strikes: Civilian Casualty Considerations—Executive Summary," June 18, 2013, Joint and Coalition Operational Analysis, at http://www.cna.org/sites/default/files/research/Drone_Strikes.pdf.

23. Afghanistan: Mid-Year Report 2013—Protection of Civilians in Armed Conflict, UNAMA, July 2013, at http://unama.unmissions.org/Default.aspx?tabid=13941&language=en-US.

24. Confirmed by ISAF to UNAMA at "deconfliction" meetings on January 9 and 12, 2014. ISAF also confirmed civilian casualties in the attack, according to a source.

25. Interview with the author, January 2014.

26. Four Helmand districts featured in the "Ten Most Violent Districts in Afghanistan," in Report on Progress toward Security and Stability in Afghanistan, US Department of Defense, April 2014, at http://www.defense.gov/pubs/April_1230_Report_Final.pdf.

27. George W. Bush: "See, they used to think they could hide. But you can't hide from the United States of America. . . . Some have met their fate by sudden justice; some are now answering questions at Guantanamo Bay. In either case, they're no longer a problem to the United States of America and our friends." Fort Hood, Texas, January 3, 2003, at http://georgewbush-whitehouse.archives.gov/news/releases/2003/01/20030103.html.

28. Cited in RAF Operational Updates published to September 2012. Archived at "UK Drone Strike Stats," Drone Wars UK, at http://dronewars.net/uk-drone-strike-list-2/.

29. Cited in Remote Control: Remotely Piloted Air Systems—Current and Future UK Use: Volume II Written evidence, Appendix A: RAF Operational Updates, House of Commons Defence Select Committee, March 11, 2014, at http://www.publications.parliament.uk/pa/cm201314/cmselect/cmdfence/772/772vw.pdf.

30. Cited in Rod Nordland, "U.S. General Apologizes after Afghan Drone Strike," *New York Times*, November 29, 2013, at http://www.nytimes.com/2013/11/30/world/asia/drone-strike-in-afghanistan.html.

31. Stanley McChrystal interview, "Afghanistan 'Needs Friends' in the West," *Today* programme, BBC Radio 4, January 21, 2014, at http://www.bbc.co.uk/programmes/p01q8v2y.

32. Interview with the author, September 2013.

33. Originally each GCS was housed in its own outdoor steel box. While these were still used for training and overseas missions, most drone squadrons had transitioned to indoor "boxes" housed within a single building.

34. Robert Evans and Brandon Bryant, "6 Myths about Drone Warfare You Probably Believe," Cracked, November 5, 2013, at http://www.cracked.com/article_20725_6-myths-about-drone-warfare-you-probably-believe.html.

35. Interview with the author November 2013.

36. Cited in The Future of Air Force Motion Imagery Exploitation, Rand: Project Air Force, 2012, at http://www.rand.org/content/dam/rand/pubs/technical_reports/2012/RAND_TR1133.pdf.

37. Lolita Baldor, "Air Force Works to Fill Need for Drone Pilots," Associated Press, August 9, 2012, at http://bigstory.ap.org/article/air-force-works-fill-need-drone-pilots. Aram Roston, "Targeted Killing: CIA's Fleet of 80+ UAVs Unlikely to be Transferred to Military," Defense News, May 15, 2013, at http://www.defensenews.com/article/20130515/C4ISR/305150026.

38. The remotely operated video enhanced receiver, or ROVER, was developed during the 2001 invasion of Afghanistan. The 2013 model, ROVER 6, allowed ground forces to observe what a drone was seeing and enabled extensive two-way communication with RPA operators.

39. Interview with the author, October 2013. However, as chapter 6 notes, Barack Obama did indeed plan to call up AFSOC operators to give the kill order for US citizen Anwar al-Awlaki in Yemen.

40. Donald Rumsfeld, Known and Unknown: A Memoir (New York: Sentinel, 2011), 390.

41. Cited by Col. James Bitzes, former chief legal advisor at the CAOC, speaking at Drones, Remote Targeting and the Promise of Law, New America Foundation, February 24, 2011, at http://counterterrorism.newamerica.net/events/2011/drones_targeting_and_law.

42. Interview with the author, background terms.

43. Interview with the author, September 2013. For more on the evolution of Kill/Capture in Iraq and the crucial role played by armed drones, see chapter 4.

44. Interview with the author, background terms.

45. Interview with the author, background terms.

46. Jeremy Scahill and Glenn Greenwald, "The NSA's Secret Role in the U.S. Assassination Program," The Intercept, February 10, 2014, at https://firstlook.org/theintercept/article/2014/02/10/the-nsas-secret-role/.

47. Brandon Bryant, interview with the author, October 2013.

48. Steve, a former USAF major, interviewed by the author, Langley AFB, December 2013. Surname withheld at the request of USAF.

49. Email to the author from ISAF Chief of Press Desk Lt. Col. Will Griffin, May 4, 2014.

50. Creech AFB listed as part of the 432nd Operations Group the following squadrons: 11th Reconnaissance Squadron (training), 15th RS, 18th RS, 20th RS, and 42nd Attack Squadron (active duty), and the 432nd Operations Support Squadron.

51. See Chris Woods, "CIA's Pakistan Drone Strikes Carried out by Regular US Air Force Personnel," *Guardian*, April 14, 2014, at http://www.theguardian.com/world/2014/apr/14/cia-drones-pakistan-us-air-force-documentary.

52. Clive Williams, "Measuring the Loss of the RQ-170 Sentinel in Iran," ABC News Australia, December 22, 2011, at http://www.abc.net.au/unleashed/3743946.html.

53. Email to author April 11, 2014, from 432nd Air Expeditionary Wing Public Affairs, Creech AFB.

54. Greg Miller, "CIA Seeks to Expand Drone Fleet, Officials Say," *Washington Post*, October 19, 2012, at http://www.washingtonpost.com/world/national-security/cia-seeks-to-expand-drone-fleet-officials-say/2012/10/18/01149a8c-1949-11e2-bd10-5ff056538b7c_story.html. Aram Roston, "Targeted Killing: CIA's Fleet of 80+ UAVs Unlikely to be Transferred to Military," Defense News, May 15, 2013, at http://www.defensenews.com/article/20130515/C4ISR/305150026.

55. "Eyes of the Warrior," Air Force Magazine, June 2002, at http://www.airforcemag.com/MagazineArchive/Magazine%20Documents/2002/June%202002/0602warrior.pdf.

56. Former AFSOC Predator operator Brandon Bryant, interviewed by Tonje Hessen Schei, New York, October 2013, observed by author.

57. Interview with the author, January 2014.

58. Dion Nissenbaum, "Blackwater's Founder Blames U.S. for Its Troubles," *Wall Street Journal*, November 17, 2013, at http://online.wsj.com/news/articles/SB10001424052702304439804579203883470837874.

59. Interview with the author, details withheld.

60. Author's archive.

61. Author's archive.

62. Chris Woods, "CIA's Pakistan Drone Strikes Carried out by Regular US Air Force Personnel," *Guardian*, April 14, 2014, at http://www.theguardian.com/world/2014/apr/14/cia-drones-pakistan-us-air-force-documentary.

63. Email to the author, April 2014.

64. Interviewed by Tonje Hessen Schei, New York, October 2013. Author present.

65. Email to the author, April 2014.

66. Jeremy Scahill, *Dirty Wars: The World Is a Battlefield* (London: Serpent's Tail, 2013), 500.

67. Jeremy Scahill, "The Secret US War in Pakistan," *The Nation*, September 23, 2009, at http://www.thenation.com/article/secret-us-war-pakistan#.

68. Interviews with former AFSOC operators, background terms.

CHAPTER 2

1. "Since the U.S. went to war in Afghanistan in 2001 and Iraq in 2003, about 2.5 million members of the Army, Navy, Marines, Air Force, Coast Guard and related Reserve and National Guard units have been deployed in the Afghanistan and Iraq wars, according to Department of Defense data." Cited

by Chris Adams, "Millions Went to War in Iraq, Afghanistan, Leaving Many with Lifelong Scars," McClatchy, March 14, 2013, at http://www.mcclatchydc.com/2013/03/14/185880/millions-went-to-war-in-iraq-afghanistan.html#.UhyD45LVApk#storylink=cpy.

2. For a detailed account of the 2001 air war in Afghanistan, see Benjamin S. Lambeth's excellent *air Power Against Terror: America's Conduct of Operation Enduring Freedom* (Santa Monica, CA: Rand Corporation, 2005).

3. Tommy Franks, *American Soldier* (New York: Regan Books, 2004), 284.

4. Interviews with the author, January 2014.

5. Donald Rumsfeld, *Known and Unknown: A Memoir* (New York: Sentinel, 2011), 389.

6. Franks, *American Soldier*, 289–294.

7. Interview with the author, December 2013.

8. Rumsfeld, *Known and Unknown*, 388.

9. Interview with the author, background terms.

10. According to a senior Pentagon official with close knowledge of the strike, a small number of Mullah Omar's bodyguards were killed. Interview with the author, background terms.

11. Scott Swanson, "War Is No Video Game – Not Even Remotely," *Breaking Defense*, November 18, 2014, at http://breakingdefense.com/2014/11/war-is-no-video-game-not-even-remotely/.

12. Interview with the author, December 2013.

13. As of April 4, 2013, 41 employee reviews of GA-ASI showed 20 were satisfied against 10 dissatisfied and 11 neutral. General Atomics Aeronautical Systems Reviews, Glassdoor, at http://www.glassdoor.com/Reviews/GA-ASI-Reviews-E15889.htm.

14. Winslow Wheeler, "4: Keeping Track of the Drones," *Time*, March 1, 2012, at http://nation.time.com/2012/03/01/4-keeping-track-of-the-drones/.

15. Defense Acquisitions: Assessments of Selected Weapon Programs, United States Government Accountability Office, Report to Congressional Committees, March 2011, at http://www.gao.gov/new.items/d11233sp.pdf.

16. US Department of Defense, Selected Acquisition Report, MQ-1B UAS PREDATOR, June 2010. Copy obtained by author.

17. The judge found in favor of General Atomics in *United States ex rel. Sam Kholi v. General Atomics et al.*, United States District Court, Southern District of California, September 18, 2003. Papers released to the author under Freedom of Information Act (FOIA).

18. See, for example, General Atomics Technologies Corporation pages at Manta, at http://www.manta.com/c/mm4wsg9/general-atomic-technologies-corporation.

19. See GATC submission to US Nuclear Regulatory Commission, May 7, 1986, archived at http://pbadupws.nrc.gov/docs/ML0303/ML030300494.pdf.

20. "Great Adventures, Flight of the Blue Bird," *Life*, April 8, 1957.

21. Di Freeze, "Linden Blue: From Disease-Resistant Bananas to UAVs," *Airport Journals*, October 1, 2005, at http://airportjournals.com/linden-blue-from-disease-resistant-bananas-to-uavs/.

22. "Earlier, at Managua, Nicaragua, [the brothers] had interviewed the late President Somoza." Cited in "Great Adventures, Flight of the Blue Bird," *Life*, April 8, 1957.

23. Charles Duhigg, "The Pilotless Plane That Only Looks Like Child's Play," *New York Times*, April 15, 2007, at http://www.nytimes.com/2007/04/15/business/yourmoney/15atomics.html.

24. Freeze, "Linden Blue."

25. Ibid.

26. Duhigg, "The Pilotless Plane."

27. Barney Gimbel, "The Predator: A Profile of Neal Blue," *Fortune* magazine, October 31, 2008, 3 of 4, at http://money.cnn.com/2008/10/28/magazines/fortune/predator_gimbel.fortune/index.htm.

28. Duhigg, "The Pilotless Plane."

29. Richard Whittle, "The Man Who Invented the Predator," *The Smithsonian Air and Space* magazine, April 2013, at http://www.airspacemag.com/flight-today/The-Man-Who-Invented-the-Predator-198846671.html.

30. Comment to the author, background terms.

31. Emailed notes to the author, October 2013.

32. Interview with the author, London, May 2013.

33. Andreas Parsch, *Leading Systems' Amber, Directory of US Military Rockets and Vehicles, Appendix 4: Undesignated Vehicles*, 2004, at http://www.designation-systems.net/dusrm/app4/amber.html.

34. Thomas Erhard, *Air Force UAVs—The Secret History*, The Mitchell Institute, July 2010.

35. Michael J. Hirschberg, *To Boldly Go Where No Unmanned Aircraft Has Gone Before: A Half-Century of DARPA's Contributions to Unmanned Aircraft*, American Institute of Aeronautics and Astronautics, January 2010, 11–13.

36. Interview with the author, London, March 2013.

37. Clarence A. Robinson Jr., "Interview with Frank W. Pace, President, Aircraft Systems Group, General Atomics Aeronautical Systems, Inc.," Defense Media Network, October 28, 2011, at http://www.defensemedianetwork.com/stories/unmanned-heritage-unmanned-future/.

38. Interview with the author, December 2013.

39. Michael R. Thirtle, Robert V. Johnson, and John L. Bidder, "The Predator ACTD: A Case Study for Transition Planning to the Formal Acquisition Process," National Defense Research Institute/Rand 1997, at http://www.dtic.mil/cgi-bin/GetTRDoc?AD=ADA337401.

40. Peter Finn, "Rise of the Drone: From Calif. Garage to Multibillion-Dollar Defense Industry," *Washington Post*, December 24, 2011, at http://www.washingtonpost.com/national/national-security/rise-of-the-drone-from-calif-garage-to-multibillion-dollar-defense-industry/2011/12/22/gIQACG8UEP_story.html.

41. "The Drone Father," *The Economist Technology Quarterly*, December 1, 2012, at http://www.economist.com/news/technology-quarterly/21567205-abe-karem-created-robotic-plane-transformed-way-modern-warfare.

42. Frank Strickland, "The Early Evolution of the Predator Drone," *Studies in Intelligence* 57, no. 1 (Extracts, March 2013), CIA Library, at https://www.cia.

gov/library/center-for-the-study-of-intelligence/csi-publications/csi-studies/
studies/vol.-57-no.-1-a/vol.-57-no.-1-a-pdfs/Strickland-Evolution%20of%20
the%20Predator.pdf.

43. Note to the author, June 2013.

44. Interview with the author, October 2013.

45. Interview with the author, April 2013.

46. General Atomics Campaign Finances, Influence Explorer, at http://
influenceexplorer.com/organization/generalatomics/691e0f84c20e487596a88
f6376eda155?cycle=1998.

47. Duhigg, "The Pilotless Plane." See also General Atomics Campaign
Finances, Influence Explorer, at http://influenceexplorer.com/organization/
general-atomics/691e0f84c20e487596a88f6376eda155?cycle=1998.

48. Retired Major General George Harrison, interview with the author March 2013.

49. Interview with Ken Israel, March 2013.

50. Mark Mazzetti, *The Way of the Knife: The CIA, a Secret Army, and a War at the
Ends of the Earth* (New York: Penguin Press, 2013), 90–91.

51. Linda D. Kozaryn, "Predators Bound for Bosnia," American Forces Press
Service, February 8, 1996, at http://www.defense.gov/News/NewsArticle.
aspx?ID=40516.

52. Stephen Trimble, "A History of Predator from the Ultimate Insider,"
Flight Global, March 17, 2011, at http://www.flightglobal.com/blogs/
the-dewline/2011/03/a-history-of-predator-from-the.html.

53. Interview with the author, London, April 2013.

54. Kenneth Israel, UAV Annual Report FY 1996, Defense Airborne Reconnaissance
Office, November 6, 1996, declassified. Archived at http://www.gwu.
edu/~nsarchiv/NSAEBB/NSAEBB63/doc5.pdf.

55. Cited by Ehrhard, *Air Force UAVs*.

56. Factsheet: 11th Reconnaissance Squadron, USAF Air Warfare Center Public
Affairs Division, January 2001, at http://www.uavm.com/images/11thRS.pdf.

57. "Indian Springs Renamed Creech Air Force Base," United States Air Force, press
release, June 20, 2005, at http://archive.is/sACO.

58. Steven L. Hampton interview, June 12, 1998, cited by Ehrhard, *Air Force UAVs*,
51 n.

59. Others took a different approach. When the RAF began seconding personnel to
USAF Predator operations in 2004, they decided all aircrew should be officers.
In contrast both the US and British Armies only used enlisted personnel to crew
their respective Gray Eagle and Watchkeeper projects.

60. John A. Tirpak, "The Robotic Air Force," September 1997, at http://
www.airforcemag.com/MagazineArchive/Pages/1997/September%20
1997/0997robotic.aspx.

61. There were differing views among interviewees about whether a Serbian tank
was also present.

62. Interview with the author, October 2013.

63. For a forensic account of the arming of Predator, see Richard Whittle, *Predator's
Big Safari*, Mitchell Institute for Airpower Studies, 2011, archived at https://
higherlogicdownload.s3.amazonaws.com/AFA/6379b747-7730-4f82-9

b45-a1c80d6c8fdb/UploadedImages/Mitchell%20Publications/Predator's%20
Big%20Safari.pdf.

64. Testimony to US Congress of Michael Scheuer, former head of the CIA's Bin Laden Unit, who authored and ran the extraordinary rendition program. *Extraordinary Rendition in US Counterterrorism Policy: The Impact on Transatlantic Relations*, US House of Representatives Foreign Affairs Committee, April 17, 2007, archived at http://www.fas.org/irp/congress/2007_hr/rendition.pdf.

65. *Black Hole: The Fate of Islamists Rendered to Egypt*, Human Rights Watch, July 2005, at http://www.hrw.org/sites/default/files/reports/egypt0505.pdf.

66. In 1999, the CIA aided in the secret capture and rendition to torture of two of al-Zawahiri's brothers. See *Black Hole: The Fate of Islamists Rendered to Egypt*, 24–30, Human Rights Watch, July 2005, at http://www.hrw.org/sites/default/files/reports/egypt0505.pdf.

67. Cited in Jane Mayer, *The Dark Side: The Inside Story of How the War on Terror Turned into a War on American Ideals* (New York: Random House, 2009), 112–115.

68. Scott Baker, "Secret Until Now: Osama Raid Avenged CIA Deaths," Associated Press, May 29, 2011, at http://www.theblaze.com/stories/2011/05/29/secret-until-now-osama-raid-avenged-cia-deaths/.

69. *Bombings of the Embassies of the United States of America at Nairobi, Kenya and Dar es Salaam, Tanzania*, FBI Executive Summary, November 18, 1998, declassified, archived at http://www.pbs.org/wgbh/pages/frontline/shows/binladen/bombings/summary.html.

70. In an extended BBC interview the author directed with the former president in 2004, Clinton noted that having to deal with Al Qaeda at the White House meant he was not having such a hard time at home: "It was a relief to have to go to work and concentrate on something else cos otherwise I would have nothing to think about all day long but what a bad fella I'd been." The Clinton Interview, BBC Panorama, presented by David Dimbleby, June 22, 2004, transcript at http://news.bbc.co.uk/nol/shared/spl/hi/programmes/panorama/transcripts/clintoninterview.txt.

71. See, for example, "U.S. Missiles Pound Targets in Afghanistan, Sudan," CNN, August 20, 1998, at http://www.cnn.co.uk/US/9808/20/us.strikes.01/.

72. Oriana Zill, "The Controversial US Retaliatory Missile Strikes," PBS, at http://www.pbs.org/wgbh/pages/frontline/shows/binladen/bombings/retaliation.html.

73. Marc Hujer, "Interview with Richard Clarke: 'Capturing Bin Laden Was Not One of Their Big Priorities,'" *Der Spiegel*, May 10, 2011, at http://www.spiegel.de/international/world/interview-with-richard-clarke-capturing-bin-laden-was-not-one-of-their-big-priorities-a-761458.html.

74. *Final Report of the National Commission on Terrorist Attacks upon the United States* [The 9/11 Commission Report], July 22, 2004, 189, at http://www.9-11commission.gov/report/.

75. The CIA's internal debates on the Predator are referenced in "The Rise of UBL and Al Qaida and the Intelligence Community Response," DCI Report,

March 19, 2004, declassified, archived at https://www.documentcloud.org/documents/368992-2004-03-19-dci-report-the-rise-of-ubl-and-al.html.

76. The 911 Commission Report, chapter 6 "From Threat to Threat," especially 188–190.

77. USAF's hands-on role is confirmed in George Tenet, "Written Statement for the Record of the Director of Central Intelligence before the 911 Commission," March 24, 2004, declassified and archived at https://www.documentcloud.org/documents/369182-2004-03-24-statement-for-the-record-of-the.html.

78. The CIA's drones were controlled by the ad hoc 32nd Expeditionary Air Intelligence Squadron, a secret USAF unit. See Richard Whittle, *Predator: The Secret Origins of the Drone Revolution* (New York: Henry Holt, 2014).

79. Steve Coll, *Ghost Wars: The Secret History of the CIA, Afghanistan, and bin Laden, from the Soviet Invasion to September 10, 2001* (New York: Penguin, 2004), 527–534.

80. Interview with the author, March 2014.

81. Interview with senior Pentagon official, background terms, December 2013.

82. In parallel General John Jumper, head of Air Combat Command, had also ordered that arming trials be conducted on the Predator. See cable from Jumper to USAF Headquarters, May 2000, archived at http://www2.gwu.edu/~nsarchiv/NSAEBB/NSAEBB484/docs/Predator-Whittle%20Document%207%20-%20ACC%20message%201%20May%202000%20re%20arming%20Predator.pdf.

83. "Both Amber and Gnat [Predator prototypes] were designed to carry under wing sensor pods such as SIGINT," notes inventor Abe Karem. Email to author, November 4, 2013.

84. To view the declassified Hellfire missile launch of January 23, 2001, and other important documents and materials related to this book, see http://www.suddenjustice.org.

85. A similar mock-up of bin Laden's Abbottabad house a decade later would help train the Special Operations Forces who finally killed him. See Barton Gellman, "A Strategy's Cautious Evolution," *Washington Post*, January 20, 2002, at http://www.washingtonpost.com/wp-dyn/content/article/2006/06/09/AR2006060900885.html.

86. Peter L. Bergen, *The Longest War: The Enduring Conflict between America and Al-Qaeda* (New York: Simon and Schuster, 2010), 45.

87. Thomas P. Christie, "Operational Test and Evaluation Report on the Predator Medium-Altitude Endurance Unmanned Aerial Vehicle (UAV)," September 2001. Copy obtained by the author.

88. General Chuck Wald, interview with the author, December 2013.

89. The "R" denoted their pure reconnaissance role.

90. Interview with the author, October 2013.

91. Gary C. Schroen, *First In: An Insider's Account of How the CIA Spearheaded the War on Terror in Afghanistan* (New York: Ballantine Books, 2005), 38.

92. Devotion to Duty: Afghanistan, CIA Library, at https://www.cia.gov/library/publications/additional-publications/devotion-to-duty/afghanistan.html.

93. Interview with the author, December 2013.

94. Schroen, *First In*, 166–167.

95. Author's interview with General Charles "Chuck" Wald, December 2013.

96. Daniel Klaidman, "Bin Laden's Poetry of Terror," *Newsweek*, March 26, 2001, at http://www.newsweek.com/bin-ladens-poetry-terror-149115.

97. Stephen Grey, "US Kills Al Qaeda Leaders by Remote Control," *Sunday Times*, November 18, 2001, archived at http://www.foxnews.com/story/2001/11/19/us-kills-al-qaeda-leaders-by-remote-control/.

98. Gary Berntsen with Ralph Pezzullo, *Jawbreaker: The Attack on bin Laden and Al Qaeda—A Personal Account by the CIA's Key Field Commander* (New York: Crown Publishers, 2005), 139.

99. Whittle, *Predator: The Secret Origins of the Drone Revolution.*

100. George Tenet, "Meritorious Unit Citation," December 12, 2002, archived at http://www2.gwu.edu/~nsarchiv/NSAEBB/NSAEBB484/docs/Predator-Whittle%20Document%2015%20-%20EAIS%20CIA%20unit%20citation%20from%20Tenet%20-%20source%20Mark%20Cooter.pdf.

101. George W. Bush address to The Citadel, December 11, 2001, transcript archived at http://www3.citadel.edu/pao/addresses/presbush01.html.

CHAPTER 3

1. Donald Rumsfeld, *Known and Unknown: A Memoir* (New York: Sentinel, 2011), 402.

2. John Sifton, "A Brief History of Drones," *The Nation*, February 27, 2012, at http://www.thenation.com/article/166124/brief-history-drones.

3. John F. Burns, "U.S. Leapt before Looking, Angry Villagers Say," *New York Times*, February 17, 2002, at http://www.nytimes.com/2002/02/17/world/a-nation-challenged-the-manhunt-us-leapt-before-looking-angry-villagers-say.html.

4. Thom Shanker and Carlotta Gall, "U.S. Attack on Warlord Aims to Help Interim Leader," *New York Times*, May 8, 2002, at http://www.nytimes.com/2002/05/09/world/us-attack-on-warlord-aims-to-help-interim-leader.html.

5. Steve Coll, *Ghost Wars: The Secret History of the CIA, Afghanistan, and bin Laden, from the Soviet Invasion to September 10, 2001* (New York: Penguin, 2004), 119–121.

6. Julian Borger, "'CIA Missile' Fails to Kill Afghan Faction Leader," *Guardian*, May 10, 2002, at http://www.theguardian.com/world/2002/may/10/afghanistan.julianborger.

7. "CIA 'Tried to Kill Afghan Warlord,'" BBC News, May 10, 2002, at http://news.bbc.co.uk/1/hi/world/south_asia/1978619.stm.

8. *Final Report of the National Commission on Terrorist Attacks upon the United States* [The 9/11 Commission Report], July 22, 2004, 211, at http://www.9-11commission.gov/report/.

9. DCIA Tenet testimony to 911 Commission, March 2004, 18, declassified June 2012, archived at https://www.documentcloud.org/documents/369182-2004-03-24-statement-for-the-record-of-the.html.

10. Presidential Executive Order 11905, United States Foreign Intelligence Activities, Section 5, Clause G: Prohibition of Assassination, February 18, 1976, archived at http://www.fas.org/irp/offdocs/eo11905.htm#SEC. 5.

11. Presidential Executive Order 12036: United States Intelligence Activities, 2-305. Prohibition on Assassination. "No person employed by or acting on behalf of the United States Government shall engage in, or conspire to engage in, assassination." January 24, 1978, archived at https://www.fas.org/irp/offdocs/eo/eo-12036.htm.

12. Casper W. Weinberger, "When Can We Target the Leaders?" *Strategic Review* 29, no. 2 (Spring 2001): 23–24.

13. W. Hays Parks, Memorandum of Law: Executive Order 12333 and Assassination, November 2, 1989, archived at https://www.law.upenn.edu/institutes/cerl/conferences/targetedkilling/papers/ParksMemorandum.pdf.

14. Osama bin Laden et al., "Fatwa Urging Jihad against Americans," originally published in *Al-Quds al-Arabi*, February 23, 1998, archived in English translation at http://www.unitedstatesaction.com/war-declaration2.htm.

15. John Rizzo, *Company Man: Thirty Years of Controversy and Crisis at the CIA* (New York: Scribner, 2014), 161–174.

16. CIA OIG Report on CIA Accountability with Respect to the 9/11 Attacks, June 2005, declassified and archived at https://www.cia.gov/library/reports/Executive%20Summary_OIG%20Report.pdf.

17. Cited in the 911 Commission Report, 188.

18. Correspondence with the author, December 2013.

19. Interview with the author, March 2014.

20. Many of the Principals at this meeting have penned their own accounts. See also the 9/11 Commission Report, 210–214.

21. Marc Hujer, "Interview with Richard Clarke: 'Capturing Bin Laden Was Not One of Their Big Priorities,'" *Der Spiegel*, May 10, 2011, at http://ml.spiegel.de/article.do?id=761458.

22. George W. Bush, *Decision Points* (New York: Virgin Books, 2010), 186.

23. The Memorandum of Notification, while still classified in 2014, appears to have been alluded to by some US officials. See, for example, the testimony of Marilyn Dorn, CIA information review officer, 34–35. *ACLU v. DoD and others*, United States District Court, Southern District of New York, January 5, 2007, archived at http://www.emptywheel.net/wp-content/uploads/2012/04/070105-cia_dorn_declaration_items_1_29_61.pdf.

24. Rizzo, *Company Man*, 173–174.

25. Interview with the author, March 2014.

26. *Black Hole: The Fate of Islamists Rendered to Egypt*, Human Right Watch, July 2005, at http://www.hrw.org/sites/default/files/reports/egypt0505.pdf.

27. Gregory D. Johnsen, *The Last Refuge: Yemen, al-Qaeda and America's War in Arabia* (New York: Norton, 2013), 39.

28. "Saleh Promises Protection for Americans," US diplomatic cable, October 7, 2001, archived by Wikileaks at http://www.cablegatesearch.net/cable.php?id=01SANAA5200&q=hull%20saleh.

29. Johnsen, *The Last Refuge*, 91.

30. "Secretary [Albright]'s Thank You to President Saleh for Cooperation with FBI," US diplomatic cable, December 7, 2000, archived by Wikileaks at http://www. cablegatesearch.net/cable.php?id=00STATE232623&q=cole%20uss.

31. "USS Cole: Investigation and Prosecution," Sana'a Embassy Cable, October 20, 2002, archived by Wikileaks at http://cablegatesearch.net/cable.php?id= 02SANAA3591&q=cole%20uss.

32. Terry Atlas, "Military Should Run Drone Strikes, Colin Powell Says," Bloomberg, May 25, 2013, at http://www.bloomberg.com/news/2013-05-24/ military-should-run-drone-strikes-colin-powell-says.html.

33. Amos Guiora, "Targeted Killing and the Law: Who Is a Legitimate Target and When Is the Target Legitimate?" Foreign Policy Research Institute, November 2013, at http://www.fpri.org/articles/2013/11/targeted-killing-and-law-who-legitimate-target-and-when-target-legitimate.

34. The term "targeted killing" first makes a concerted appearance from late 2000 onward and remains the preferred Israeli term for its program.

35. September 29, 2000, to March 31, 2014. Data provided by B'Tselem to the author April 6, 2014. See also http://www.btselem.org/statistics.

36. See, for example, Suzanne Goldenberg, "Israel Accused of Policy of Murder," January 11, 2001, at http://www.theguardian.com/world/2001/jan/11/israel1.

37. Interview with the author, background terms, March 2014.

38. Daniel Byman, A High Price: The Triumphs and Failures of Israeli Counterterrorism (New York: Oxford University Press, 2011), 315.

39. Interview with the author, background terms, March 2014.

40. George Mitchell et al., "Sharm El-Sheikh Fact-Finding Committee Report aka the Mitchell Report, April 30, 2001, archived at http://ue.eu.int/ueDocs/cms_ Data/docs/pressdata/EN/reports/ACF319.pdf.

41. Joel Greenberg, "Israel Affirms Policy of Assassinating Militants," New York Times, July 5, 2001, at http://www.nytimes.com/2001/07/05/world/israel-affirms-policy-of-assassinating-militants.html.

42. "US Says Opposes Targeted Killing by Israel," Reuters, October 15, 2001, archived at http://www.freerepublic.com/focus/f-news/548707/posts.

43. Barton Gellman, "CIA Weighs 'Targeted Killing' Missions," Washington Post, October 28, 2001, partially archived at http://www.dailykos.com/ story/2009/07/17/754449/-CIA-Weighs-Targeted-Killing-Missions-WaPo-10-28-01.

44. Interview with the author, February 2014.

45. Ibid.

46. Ori Nir, "Bush Seeks Israeli Advice on 'Targeted Killings,'" The Jewish Daily Forward, February 7, 2003, archived at http://electronicintifada.net/content/ bush-seeks-israeli-advice-targeted-killings/4391.

47. Email to the author, March 2014.

48. Interview with the author, background terms, March 2014.

49. Interview with the author, background terms.

50. Interview with the author, January 2014.

51. Interview with senior Pentagon official, background terms, December 2013.

52. Philip Smucker, "The Intrigue behind the Drone Strike," *Christian Science Monitor*, November 12, 2002, at http://www.csmonitor.com/2002/1112/p01s02-wome.html.

53. Known as the National Geospatial-Intelligence Agency since 2003.

54. Dana Priest, "NSA Growth Fueled by Need to Target Terrorists," *Washington Post*, July 22, 2013, at http://www.washingtonpost.com/world/national-security/nsa-growth-fueled-by-need-to-target-terrorists/2013/07/21/24c93cf4-f0b1-11e2-bed3-b9b6fe264871_story_2.html.

55. Johnsen, *The Last Refuge*, 121.

56. Transcript 6, "Top Secret America," PBS Frontline, 2010, at http://www.pbs.org/wgbh/pages/frontline/iraq-war-on-terror/topsecretamerica/transcript-6/.

57. "Yemen Arrests 'al-Qaeda Members,'" BBC News, March 4, 2004, at http://news.bbc.co.uk/1/hi/world/middle_east/3531657.stm.

58. Richard Boucher, US State Department official spokesman, Daily Press Briefing, November 5, 2002, archived at http://2001-2009.state.gov/r/pa/prs/dpb/2002/14920.htm.

59. Asma Jahangir, Report of the Special Rapporteur on Extrajudicial, Summary or Arbitrary Executions, United Nations Economic and Social Council, 60th Session, March 24, 2004, 16, at http://www.unhchr.ch/Huridocda/Huridoca.nsf/0/46215e3ae5d1abe0c1256cdf005721d1/$FILE/G0310327.pdf.

60. "The Sanaa Special Penal Court ordered the release of Abdel Rauf Nassib, who had been tried and acquitted in 2004 of charges that he forged official documents for the USS Cole attackers." Cited in "Terror Trials Update: Defendants Released and Rumours Unconfirmed," leaked US embassy cable, February 22, 2004, archived by Wikileaks at http://www.cablegatesearch.net/cable.php?id=06SANAA448&q=abdel%20nassib%20rauf.

61. "'222 dead' in Qaeda Battle for Yemen's Loder," Agence France Press, April 14, 2012, archived at http://www.buddygag.com/news/222-dead-in-qaida-battle/.

62. JTF-GTMO Detainee Assessment: Abd al-Rahim al-Nashiri, December 8, 2006, obtained and archived by Wikileaks at http://wikileaks.org/gitmo/pdf/sa/us9sa-010015dp.pdf.

63. David Johnston and David E. Sanger, "Hunt for Suspects: Fatal Strike in Yemen Was Based on Rules Set Out by Bush," *New York Times*, November 6, 2002, at http://www.nytimes.com/2002/11/06/world/threats-responses-hunt-for-suspects-fatal-strike-yemen-was-based-rules-set-bush.html?pagewanted=all&src=pm.

64. Johnsen, *The Last Refuge*, 95–97.

65. A month before the *Limburg* attack, an FBI interrogator in Pakistan learned of an imminent attack on an unnamed western oil tanker off the Yemen coast: his warnings were reportedly dismissed by the CIA. See, for example, Katherine Hawkins, "The Terrorism That Torture Didn't Stop," *The Nation*, November 7, 2013, at http://www.thenation.com/article/177006/terrorism-torture-didnt-stop#.

66. For a detailed study of the Lackawanna Six case, see Dina Temple-Raston, *The Jihad Next Door: The Lackawanna Six and Rough Justice in the Age of Terror* (New York: Public Affairs, 2007).

67. George W. Bush, State of the Union Address, January 28, 2003, archived at http://www.washingtonpost.com/wp-srv/onpolitics/transcripts/bushtext_012803.html.

68. Duncan Campbell and Brian Whittaker, "US Elite Force Gets Ready for Yemen Raid," *The Guardian*, September 18, 2002, at http://www.theguardian.com/world/2002/sep/19/duncancampbell.brianwhitaker.

69. Matthew Cole, Richard Esposito, and Brian Ross, "U.S. Mulls Legality of Killing American Al Qaeda 'Turncoat,'" ABC News, January 25, 2010, at http://abcnews.go.com/Blotter/anwar-awlaki-us-mulls-legality-killing-american-al-qaeda-turncoat/story?id=9651830&page=1.

70. Dana Priest, "U.S. Military Teams, Intelligence Deeply Involved in Aiding Yemen on Strikes," *Washington Post*, January 26, 2010, at http://www.washingtonpost.com/wp-dyn/content/article/2010/01/26/AR2010012604239_pf.html.

71. Interview with the author, January 2014.

72. For more on the killing of Derwish and other US citizens in drone strikes during the Bush presidency, see chapter 6.

73. Fifth Amendment of the US Constitution, adopted as part of the Bill of Rights December 15, 1791.

74. Mark Mazzetti, *The Way of the Knife: The CIA, a Secret Army, and a War at the Ends of the Earth* (New York: Penguin Press, 2013), 85–87.

75. Philip Smucker, "The Intrigue behind the Drone Strike," *Christian Science Monitor*, November 12, 2002, at http://www.csmonitor.com/2002/1112/p01s02-wome.html.

76. "A Wedding that Became a Funeral: US Drone Attack on Marriage Procession in Yemen," Human Rights Watch, February 19, 2014, at http://www.hrw.org/sites/default/files/reports/yemen0214_ForUpload_0.pdf.

77. Paul Wolfowitz, "Transcript: Interview with Maria Ressa," CNN, November 5, 2002, at http://www.defense.gov/transcripts/transcript.aspx?transcriptid=3264.

78. Smucker, "The Intrigue behind the Drone Strike."

79. Tony Karon, "Yemen Strike Opens New Chapter in War on Terror," *Time*, November 5, 2002, at http://content.time.com/time/world/article/0,8599,387571,00.html.

80. "2002 Human Rights Report for Yemen Must be Credible," US embassy cable, February 26, 2003, archived by Wikileaks at http://cablegatesearch.net/cable.php?id=03SANAA374&q=cole%20uss.

81. Country Reports on Human Rights Practices: Yemen, US State Department, March 31, 2003, archived at http://www.state.gov/j/drl/rls/hrrpt/2002/18293.htm.

82. Ben Emmerson QC, address to joint session of UK All Party Parliamentary Groups on the United Nations and Drones, December 13, 2013. Author's transcript.

83. Interview with the author, March 2014.

84. S.J. Res. 23 (107th): Authorization for Use of Military Force, September 18, 2001, archived at https://www.govtrack.us/congress/bills/107/sjres23/text.

85. Secretary of State Colin Powell to US Mission Geneva, April 9, 2003, declassified June 29, 2011, archived at https://www.aclu.org/files/dronefoia/dos/drone_dos_20110720DOS_DRONE001925.pdf.

86. "Opinion Paper: How Is the Term 'Armed Conflict' Defined in International Humanitarian Law?" ICRC, March 2008, at http://www.icrc.org/eng/assets/files/other/opinion-paper-armed-conflict.pdf.

87. Cited in "International Human Rights Law and the Role of the Legal Professions: A General Introduction," Office of the High Commissioner for Human Rights, March 24, 1999, at http://www.ohchr.org/Documents/Publications/training9chapter1en.pdf.

88. See George W. Bush, "Humane Treatment of Al Qaeda and Taliban Detainees: Memorandum for the Vice President et al.," February 7, 2002, archived at http://www.lawfareblog.com/wp-content/uploads/2013/05/Memorandum-from-President-to-Vice-President-et-al.-Humane-Treatment-of-al-Qaeda-and-Taliban-Detainees-Feb-7-2002.pdf.

89. See, for example, Silvia Boreli, "Casting Light on the Legal Black Hole: International Law and Detentions Abroad in the "War on Terror," *International Review of the Red Cross* 87, no. 857, March 2005, at http://www.icrc.org/eng/assets/files/other/irrc_857_borelli.pdf.

90. *Hamdan v. Rumsfeld*, US Supreme Court, June 29, 2006, at http://www.supremecourt.gov/opinions/05pdf/05-184.pdf.

91. As a major study by Stanford and New York University law schools later helpfully summarized: " 'Targeted killings' as typically understood (intentional and premeditated killings) cannot be lawful under IHRL, which allows intentional lethal force only when necessary to protect against a threat to life, and where there are no other means, such as capture or non-lethal incapacitation, of preventing that threat to life." Jim Cavallaro, Sarah Knuckey, and Stephan Sonnenberg, "Living under Drones," September 2012, 117, at http://www.livingunderdrones.org/wp-content/uploads/2013/10/Stanford-NYU-Living-Under-Drones.pdf.

92. Bootie Cosgrove-Mather, "Remote-Controlled Spy Planes," CBS News, November 6, 2002, at http://www.cbsnews.com/news/remote-controlled-spy-planes/.

93. "Yemen/USA: Government Must Not Sanction Extra-Judicial Executions," Amnesty International, press release, November 8, 2002, at http://www.amnesty.org/en/library/asset/AMR51/168/2002/en/ac72c772-fae9-11dd-8917-49d72d0853f5/amr511682002en.pdf.

94. Kenneth Roth (2003) "Debating the Issues," *International Law Studies* 81 (reprint 2006), archived at https://www.usnwc.edu/Research---Gaming/International-Law/New-International-Law-Studies-(Blue-Book)-Series/International-Law-Blue-Book-Articles.aspx?Volume=81.

95. Known as the UN Commission on Human Rights until its reform in 2006.

96. Asma Jahangir, UN Special Rapporteur on Extrajudicial, Summary or Arbitrary Executions, *Civil and Political Rights, including the Questions of Disappearances and Summary Executions,* January 13, 2003, archived at http://www.unhchr.ch/Huridocda/Huridoca.nsf/0/46215e3ae5d1abe0c1256cdf005721d1/$FILE/G0310327.pdf.

97. Asma Jahangir, Report of the Special Rapporteur, on Extrajudicial, Summary or Arbitrary Executions, United Nations Economic and Social Council, 60th Session, March 24, 2004.

98. Secretary of State Colin Powell to US Mission Geneva, April 9, 2003, declassified June 29, 2011, archived at https://www.aclu.org/files/dronefoia/dos/drone_dos_20110720DOS_DRONE001925.pdf.

99. Ben Emmerson QC, All-Party Parliamentary Groups on the UN and on Drones, December 4, 2013 (transcript author's own), at http://www.una.org.uk/media/audio/4-december-2013-ben-emmerson-qc-and-professor-clarke-parliamentary-event-drones-part-1.

100. Interview with the author, background terms.

101. Ibid.

102. "Additional Pre-Hearing Questions for Ms. Caroline D. Krass upon Her Nomination to be General Counsel for the CIA," SSCI, December 17, 2013, at http://www.intelligence.senate.gov/131217/krassprehearing.pdf.

103. RPAs were reported to have played a "spotter" role, for example, in the killing of Hamas spiritual adviser Sheikh Ahmed Yassin. Chris Mcgreal, " 'He'll Kill More in Death than He Did Alive,' " The Guardian, March 23, 2004, at http://www.theguardian.com/world/2004/mar/23/israel.

104. "People and Power: Israel's Drone Dealers," Directed by Yotam Feldman, Al Jazeera, May 1, 2014, at http://www.aljazeera.com/programmes/peopleandpower/2014/04/201442911431250545.html.

105. "Armed Israeli Drones Hunt Palestinians," Al Jazeera English, September 14, 2004, at http://www.aljazeera.com/archive/2004/09/200841014731539330.html.

106. Operation Pillar of Defense: Summary of Events, Israel Defense Forces, November 22, 2012, at http://www.idfblog.com/2012/11/22/operation-pillar-of-defense-summary-of-events/.

107. Philip Alston, "Interim Report of the Special Rapporteur of the Commission on Human Rights on Extrajudicial, Summary or Arbitrary Executions," UN General Assembly, September 1, 2004 archived at http://www.extrajudicialexecutions.org/application/media/59%20GA%20SR%20Report%20%28A_59_319%29.pdf.

108. Matthew Tempest, "UK Condemns 'Unlawful' Yassin Killing," The Guardian, March 22, 2004, at http://www.theguardian.com/politics/2004/mar/22/foreignpolicy.israel.

109. Public Committee against Torture in Israel v. Government of Israel, Supreme Court of Israel, HCJ 769/02 (13 Dec 2006) at https://www.law.upenn.edu/institutes/cerl/conferences/targetedkilling/papers/IsraeliTargetedKillingCase.pdf.

110. Interview with the author, background terms.

111. Interview with the author, March 2014.

112. Interview with the author, February 2014.

113. Ben Emmerson QC, Interim Report to UN General Assembly, released September 18, 2013, at http://justsecurity.org/wp-content/uploads/2013/10/2013EmmersonSpecialRapporteurReportDrones.pdf.

114. "Precisely Wrong: Gaza Civilians Killed by Israeli Drone-Launched Missiles," Human Rights Watch, June 30, 2009, at http://www.hrw.org/node/84077/section/1.

115. Cited by Human Rights Watch, "Precisely Wrong."

116. See, for example, "Faulty Intelligence, Wanton Recklessness, or a Combination of the Two," Amnesty International blog, February 2, 2009, at http://livewire.amnesty.org/2009/02/02/faulty-intelligence-wanton-recklessness-or-a-combination-of-the-two/.

117. Report of UN High Commissioner for Human Rights on the Implementation of Human Rights Council Resolutions S-9/1 and S-12/1, March 6, 2013, at http://www.ohchr.org/Documents/HRBodies/HRCouncil/RegularSession/Session22/A.HRC.22.35.Add.1_AV.pdf.

118. "Israel: Gaza Airstrikes Violated Laws of War," Human Rights Watch, February 12, 2013, at http://www.hrw.org/news/2013/02/12/israel-gaza-airstrikes-violated-laws-war.

119. Israeli news outlet YNet cited an IDF official as stating that by early August 2014, "1,768 Palestinians were killed and some 9,300 were injured in the Gaza Strip. The IDF estimates that 750 to 1,000 of the dead were terrorists." Yoav Zitun, "IDF Operation Protective Edge, in Numbers," YNet News, August 5, 2014, at http://www.ynetnews.com/articles/0,7340,L-4555441,00.html.

120. John Brennan, "The Ethics and Efficacy of the President's Counterterrorism Strategy," April 30, 2012, at http://www.cfr.org/counterterrorism/brennans-speech-counterterrorism-april-2012/p28100.

CHAPTER 4

1. "We went off to fight on the wrong battlefield, with no appreciation of how many enemies we would create, and no plan for how to get out. Because of a war in Iraq that should never have been authorized and should never have been waged, we are now less safe than we were before 9/11." Senator Barack Obama, Woodrow Wilson Center, Washington, DC, August 1, 2007, archived at http://www.cfr.org/elections/obamas-speech-woodrow-wilson-center/p13974.

2. Iraq Body Count estimates some 127,000 civilians died as a direct result of conflict between 2003 and 2011, at http://www.iraqbodycount.org/analysis/numbers/2011/iCasualties. Icasualties records 4,804 Coalition fatalities in the same period, not counting Iraqi military personnel, at http://icasualties.org/Iraq/index.aspx. Few public organizations are known to have collated overall insurgency casualty data, although Iraq War Logs provisionally estimated 20,500 insurgents killed. US and UK Special Forces alone are estimated to have killed around 3,500 insurgents. Mark Urban, *Task Force Black: The Explosive True Story of the SAS and the Secret War in Iraq* (London: Little, Brown, 2010), 270.

3. Cited in Anthony Cordesman, "Iraq: Putting US Withdrawal in Perspective," CSSI paper, December 2011, at http://csis.org/files/publication/111214_Iraq_US_Withdrawal.pdf.

4. Cited in "Former Drone Pilot, Lieutenant-Colonel: Obama Personally Orders Drone Killings," *Russia Today*, November 29, 2013, at http://rt.com/shows/sophieco/weapon-drones-industry-demand-465/.

5. America's Reapers and Predators returned to Iraq's skies in August 2014, after much of the country was overrun by Al Qaeda successor the Islamic State. An intensive US bombing campaign, soon expanded to Syria, saw more than 1,500 airstrikes against ISIS targets by year's end, with armed drones playing a key role.

6. Lt. General N. A. Schwarz, Operation Iraqi Freedom (OIF) History Brief, May 14, 2003, declassified May 8, 2013, at http://nsarchive.files.wordpress.com/2010/10/oif-history.pdf.

7. "Iraq Says U.S. Helicopter Shot Down," CBC News, April 4, 2003, at http://www.cbc.ca/news/world/iraq-says-u-s-helicopter-shot-down-1.401123.

8. George W. Bush, USS *Abraham Lincoln*, May 1, 2003, transcript via http://edition.cnn.com/2003/US/05/01/bush.transcript/.

9. The BBC was one of the few international news organizations to maintain a permanent presence in the "red zone" for the duration of the war. Armed bodyguards were only introduced for personnel from mid-2004 onward, as the threat of suicide bombings and kidnap escalated.

10. George Tenet, *At the Center of the Storm: My Years at the CIA* (New York: Harper Luxe, 2007), 516–541.

11. For a critique of various Bush administration claims of Iraq's links to Al Qaeda, see *Postwar Findings about Iraq's WMD Programs and Links to Terrorism and How They Compare with Prewar Assessments*, US Senate Select Committee on Intelligence, September 8, 2006, at http://www.gpo.gov/fdsys/pkg/CRPT-109srpt331/pdf/CRPT-109srpt331.pdf.

12. Intercepted letter from Abu Musab al-Zarqawi to Osama bin Laden, Coalition Provisional Authority translation, February 2004, archived at http://www.au.af.mil/au/awc/awcgate/state/31694.htm.

13. General Stanley McChrystal, *My Share of the Task: A Memoir* (New York: Portfolio Penguin, 2013), 236.

14. Figures cited in "Killing bin Laden: A "Routine Mission" for War-Tested SEALs," PBS Newshour, May 6, 2011, transcript at http://www.pbs.org/newshour/bb/military/jan-june11/specialops_05-06.html.

15. Urban, *Task Force Black*, 270–271.

16. Bob Woodward, *The War Within: A Secret White House History 2006-2008* (London: Simon & Schuster, 2009), 380.

17. Robert M. Gates, *Duty: Memoirs of a Secretary of War* (New York: W. H. Allen, 2014), 254.

18. McChrystal, *My Share of the Task*, 202–203.

19. "No Blood, No Foul: Soldiers' Accounts of Detainee Abuse in Iraq," *Human Rights Watch* 18, no. 3 (G), July 2006, at http://www.hrw.org/reports/2006/us0706/us0706web.pdf.

20. Eric Schmitt and Carolyn Marshall, "In Secret Unit's 'Black Room,' a Grim Portrait of U.S. Abuse," *New York Times*, March 19, 2006, at http://www.nytimes.com/2006/03/19/international/middleeast/19abuse.html.

21. Stanley McChrystal, "It Takes a Network: The New Front Line of Modern Warfare," *Foreign Policy*, February 22, 2011, at http://www.foreignpolicy.com/articles/2011/02/22/it_takes_a_network?page=ful.

22. Background interview with former NSA analyst attached to JSOC. Time, date, and location of assignment and interview withheld by request.

23. Interview with the author, January 2014.

24. McChrystal, *My Share of the Task*, 160.

25. Interview with retired Colonel Pete Forrest, former AFSOC, 3rd SOS, January 2014.

26. Interview with the author, January 2014.

27. Interview with the author, December 2013.

28. "After a visit to Israel in February I'd wanted SOCOM to bypass the creaky acquisition process and buy ready-made Israeli models." McChrystal, *My Share of the Task*, 156–157.

29. Interview with the author.

30. Interview with the author, October 2013.

31. Interview with the author, January 2014.

32. Michael Hoffman, "Air Force under Pressure to Meet the Growing Demand," *Military Times*, April 28, 2008, archived at http://www.ar15.com/archive/topic.html?b=1&f=5&t=701797.

33. Gary Emery, "New Intel Squadron Turns Aerial Eye on Terrorists," American Forces Press Service, August 30, 2006, at http://www.defense.gov/News/NewsArticle.aspx?ID=634.

34. See, for example, Robert F. Worth, "Blast Destroys Shrine in Iraq, Setting Off Sectarian Fury," *New York Times*, February 22, 2006, at http://www.nytimes.com/2006/02/22/international/middleeast/22cnd-iraq.html.

35. McChrystal, *My Share of the Task*, 89–90.

36. Rumsfeld "snowflake" to Stephen Cambone, Under-Secretary of Defense for Intelligence, who oversaw "black" Special Forces operations; and to General Richard Myers, CJCS. The Rumsfeld Papers, May 19, 2005, archived at http://library.rumsfeld.com/doclib/sp/463/To%20General%20Dick%20Myers%20re%20Meeting%20with%20POTUS%2005-19-2005.pdf.

37. Urban, *Task Force Black*, 70–71.

38. Interview with the author.

39. Interview with the author, name and date withheld.

40. Interview with the author, January 2014.

41. Interview with General James Poss, former Director of Intelligence, USAF, October 2013.

42. Interview with Pete Forrest, January 2014.

43. McChrystal, *My Share of the Task*, 219.

44. For a forensic description of the surveillance that led to al-Zarqawi's death, see McChrystal, *My Share of the Task*, 215–236.

45. George W. Bush, *Decision Points* (New York: Virgin Books, 2010), 365.

46. Interview with retired AFSOC Colonel Pete Forrest, January 2014.

47. Matt J. Martin, with Charles W. Sasser, *Predator: The Remote Control Air War over Iraq and Afghanistan—a Pilot's Story* (Minneapolis, MN: Zenith Press, 2010), 265.

48. Interview with the author, background terms.

49. Interview with the author, November 2013.

50. Ibid.

51. Interview with the author, January 2014.

52. CNN ImageSource log of August 4, 2004, video clip issued by USAF February 2005.

53. Interview with the author, January 2014.

54. Gates, *Duty*, 126–135.

55. Interview with the author, January 2014.

56. Interview with the author, London, September 2013.

57. In late 2013 YouTube banned a number of popular compilations of Predator attacks in Iraq, which had been on the site for some years, noting that "This video has been removed as a violation of YouTube's policy on violence."

58. Despite insisting his actions in leaking the Apache tapes and hundreds of thousands of classified military and diplomatic cables was in the public interest, Manning was later jailed for 35 years by a US military court.

59. CNN ImageSource logs of four video clips issued by USAF, February 2005, kindly provided to author.

60. "New Videos Show Predators at Work in Iraq," CNN, February 9, 2005, at http://edition.cnn.com/2005/WORLD/meast/02/08/predator.video/.

61. Noah Max, "Predator Attacks on Tape," DefenseTech, February 9, 2005, at http://defensetech.org/2005/02/09/predator-attacks-on-tape/.

62. "RAF Reaper Strikes Insurgent IED Team," MoD YouTube channel, November 25, 2010, at https://www.youtube.com/watch?v=GShSMMLooJg.

63. Interview with the author, March 2014.

64. Ben Emmerson QC, Interim Report to UN General Assembly, September 18, 2013, at http://justsecurity.org/wp-content/uploads/2013/10/2013Emmerson SpecialRapporteurReportDrones.pdf.

65. See, for example, Scott Shane, "Contrasting Reports of Drone Strikes," *New York Times*, August 11, 2011, at http://www.nytimes.com/2011/08/12/world/asia/12droneside.html.

66. Rebecca Grant, "The Bekaa Valley War," *Air Force Magazine*, June 2002, at http://www.airforcemag.com/MagazineArchive/Pages/2002/June%20 2002/0602bekaa.aspx.

67. Gili Cohen, "Israel Is World's Largest Exporter of Drones, Study Finds," Haaretz, May 19, 2013, at http://www.haaretz.com/news/diplomacy-defense/israel-is-world-s-largest-exporter-of-drones-study-finds.premium-1.524771.

68. John Reed, "Israeli Drone Makers Fight Off Export Rivals," *Financial Times*, February 5, 2014, at http://www.ft.com/cms/s/0/2d949c8a-8a6b-11e3-ba54-00144feab7de.html.

69. "People and Power: Israel's Drone Dealers," Directed by Yotam Feldman, Al Jazeera, May 1, 2014, at http://www.aljazeera.com/programmes/peopleandpower/2014/04/201442911431250545.html.

70. Peter Luff MP, Minister of Defence, Hansard Written Answer 1 Dec 2011: Column 1062W, at http://www.publications.parliament.uk/pa/cm201011/cmhansrd/cm111201/text/111201w0002.htm.

71. Nicholas de Larrinaga, "UK's Watchkeeper UAV Inches towards Release to Service," *Jane's Defence Weekly*, October 7 2013, at http://www.janes.com/article/28053/uk-s-watchkeeper-uav-inches-towards-release-to-service.

72. Cited in "Defence Secretary Salutes First Afghan Officer Cadets," Ministry of Defence release, September 24, 2014, at https://www.gov.uk/government/news/defence-secretary-salutes-first-afghan-officer-cadets.

73. Defense Acquisitions: Assessments of Selected Weapon Programs, 101–102, US Government Accountability Office, March 2013, at http://www.gao.gov/assets/660/653379.pdf.

74. Interview with the author, October 2013.

75. According to RAF officials dual-badged British personnel continued to fly missions in Iraq until the US withdrawal in 2011—two years after the last British ground forces had departed. "Dual-badging" on USAF Predators in Afghanistan was still ongoing in spring 2014. See also "Written Answers to Questions: Defence," Hansard, April 24, 2013: Column 906W, at http://www.publications.parliament.uk/pa/cm201213/cmhansrd/cm130424/text/130424w0001.htm#130424w0001.htm_wqn18.

76. Interview with the author, October 2013.

77. Interview with the author, background terms, March 2014.

78. Francis Harris, "In Las Vegas a Pilot Pulls the Trigger: In Iraq a Predator Fires its Missile," *Daily Telegraph*, June 2, 2006, at http://www.telegraph.co.uk/news/worldnews/asia/afghanistan/1520143/In-Las-Vegas-a-pilot-pulls-the-trigger.-In-Iraq-a-Predator-fires-its-missile.html.

79. Interview with the author, December 2013.

80. For more on differing RoEs, see chapter 10.

81. Discussion with the author, background terms.

82. Martin, *Predator*, 284–285.

83. Interviewed by the author, Langley AFB, December 2013. Surname withheld by request of USAF.

84. Interview with the author, February 2014.

85. Operators later complained that their sensors were not upgraded as frequently as those of their US colleagues. Madeleine Moon MP to All Party Parliamentary Group on Drones, December 2013. Author's notes.

CHAPTER 5

1. All but 23 of 390 US drone strikes carried out to August 2014 took place in Waziristan, according to the Bureau of Investigative Journalism. Waziristan's land mass is given as 5,800 square miles—demographics via the official FATA website at http://fata.gov.pk/index.php?option=com_content&view=article&id=56&Itemid=92.

2. Interview with the author, January 2014.

3. Ben Emmerson QC, address to joint session of UK All Party Parliamentary Groups on the United Nations and Drones, December 13, 2013. Author's transcript.

4. Since renamed Khyber Pakhtunkhwa Province (KPK).

5. Interview with the author, March 2014.

6. Anwarullah Khan, "82 Die as Missiles Rain on Bajaur: Pakistan Owns up to Strike; Locals Blame US Drones," *Dawn*, October 31, 2006, at http://www.dawn.com/news/216918/82-die-as-missiles-rain-on-bajaur-pakistan-owns-up-to-strike-locals-blame-us-drones.

7. Yousaf Ali, "'Most Bajaur Victims Were under 20,'" *The News International*, November 5, 2006, at http://www.thenews.com.pk/TodaysPrintDetail.aspx?ID=4043&Cat=13&dt=11/5/2006.

8. *Details of Attacks by NATO Forces/Predator Drones*, FATA Secretariat compilation report 2006-2013.

9. "Official list of Bajaur victims released," *The News International*, November 8, 2006, at http://www.thenews.com.pk/TodaysPrintDetail.aspx?ID=31085&Cat=6&dt=11/8/2006.

10. Carlotta Gall, "Dozens Killed in Suicide Bombing in Pakistan," *New York Times*, November 8, 2006, at http://www.nytimes.com/2006/11/08/world/asia/08cnd-pakistan.html?pagewanted=all.

11. Christina Lamb, "US Carried Out Madrasah Bombing," *Sunday Times*, November 26, 2006, at http://www.thesundaytimes.co.uk/sto/news/world_news/article173354.ece.

12. Unpublished transcript of interview with General Pervez Musharraf, July 2012, courtesy of Jemima Khan.

13. Interview with the author, November 2013.

14. Interview by the author with former senior US intelligence official, background terms.

15. Gareth Porter, "Why Pakistani Military Demands a Veto on Drone Strikes," IPS News, August 16, 2011, at http://www.ipsnews.net/2011/08/why-pakistani-military-demands-a-veto-on-drone-strikes/.

16. Interview with the author, November 2014.

17. Winston Churchill, *The Story of the Malakand Field Force: An Episode of Frontier War* (1898), chapter 1, ebook at http://www.gutenberg.org/files/9404/9404-h/9404-h.htm.

18. For a good overview of the Royal Air Force's bombing campaign, see Andrew M. Roe's *Waging War in Waziristan*.

19. Report by Air-Marshall Sir John Salmond on the Royal Air Force in India, August 1922. RAF Museum Hendon, cited in Andrew M. Roe, *Waging War in Waziristan: The British Struggle in the Land of Bin Laden, 1849-1947* (Lawrence: University Press of Kansas, 2010), 132.

20. Colonel F. S. Keen, cited in Roe, *Waging War in Waziristan*, 132.

21. Interview with the author, London, March 2014.

22. Population Demography, Federally Administered Tribal Areas website, at http://fata.gov.pk/index.php?option=com_content&view=article&id=56&Itemid=92.

23. For a detailed review of the role of the CIA and Saudi Arabia in bankrolling Islamist groups, see Steve Coll, *Ghost Wars: The Secret History of the CIA, Afghanistan, and Bin Laden, from the Soviet Invasion to September 10, 2001* (New York: Penguin, 2004).

24. Paul Pillar, former deputy of the CIA's Counter Terrorism Center, correspondence with the author, December 2013.
25. Pervez Musharraf, *In the Line of Fire: A Memoir* (New York: Simon & Schuster, 2006), 200–201.
26. Senior former ISI official, interviewed by the author Pakistan, November 2012.
27. A flurry of US Defense Secretary Donald Rumsfeld's "snowflake" memos give a sense of the administration's concern: "If Pakistan goes under, we have serious problem," The Rumsfeld Papers, March 10, 2003, at http://library.rumsfeld.com/doclib/sp/1632/2003-03-10%20to%20Doug%20Feith%20re%20Pakistan.pdf.
28. John Rizzo, *Company Man: Thirty Years of Controversy and Crisis at the CIA* (New York: Scribner, 2014), 298.
29. Interviewed by the author, Islamabad, November 2012.
30. Kiriakou was later jailed by the Obama administration for leaking the name of a fellow CIA agent involved in the CIA's torture program.
31. Jennifer Matthews, the CIA team leader who coordinated the overall effort to track Zubaydah down, was subsequently killed in a 2009 Pakistan Taliban revenge attack against drone strikes.
32. John Kiriakou, with Michael Ruby, *The Reluctant Spy: My Secret Life in the CIA's War on Terror* (New York: Random House, 2009), xiv–xix.
33. Conversations between the author and senior Pakistani military officials, background terms.
34. Interview with the author, background terms.
35. Syed Saleem Shahzad, *Inside Al Qaeda and the Taliban: Beyond Bin Laden and 9/11* (London: Pluto Press, 2011), 5–6.
36. Interview with Brigadier Asad Munir, Islamabad, November 2012.
37. US secret Afghanistan military cables via Wikileaks, at https://wikileaks.org/tag/AF_0.html.
38. Yuldashev was finally killed in a CIA drone strike on August 27, 2009.
39. Anatol Lieven, *Pakistan: A Hard Country* (New York: Allen Lane, 2011), 414–416.
40. Cited by Shahzad, who lays out the terms of the agreement in some detail, *Inside Al Qaeda and the Taliban*, 13–14.
41. Ismail Khan and Dilawar Khan Wazir, "Night Raid Kills Nek, Four Other Militants: Wana Operation," *Dawn*, June 19, 2004, archived at http://archive.is/IgLr4#selection-529.1-529.59.
42. Iqbal Khattak, "Nek Killed in Missile Strike," *Daily Times*, June 19, 2004, archived at http://counterterrorism.newamerica.net/sites/newamerica.net/files/program_pages/attachments/2004-7%20Sources.pdf.
43. David Rohde and Mohammed Khan, "Ex Taliban Fighter Dies in Strike in Pakistan," *New York Times*, June 19, 2004, at http://www.nytimes.com/2004/06/19/international/asia/19STAN.html.
44. Mark Mazzetti, "A Secret Deal on Drones, Sealed in Blood," *New York Times*, April 6, 2013, at http://www.nytimes.com/2013/04/07/world/asia/origins-of-cias-not-so-secret-drone-war-in-pakistan.html.
45. "Pakistan: Attempted Intercepts of Coalition Aircraft," leaked US embassy cable December 14, 2007, archived by Wikileaks at http://www.cablegatesearch.net/cable.php?id=07ISLAMABAD5283&q=boulevard%20pakistan.

46. "CJCS Mullen's Meeting with COAS General Kayani," leaked US embassy cable, March 24, 2008, archived by Wikileaks at http://www.cablegatesearch. net/cable.php?id=08ISLAMABAD1272&q=kayani.

47. Gregory W. Pedlow and Donald E. Weizenbach, "The Central Intelligence Agency and Overhead Reconnaissance: The U2 and Oxcart Programs 1954-1974," CIA, 1992 (declassified June 2013) archived at http://www2.gwu.edu/~nsarchiv/ NSAEBB/NSAEBB434/docs/U2%20-%20Cover-Contents-Foreword-Preface.pdf.

48. Jeremy Page, "Google Earth Reveals Secret History of US Base in Pakistan," *London Times*, February 19, 2009, paywalled at http://www.timesonline.co.uk/ tol/news/world/asia/article5762371.ece.

49. Interview with the author, Islamabad, December 2012.

50. Interview with the author.

51. See, for example, Mark Mazzetti, *The Way of the Knife: The CIA, a Secret Army, and a War at the Ends of the Earth* (New York: Penguin Press, 2013), 108–110.

52. Iqbal Khattak, "Wana Calm after Nek Killing," *Daily Times*, June 20, 2004, archived at http://stagingarchives.dailytimes.com.pk/national/20-Jun-2004/ wana-calm-after-nek-s-killing.

53. "Exclusive: CIA Aircraft Kills Terrorist," ABC News, May 13, 2005, at http:// abcnews.go.com/WNT/Investigation/story?id=755961.

54. "USA: An Extrajudicial Execution by the CIA?" Amnesty International, May 18, 2005, at http://www.amnesty.org/en/library/asset/AMR51/079/2005/en/ bcffa8d8-d4ea-11dd-8a23-d58a49c0d652/amr510792005en.html.

55. Dana Priest, "Surveillance Operation in Pakistan Located and Killed Al Qaeda Official," *Washington Post*, May 15, 2005, at http://www.washingtonpost.com/ wp-dyn/articles/A60743-2005May15.html.

56. Philip Alston, UN Special Rapporteur for Extrajudicial, Summary or Arbitrary Executions: UN Doc: E/CN.4.2005/7, page 15 para. 41, December 22, 2004, at http://daccess-dds-ny.un.org/doc/UNDOC/GEN/G05/101/34/PDF/G0510134. pdf?OpenElement.

57. "SR on Extrajudicial, Summary or Arbitrary Executions Requests Information on Haitham al-Yemeni," leaked US embassy cable, September 6, 2005, archived by Wikileaks at http://www.cablegatesearch.net/search.php?q=Yemeni+Alston &qo=0&qc=0&qto=2010-02-28.

58. Philip Alston, "Report of the Special Rapporteur on Extrajudicial, Summary or Arbitrary Executions: Addendum—Summary of Cases Transmitted to Government and Replies Received," 245, March 12, 2007, archived at http:// www.geneva-academy.ch/RULAC/pdf_state/Extrajudicial-executions-report-Ireland-2007.pdf.

59. "UN Expert on Extrajudicial Killings Tells United States War on Terror Could Undermine Human Rights Accountability," UNHRC press release, March 28, 2007, at http://www.unhchr.ch/huricane/huricane.nsf/view01/2e076b5840ae 2d0fc12572ac006fa39f?opendocument.

60. For more on the deaths of Spanish citizens Raquel Burgos Garcia and Amer Azizi in this strike, see chapter 6.

61. "Pakistani Journalist Abducted in December is Found Dead," Reuters, June 17, 2006, at http://www.washingtonpost.com/wp-dyn/content/article/2006/06/17/AR2006061700160.html.

62. "FATA: Missing Pakistan Journalist Found Dead in Waziristan," leaked US embassy cable, June 20, 2006, archived by Wikileaks at http://www.cablegatesearch.net/cable.php?id=06ISLAMABAD11675&q=hayatullah%20khan.

63. Philip Alston, "Report of the Special Rapporteur on Extrajudicial, Summary or Arbitrary Executions: Summary of Cases Transmitted to Government and Replies Received," UN General Assembly, March 12, 2007, at http://www.extrajudicialexecutions.org/application/media/Add%201).pdf.

64. "Slain Tribal Area Journalist's Widow Murdered," Reporters Without Borders, November 17, 2007, at http://archives.rsf.org/article.php3?id_article=24417.

65. "FATA: Missing Pakistan Journalist Found Dead in Waziristan," leaked US embassy cable, June 20, 2006, archived by Wikileaks at http://www.cablegatesearch.net/cable.php?id=06ISLAMABAD11675&q=hayatullah%20khan.

66. Elizabeth Rubin, *Roots of Impunity: Pakistan's Endangered Press and the Perilous Web of Militancy, Security, and Politics*, Committee to Protect Journalists Special Report, May 2013, at https://www.cpj.org/reports/CPJ.Pakistan.Roots.of.Impunity.pdf.

67. Interview with the author. Identity withheld.

68. Cited in Rubin, *Roots of Impunity*, 17.

69. "Pakistan 'Approved Saleem Shahzad Murder' Says Mullen," BBC News, July 8, 2011, at http://www.bbc.co.uk/news/world-south-asia-14074814.

70. Sophia Saifi, "Pakistan Anti-Drone Activist Kareem Khan Freed after Abduction," CNN, February 15, 2014, at http://edition.cnn.com/2014/02/15/world/asia/pakistan-drone-activist/.

71. Committee to Protect Journalists: Journalists Killed by Country at https://www.cpj.org/killed/.

72. Interviewed by the author, Islamabad, December 2012. For an extended discussion with Yusufzai on the challenges of reporting from FATA, see Chris Woods, 'Interview: 'Ask the Wrong People about Drone Deaths and You can be Killed,'" Bureau of Investigative Journalism, August 1, 2013, at http://www.thebureauinvestigates.com/2013/08/01/interview-ask-the-wrong-people-about-drone-deaths-and-you-can-be-killed/.

73. Comments to the author, background terms.

74. "Hamid Mir Undergoes 'Successful Operation' after Being Shot," *The News*, April 19, 2014, at http://www.thenews.com.pk/article-145131-Hamid-Mir-shot,-injured-in-Karachi.

75. Chris Woods, "Attacking the Messenger: How the CIA Tried to Undermine Drone Study," Bureau of Investigative Journalism, August 12, 2011, at http://www.thebureauinvestigates.com/2011/08/12/attacking-the-messenger-how-the-cia-tried-to-undermine-drone-study/.

76. Scott Shane, "U.S. Said to Target Rescuers at Drone Strike Sites," *New York Times*, February 5, 2012, at http://www.nytimes.com/2012/02/06/world/asia/us-drone-strikes-are-said-to-target-rescuers.html.

77. Mohammed Khan and Carlotta Gall, "A Qaeda Bomb Expert Killed in Pakistan Was a Paymaster," *New York Times*, April 22, 2006, at http://www.nytimes.com/2006/04/22/world/middleeast/22qaeda.html.

78. Jonathan Landay, "Al Qaida Operative Who Helped Direct London Bombings is Dead," McClatchy, April 8, 2008, archived at http://web.archive.org/web/20080410225338/http://www.mcclatchydc.com/world/story/33057.html.

79. Pir Zubair Shah, "My Drone War," *Foreign Policy*, February 27, 2012, at http://www.foreignpolicy.com/articles/2012/02/27/my_drone_war?page=0,1.

80. Alice K. Ross, "Leaked Official Document Records 330 Drone Strikes in Pakistan," Bureau of Investigative Journalism, January 29, 2014, at http://www.thebureauinvestigates.com/2014/01/29/leaked-official-document-records-330-drone-strikes-in-pakistan/.

81. Carlotta Gall, "Airstrike by US Draws Protest from Pakistanis," *New York Times*, January 15, 2006, at http://query.nytimes.com/gst/fullpage.html?res=9e07e5d d143ff936a25752c0a9609c8b63&pagewanted=all.

82. Imtiaz Ali and Massoud Ansari, "Pakistan Fury as CIA Airstrike on Village Kills 18," *Daily Telegraph*, January 15, 2006, at http://www.telegraph.co.uk/news/worldnews/asia/pakistan/1507895/Pakistan-fury-as-CIA-airstrike-on-village-kills-18.html.

83. Antonio Giustozzi, *Decoding the New Taliban: Insights From The Afghan Field* (London: Oxford University Press, 2012), 34.

84. Bizarrely a State Department website claimed in 2014 that "the U.S. Embassy [in Kabul] closed in 1989 due to concerns that the new Taliban regime would be unable to maintain security or adequately protect diplomats following the final Soviet departure." Yet the Taliban was not founded until 1994 and only took power two years later. See http://diplomacy.state.gov/discoverdiplomacy/explorer/places/170250.htm.

85. A factor in that strategic decision was Pakistan's continued support for terrorist/militant groups in Kashmir, and its key role in facilitating the rise to power of the Afghan Taliban.

86. Unpublished extract, on the record interview of Pervez Musharraf for the *New Statesman*. Used by kind permission of Jemima Khan.

87. "Attack Threat RPT Unknown," leaked Afghan war logs, September 17, 2004, archived by Wikileaks at http://wardiary.wikileaks.org/id/777EA79A-2219-0 B3F-9F6E4A8BB5C80A89/.

88. Sean D. Naylor, "US Officer: Pakistani Forces Aided Taliban," *Army Times*, September 23, 2008, archived at http://www.liveleak.com/view?i=cba_1224103966.

89. *Joint Task Force Guantánamo Matrix of Threat Indicators for Enemy Combatants*, The Government's Guide to Assessing Prisoners, *New York Times*, April 2, 2011, leaked to Wikileaks and archived at http://www-nc.nytimes.com/interactive/2011/04/24/world/guantanamo-guide-to-assessing-prisoners.html.

90. Interview with the author, background terms.

91. Interview with the author, Lal Masjid, Islamabad, November 2012.

92. Syed Saleem Shahzad, "US on the Scent of Terror Money in Pakistan," *Asia Times*, December 6, 2005, at http://www.atimes.com/atimes/South_Asia/GL06Df01.html.

93. Former Pakistani intelligence official with close knowledge of events, interviewed by the author 2011. Name and location withheld.

94. Shahzad, *Inside Al Qaeda and the Taliban*, 165.

95. Cited in Karen DeYoung and Karin Brulliard, "Obama Administration is Divided over Future of U.S.-Pakistan Relationship," *Washington Post*, May 15, 2011, at http://www.washingtonpost.com/world/national-security/obama-administration-remains-divided-over-future-of-us-pakistan-relationship/2011/05/13/AFOJcj3G_story.html.

96. Former high-ranking RAW intelligence official interviewed by the author, date and location withheld.

97. Interview with the author, background terms.

98. "Top Al Qaeda Terrorist Abu Zubair al-Masri 'was Missile Target in Bush Campaign for Favourable Legacy,'" *London Times*, November 24, 2008, paywalled at http://www.timesonline.co.uk/tol/news/world/us_and_americas/article5225966.ece.

99. Michael T. Flynn, Rich Jurgens, and Thomas L. Cantrell, *Employing ISR: SOF Best Practices*, Joint Forces Quarterly issue 50, 3rd quarter 2008, at http://www.dtic.mil/doctrine/docnet/courses/intelligence/intel/jfq_50_art-2.pdf.

100. David S. Cloud, "CIA Drones Have Broader List of Targets," *Los Angeles Times*, May 5, 2010, at http://articles.latimes.com/2010/may/05/world/la-fg-drone-targets-20100506.

101. Interview with the author, May 2014.

102. Interview with the author, background terms.

103. Jemima Khan, "Pervez Musharraf: If You Are Weak, Anyone Can Come and Kick You," *New Statesman*, June 13, 2012, at http://www.newstatesman.com/politics/politics/2012/06/pervez-musharraf-if-weak-anyone-kick-you.

104. "Immunity for Musharraf Likely after Zardari's Election as President," leaked US embassy cable, August 23, 2008, archived by Wikileaks at http://www.cablegatesearch.net/cable.php?id=08ISLAMABAD2802&q=assembly%20gilani%20ignore%20national%20protest.

105. Cited by Bob Woodward, *Obama's Wars: The Inside Story* (London: Simon & Schuster, 2010), 26.

106. "Gilani to Codel Snowe: Help Us to Hit Targets," leaked US embassy cable, November 13, 2008, archived by Wikileaks at http://www.cablegatesearch.net/cable.php?id=08ISLAMABAD3586&q=drone%20gilani.

107. "MFA Again Convokes Ambassador re. Drone Strikes," leaked US embassy cable, November 20, 2008, archived by Wikileaks at http://www.cablegatesearch.net/cable.php?id=08ISLAMABAD3654&q=drone%20gilani.

108. "Gilani to Kerry: No Conditionality, No Drones," leaked US embassy cable, April 16, 2009, archived by Wikileaks at http://www.cablegatesearch.net/cable.php?id=09ISLAMABAD807&q=drone%20gilani.

109. "SRAP Holbrooke's June 5 Meeting with FM Qureshi," leaked US embassy cable, June 13, 2009, archived by Wikileaks at http://www.cablegatesearch.net/cable.php?id=09ISLAMABAD1299&q=drone%20gilani.

110. David E. Sanger, *The Inheritance: The World Obama Confronts and the Challenges to American Power* (New York: Random House, 2009), 255–257.

111. Woodward, *Obama's Wars*, 8.

112. "U.S., Pakistan Deny Reports of Helicopter Shooting," Radio Free Europe, September 16, 2008, at http://www.rferl.org/content/US_Pakistan_Deny_ Reports_Of_Helicopter_Shooting/1200288.html.

113. George W. Bush, *Decision Points* (New York: Virgin Books, 2010), 217.

114. Anne Patterson, "Reaction to Alleged Drone Attacks in Bannu," leaked US embassy cable, November 24, 2008, archived by Wikileaks at http://www. cablegatesearch.net/search.php?q=strikes+mainland+pakistan+stripes&qo= 0&qc=0&qto=2010-02-28.

115. Estimates via "The Bush Years: Pakistan Strikes 2004–2009," Bureau of Investigative Journalism, at http://www.thebureauinvestigates.com/2011/ 08/10/the-bush-years-2004-2009/.

CHAPTER 6

1. Catherine Herridge, Pamela Browne, Cyd Upson, and Gregory Johnsen, "New Details Emerge of Radical Imam's Lunch at the Pentagon," Fox News, May 20, 2011, at http://www.foxnews.com/politics/2011/05/19/ exclusive-new-details-emerge-al-qaeda-terror-chiefs-lunch-pentagon/.

2. Interviewed by Norwegian filmmaker Tonje Schei, author present, New York, October 2013.

3. Craig Whitlock, "Remote U.S. Base at Core of Secret Operations," *Washington Post*, October 26, 2012, at http://www.washingtonpost.com/world/national-security/remote-us-base-at-core-of-secret-operations/2012/10/25/a26a9392-197a-11e2-bd10-5ff056538b7c_story.html.

4. Interview with the author, November 2013.

5. The sole exception is Israel, which has openly practiced a policy of targeted killings since the 1990s and on which its Supreme Court has ruled.

6. Dr. Hans-Christian Ströbele addressing British parliamentarians, November 19, 2013. Author's notes.

7. According to the BIJ's research, the national or regional origins of 374 of atleast 410 of those killed could reasonably be determined. Of these, 195 were Pakistanis; 23 were Afghans; and a further 42 were indeterminate Pashtuns of one or other nation. An additional 30 of those killed originated from the immediate region. Some three-quarters then were locals, most likely militants engaged in the Afghan or Pakistani insurgencies, or civilian noncombatants. The Bureau also found evidence for 71 Arab and North African deaths (19%). Two Canadians, a Briton, and two Spaniards were also among those killed. Nationals of at least fifteen countries were targeted in total.

8. Interview with the author, March 2014.

9. Of at least 2,000 people estimated killed in drone bombings in Pakistan between 2009 and 2013, the nationalities of 1,886 could be reasonably determined. Some 85% (1,437 individuals) were recorded as being Afghans, Pakistanis, Uzbeks, and others from the immediate region. Arabs and North Africans represented a further 150 deaths—less than one in ten of those identified.

10. Jonathan Landay, "Obama's Drone War Kills 'Others,' Not Just al Qaida Leaders," McClatchy, April 9, 2013, at http://www.mcclatchydc.com/2013/04/09/188062/obamas-drone-war-kills-others.html.

11. Interview with the author, background terms.

12. Abdi Sheikh, "Four Foreign Militants Killed in Somalia Missile Strike," Reuters, February 24, 2012, at http://in.reuters.com/article/2012/02/24/somalia-conflict-idINDEE81N0C820120224.

13. Interview with the author. Also see Chris Woods, "Where Is the Evidence My Son Was a Terrorist?" *The Independent*, March 15, 2013, at http://www.independent.co.uk/news/uk/crime/where-is-the-evidence-my-son-was-a-terrorist-8537013.html.

14. The Biography of the Martyr, "Bilal Al Birjawi al-Lubani (Abu Hafs)," February 2013 (translated from Arabic).

15. Berjawi's own testimony under the pseudonym "Abu Omar," in *The Horn of Africa Inquisition*, CagePrisoners, 2010, at http://www.therenditionproject.org.uk/pdf/PDF%2046%20%5BCP-2010-04-REP%20The%20Horn%20of%20Africa%20Inquisition%5D.pdf.

16. Alice K. Ross and Patrick Galey, "Rise in Citizenship-Stripping as Government Cracks Down on UK Fighters in Syria," Bureau of Investigative Journalism, December 23, 2013, at http://www.thebureauinvestigates.com/2013/12/23/rise-in-citizenship-stripping-as-government-cracks-down-on-uk-fighters-in-syria/.

17. Letter from British Home Secretary Theresa May MP to Mohamed Sakr, September 23, 2010, copy obtained by author.

18. *Open Judgement: J1 and Secretary of State for the Home Department*, Special Immigration Appeals Commission, April 15, 2011, at http://www.siac.tribunals.gov.uk/Documents/outcomes/J1_SubstantiveJudgmnt_150411.pdf.

19. Barbara Starr, "U.S. Strikes Al Qaeda Affiliate in Somalia," CNN, June 28, 2011, at http://security.blogs.cnn.com/2011/06/28/u-s-strikes-al-qaeda-affiliate-in-somalia/.

20. "Somalia's al-Shabab Join al-Qaeda," BBC News, February 10, 2012, at http://www.bbc.co.uk/news/world-africa-16979440.

21. The Biography of the Martyr, "Bilal Al Birjawi al-Lubani (Abu Hafs)."

22. Author's copy.

23. US Secretary of State Hillary Clinton, speaking at the London Conference on Somalia, January 23, 2012, video at https://www.youtube.com/watch?v=FCtOh3ZozKk.

24. Unpublished transcript, interview with the author, March 2013.

25. See, for example, Baroness Helena Kennedy QC, "Citizenship is not a privilege, it is a protected legal status," March 20, 2014, Bureau of Investigative Journalism, at http://www.thebureauinvestigates.com/2014/03/20/comment-the-home-offices-attack-on-the-right-to-have-rights/.

26. Karen DeYoung, "CIA Idles Drone Flights from Base in Pakistan," *Washington Post*, July 2, 2011, at http://www.washingtonpost.com/world/national-security/cia-idles-drone-flights-from-base-in-pakistan/2011/07/01/AGpOiKuH_story.html.

27. See, for example, Nick Hopkins and Julian Borger, "NSA Pays £100m in Secret Funding for GCHQ," *Guardian*, August 1, 2013, at http://www.theguardian. com/uk-news/2013/aug/01/nsa-paid-gchq-spying-edward-snowden.

28. Ben Emmerson QC, address to joint session of UK All Party Parliamentary Groups on the United Nations and Drones, December 13, 2013. Author's transcript.

29. Matthew Tempest, "UK Condemns 'Unlawful' Yassin Killing," *Guardian*, March 22, 2004, at http://www.theguardian.com/politics/2004/mar/22/ foreignpolicy.israel.

30. Interview with the author, March 2012.

31. Chris Woods and Alice K. Ross, "Former British Citizens Killed by Drone Strikes after Passports Revoked," Bureau of Investigative Journalism, February 27, 2013, at http://www.thebureauinvestigates.com/2013/02/27/ former-british-citizens-killed-by-drone-strikes-after-passports-revoked/.

32. Sir John Sawer in evidence to the Intelligence and Security Committee, British parliament, November 7, 2013, via http://isc.independent.gov.uk/.

33. See, for example, Colum Lynch, "Exclusive: U.S Boycotts U.N. Drone Talks," March 19, 2014, at http://foreignpolicy.com/2014/03/19/exclusive-u-s-boycotts-u-n-drone-talks/.

34. Holger Stark, "Germany Limits Information Exchange with US Intelligence," *Der Spiegel*, May 17, 2011, at http://www.spiegel.de/international/germany/ drone-killing-debate-germany-limits-information-exchange-with-us-intelligence-a-762873.html.

35. Richard Norton-Taylor, "US Drone 'Kills Eight Germans' in Pakistan amid Terror Plot Fears," *The Guardian*, October 4, 2010, at http://www.theguardian. com/world/2010/oct/04/us-kills-eight-militants-pakistan.

36. "US Issues Europe Travel Alert as Intel Shows Terror Plot Targeting Paris, Berlin Landmarks," Fox News, October 3, 2010, at http://www. foxnews.com/politics/2010/10/03/administration-issues-travel-alert-americans-europe-terror-threat/.

37. Karolina Tagaris, Estelle Shirbon, William Maclean, Philip Stewart, and Mark Hosenball, "Plot to Attack European Cities Foiled: Report," Reuters, September 29, 2010, at http://uk.reuters.com/article/2010/09/29/ us-britain-security-idUKTRE68R5ZS20100929.

38. Email from Emrah Erdogan to Hans-Christian Ströbele MP, early 2011.

39. Extract from witness interview statement taken by Andreas Schueller, European Centre for Constitutional and Human Rights, Germany, February 28, 2013.

40. Interview with the author, Berlin, January 2014.

41. "Sieben Jahre Haft für Auslöser von Terroralarm im Bundestag," *Frankfurter Allgemeine*, January 23, 2014, at http://www.faz.net/aktuell/politik/ anschlagdrohung-sieben-jahre-haft-fuer-ausloeser-von-terroralarm-im-bundestag-12765861.html.

42. Speaking to Deutschlandfunk Radio, cited in "The World from Berlin: 'Germany Must Do More to Combat Homegrown Terrorism,'" Spiegel Online, October 6, 2010, at http://www.spiegel.de/international/

world/the-world-from-berlin-germany-must-do-more-to-combat-home-grown-terrorism-a-721584.html.

43. A. Böhm, C. Elmer, and N. Plonka, "Aus dem Leben zweier deutscher Islamisten," Stern Investigativ, March 29, 2012, at http://www.stern.de/investigativ/projekte/terrorismus/us-drohnenopfer-aus-dem-leben-zweier-deutscher-islam isten-1806355.html.

44. In the wake of the Edward Snowden revelations in 2013, it was later reported that "Chancellery minister Ronald Pofalla told a closed parliamentary committee that GSM data, which the BND has admitted sending to other foreign secret services, was not specific enough to pinpoint exact locations." Louise Osborne, "Germany Denies Phone Data Sent to NSA Used in Drone Attacks," Guardian, August 12, 2013, at http://www.theguardian.com/world/2013/aug/12/germany-phone-data-nsa-drone.

45. Florian Flade, "German Judge Presses Charges after Drone Killing," Jih@d blog, November 1, 2011, at http://ojihad.wordpress.com/2011/01/11/german-judge-presses-charges-after-drone-killing/.

46. Interview with the author, May 2014.

47. Cited in Bill Roggio, "IMU Lauds Another German Killed in US Drone Strike," Long War Journal, April 18, 2013, at http://www.longwarjournal.org/archives/2013/04/imu_lauds_another_ge.php.

48. Interview with the author, Berlin, January 2014.

49. Wajid Shamsul Hasan, Pakistan's High Commissioner to the UK, interview with the author July 2012. See also Chris Woods, "CIA Drone Strikes Violate Pakistan's Sovereignty, Says Senior Diplomat," The Guardian, August 3, 2012, at http://www.theguardian.com/world/2012/aug/03/cia-drone-strikes-violate-pakistan.

50. Interview with the author, background terms, February 2014.

51. Nic Robertson, Paul Crookshank, and Tim Lister, "Documents Give New Details on al Qaeda's London Bombings," CNN, April 30, 2012, at http://edition.cnn.com/2012/04/30/world/al-qaeda-documents-london-bombings/.

52. For a detailed study of Azizi's role in Al Qaeda and his links to the Madrid bombings, see Fernando Reinares, "The Evidence of Al-Qa`ida's Role in the 2004 Madrid Attack," West Point Combating Terrorism Center, March 22, 2012, at http://www.ctc.usma.edu/posts/the-evidence-of-al-qaidas-role-in-the-2004-madrid-attack.

53. "Evidence Suggests US Missile Used in Strike," NBC News, December 5, 2005, at http://www.nbcnews.com/id/10303175/#.UsFpWvRdXA0.

54. Manuel Marlasca and Luis Rendueles, "La CIA mató a una española en Pakistán," May 27, 2011, at http://www.interviu.es/reportajes/articulos/la-cia-mato-a-una-espanola-en-pakistan.

55. Brian Ross, "Exclusive: Suicide Bomb Teams Sent to U.S., Europe," ABC News, June 18, 2007, at http://abcnews.go.com/blogs/headlines/2007/06/exclusive_suici/.

56. Colin Freeze, "Former CIA Director Knew of Canada's 'Lost Boys,'" Globe and Mail, August 23, 2012, at http://m.theglobeandmail.com/news/national/former-cia-director-knew-of-canadas-lost-boys/article1807149/?service=mobile.

57. Interview with the author, background terms, February 2014.

58. "Two Canadians Killed in Wana Missile Attack," Dawn/AFP, August 31, 2008, at http://www.dawn.com/news/319095/two-canadians-killed-in-wana-missile-attack.

59. Counterterrorism officers from the Royal Canadian Mounted Police had earlier issued arrest warrants for two men named as Ferid Ahmed Imam and Maiwand Yar, for example, following "evidence that two Canadian citizens conspired to travel to Pakistan [in 2007] for terrorist training." However, there was no indication that either man had been killed by the United States, with the RCMP noting to the author in 2012 that "We have no information to suggest that either Imam or Yar are deceased." RCMP email to author, May 2012.

60. For a full list of Westerners reported killed by the United States, see Appendix A.

61. Chris Woods, "Mystery of 'Australian' Slain by Drone Deepens," Bureau of Investigative Journalism, August 25, 2011, at http://www.thebureauinvestigates.com/2011/08/25/mystery-of-australian-slain-by-drone-deepens/.

62. Paul Maley and Mark Schliebs, "Aussies Killed in US Drone Strike in Yemen," The Australian, April 16, 2014, paywalled at http://www.theaustralian.com.au/national-affairs/policy/aussies-killed-in-us-drone-strike-in-yemen/story-fn59nm2j-1226885783804#.

63. Marc Corcoran, "Drone Strikes Based on Work at Pine Gap Could See Australians Charged, Malcolm Fraser Says," ABC Australia, April 28, 2014, at http://www.abc.net.au/news/2014-04-28/australians-could-be-charged-over-us-drone-strikes-fraser/5416224.

64. Paul Maley, "Pine Gap 'Supports US Drone Hits,'" The Australian, May 20, 2014, at http://www.theaustralian.com.au/national-affairs/policy/pine-gap-supports-us-drone-hits/story-e6frg8yo-1226923350422#.

65. Philip Dorling, "Pine Gap Drives US Drone Kills," The Age, July 21, 2013, at http://www.theage.com.au/national/pine-gap-drives-us-drone-kills-20130720-2qbsa.html.

66. "Rashid Rauf remains the subject of an order for extradition and repatriation," West Midlands Police told the author in May 2012. "Unsubstantiated reports suggest Rashid Rauf was killed in a military strike, but we are awaiting official confirmation of this from the authorities in Pakistan."

67. Nic Robertson, Paul Cruickshank, and Tim Lister, "Documents Give New Details on Al Qaeda's London Bombings," CNN, April 30, 2012, at http://edition.cnn.com/2012/04/30/world/al-qaeda-documents-london-bombings/index.html.

68. "Both Pakistani and British intelligence sources told Human Rights Watch that Rauf was beaten and mistreated while in the custody of the ISI." Cited in "Cruel Britannia: British Complicity in the Torture and Ill-treatment of Terror Suspects in Pakistan," Human Rights Watch, November 2009, at http://www.hrw.org/sites/default/files/reports/uk1109webwcover_0.pdf.

69. "Police Fired for Negligence in Rauf Case," leaked US embassy cable, January 18, 2008, archived by Wikileaks at http://www.cablegatesearch.net/cable.php?id=08ISLAMABAD290&q=prayer%20rashid%20rauf.

70. David Leppard, "GCHQ Finds Al-Qaeda for American Strikes," *Sunday Times*, July 25, 2010, paywalled at http://www.thesundaytimes.co.uk/sto/news/uk_news/Defence/article353492.ece.

71. Chris Allbriton, "Pakistan Helps US Drone Campaign," Reuters, January 22, 2012, at http://www.thefiscaltimes.com/Articles/2012/01/22/Pakistan-Helps-US-Drone-Campaign.

72. Interview with the author, background terms.

73. Amardeep Bassey, "Family of Al Qaida Terrorist Rashid Rauf to Sue British Government for Murder," *Birmingham Mail*, October 27, 2012, at http://www.birminghammail.co.uk/news/local-news/al-qaida-terrorist-rashid-raufs-270221.

74. *Noor Khan and Secretary of State for Foreign and Commonwealth Affairs: Detailed Statement of Facts and Grounds*, High Court of Justice Queen's Bench Division, March 13, 2012.

75. Alice Ross, "High Court Rejects First UK Challenge to CIA's Drone Campaign," Bureau of Investigative Journalism, December 22, 2012, at http://www.thebureauinvestigates.com/2012/12/22/court-of-appeal-rejects-first-uk-challenge-to-cias-drone-campaign/.

76. *United States of America v. Jude Kenan Mohammad and others*, District Court for the Eastern District of North Carolina, September 24, 2009, archived at http://www.investigativeproject.org/documents/case_docs/1075.pdf.

77. Scott Shane and Eric Schmitt, "One Drone Victim's Trail from Raleigh to Pakistan," *New York Times*, May 22, 2013, at http://www.nytimes.com/2013/05/23/us/one-drone-victims-trail-from-raleigh-to-pakistan.html.

78. "Special Issue: The Greatest Special Operation of All Time," *Inspire*, no. 7, published September 27, 2011.

79. Letter from Eric Holder, US Attorney General to Patrick Leahy, Chairman of the Senate Judiciary Committee, May 22, 2013, at http://www.justice.gov/ag/AG-letter-5-22-13.pdf.

80. Dana Priest, "U.S. Military Teams, Intelligence Deeply Involved in Aiding Yemen on Strikes," *Washington Post*, January 27, 2010, at http://www.washingtonpost.com/wp-dyn/content/article/2010/01/26/AR2010012604239.html.

81. John Brennan, cited in Eli Lake, "Dozens of Americans Believed to Have Joined Terrorists," *Washington Times*, June 24, 2010, at http://www.washingtontimes.com/news/2010/jun/24/dozens-from-us-on-list-of-targets-as-terrorists/?page=all#pagebreak.

82. Leon Panetta, director Central Intelligence Agency to Jake Tapper, This Week transcript, ABC News, June 27 2010, at http://abcnews.go.com/ThisWeek/week-transcript-panetta/story?id=11025299&singlePage=true.

83. Professor Christof Heyns, UN Special Rapporteur on extrajudicial summary or arbitrary executions, Human Rights Council Seventeenth session Agenda item 3 advance version, May 27, 2011, at http://www2.ohchr.org/english/bodies/hrcouncil/docs/17session/A-HRC-17-28-Add1.pdf.

84. http://www.cablegatesearch.net/search.php?q=awlaqi&qo=0&qc=0&qto=2010-02-28.

85. "Lawfulness of a Lethal Operation Directed against a US Citizen Who Is a Senior Operational Leader of al-Qaida or an Associated Force," Department of Justice White Paper, leaked to NBC News, February 4, 2013, at http://msnbc-media.msn.com/i/msnbc/sections/news/020413_DOJ_White_Paper.pdf.

86. See, for example, Marcy Wheeler, "AQAP Drone Strikes Obama's Awlaki Drone Story," EmptyWheel, June 27, 2014, at http://www.emptywheel.net/2014/06/27/arab-propagandists-drone-strike-obamas-awlaki-drone-story/.

87. At a meeting between CENTCOM commander David Petraeus and President Saleh of Yemen in early January 2010 the attempt to kill the American cleric was secretly discussed: "AQAP leader Nassr al-Wahishi and extremist cleric Anwar al-Awlaki may still be alive, Saleh said, but the December strikes had already caused al-Qaeda operatives to turn themselves in to authorities and residents in affected areas to deny refuge to al-Qaeda." http://www.cablegatesearch.net/cable.php?id=10SANAA4&q=awlaki.

88. Philip J Crowley, Designations of Al-Qa'ida in the Arabian Peninsula (AQAP) and Senior Leaders, US State Department, January 19, 2010, at http://www.state.gov/r/pa/prs/ps/2010/01/135364.htm. See also Treasury Designates Anwar Al-Aulaqi, Key Leader of Al-Qa'ida in the Arabian Peninsula, US Treasury press statement, July 16, 2010, at http://www.treasury.gov/press-center/press-releases/Pages/tg779.aspx.

89. Sudarsan Raghavan and Michael D. Shear, "U.S.-Aided Attack in Yemen Thought to Have Killed Aulaqi, 2 al-Qaeda Leaders," *Washington Post*, December 25, 2009, at http://www.washingtonpost.com/wp-dyn/content/article/2009/12/24/AR2009122400536.html.

90. "General Petraeus' Meeting with Saleh on Security Assistance, AQAP Strikes," leaked US embassy cable, January 4, 2010, archived by Wikileaks at http://www.cablegatesearch.net/cable.php?id=10SANAA4&q=petraeus%20yemen.

91. *Final Report of the William H. Webster Commission on The Federal Bureau of Investigation, Counterterrorism Intelligence, and the Events at Fort Hood, Texas, on November 5, 2009*, June 2012, at http://www.fbi.gov/news/pressrel/press-releases/final-report-of-the-william-h.-webster-commission.

92. Interview with the author, November 2013.

93. "Lawfulness of a Lethal Operation Directed against a US Citizen Who Is a Senior Operational Leader of al-Qaida or an Associated Force," Department of Justice White Paper, leaked to NBC News, February 4, 2013, at http://msnbc-media.msn.com/i/msnbc/sections/news/020413_DOJ_White_Paper.pdf.

94. Charlie Savage, "Justice Department Memo Approving Targeted Killing of Anwar Al-Awlaki," *New York Times*, June 23, 2014, at http://www.nytimes.com/interactive/2014/06/23/us/23awlaki-memo.html.

95. Interview with the author, March 2014.

96. See, for example, Hakim Almasmari, "Official: Drone Attack Kills Awlaki's Son in Yemen," CNN, October 15, 2011, at http://edition.cnn.com/2011/10/15/world/meast/yemen-drone-attack/index.html.

97. Jeremy Scahill, *Dirty Wars: The World Is a Battlefield* (London: Serpent's Tail, 2013), 496.

98. "The Family Mourns: The Family of Abdulrahman and Anwar Al Awlaki Statement," November 23, 2011, at http://upstatedroneaction.org/wordpress /2011/11/23/a-family-mourns/.

99. Jeremy Scahill, "Inside America's Dirty Wars," *The Nation*, April 13, 2013, at http://www.thenation.com/article/173980/inside-americas-dirty-wars? page=0,3#.

100. Bob Woodward, *Obama's Wars: The Inside Story* (London: Simon & Schuster, 2010), 25–26.

101. Interview with the author, background terms.

102. Mark Mazzetti and Eric Schmitt, "U.S. Militant, Hidden, Spurs Drone Debate," *New York Times*, February 28, 2014, at http://www.nytimes.com/2014/02/28/ world/asia/us-militant-hidden-spurs-drone-debate.html.

103. Hina Shamsi, "Violating the Ideals He Pledged to Uphold," American Civil Liberties Union, March 2, 2014, archived at http://www.philly.com/philly/ opinion/20140302_Violating_the_ideals_he_pledged_to_uphold.html.

104. Research by the Bureau of Investigative Journalism.

105. Cited in "5-Point Plan for Reforming U.S. Drone Strike Policy to Prevent Extrajudicial Executions," Amnesty International, at http://www.amnestyusa. org/pdfs/5PointPlanForReformingUSDroneStrikePolicy.pdf.

CHAPTER 7

1. Carlotta Gall and Jeff Zeleny, "Obama Opens a Foreign Tour in Afghanistan," *New York Times*, July 20, 2008, at http://www.nytimes.com/2008/07/20/us/ politics/20OBAMA.html.

2. "Statement from Obama Delegation," Politico, July 20, 2008, at http://www. politico.com/news/stories/0708/11899.html.

3. Barack Obama interviewed by Tom Brokaw, NBC News Meet the Press, July 27, 2008, transcript archived at http://www.presidency.ucsb.edu/ws/index. php?pid=77724#axzz1NZhuU6KV.

4. Mark Mazzetti, "U.S. Aborted Raid on Qaeda Chiefs in Pakistan in '05," *New York Times*, July 8, 2007, at http://www.nytimes.com/2007/07/08/ washington/08intel.html.

5. Barack Obama, "The War We Need to Win," Woodrow Wilson International Center, August 1, 2007, archived at http://www.cfr.org/elections/obamas- speech-woodrow-wilson-center/p13974.

6. "The Terrorist Threat to the Homeland," US National Intelligence Estimate (unclassified version), July 2007, at http://www.dni.gov/files/documents/ NIE_terrorist%20threat%202007.pdf.

7. Interview with the author, background terms.

8. AFL-CIO Democratic Presidential Debate: Chicago, August 7, 2007, tran- script at http://www.democracynow.org/2007/8/8/afl_cio_host_demo- cratic_presidential_debate.

9. Democratic debate transcript: Ohio, NBC News, February 26, 2008, archived at http://www.msnbc.msn.com/id/23354734/ns/politics-the_debates/t/feb- democratic-debate-transcript/#.UFMBVK6z6So.

10. Cited in Helene Cooper, "Choosing Which War to Fight," *New York Times*, February 24, 2008, at http://www.nytimes.com/2008/02/24/weekinreview/24cooper.html.

11. Dana Priest and Ann Scott Tyson, "Bin Laden Trail 'Stone Cold,'" *Washington Post*, September 10, 2006, at http://www.washingtonpost.com/wp-dyn/content/article/2006/09/09/AR2006090901105_pf.html.

12. Matthew M. Aid, *Intel Wars: The Secret History of the Fight against Terror* (New York: Bloomsbury Press, 2012), 67.

13. Interview with the author, November 2013.

14. "UNAMA recorded 552 civilian casualties of this nature in 2008. This constitutes 64% of the 828 non-combatant deaths attributed to actions by pro-government forces in 2008, and 26% of all civilians killed as a result of armed conflict in 2008." United Nations Assistance Mission to Afghanistan: Annual Report on Protection of Civilians in Armed Conflict, 2008, at http://unama.unmissions.org/Portals/UNAMA/human%20rights/UNAMA_09february-Annual%20Report_PoC%202008_FINAL_11Feb09.pdf.

15. Interview with the author, London, 2014.

16. "Karzai 'Demands' Obama End Civilian Deaths after Latest Incident," Associated Press, November 11, 2008, at http://usatoday30.usatoday.com/news/world/2008-11-05-afghanistan-violence_N.htm.

17. Stanley McChrystal, *My Share of the Task: A Memoir* (New York: Portfolio Penguin, 2013), 311.

18. Interview with the author, background terms, December 2013.

19. Cited by David Wood, "Holding Fire Afghanistan," *Air Force Magazine*, January 2010, at http://www.airforcemag.com/MagazineArchive/Pages/2010/January%202010/0110afghanistan.aspx.

20. McChrystal, *My Share of the Task*, 310.

21. Michael T. Flynn, Matt Pottinger, and Paul D. Batchelor, "Fixing Intel: A Blueprint for Making Intelligence Relevant in Afghanistan," Center for a New American Security, January 2010, archived at http://www.cnas.org/files/documents/publications/AfghanIntel_Flynn_Jan2010_code507_voices.pdf.

22. Interview with the author, Langley AFB, December 2013. Surname withheld at request of USAF.

23. Interview with the author.

24. Interview with the author, background terms.

25. Comments to the author, background terms.

26. See, for example, the description of a visit by McChrystal to a forward base in Michael Hastings, "The Runaway General," June 22, 2010, at http://www.rollingstone.com/politics/news/the-runaway-general-20100622.

27. "Annual Report on Protection of Civilians in Armed Conflict: Afghanistan 2009," UNAMA, February 2010, at http://unama.unmissions.org/Portals/UNAMA/human%20rights/Protection%20of%20Civilian%202009%20report%20English.pdf.

28. There was much for the new US administration to distrust. On November 26, 2008, the militant Pakistani group Lashkar e-Taiba had launched terrorist

attacks on the city of Mumbai that killed 160 people. It later emerged that elements of Pakistan's spy agency the ISI had assisted the attack.

29. "CODEL Biden's Meeting with COAS Kayani and ISI Pasha," leaked US embassy cable, February 6, 2009, archived by Wikileaks at http://www.cablegatesearch. net/cable.php?id=09ISLAMABAD270&q=pasha.

30. Mushtaq Yusufzai, "Militants Threaten to Scrap Peace Accord," *The News International*, November 2, 2008, at http://www.thenews.com.pk/ TodaysPrintDetail.aspx?ID=18122&Cat=13&dt=11/4/2008.

31. Shortly after Obama took office, Nazir put aside squabbles with other Taliban leaders and united to face "the American and Pakistani aggressors." For good measure, he swore loyalty to Osama bin Laden and Mullah Omar, head of Afghanistan's Taliban. Nazir coincidentally restated his loyalties to Al Qaeda in an interview in May 2011, conducted on the day of bin Laden's death. In 2013 the CIA finally killed Nazir and his most senior commanders in a devastating strike.

32. Mushtaq Yusufzai, "US Sleuths Took Part in Bara Swoop," *The News International*, January 23, 2009, at http://www.thenews.com.pk/TodaysPrintDetail.aspx?ID= 19823&Cat=13&dt=1/24/2009.

33. Matthew Rosenberg, "Pakistan Lends Support for U.S. Military Strikes," *Wall Street Journal*, February 18, 2009, at http://online.wsj.com/news/articles/ SB123491516776204073.

34. Daniel Klaidman, *Kill or Capture: The War on Terror and the Soul of the Obama Presidency* (New York: Houghton Mifflin Harcourt, 2012), 38–39.

35. Now known as the Center for Civilians in Conflict.

36. "Colleteral [*sic*] Damages," note from Assistant Political Agent, South Waziristan on meeting with Ganghi Khel jirga, February 3, 2009, copy provided to the author.

37. "Pakistani Deaths Exceed Afghan in Terror War: Report," *Dawn*, December 10, 2009, at http://www.dawn.com/news/590011/pakistani-civilian-deaths-exceed-afghan-in-terror-war-report.

38. Woodward, *Obama's Wars*, 93.

39. Klaidman, *Kill or Capture*, 40.

40. Aid, *Intel Wars*, 118.

41. See, for example, Owais Tohid, "Pakistani Teen Tells of His Recruitment, Training as Suicide Bomber," *Christian Science Monitor*, June 16, 2011, at http:// www.csmonitor.com/World/Asia-South-Central/2011/0616/Pakistani-teen-tells-of-his-recruitment-training-as-suicide-bomber.

42. Jason Burke, "Taliban and Pakistan Officials Agree Permanent Ceasefire in Swat Valley," *Guardian*, February 21, 2009, at http://www.guardian.co.uk/ world/2009/feb/21/pakistan-afghanistan.

43. Hillary Clinton, "New Beginnings: Foreign Policy Priorities in the Obama Administration," House Foreign Affairs Committee, April 22, 2009, at http:// democrats.foreignaffairs.house.gov/111/48841.pdf.

44. "Pakistan: Extrajudicial Executions by Army in Swat," Human Rights Watch, July 16, 2009, at http://www.hrw.org/news/2010/07/16/pakistan-extrajudicial-executions-army-swat.

45. David Rohde, "A Drone and Dwindling Hope," *New York Times*, October 20, 2009, at http://www.nytimes.com/2009/10/21/world/asia/21hostage.html.

46. Cited in Joby Warrick, "CIA Places Blame for Bhutto Assassination," *Washington Post*, January 18, 2008, at http://www.washingtonpost.com/wp-dyn/content/article/2008/01/17/AR2008011703252.html.

47. Cited in Pir Zubair Shah, Sabrina Tavernise, and Mark Mazzetti, "Taliban Leader in Pakistan Is Reportedly Killed," *New York Times*, August 7, 2009, at http://www.nytimes.com/2009/08/08/world/asia/08pstan.html.

48. "Obama: We Took Out Pakistani Taliban Chief," ABC News Australia, August 22, 2009, at http://www.abc.net.au/news/2009-08-21/obama-we-took-out-pakistani-taliban-chief/1399370.

49. "Scenesetter for General Kayani's Visit to Washington," leaked US embassy cable, February 19, 2009, at http://www.cablegatesearch.net/cable.php?id=09I SLAMABAD365&q=kayani.

50. Embedded visit with the Pakistan Army to South Waziristan by the author, November 2012.

51. Leon Panetta, "Director's Remarks at the Pacific Council on International Policy," Central Intelligence Agency, May 18, 2009, at https://www.cia.gov/news-information/speeches-testimony/directors-remarks-at-pacific-council.html.

52. The US Rewards for Justice page on Mehsud, which offered a $5 million reward for the terrorist, focused heavily on his operations within Pakistan, although also noted that "in addition, Mehsud has stated his intention to attack the United States. He has conducted cross-border attacks against U.S. forces in Afghanistan, and poses a clear threat to American persons and interests in the region." Rewards for Justice: Baitullah Mehsud, March 25, 2009, at http://www.state.gov/r/pa/prs/ps/2009/03/120863.htm.

53. Carlotta Gall, "Pakistan and Afghan Taliban Close Ranks," March 26, 2009, at http://www.nytimes.com/2009/03/27/world/asia/27taliban.html.

54. Joby Warrick, *The Triple Agent: The Al-Qaeda Mole Who Infiltrated the CIA* (New York: Doubleday, 2011), 64.

55. Chris Woods, "The CIA, a Dirty Bomb Plot and Drones: An Interview with Joby Warrick," Bureau of Investigative Journalism, November 2, 2011, at http://www.thebureauinvestigates.com/2011/11/02/the-cia-a-dirty-bomb-plot-and-drones-an-interview-with-joby-warrick/.

56. Ben Emmerson QC, UN Special Rapporteur on the Promotion and Protection of Human Rights and Fundamental Freedoms while Countering Terrorism, 3rd Annual Report, March 11, 2014, archived at http://justsecurity.org/wp-content/uploads/2014/02/Special-Rapporteur-Rapporteur-Emmerson-Drones-2014.pdf.

57. Chris Woods, "Drone Strikes in Pakistan: Witnesses Speak Out," February 4, 2012, at http://www.thebureauinvestigates.com/2012/02/04/witnesses-speak-out/.

58. Ben Emmerson QC, address to joint session of UK All Party Parliamentary Groups on the United Nations and Drones, December 13, 2013. Author's transcript.

59. Interview with the author, March 2014.

60. Mushtaq Yusufzai, Mumtaz Khan, and Haji Mujtaba, "40 Militants Die in NWA Drone Strikes," *The News International*, May 17, 2009, at http://www.thenews. com.pk/TodaysPrintDetail.aspx?ID=22177&Cat=13&dt=5/17/2009.

61. "According to a health professional familiar with North Waziristan, one humanitarian organization had a 'policy to not go immediately [to a reported drone strike] because of follow up strikes. There is a six hour mandatory delay.'" Cited in *Living under Drones*, 76.

62. Chris Woods, "Get the Data: Obama's Terror Drones," Bureau of Investigative Journalism, February 4, 2012, at http://www.thebureauinvestigates. com/2012/02/04/get-the-data-obamas-terror-drones/.

63. Christof Heyns, "Armed Drones and the Right to Life," UN General Assembly, September 13, 2013, at http://justsecurity.org/wp-content/uploads/2013/10/ UN-Special-Rapporteur-Extrajudicial-Christof-Heyns-Report-Drones.pdf.

64. Ben Emmerson QC: "Christof Heyns . . . has described such attacks, if they prove to have happened, as war crimes. I would endorse that view." Cited in "UN Team to Investigate Civilian Drone Deaths," October 25, 2012, at http://www. thebureauinvestigates.com/2012/10/25/united-nations-team-to-investigate-civilian-drone-deaths/.

65. "Will I Be Next? US Drone Strikes in Pakistan," Amnesty International, 2013, 28-31, at http://www.amnestyusa.org/sites/default/files/asa330132013en.pdf.

66. *Living under Drones*, 74–76, at http://www.livingunderdrones.org/wp-content/ uploads/2013/10/Stanford-NYU-Living-Under-Drones.pdf. Scott Shane, "U.S. Said to Target Rescuers at Drone Strike Sites," *New York Times*, February 5, 2012, at http://www.nytimes.com/2012/02/06/world/asia/ us-drone-strikes-are-said-to-target-rescuers.html.

67. Richard Hoagland, cited in Robert Naiman, "Americans Press US Ambassador for End to Drone Strikes in Pakistan, and the Ambassador Responds," TruthOut, October 5, 2012, at http://truth-out.org/news/item/11963-americans-press-us-ambassador-for-end-to-drone-strikes-in-pakistan-and-the-ambassador-responds.

68. This rule applied to US military operations in both Iraq and Afghanistan. See MultiNational Corps Iraq Rules of Engagement (ROE) Annotated Version, July 27, 2005 (declassified), cited in Neta C. Crawford, *Accountability for Killing: Moral Responsibility for Collateral Damage in America's Post-9/11 Wars* (London: Oxford University Press, 2013), 357.

69. Alice K. Ross and Jack Serle, "Most US Drone Strikes in Pakistan Attack Houses," Bureau of Investigative Journalism, May 23, 2014, at http://www. thebureauinvestigates.com/2014/05/23/most-us-drone-strikes-in-pakistan-attack-houses/.

70. Interview with the author, March 2014.

71. Interview with the author, March 2012.

72. "Clinton Faces Pakistani Anger at Drone Attacks," Associated Press, October 30, 2009, archived at http://www.foxnews.com/politics/2009/10/30/clinton-faces-pakistani-anger-drone-attacks/#_blank.

73. Ann Patterson, "Reviewing Our Afghanistan/Pakistan Strategy," leaked US embassy cable, September 23, 2009, archived by Wikileaks at http://www.wikileaks.org/plusd/cables/09ISLAMABAD2295_a.html.

74. Woodward, *Obama's Wars*, 207–209; and Michael Hirsh, "Slow Dance: Obama's Romance with the CIA," *National Journal*, May 11, 2011, at http://www.nationaljournal.com/magazine/secret-love-obama-s-budding-romance-with-the-cia-20110511.

75. As Scahill notes, Pentagon spokesman Geoff Morrell misled journalists in November 2009 by insisting that US SOF were only in Pakistan as trainers: "that's the extent of four—our, you know, military boots on the ground in Pakistan." http://www.thenation.com/blog/156765/not-so-secret-anymore-us-war-pakistan#.

76. "Suicide Bomber Chapman," leaked US military files Afghanistan, December 30, 2009, archived by Wikileaks at https://wikileaks.org/afg/event/2009/12/AFG20091230n2388.html.

77. For a detailed study of al-Balawi's background, see Warrick's *The Triple Agent*.

78. Joby Warrick, "Systemic Failures Led to Suicide Attack, CIA Says," *Washington Post*, October 20, 2010, at http://www.washingtonpost.com/wp-dyn/content/article/2010/10/19/AR2010101906416.html.

79. Cited in Warrick, *The Triple Agent*, 190.

80. "Complaint to UNHRC Against the United States of America for the Killing of Innocent Citizens of the Islamic Republic of Pakistan," Reprieve, February 22, 2012, at http://www.reprieve.org.uk/wp-content/uploads/2015/03/2012_02_22_PUB-FINAL-UN-HRC-Complaint.pdf.

81. Behram's notes of his visit provided to the author. Anonymous US intelligence officials implied to the author and others that Noor Behram had links with the Taliban, though offered no proof.

82. Hazrat Ali Bacha, "Bomb in Pakistan Kills 3 U.S. Soldiers, 3 Children," Reuters, February 3, 2010, at http://www.reuters.com/article/2010/02/03/us-pakistan-blast-idUSTRE6120UH20100203.

83. Laith Alkhouri, "Video of Times Square Bomber Faisal Shahzad with Taliban Commander Hakimullah Mehsud," Flashpoint Partners, July 22, 2010, archived at https://web.archive.org/web/20100725071558/http://www.flashpoint-intel.com/library/pakistan/631-flashpoint-exclusive-video-of-times-square-bomber-faisal-shahzad-with-taliban-commander-hakimullah-mehsud.html.

84. Cited in Benjamin Weiser, "A Guilty Plea in Plot to Bomb Times Square," *New York Times*, June 22, 2010, at http://www.nytimes.com/2010/06/22/nyregion/22terror.html.

85. "Clinton War on Terror, Pakistan," CBS News video, May 7, 2010, at http://www.cbsnews.com/videos/clinton-on-war-on-terror-pakistan/.

86. In 2013 Washington resumed strikes on the TTP's leadership, with devastating results. For more, see chapter 10.

87. Interview with the author, March 2014.

88. Ayalon was Shin Bet chief from 1996 to 2000. *The Gatekeepers*, directed by Dror Moreh, Cinephil, 2012.

CHAPTER 8

1. Interview with the author, November 2013. Chad Bruton, a former Predator pilot with the 15th RS, also recalled for the author missions involving helicopters: "I particularly remember the ones with the Apaches because those guys believe in overkill. I mean after they've shot everybody, if a body so much as twitched they would come through and rake it again which was just like—bang. I mean seriously, it's dead man. Leave it be."

2. Interviews with the author, November 2013–January 2014.

3. In 2002, for example, CENTCOM Commander General Tommy Franks told reporters "You know we don't do body counts." Cited by Edward Epstein, "Success in Afghan War Hard to Gauge," *San Francisco Chronicle*, March 23, 2002, archived at http://www.globalsecurity.org/org/news/2002/020323-attack01.htm.

4. Jeff Schogal, "AF Disputes Drone Operator's Claim," *Air Force Times*, June 14, 2013, archived at http://www.airforcetimes.com/article/20130614/NEWS04/306140020/AF-disputes-drone-operator-s-claim.

5. Interview with the author, October 2013.

6. Interview with the author, November 2013.

7. Interview with the author, January 2014.

8. Major Chad Bruton, interview with the author.

9. Interview with the author, background terms.

10. Interview with the author, Langley AFB, December 2013. Surname withheld at request of USAF.

11. Philip Alston, Report of the Special Rapporteur on Extrajudicial, Summary or Arbitrary Executions, UN Human Rights Council 14th session, May 28, 2010, 25, archived at http://vcnv.org/files/A_HRC_14_24_Add6.pdf.

12. Interview with the author, February 2014.

13. Notes provided to the author dated May 2012.

14. Interview with the author, November 2013.

15. Matt J. Martin, with Charles W. Sasser, *Predator: The Remote Control Air War over Iraq and Afghanistan—a Pilot's Story* (Minneapolis, MN: Zenith Press, 2010), 88, 54, and 211.

16. See, for example, Neta Bar and Eyal Ben-Ari, "Israeli Snipers in the Al-Aqsa Intifada: Killing, Humanity and Lived Experience," *Third World Quarterly* 26, no. 1 (2005): 133–152, at http://www.academia.edu/3472756/Israeli_snipers_in_the_Al-Aqsa_intifada_killing_humanity_and_lived_experience.

17. Interview with the author, October 2013.

18. Unpublished interview by film-maker Tonje Schei, author's copy.

19. Cited in DRONE, Flimmer Films, April 2014, directed by Tonje Hessen Schei.

20. Interview with the author, Langley AFB, December 2013. Surname withheld at request of USAF.

21. "Remote Control: Remotely Piloted Air Systems—Current and Future UK Use," House of Commons Defence Select Committee, March 11, 2014, at http://www.publications.parliament.uk/pa/cm201314/cmselect/cmdfence/772/772.pdf.

22. Interview with the author, January 2014.

23. Interview with the author, October 2013.

24. Cited in "The Future of Air Force Motion Imagery Exploitation," Rand: Project Air Force, 2012, at http://www.rand.org/content/dam/rand/pubs/technical_reports/2012/RAND_TR1133.pdf.

25. Colonel Bradley T. Hoagland, "Manning the Next Unmanned Air Force: Developing RPA Pilots of the Future," Brookings Institution, August 2013, at http://www.brookings.edu/~/media/research/files/papers/2013/08/06%20 air%20force%20drone%20pilot%20development%20hoagland/manning%20 unmanned%20force_final_08052013.pdf.

26. Lee Ferran, "Drone 'Stigma' Means 'Less Skilled' Pilots at Controls of Deadly Robots," ABC News, April 29, 2014, at http://abcnews.go.com/Blotter/ drone-stigma-means-skilled-pilots-controls-deadly-robots/story?id=23475968.

27. Major Chad Bruton, interview with the author.

28. Retired Colonel Don Hudson is Technical Director of the 480th ISR Wing and a former vice-commander of the unit. Interviewed by the author, Langley AFB Virginia, December 2013.

29. Interview with the author, Langley AFB, December 2013. Surname withheld at request of USAF.

30. "Actions Needed to Strengthen Management of Unmanned Aerial System Pilots," Government Accountability Office, April 2014, at http://www.gao.gov/ assets/670/662467.pdf.

31. Interview with the author, January 2014.

32. Critics seemed particularly offended that the proposed medal would rank above the Purple Heart, awarded for injuries sustained on the battlefield. See, for example, Gordon Lubold, "Medals for Drone Pilots? Hagel Faces Tough Choices," Foreign Policy, January 27, 2014, at http://complex.foreignpolicy.com/ posts/2014/01/27/medals_for_drone_pilots_hagel_still_cant_decide.

33. Brendan Cullerton, "Pentagon to Consider Whether Drone Pilots Deserve Top Military Honors," ABC News, April 28, 2014, at http://abcnews.go.com/Politics/ pentagon-drone-pilots-deserve-top-military-honors/story?id=23501910.

34. Interview with the author, February 2014.

35. Interview with the author, 480th ISR HQ, Langley AFB Virginia, December 2013.

36. Interview with the author, Langley AFB Virginia, December 2013. Surname withheld at request of USAF.

37. Attempts to rebrand as the more public-friendly "Sentinel" system never caught on, with that name eventually appropriated for the CIA's RQ-170 stealth drone.

38. Mark Francois, UK Defence Minister, "Written Answers to Questions," Hansard, HC Deb c414W, November 11, 2013, at http://www.publications.parliament.uk/ pa/cm201314/cmhansrd/cm131111/text/131111w0001.htm#131111w0001. htm_wqn9.

39. Interview with the author, January 2014.

40. Interview with the author, November 2013.

41. James Fenton, "Retired Military Drone Operator Shares Experience of Remote Piloting," Daily Times, Four Corner News, November 25, 2013, at http://

www.daily-times.com/four_corners-news/ci_24600432/retired-military-drone-operator-shares-experience-remote-piloting.

42. Noah Shachtman, "Exclusive: Computer Virus Hits U.S. Drone Fleet," *Wired*, October 7, 2011, at http://www.wired.com/dangerroom/2011/10/virus-hits-drone-fleet/.

43. "Flying Operations of Remotely Piloted Aircraft Unaffected by Malware," Media Advisory, Air Force Space Command, October 12, 2011.

44. See, for example, Wayne Chappelle et al., *Prevalence of High Emotional Distress and Symptoms of Post-Traumatic Stress Disorder in U.S. Air Force Active Duty Remotely Piloted Aircraft Operators*, Air Force Research Laboratory, December 2012.

45. Unpublished interview with Tonje Schei, author's copy.

46. Heather Linebaugh, "I Worked on the US Drone Program: The Public Should Know What Really Goes On," *Guardian*, December 29, 2013, at http://www.theguardian.com/commentisfree/2013/dec/29/drones-us-military.

47. Andrew Robathan, UK Minister of Defence, Written Answers: Unmanned Aerial Vehicles, Hansard, February 25, 2013, archived at http://www.publications.parliament.uk/pa/cm201213/cmhansrd/cm130225/text/130225w0002.htm.

48. Background interview with the author, Langley AFB, December 2013.

49. Correspondence between AFSOC and the author, June 2014.

50. "Actions Needed to Strengthen Management of Unmanned Aerial System Pilots," Government Accountability Office, April 2014, at http://www.gao.gov/assets/670/662467.pdf.

51. Barack Obama, "Remarks by the President on the Situation in Iraq," White House, June 19, 2014, at http://www.whitehouse.gov/the-press-office/2014/06/19/remarks-president-situation-iraq.

CHAPTER 9

1. Vivian Salama, "Death from Above: How American Drone Strikes Are Devastating Yemen," *Rolling Stone*, April 14, 2014, at http://www.rollingstone.com/politics/news/death-from-above-how-american-drone-strikes-are-devastating-yemen-20140414.

2. Eyewitness details via "A Wedding that Became a Funeral: US Drone Attack on Marriage Procession in Yemen," Human Rights Watch, February 20, 2014, at http://www.hrw.org/sites/default/files/reports/yemen0214_ForUpload.pdf.

3. Interview with the author, February 2014.

4. Mohammed Ghobari, "Yemen Says Air Strike Targeted al Qaeda Leaders," Reuters, December 14, 2013, at http://uk.reuters.com/article/2013/12/14/uk-yemen-strike-statement-idUKBRE9BD07920131214.

5. Nasser al-Sakkaf, "Government Offers Guns and Money to Families of Those Killed in al-Beida'a Airstrike," *Yemen Times*, December 17, 2013, at http://www.yementimes.com/en/1738/news/3238/Government-offers-guns-and-money-to-families-of-those-killed-in-Al-Beida%E2%80%99a-airstrike.htm.

6. Interview and emails with the author, March 2014.

7. See also, for example, Iona Craig, "What Really Happened When a U.S. Drone Hit a Yemeni Wedding Convoy?" Al Jazeera America, January 20, 2014, at

http://america.aljazeera.com/watch/shows/america-tonight/america-tonight-blog/2014/1/17/what-really-happenedwhenausdronehitayemeniwedding-convoy.html.

8. UN special rapporteurs Christof Heyns and Juan Mendez, "UN Experts Condemn Lethal Drone Airstrikes in Yemen," United Nations Human Rights Council, press release, December 26, 2013, at http://www.ohchr.org/EN/NewsEvents/Pages/DisplayNews.aspx?NewsID=14145&LangID=E.

9. Pakistan's upper and lower chambers voted unanimously in 2012 for an end to US drone strikes following a three-week debate. See, for example, Haris Anwar, "Pakistan Parliament Approves Guidelines to Change U.S. Ties," *Bloomberg Business Week*, April 13, 2012, at http://www.businessweek.com/news/2012-04-13/pakistan-parliament-approves-guidelines-to-reset-ties-with-u-dot-s-dot.

10. Hakim Almasmari, "Drone Strikes Must End, Yemen's Parliament Says," CNN, December 15, 2013, at http://edition.cnn.com/2013/12/15/world/meast/yemen-drones/.

11. Stanley McChrystal, *My Share of the Task: A Memoir* (New York: Portfolio Penguin, 2013), 310–311.

12. Casualty data from the Bureau of Investigative Journalism, via Get The Data: Drone Wars, at http://www.thebureauinvestigates.com/category/projects/drones/drones-graphs/?view=all.

13. Interview with the author, background terms.

14. Kimberly Dozier, "Report: US Drone May Have Killed Dozen Civilians," Associated Press, February 19, 2014, archived at http://www.pbs.org/newshour/rundown/report-u-s-drones-may-killed-civilians/.

15. Michael Isikoff, "US Investigates Yemenis' Charge That Drone Strike 'Turned Wedding into a Funeral,'" NBC News, January 7, 2014, at http://investigations.nbcnews.com/_news/2014/01/07/22163872-us-investigates-yemenis-charge-that-drone-strike-turned-wedding-into-a-funeral?lite.

16. Interview with the author, March 2014.

17. Cited in Azmat Khan, "Understanding Yemen's Al Qaeda Threat," PBS Frontline, May 29, 2012, at http://www.pbs.org/wgbh/pages/frontline/foreign-affairs-defense/al-qaeda-in-yemen/understanding-yemens-al-qaeda-threat/.

18. Interview with the author, background terms.

19. For a detailed description of the origins of Al Qaeda in the Arabian Peninsula, see Gregory D. Johnsen, *The Last Refuge: Yemen, al-Qaeda and America's War in Arabia* (New York: Norton, 2013), 195–219.

20. Jabber Elbaneh was sentenced by a Yemeni court to 10 years (later reduced to five) for his role in a 2002 plot to attack an oil installation. For more on Susan Elbaneh, see Ivan Watson, "Embassy Attack Marks Rise of Al-Qaida in Yemen," NPR, September 29, 2008, at http://www.npr.org/templates/story/story.php?storyId=95102921.

21. The name had first been coined by the Saudi group in March 2004. See Thomas Small and Jonathan Hacker, *Path of Blood: The Story of Al Qaeda's War on the House of Saud* (London: Simon & Schuster, 2014), 205.

22. "Counter-terrorism Adviser Brennan's Meeting with Saudi King Abdullah," leaked US embassy cable, March 22, 2009, archived by Wikileaks at http://www.cablegatesearch.net/cable.php?id=09RIYADH447&q=brennan.

23. "Brennan-Saleh Meeting Sep. 6 2009," leaked US embassy cable, September 15, 2009, archived by Wikileaks at http://www.cablegatesearch.net/cable.php?id=09SANAA1669&q=brennan%20yemen.

24. "President Saleh Receives the Commander of US Special Operations," Office of President Saleh, press release, October 4, 2010, at http://www.presidentsaleh.gov.ye/shownews.php?Ing=en&_nsid=7743 [Arabic].

25. "Yemen: Cracking Down under Pressure," Amnesty International, 31–33, August 2010, at http://www.amnesty.org/en/library/asset/MDE31/010/2010/en/da8bd0cc-37ab-4472-80b3-bcf8a48fc827/mde310102010en.pdf.

26. Alleged targets cited by state media in Mohammad Taher, "Complete Details on Recent Deadly Operations against al-Qaeda," Saba News Agency, January 3, 2010, at http://www.sabanews.net/en/news202231.htm.

27. Sheikh Hamir Ben Abdullah Ben Hussein Al-Ahmar, *Yemen Parliamentary Commission of Inquiry into the Security Incidents in Abyan Province*, February 7, 2010. Author's copy.

28. "ROYG Looks Ahead Following CT Operations, But Perhaps Not Far Enough," leaked US embassy cable, December 21, 2009, archived by Wikileaks at http://www.cablegatesearch.net/cable.php?id=09SANAA2251&q=seche.

29. "General Petraeus' Meeting with Saleh No Security Assistance, AQAP Strikes," leaked US embassy cable, January 4, 2010, archived by Wikileaks at http://www.cablegatesearch.net/cable.php?id=10SANAA4&q=petraeus%20yemen.

30. Attempted Terrorist Attack on NorthWest Airlines Flight 253: Report of the Senate Committee on Intelligence, unclassified version, May 24, 2010, at http://www.intelligence.senate.gov/pdfs/111199.pdf.

31. Al-Awlaki's anger may have been stoked after JSOC had tried to kill him just days after the al-Majala attack. See *Inspire* magazine, al-Malahem Media, no. 1 (June 2010): 57.

32. "Annex 2: The Targeted Killing of Jaber Al-Shabwani, Ma'rib, 24 May 2010," 75–76, *Licence to Kill: Why the American Drone War on Yemen Violates International Law*, Alkarama, July 2013, at http://en.alkarama.org/documents/ALK_USA-Yemen_Drones_PublicReport_EN.pdf.

33. Cited by Don Rassler et al., "Letters from Abbottabad: Bin Ladin Sidelined?" West Point CTC, May 3, 2012, at http://www.ctc.usma.edu/wp-content/uploads/2012/05/CTC_LtrsFromAbottabad_WEB_v2.pdf.

34. Johnsen, *The Last Refuge*, 73.

35. James Bamford, "*Inspire* Magazine: The Most Dangerous Download on Earth," *GQ* magazine, December 2013, at http://www.gq.com/news-politics/newsmakers/201312/inspire-magazine-al-qaeda-boston-bombing.

36. *Inspire* magazine, al-Malahem Media, no. 1 (June 2010).

37. Daniel Klaidman, "Drones: The Silent Killers," *Newsweek*, May 28, 2012, at http://www.newsweek.com/drones-silent-killers-64909.

38. Bamford, "*Inspire* Magazine: The Most Dangerous Download on Earth."

39. "The Greatest Special Operation of All Time," *Inspire* magazine, no. 7 (September 27, 2011).

40. As with the Osama bin Laden operation weeks earlier, there appeared to be little interest in capturing rather than assassinating Anwar al-Awlaki.

41. Duncan Gardham, "MI6 Attacks Al-Qaeda in 'Operation Cupcake,'" *Daily Telegraph*, June 2, 2011, at http://www.telegraph.co.uk/news/uknews/ terrorism-in-the-uk/8553366/MI6-attacks-al-Qaeda-in-Operation-Cupcake. html.

42. Interview with the author, January 2014.

43. "'Between a Drone and Al-Qaeda': The Civilian Cost of US Targeted Killings in Yemen," Human Rights Watch, October 2013, 53–60, at http://www.hrw.org/ sites/default/files/reports/yemen1013_ForUpload_1.pdf.

44. Sudarsan Raghavan, "When U.S. Drones Kill Civilians, Yemen's Government Tries to Conceal It," December 25, 2012, at http://www. washingtonpost.com/world/middle_east/when-us-drones-kill-civi lians-yemens-government-tries-to-conceal-it/2012/12/24/bd4d7ac2-486d-1 1e2-8af9-9b50cb4605a7_print.html.

45. "The U.S. military has also been working closely with the Yemeni government to operationally dismantle and ultimately eliminate the terrorist threat posed by al-Qa'ida in the Arabian Peninsula (AQAP), the most active and danger- ous affiliate of al-Qa'ida today." Barack Obama, "Presidential Letter—2012 War Powers Resolution 6-Month Report," White House, June 15, 2012, at http://www.whitehouse.gov/the-press-office/2012/06/15/presidential-letter-2 012-war-powers-resolution-6-month-report.

46. *Inspire* magazine, no. 6 (Summer 2011).

47. Dana Priest and William M. Arkin, "'Top Secret America': A Look at the Military's Joint Special Operations Command," *Washington Post*, September 2, 2011, at http://www.washingtonpost.com/world/national-security/top- secret-america-a-look-at-the-militarys-joint-special-operations-comm and/2011/08/30/gIQAvYuAxJ_story.html.

48. Kimberly Dozier, "Report: US Drone May Have Killed Dozen Civilians," Associated Press, February 19, 2014, archived at http://news.yahoo.com/report- us-drone-may-killed-yemeni-civilians-052920306.html.

49. "Get the Data: Drone Wars," TBIJ, at http://www.thebureauinvestigates.com/ category/projects/drones/drones-graphs/.

50. Glenn Greenwald, *No Place to Hide*, 43.

51. Jeremy Scahill and Glenn Greenwald, "The NSA's Secret Role in the U.S. Assassination Program," *The Intercept*, February 10, 2014, at https://firstlook. org/theintercept/article/2014/02/10/the-nsas-secret-role/.

52. Barack Obama, "Remarks by the President at the National Defense University," White House, May 23, 2013, at http://www.whitehouse.gov/ the-press-office/2013/05/23/remarks-president-national-defense-university.

53. Interview with the author, background terms.

54. Senator Dianne Feinstein, "Letter to the Editor: Re. Coming Clean on Drones," *Los Angeles Times*, May 17, 2012, at http://articles.latimes.com/2012/may/17/ opinion/la-le-0517-thursday-feinstein-drones-20120517.

55. Interview with the author, February 2014.

56. In a background briefing accompanying Obama's May 2013 NDU speech, senior Administration officials noted there was "the preference that the United States military have the lead for the use of force not just in war zones like Afghanistan, but beyond Afghanistan where we are fighting against al-Qaida and its associated forces." Background Briefing by Senior Administration Officials on the President's Speech on Counterterrorism, White House, May 23, 2013, at http://www.whitehouse.gov/the-press-office/2013/05/23/background-briefing-senior-administration-officials-presidents-speech-co.

57. Barack Obama, "Remarks by the President at the United States Military Academy Commencement Ceremony," White House, May 28, 2014, at http://www.whitehouse.gov/the-press-office/2014/05/28/remarks-president-west-point-academy-commencement-ceremony.

58. John Brennan, Open Hearing on Nomination to be Director of the Central Intelligence Agency, SSCI, February 7, 2013, at http://www.intelligence.senate.gov/130207/transcript.pdf.

59. Interview with the author, background terms.

60. Cited by Todd Eastham, "Al Qaeda Bomb Maker Is Top Threat, Must Be Killed: U.S. Senator," Reuters, May 13, 2012, at http://www.reuters.com/article/2012/05/13/us-usa-security-aqap-idUSBRE84C0A720120513.

61. Congressman Mike Rogers, "Opening Statement: World Wide Threats Hearing—Open Session," HPSCI, February 4, 2014, at http://intelligence.house.gov/sites/intelligence.house.gov/files/documents/chairstatement02042014.pdf.

62. Mustafa Qadri, "Will I Be Next? US Drone Strikes in Pakistan," Amnesty International, October 2013, at http://amnesty.org/en/library/asset/ASA33/013/2013/en/041c08cb-fb54-47b3-b3fe-a72c9169e487/asa330132013en.pdf.

63. Ken Dilanian, "Congress Zooms In on Drone Killings," Los Angeles Times, June 25, 2012, at http://articles.latimes.com/2012/jun/25/nation/la-na-drone-oversight-20120625.

64. Chris Woods, "No Evidence Congressional Committee Does "Utmost" to Follow Up Drone Civilian Death Claims," Bureau of Investigative Journalism, February 27, 2013, at http://www.thebureauinvestigates.com/2013/02/27/no-evidence-congressional-committee-does-utmost-to-follow-up-drone-civilian-death-claims/.

65. See, for example, "Man Crucified by Al-Qaeda-Affiliated Ansar Al-Shari'a for Allegedly Directing U.S. Drones in Yemen," MEMRI, August 29, 2012, at http://www.memri.org/report/en/0/0/0/0/0/0/6632.htm.

66. Interview with the author, May 2014.

67. Ahmed al-Haj, "Yemen Clashes Kill 13 al-Qaida Militants, 4 Troops," Associated Press, May 16, 2012, at http://mobile.seattletimes.com/story/today/2018209939/track-.-.-./.

68. Alkarama submission, Hearing before the Senate Judiciary Subcommittee on the Constitution, Civil Rights, and Human Rights, April 23, 2013, at http://ccrjustice.org/files/HOOD,_Alkarama,_CCR_SJC_Submission.pdf.

69. Jack Serle, "Yemen's 'Barely Functional' Air Force Points to US Involvement in Strikes," Bureau of Investigative Journalism, March 12, 2012, at http://www.thebureauinvestigates.com/2012/03/29/barely-functional-why-us-is-likely-to-be-behind-yemens-precision-airstrikes/.

70. Greg Miller, "In Interview, Yemeni President Acknowledges Approving U.S. Drone Strikes," *Washington Post*, September 29, 2012, at http://www.washingtonpost.com/world/national-security/yemeni-president-acknowledges-approving-us-drone-strikes/2012/09/29/09bec2ae-0a56-11e2-afff-d6c7f20a83bf_story.html.

71. Scott Shane, "Yemen's Leader Praises U.S. Drone Strikes," *New York Times*, September 29, 2012, at http://www.nytimes.com/2012/09/29/world/middleeast/yemens-leader-president-hadi-praises-us-drone-strikes.html.

72. Hooria Mashhour, "The United States' Bloody Messes in Yemen," *Washington Post*, January 14, 2014, at http://www.washingtonpost.com/opinions/hooria-mashhour-the-united-states-bloody-messes-in-yemen/2014/01/14/c21dfcec-7653-11e3-b1c5-739e63e9c9a7_story.html.

73. Interview with the author on background terms.

74. "Libya and the War Powers Act," *New York Times* editorial, June 16, 2011, at http://www.nytimes.com/2011/06/17/opinion/17fri1.html. For more on the Libya air war, see chapter 12.

75. John Brennan, "The Ethics and Efficacy of the President's Counterterrorism Strategy," April 30, 2012, at http://www.cfr.org/counterterrorism/brennans-speech-counterterrorism-april-2012/p28100.

76. "Unofficial Transcript: Hour 1—Sen. Rand Paul Filibuster of Brennan Nomination," March 6, 2013, at http://www.paul.senate.gov/?p=press_release&id=727.

77. Jeh Johnson, "National Security Law, Lawyers and Lawyering in the Obama Administration," Yale Law School, February 22, 2012, archived at http://www.cfr.org/defense-and-security/jeh-johnsons-speech-national-security-law-lawyers-lawyering-obama-administration/p27448.

78. Comments to the author, Chicago, April 2013.

79. Barack Obama, "Remarks by the President at the National Defense University," May 23, 2013, at http://www.whitehouse.gov/the-press-office/2013/05/23/remarks-president-national-defense-university.

80. Barack Obama, "Statement by the President on H.R. 1540," White House, December 31, 2011, at http://www.whitehouse.gov/the-press-office/2011/12/31/statement-president-hr-1540.

81. "Drones in Yemen Causing a "Psychological Emergency," Psychologist Tells MPs," Reprieve press release, March 5, 2013, at http://www.reprieve.org.uk/press/2013_03_05_drones_in_yemen_psychological_emergency/.

82. Interviewed by the author, February 2014.

83. See, for example, "Gregory Johnsen on Yemen, the U.S., and Drones," Open Canada, December 14, 2012, at http://opencanada.org/features/the-think-tank/interviews/gregory-johnsen-on-yemen-the-u-s-and-drones/.

84. Interview with the author, April 2014.

85. "Yemen Suicide Attack Kills 96," Xinhua, May 21, 2012, at http://www.china. org.cn/world/2012-05/21/content_25437357.htm.

86. Ben Emmerson, 3rd Annual Report of the Special Rapporteur on the Promotion and Protection of Human Rights and Fundamental Freedoms While Countering Terrorism, March 11, 2014, at http://justsecurity.org/wp-content/ uploads/2014/02/Special-Rapporteur-Rapporteur-Emmerson-Drones-2014. pdf.

87. Jack Serle, "US and Others Have 'Licence to Ignore International Law' in Somalia," Bureau of Investigative Journalism, September 24, 2012, at http://www.thebureauinvestigates.com/2012/09/24/us-and-others-given-licence-to-ignore-international-law-in-somalia/.

88. United Nations Monitoring Group on Somalia and Eritrea, Annual Report 2011, published June 27, 2012, at http://www.un.org/ga/search/view_doc. asp?symbol=S/2012/544.

89. Jeremy Scahill, Dirty Wars: The World is a Battlefield (London: Serpent's Tail, 2013), 295–296.

90. "CT in Horn of Africa; Results and Recommendations from May 23-24 RSI Chiefs of Mission," Embassy Dar es Salaam, leaked US diplomatic cable, July 3, 2006, archived at http://www.cablegatesearch.net/cable. php?id=06DARESSALAAM1076&q=socom%20somalia.

91. Sean D. Naylor, "Clandestine Somalia Missions Yield AQ Targets," Army Times, November 14, 2011, at http://www.armytimes.com/article/20111114/ NEWS/111140317/Clandestine-Somalia-missions-yield-AQ-targets.

92. Stig Jarle Hansen, Al-Shabaab in Somalia: The History and Ideology of a Militant Islamist Group 2005-2012 (London: Hurst, 2013), 26.

93. Martin Scheinin, "Joint Study on Global Practices in Relation to Secret Detention in the Context of Countering Terrorism of the Special Rapporteur on the Promotion and Protection of Human Rights and Fundamental Freedoms While Countering Terrorism," 155–156, UN Human Rights Council 13th Session, February 19, 2010, at http://www2.ohchr.org/english/ bodies/hrcouncil/docs/13session/A-HRC-13-42.pdf.

94. Sondra Crosby, MD, "A Doctor's Response to Torture," Annals of Internal Medicine 156 (2012): 471–472.

95. Interview with the author, January 2013.

96. Matthew M. Aid, Intel Wars: The Secret History of the Fight against Terror (New York: Bloomsbury Press, 2012), 137–139.

97. Jeffrey Gettleman, "More Than 50 Die in U.S. Strikes in Somalia," New York Times, January 9, 2007, at http://www.nytimes.com/2007/01/09/world/ africa/09cnd-somalia.html.

98. "U.S. Strikes in Somalia Reportedly Kill 31," Associated Press, February 11, 2009, at http://www.cbsnews.com/stories/2007/01/08/world/main2335451. shtml.

99. Cited in "A Strike from the Skies That Missed," US News, January 14, 2007, archived at https://web.archive.org/web/20130302062212/.

100. McChrystal, My Share of the Task, 270–271.

101. "Somalia: A Targeted Killing," *Africa Confidential* 49, no. 11, May 23, 2008, paywalled at http://www.africa-confidential.com/article-preview/id/2619/A_targeted_killing.

102. "Djibouti EAC: Implications of Somalia Airstrikes," leaked US embassy cable, May 6, 2008, archived by Wikileaks at http://www.cablegatesearch.net/cable.php?id=08DJIBOUTI436&q=ayrow.

103. Graham Turbiville, Josh Meservey, and James Forest, "Countering the al-Shabaab Insurgency in Somalia: Lessons for U.S. Special Operations Forces," JSOU Report 14-1, February 2014, at https://jsou.socom.mil/PubsPages/al_Shabaab_Feb_2014%20PDF.pdf.

104. "Somalia: Codel Marshall Scenesetter: How Iraq/Afghanistan Relate to Somalia," Embassy Nairobi, leaked US diplomatic cable, August 26, 2009, archived by Wikileaks at http://www.cablegatesearch.net/cable.php?id=09NAIROBI1801&q=somalia.

105. "Somalia: Reported US Covert Actions 2001–2015," Bureau of Investigative Journalism, ongoing project, at http://www.thebureauinvestigates.com/2012/02/22/get-the-data-somalias-hidden-war/.

106. United Nations Monitoring Group on Somalia and Eritrea, Annual Report 2011, published June 27, 2012, at http://www.un.org/ga/search/view_doc.asp?symbol=S/2012/544.

107. In August 2013 armed US drone flights from Lemonnier finally ended after a series of crashes and near-collisions, with a new base opened at Chabelly to the south-west of the capital. Satellite images later showed three Predators and two Reapers on the facility's runway apron. "CIA-DoD Chabelly Djibouti Drone Base," Cryptome, March 30, 2014, at http://cryptome.org/2014-info/chabelly/chabelly-drone-base.htm.

108. Daniel Klaidman, *Kill or Capture: The War on Terror and the Soul of the Obama Presidency* (New York: Houghton Mifflin Harcourt, 2012), 213, 221.

109. Aweys Cadde, "Airstrikes Hit Lower Juba Again," Somalia Report, July 6, 2011, at http://www.somaliareport.com/index.php/post/1105/Airstrikes_Hit_Lower_JubaAgain.

110. Katharine Houreld, "Who's Bombing Somalia? French, US Trade Blame," Associated Press, November 16, 2011, at http://www.boston.com/news/world/africa/articles/2011/11/16/whos_bombing_somalia_french_us_trade_blame/.

111. "Press TV's Somalia Claims 2011-12," Bureau of Investigative Journalism, at http://www.thebureauinvestigates.com/2011/12/02/the-press-tv-claims/.

112. Emma Slater and Chris Woods, "Iranian TV Station Accused of Faking Reports of Somalia Drone Strikes," *The Guardian*, December 2, 2011, at http://www.guardian.co.uk/world/2011/dec/02/iranian-tv-fake-drone-somalia.

113. Winners listed at http://www.pressgazette.co.uk/david-walsh-scoops-journalist-year-win-british-journalism-awards.

114. Email to the author citing senior US counterterrorism official, July 2011.

115. Barack Obama, "Remarks by the President at the United States Military Academy Commencement Ceremony," White House, May 28, 2014, at http://

www.whitehouse.gov/the-press-office/2014/05/28/remarks-president-west-point-academy-commencement-ceremony.

CHAPTER 10

1. "Airbase near Jacobabad under US Control, Senate Panel Told," *Dawn*, August 19, 2010, at http://dawn.com/news/856711/airbase-near-jacobabad-under-us-control-senate-panel-told.
2. "Correction for the Record: Shahbaz Air Base," US Embassy Islamabad, August 19, 2010, at http://islamabad.usembassy.gov/pr-10081901.html.
3. Chris Woods, "CIA Drones Quit One Pakistan Site—But US Keeps Access to Other Airbases," Bureau of Investigative Journalism, December 15, 2011, at http://www.thebureauinvestigates.com/2011/12/15/cia-drones-quit-pakistan-site-but-us-keeps-access-to-other-airbases/.
4. The CIA additionally used Shamsi airfield for seven years to fly its armed Predators, though was finally expelled in December 2011 after US forces based in Afghanistan accidentally killed 28 Pakistan border troops.
5. "Taliban Unscathed by US Strikes," *Washington Post*, Greg Miller, October 21, 2010, at http://www.washingtonpost.com/wp-dyn/content/article/2010/10/26/AR2010102606987_2.html.
6. Cited in Rania Abouzeid, "Despite Aid, Pakistanis Are Suspicious of the U.S.," *Time*, August 30, 2010, at http://content.time.com/time/world/article/0,8599,2014480,00.html.
7. Estimates provided by the Bureau of Investigative Journalism.
8. Michael Hastings, "The Runaway General," *Rolling Stone*, June 22, 2010, at http://www.rollingstone.com/politics/news/the-runaway-general-20100622.
9. Data provided to the author by AFCENT. Between August and November 2009, 1,478 missiles and bombs were reported dropped.
10. Data from UNAMA Annual Reports on the Protection of Civilians, 2010 and 2011, at http://unama.unmissions.org/Default.aspx?tabid=13941&language=en-US.
11. The number of Afghan security personnel also killed in this period is not known, although of 13,000 Afghan military and police fatalities since 2001, "most" reportedly took place after 2010, with as many as 400 killed per month in the 2013 Afghan fighting season. Data via Afghan Ministries of Defence and Interior, 2013.
12. Interview with the author, October 2013.
13. Both secret detention and extraordinary rendition did however continue under Obama, with a number of terrorist suspects secretly captured, detained, and later transported to the United States without due process. See, for example, the case of Ahmed Abdulkadir Warsame cited in Mike Levine, "Terror Suspect Interrogated on Navy Ship for Two Months Arrives in U.S.," Fox News, July 5, 2011, at http://www.foxnews.com/politics/2011/07/05/terror-suspect-interrogated-on-navy-ship-for-two-months-arrives-in-us/. Barack Obama, "Executive Order 13491: Ensuring Lawful Interrogations," January 22, 2009, at http://frwebgate.access.gpo.gov/cgi-bin/getpage.cgi?dbname=2009_register&position=all&page=4893.

14. Tom Junod, "The Lethal Presidency of Barack Obama," May 23, 2013, at http://www.esquire.com/features/obama-lethal-presidency-0812-4.

15. Karen de Young and Joby Warrick, "Under Obama, More Targeted Killings than Captures in Counterterrorism Efforts," *Washington Post*, February 14, 2010, at http://www.washingtonpost.com/wp-dyn/content/article/2010/02/13/AR2010021303748.html.

16. Nick Davies, "Afghanistan War Logs: Task Force 373—Special Forces Hunting Top Taliban," *Guardian*, July 25, 2010, at http://www.theguardian.com/world/2010/jul/25/task-force-373-secret-afghanistan-taliban.

17. Interview with the author, background terms.

18. Interview with the author, May 2014.

19. Interview with the author, May 2014.

20. Michael Hirsh, "Slow Dance: Obama's Romance with the CIA," *National Journal*, May 11, 2011, at http://www.nationaljournal.com/magazine/secret-love-obama-s-budding-romance-with-the-cia-20110511.

21. Interview with the author, May 2014.

22. Interview with the author, background terms, December 2013.

23. Interview with the author, background terms, March 2014.

24. "Between 2007 and mid-2009, SOF targeting operations (including SOF-directed airstrikes) caused about half of all US-caused civilian casualties." Sarah Sewall and Larry Lewis, "Joint Civilian Casualty Study: Executive Summary," Harvard University for ISAF, August 2010, at http://www.cna.org/sites/default/files/research/JCCS_EXSUM.pdf.

25. Dion Nissenbaum and Habib Khan Totakhil, "U.S. Raid Kills Karzai Cousin," *Wall Street Journal*, March 11, 2011, at http://online.wsj.com/news/articles/SB10001424052748704823004576192421301753248.

26. Harold Hongju Koh, "The Obama Administration and International Law," Annual Meeting of the American Society of International Law, March 25, 2010, at http://www.state.gov/s/l/releases/remarks/139119.htm.

27. Jonathan Evans, "Address at the Worshipful Company of Security Professionals by the Director General of the Security Service," September 17, 2010, transcript at https://www.mi5.gov.uk/home/about-us/who-we-are/staff-and-management/director-general/speeches-by-the-director-general/the-threat-to-national-security.html.

28. Barack Obama, "The President's News Conference," September 10, 2010, at http://www.presidency.ucsb.edu/ws/?pid=88429.

29. Greg Miller, "Al-Qaeda Targets Dwindle as Group Shrinks," *Washington Post*, November 23, 2011, at http://www.washingtonpost.com/world/national-security/al-qaeda-targets-dwindle-as-group-shrinks/2011/11/22/gIQAbXJNmN_story.html.

30. Jonathan S. Landay, "Obama's Drone War Kills 'Others,' Not Just Al Qaida Leaders," April 9, 2013, at http://www.mcclatchydc.com/2013/04/09/188062/obamas-drone-war-kills-others.html.

31. Barack Obama, "Remarks by the President at the National Defense University," May 23, 2013, at http://www.whitehouse.gov/the-press-office/2013/05/23/remarks-president-national-defense-university.

32. Interview with the author, Islamabad, December 2012.

33. Ann Patterson, "Reviewing Our Afghanistan/Pakistan Strategy," leaked US embassy cable, September 23, 2009, archived by Wikileaks at http://www.wikileaks.org/plusd/cables/09ISLAMABAD2295_a.html.

34. Bruce Riedel, Ambassador Richard Holbrooke, and Michelle Flournoy, Press Briefing on the New Strategy for Afghanistan and Pakistan, White House, March 27, 2009, at http://www.whitehouse.gov/the_press_office/Press-Briefing-by-Bruce-Riedel-Ambassador-Richard-Holbrooke-and-Michelle-Flournoy-on-the-New-Strategy-for-Afghanistan-and-Pakistan.

35. Mark Mazzetti and Dexter Filkins, "US Seeks to Expand Raids in Pakistan," *New York Times*, December 20, 2010, at http://www.nytimes.com/2010/12/21/world/asia/21intel.html.

36. Tahir Khalil, "Pakistan Ignored US Warnings of Unilateral Action," May 9, 2011, at http://www.thenews.com.pk/TodaysPrintDetail.aspx?ID=5858&Cat=13&dt=5/9/2011.

37. Interview with the author, background terms.

38. According to data provided to the author by the Pakistan military's media wing the ISPR, Pakistan lost 799 troops in 2009 with a further 3,004 injured.

39. "2009 Report on Terrorism," US National Counterterrorism Center, April 30, 2010, archived at http://www.riskintel.com/wp-content/uploads/downloads/2011/10/2009_report_on_terrorism.pdf.

40. "Nine Pakistani Troops Killed in Militant Ambush," Reuters, June 5, 2012, at http://www.dawn.com/news/716184/militants-attack-military-convoy-officials.

41. Cited in "Kayani was Reluctant to Launch N Waziristan Operation," *Dawn*, June 30, 2014, at http://www.dawn.com/news/1116115.

42. Comments to the author, December 2013.

43. Cited in Chris Woods, "Attacking the Messenger: How the CIA Tried to Undermine Drone Study," Bureau of Investigative Journalism, August 12, 2011, at http://www.thebureauinvestigates.com/2011/08/12/attacking-the-messenger-how-the-cia-tried-to-undermine-drone-study/.

44. David Rose, "CIA Chiefs Face Arrest over Horrific Evidence of Bloody 'Video-Game' Sorties by Drone Pilots," *Daily Mail*, October 21, 2012, at http://www.dailymail.co.uk/news/article-2220828/US-drone-attacks-CIA-chiefs-face-arrest-horrific-evidence-bloody-video-game-sorties.html.

45. Interview with the author, March 2014.

46. Now known as the Center for Civilians in Armed Conflict.

47. Interview with the author, New York, October 2013.

48. Email to the author, May 2014.

49. Christopher Rogers, "Civilian Harm and Conflict in Northwest Pakistan," Center for Civilians in Conflict, September 2010, at http://civiliansinconflict.org/uploads/files/publications/Pakistan_Report_2010_%282013%29.pdf.

50. "Registration of FIR against Jonathan Banks, CIA Station Chief, Islamabad," December 13, 2010, author's copy.

51. Interview with the author, March 2014.

52. *Nachman Holtzberg et al. v. LeT, ISI, Ahmed Shuja Pasha and others,* filed November 19, 2010, United States District Court, Eastern District of New York. Author's copy.

53. US Statement of Interest, filed December 17, 2012.

54. Based on discussions by the author with Pakistan government officials, diplomats, and others stationed in Islamabad at the time.

55. Interview with the author, New York, October 2013.

56. Cited in Zahid Gishkari, "Gross Offences: In Fury at Drone Strikes, PTI 'Outs CIA Station Chief,'" *Express Tribune,* November 28, 2013, at http://tribune.com.pk/story/638190/gross-offences-in-fury-at-drone-strikes-pti-outs-cia-station-chief/.

57. "Scenesetter for FBI Director Mueller's February 24 Visit," leaked US Embassy cable, February 22, 2010, archived by Wikileaks at http://www.cablegatesearch.net/cable.php?id=10ISLAMABAD416&q=sihala%20tdyers.

58. Bari Baloch, "Three US Diplomats Arrested, Says CM," *The Nation* (Pakistan), January 10, 2010, at http://www.nation.com.pk/islamabad/10-Jan-2010/Three-US-diplomats-arrested-says-CM.

59. Interview with the author. Location and date withheld.

60. Interview with the author, background terms.

61. "About 22,000 Flee Mohmand Offensive—UN," *Dawn,* February 3, 2011, at http://www.dawn.com/news/603562/about-22000-flee-mohmand-offensive-un.

62. Ibid.

63. Eric Schmitt, "U.S. Officers Kill Armed Civilians in Yemen Capital," *New York Times,* May 9, 2014, at http://www.nytimes.com/2014/05/10/world/middleeast/us-officers-kill-armed-civilians-in-yemen-capital.html.

64. Barack Obama, "Press Conference by the President," White House, February 15, 2011, at http://www.whitehouse.gov/the-press-office/2011/02/15/press-conference-president.

65. According to a former senior Indian intelligence official interviewed by the author, they may instead have been agents of the group Lashkar e-Taiba.

66. "Raymond Davis Tried to Trick Investigators," *Daily Times,* February 15, 2011, at http://archives.dailytimes.com.pk/national/15-Feb-2011/raymond-davis-tried-to-trick-investigators.

67. Figure provided to the author by a senior Pakistani defence official.

68. Mark Mazzetti et al., "American Held in Pakistan Worked with C.I.A.," *New York Times,* February 21, 2011, at http://www.nytimes.com/2011/02/22/world/asia/22pakistan.html.

69. Interview with the author, Islamabad, November 2012.

70. Jill Dougherty and Charley Keyes, "U.S. Rep: Crisis over Detained Diplomat May Imperil Pakistan Aid," CNN, February 9, 2011, at http://edition.cnn.com/2011/POLITICS/02/08/us.pakistan.diplomat/.

71. See, for example, "Raymond Davis Does Not Enjoy Blanket Immunity: Qureshi," *Dawn,* February 16, 2011, at http://www.dawn.com/news/606673/us-should-realise-pakistans-sacrifices-in-terror-war-shah-mehmood-qureshi.

72. "Widow of Pakistani shot by Raymond Davis Kills Herself," BBC News, February 7, 2011, at http://www.bbc.co.uk/news/world-south-asia-12379038.

73. Kathy Gannon, "Timing of US Drone Strike Questioned," Associated Press, August 2, 2011, at http://www.knoxnews.com/news/2011/aug/02/ap-exclusive-timing-of-us-drone-strike/?print=1.

74. Bill Roggio, "US Predators Strike in Datta Khel Area in North Waziristan," Long War Journal, March 16, 2011, at http://www.longwarjournal.org/archives/2011/03/us_predators_strike_21.php.

75. Chris Woods and Christina Lamb, "CIA Tactics in Pakistan Include Targeting Rescuers and Funerals," Sunday Times/Bureau of Investigative Journalism, February 4, 2012, at http://www.thebureauinvestigates.com/2012/02/04/obama-terror-drones-cia-tactics-in-pakistan-include-targeting-rescuers-and-funerals/.

76. Scott Shane, "Contrasting Reports of Drone Strikes," New York Times, August 11, 2011, at http://www.nytimes.com/2011/08/12/world/asia/12droneside.html.

77. Correspondence with the author, December 2013.

78. Kathy Gannon, "Timing of US Drone Strike Questioned," Associated Press, August 2, 2011, at http://www.knoxnews.com/news/2011/aug/02/ap-exclusive-timing-of-us-drone-strike/?print=1.

79. Interview with the author, November 2014.

80. Chris Woods, "Evidence in British Court Contradicts CIA Drone Claims," Bureau of Investigative Journalism, April 24, 2012, at http://www.thebureauinvestigates.com/2012/04/24/british-legal-case-shines-fesh-light-on-civilian-drone-deaths/.

81. "Detail of Attacks by NATO Forces/Predators in FATA," leaked FATA Secretariat report, January 13, 2006-September 30, 2013, at http://www.thebureauinvestigates.com/2014/01/29/get-the-data-pakistani-governments-secret-report-on-drone-strikes/.

82. "Agencies: Zardari Urges US to Stop Drone Attacks," Dawn, March 24, 2011, at http://dawn.com/news/615531/us-should-stop-drone-attacks-says-zardari.

83. General Ashfaq Kayani, Inter Services Public Relations, press release, March 17, 2011, at http://www.ispr.gov.pk/front/main.asp?o=t-press_release&date=2011/3/17.

84. Nick Paton Walsh, Nasir Habib, and Pam Benson, "Pakistani Sources Say U.S. Strike Killed 6 Suspected Militants," CNN, April 13, 2011, at http://edition.cnn.com/2011/WORLD/asiapcf/04/13/pakistan.drone.strike/?hpt=T2.

85. Eric Schmitt, "New C.I.A. Drone Attack Draws Rebuke from Pakistan," New York Times, April 13, 2011, at http://www.nytimes.com/2011/04/14/world/asia/14pakistan.html.

86. "Pakistan: US Drones Are 'Core Irritant' in Terror Fight," BBC News, April 14, 2011, at http://www.bbc.co.uk/news/world-south-asia-13077365.

87. Adam Entous, Siobhan Gorman, and Evan Perez, "U.S. Unease over Drone Strikes," Wall Street Journal, September 26, 2012, at http://online.wsj.com/news/articles/SB10000872396390444100404577641520858011452?mg=reno64-wsj&url=http%3A%2F%2Fonline.wsj.com%2Farticle%2FSB10000872396390444100404577641520858011452.html.

88. Jemima Khan, "Pervez Musharraf: If You Are Weak, Anyone Can Come and Kick You," *New Statesman*, June 13, 2012, at http://www.newstatesman.com/politics/politics/2012/06/pervez-musharraf-if-weak-anyone-kick-you.

89. Karen Brulliard, "Pakistan's Top Officials Continue to Express Anger Day after NATO Airstrike," *Washington Post*, November 26, 2011, at http://www.washingtonpost.com/world/pakistani-officials-say-alleged-nato-attack-kills-at-least-12/2011/11/26/gIQA2mqtxN_story.html.

90. "Get the Data: Drone Wars," Bureau of Investigative Journalism, at http://www.thebureauinvestigates.com/category/projects/drones/drones-graphs/.

91. Barack Obama, Google "Town Hall" debate, January 29, 2012, transcript archived at http://www.thebureauinvestigates.com/2012/02/01/analysis-obama-outs-secret-cia-drone-campaign-but-do-his-words-add-up/.

92. Interview with the author, background terms.

93. Correspondence with the author, December 2013.

94. In contrast, noncombatant deaths from drone strikes had tripled across the border in Afghanistan. See chapter 1.

95. Lesley Wroughton, "After Militant's Killing, Kerry Says Sensitive to Pakistan Concerns," Reuters, November 4, 2013, at http://www.reuters.com/article/2013/11/04/us-pakistan-drone-usa-kerry-idUSBRE9A30N220131104.

96. Correspondence with the author, December 2013.

97. "Pakistani Public Opinion Ever More Critical of U.S.," June 27, 2012, at http://www.pewglobal.org/2012/06/27/pakistani-public-opinion-ever-more-critical-of-u-s/.

CHAPTER 11

1. "No Drone Strike Took Place Today: ISPR," *The Nation*, December 10, 2009, at http://www.nation.com.pk/politics/10-Dec-2009/No-drone-strike-took-place-today-ISPR.

2. Iftikar A. Khan, "Nearly 580 Terrorists Killed in S. Waziristan, Says ISPR," *Dawn*, December 10, 2009, at http://www.dawn.com/news/507767/nearly-580-terrorists-killed-in-s-waziristan-says-ispr.

3. Bill Roggio, "US Strike Kills 4 Al Qaeda, 2 Taliban in South Waziristan," Long War Journal, December 10, 2009, at http://www.longwarjournal.org/archives/2009/12/us_strike_kills_four.php.

4. Barack Obama, "Nobel Lecture: A Just and Lasting Peace," Nobel Peace Prize Ceremony, December 10, 2009, at http://www.nobelprize.org/nobel_prizes/peace/laureates/2009/obama-lecture_en.html.

5. "The President Donates Nobel Prize Money to Charity," White House Press Office, March 11, 2010, at http://www.whitehouse.gov/the-press-office/president-donates-nobel-prize-money-charity.

6. "Unofficial Transcript: Hour 1—Sen. Rand Paul Filibuster of Brennan Nomination," March 6, 2013, at http://www.paul.senate.gov/?p=press_release&id=727.

7. In Iraq an estimated 14,000 were killed by occupying, mostly US forces. Iraq Body Count at https://www.iraqbodycount.org/database/. In Afghanistan, the

United Nations recorded more than 3,500 civilians killed from 2007 to 2013 alone in actions by pro-government (mostly US) troops. UNAMA Annual Reports at http://unama.unmissions.org/Default.aspx?tabid=13941&language =en-US. At least 500 noncombatants were also credibly reported killed in drone strikes in Pakistan, Yemen, and Somalia.

8. George W. Bush, "Presidential Speech Launching Iraq Invasion," March 19, 2003, archived at http://uspolitics.about.com/od/warinkiraq/a/bush_2003march. htm.

9. Lt. General Michael Moseley, "Operation Iraqi Freedom—By the Numbers," USAF Assessment and Analysis Division, April 30, 2003, at http:// www.globalsecurity.org/military/library/report/2003/uscentaf_oif_ report_30apr2003.pdf.

10. Interview with the author, March 2014.

11. Gregory McNeal, "Are Targeted Killings Unlawful? A Case Study in Empirical Claims without Empirical Evidence," in Claire Finkelstein, Jens David Ohlin, and Andrew Altman (eds.), *Targeted Killings: Law and Morality in an Asymmetrical World* (Oxford: Oxford University Press, 2012), 330.

12. Emma Slater and James Ball, "The Impact of Escalation of Force on Civilians in Iraq," Action on Armed Violence, June 3, 2013, at http://aoav.org.uk/2013/ the-impact-of-escalation-of-force-on-civilians-in-iraq/.

13. Interview with the author, London, September 2013.

14. Some 890 civilian deaths were reportedly caused by the Coalition in 2006. Total civilian casualties for 2007 were 5,100 killed. All data from Iraq Body Count at http://www.iraqbodycount.org/analysis/numbers/2011/.

15. Data released by AFCENT.

16. "General Petraeus Issues Updated Tactical Directive," ISAF News, August 1, 2010, at http://www.isaf.nato.int/article/isaf-releases/general-petraeus-issues -updated-tactical-directive-emphasizes-disciplined-use-of-force.html.

17. "Consolidated Rules of Engagement," MNF Iraq, obtained and distributed by Wikileaks, archived at http://wlstorage.net/file/us-iraq-rules-of-engagement.pdf.

18. Interview with the author.

19. Interview with the author, December 2013.

20. Interview with the author, November 2013.

21. "Troops in Contact": Airstrikes and Civilian Deaths in Afghanistan, Human Rights Watch, September 8, 2008, at http://www.hrw.org/sites/default/files/ reports/afghanistan0908webwcover_0.pdf.

22. Interview with the author, February 2014.

23. Interview with the author, background terms.

24. Interview with the author, November 2013.

25. Comment to the author, background terms.

26. Interview with the author, background terms, March 2014.

27. Ben Emmerson QC, address to joint session of UK All Party Parliamentary Groups on the United Nations and Drones, December 13, 2013. Author's transcript.

28. Interview with the author, background terms.

29. Chris Cole, "New British Drone Strike Stats Released to Drone Wars UK," Drone Wars UK, February 6, 2014, at http://dronewars.net/2014/02/06/new-british-d rone-strike-stats-released-to-drone-wars-uk/.

30. Nick Hopkins, "Afghan Civilians Killed by RAF Drone," Guardian, July 5, 2011, at http://www.theguardian.com/uk/2011/jul/05/afghanistan-raf-drone-civilian-deaths.

31. Nick Hopkins, "British Reliance on Drones in Afghanistan Prompts Fears for Civilians," Guardian, June 12, 2012, at http://www.theguardian.com/world/2012/jun/18/british-drones-afghanistan-taliban.

32. Chris Cole, "UK Drone Strike Casualty Figures: Incredible or Just Not Credible?" Drone Wars UK, November 2, 2011, at http://dronewars.net/2012/11/02/uk-drone-strike-casualty-figures-incredible-or-just-not-credible/.

33. Ben Emmerson QC, "Report of the Special Rapporteur on the Promotion and Protection of Human Rights and Fundamental Freedoms While Countering Terrorism," UN Human Rights Council, 25th session, February 28, 2014, archived at http://justsecurity.org/wp-content/uploads/2014/02/Special-Rapporteur-Rapporteur-Emmerson-Drones-2014.pdf.

34. Interview with the author, February 2014.

35. Interview with the author, background terms.

36. Barack Obama, "Remarks by the President at the National Defense University," White House, May 23, 2013, at http://www.whitehouse.gov/the-press-office/2013/05/23/remarks-president-national-defense-university.

37. Chris Woods and Alice K. Ross, "Revealed: US and Britain Launched 1,200 Drone Strikes in Recent Wars," Bureau of Investigative Journalism, December 4, 2012, at http://www.thebureauinvestigates.com/2012/12/04/revealed-us-and-britain-launched-1200-drone-strikes-in-recent-wars/.

38. Brian Everstine and Aaron Mehta, "DoD: Media Must Request Drone Strike Data," Defense News, March 14, 2013, at http://www.defensenews.com/article/20130314/DEFREG02/303140011/DoD-Media-must-request-drone-strike-data.

39. Freedom of Information Act: Request for Data on Conventional RPA Use, letter to the author from US Department of the Air Force, March 11, 2014.

40. Afghanistan Annual Report 2013: Protection of Civilians in Armed Conflict, UNAMA, February 8, 2014, at http://unama.unmissions.org/Portals/UNAMA/human%20rights/Feb_8_2014_PoC-report_2013-Full-report-ENG.pdf.

41. Interview with the author, background terms.

42. "Afghanistan Mid-Year Report on Protection of Civilians in Armed Conflict: 2013," UNAMA, July 2013, at http://unama.unmissions.org/LinkClick.aspx?fileticket=EZoxNuqDtps%3d&tabid=12254&language=en-US.

43. Round-table discussion with the author, Langley AFB. Surnames withheld at request of USAF.

44. Christopher Rogers, "Civilian Harm and Conflict in Northwest Pakistan," Center for Civilians in Conflict, September 2010, at http://civiliansinconflict.org/uploads/files/publications/Pakistan_Report_2010_%282013%29.pdf.

45. Interview with the author, February 2014.

46. Ken Dilanian, "CIA Drones May Be Avoiding Pakistani Civilians," *Los Angeles Times*, February 22, 2011, at http://articles.latimes.com/2011/feb/22/world/la-fg-drone-strikes-20110222.

47. Sebastian Abbott, "AP Impact: New Light on Drone War's Death Toll," Associated Press, February 25, 2012, archived at http://www.deseretnews.com/article/765554274/AP-IMPACT-New-light-on-drone-wars-death-toll.html.

48. John Brennan, "Ensuring al-Qa'ida's Demise: Question and Answer Session," C-Span, June 29, 2011, at http://www.c-span.org/video/?300266-1/obama-administration-counterterrorism-strategy.

49. Email to the author from US counterintelligence official, background terms, July 2011.

50. For more on this March 17, 2011, attack which killed up to 42 people, see chapter 10.

51. Chris Woods and Rahimullah Yousufzai, "Get the Data: Twenty-Five Deadly Strikes," Bureau of Investigative Journalism, July 18, 2011, at http://www.thebureauinvestigates.com/2011/07/18/get-the-data-twenty-five-deadly-strikes/.

52. Chris Woods, "US Claims of 'No Civilian Deaths' Are Untrue," Bureau of Investigative Journalism, July 18, 2011, at http://www.thebureauinvestigates.com/2011/07/18/washingtons-untrue-claims-no-civilian-deaths-in-pakistan-drone-strikes/.

53. Jonathan S. Landay, "Obama's Drone War Kills 'Others,' Not Just Al Qaida Leaders," McClatchy, April 9, 2013, at http://www.mcclatchydc.com/2013/04/09/188062/obamas-drone-war-kills-others.html.

54. Chris Woods, "Drone War Exposed—the Complete Picture of CIA Strikes in Pakistan," Bureau of Investigative Journalism, August 10, 2011, at http://www.thebureauinvestigates.com/2011/08/10/most-complete-picture-yet-of-cia-drone-strikes/.

55. Excerpt from CIA press office briefing for journalists, August 2011, subsequently leaked to the author.

56. "The Drone Problem: Micah Zenko in Conversation," *The Straddler*, December 2013, at http://www.thestraddler.com/201412/piece3.php.

57. For a more detailed study of this topic, see Chris Woods, "Understanding the Gulf between Public and US Government Estimates of Civilian Casualties in Covert Drone Strikes," in David Cortright, Rachel Fairhurst, and Kristen Wall (eds.), *Drones and the Future of Armed Conflict: Ethical, Legal and Strategic Implications* (Chicago: University of Chicago Press, 2015).

58. Chris Woods, "Leaked Pakistani Report Confirms High Civilian Death Toll in CIA Drone Strikes," Bureau of Investigative Journalism, July 22, 2013, at http://www.thebureauinvestigates.com/2013/07/22/exclusive-leaked-pakistani-report-confirms-high-civilian-death-toll-in-cia-drone-strikes/.

59. Ben Emmerson QC, "Statement of the Special Rapporteur Following Meetings in Pakistan," Office of the UN High Commissioner for Human Rights, March 14, 2013, at http://www.ohchr.org/EN/NewsEvents/Pages/DisplayNews.aspx?NewsID=13146&LangID=E.

60. See, for example, Christine Fair, "The Problems with Studying Civilian Casualties from Drone Usage in Pakistan: What We Can't Know," The Monkey Cage, August 17, 2011, at http://themonkeycage.org/2011/08/17/the-problems-with-studying-civilian-casualties-from-drone-usage-in-pakistan-what-we-can%E2%80%99t-know/.

61. Handbook on International Rules Governing Military Operations, ICRC, December 2013, at http://www.icrc.org/eng/assets/files/publications/icrc-002-0431.pdf.

62. Nils Melzer, "Interpretive Guidance on the Notion of Direct Participation in Hostilities under International Humanitarian Law," ICRC, May 2009, at http://www.icrc.org/eng/assets/files/other/icrc-002-0990.pdf.

63. Betr: Drohneneinsatz vom 4. Oktober 2010 in Mir Ali/Pakistan—Verfügung des Generalbundesanwalts vom 20. Juni 2013—3 BJs 7/12-4, at http://www.generalbundesanwalt.de/docs/drohneneinsatz_vom_04oktober2010_mir_ali_pakistan.pdf.

64. Interview with the author, background terms.

65. Jo Becker and Scott Shane, "Secret 'Kill List' Proves a Test of Obama's Principles and Will," New York Times, May 29, 2012, at http://www.nytimes.com/2012/05/29/world/obamas-leadership-in-war-on-al-qaeda.html.

66. Footnote 1, US Policy Standards and Procedures for the Use of Force in Counterterrorism Operations outside the United States and Areas of Active Hostilities, White House, May 23, 2013, at http://www.whitehouse.gov/sites/default/files/uploads/2013.05.23_fact_sheet_on_ppg.pdf.

67. Interview with the author, March 2014.

68. Heather Linebaugh, "I Worked on the US Drone Program. The Public Should Know What Really Goes On," Guardian, December 29, 2013, at http://www.theguardian.com/commentisfree/2013/dec/29/drones-us-military.

69. Major General Timothy McHale, "AR 15-6 Investigation, 21 February 2010 US Air-To-Ground Engagement in the Vicinity of Shahidi Hassas, Uruzgan District, Afghanistan," May 21, 2010, partially declassified under Freedom of Information Act.

70. "Definition of Civilian and Civilian Population," Protocol Additional to the Geneva Conventions of 12 August 1949, and relating to the Protection of Victims of International Armed Conflicts (Protocol I), June 8, 1977, at http://www.icrc.org/applic/ihl/ihl.nsf/Article.xsp?action=openDocument&documentId=E1F8F99C4C3F8FE4C12563CD0051DC8A.

71. Interview with the author, November 2013.

72. "Pakistani CIA Informant: 'Drone Attacks Are the Right Thing to Do,'" Der Spiegel, December 4, 2013, at http://www.spiegel.de/international/zeitgeist/interview-pakistani-cia-informant-on-drone-warfare-and-taliban-a-937045.html.

73. Nils Melzer, "Interpretive Guidance on the Notion of Direct Participation in Hostilities under International Humanitarian Law," ICRC, May 2009, at http://www.icrc.org/eng/assets/files/other/icrc-002-0990.pdf.

74. "No-Strike and the Collateral Damage Estimation Methodology," Chairman of the Joint Chiefs of Staff Instruction, February 13, 2009, archived at https://www.aclu.org/files/dronefoia/dod/drone_dod_3160_01.pdf.

75. Interview with the author, February 2014.

76. Interview with the author, March 2014.

77. Al-Rabia was killed less than a month later in another CIA strike which also killed a Spanish husband and wife, and two children. See chapter 6.

78. Graeme Smith, "Pakistan's Deadly Robots in the Sky," *Globe and Mail*, October 1, 2010, at http://www.theglobeandmail.com/news/world/asia-pacific/pakistans-deadly-robots-in-the-sky/article1739172/page3/.

79. Alice K. Ross and Jack Serle, "Most US Drone Strikes in Pakistan Attack Houses," Bureau of Investigative Journalism, May 23, 2014, at http://www.thebureauinvestigates.com/2014/05/23/most-us-drone-strikes-in-pakistan-attack-houses/.

80. Jonathan S. Landay, "Obama's Drone War Kills 'Others,' Not Just Al Qaida Leaders," McClatchy, April 9, 2013, at http://www.mcclatchydc.com/2013/04/09/188062/obamas-drone-war-kills-others.html.

81. "Senior Administration Officials on the Terrorist Designation of the Haqqani Network," State Department Special Briefing, September 7, 2012, at http://www.state.gov/r/pa/prs/ps/2012/09/197495.htm.

82. Ben Emmerson QC, address to joint session of UK All Party Parliamentary Groups on the United Nations and Drones, December 13, 2013. Author's transcript.

83. Bob Dreyfuss, "Mass-Casualty Attacks in the Afghan War," *The Nation*, September 19, 2013, at http://www.thenation.com/article/176262/mass-casualty-attacks-afghan-war.

84. Rob Blackhurst, "The Air Force Men Who Fly Drones in Afghanistan by Remote Control," *Daily Telegraph*, September 24, 2012, at http://www.telegraph.co.uk/news/uknews/defence/9552547/The-air-force-men-who-fly-drones-in-Afghanistan-by-remote-control.html.

85. Document 15, from Osama bin Laden to unstated recipient October 2010, published by the West Point Counter-Terrorism Center, May 3 2012, English translation at http://www.ctc.usma.edu/posts/letters-from-abbottabad-bin-ladin-sidelined.

86. Interview with the author, May 2013.

87. Reid Cherlin, "Obama's Drone-Master," *GQ Magazine*, June 17, 2013, at http://www.gq.com/news-politics/big-issues/201306/john-brennan-cia-director-interview-drone-program.

88. "Open Hearing on the Nomination of John O. Brennan to be Director of the Central Intelligence Agency," Senate Select Committee on Intelligence, February 7, 2013, at http://www.intelligence.senate.gov/130207/transcript.pdf.

89. Glenn Greenwald, "UK detention of Reprieve activist consistent with NSA's view of drone opponents as 'threats' and 'adversaries,'" *Guardian*, September 25, 2013, at http://www.theguardian.com/commentisfree/2013/sep/25/nsa-uk-drone-opponents-threats.

90. "Post-Confirmation Hearing Questions for the Record: Mr John Brennan," Senate Select Committee on Intelligence, February 7, 2013, at http://www.intelligence.senate.gov/130207/posthearing.pdf.

91. James Clapper, Letter to Senators Dianne Feinstein and Saxby Chambliss, April 18, 2014, at http://www.theguardian.com/world/interactive/2014/apr/29/cia-us-national-security.

92. The United Nations "recorded 59 civilian casualties (45 civilian deaths and 14 injured) from 19 incidents of unmanned aerial vehicle (UAV)/RPA strikes" in Afghanistan. Afghanistan Annual Report 2013: Protections of Civilians in Armed Conflict, UNAMA, published February 2014.

93. Interview with the author, Pentagon, December 2013.

94. Larry Lewis, "Reducing and Mitigating Civilian Casualties: Enduring Lessons," Joint and Coalition Operational Analysis, April 12, 2013, at http://www.cna.org/sites/default/files/research/CIVCAS_Enduring_Lessons.pdf.

95. Interview with the author, February 2014.

96. Interview with the author.

97. Interview with the author, May 2014.

98. For 2009 to 2013, the Long War Journal reported 105 civilians among 2,197 killed by the CIA in Pakistan; New America Foundation cited at least 157 civilians killed among 2,374 fatalities; and BIJ estimated 249 or more noncombatant deaths from an overall minimum tally of 1,892 killed. Data correct as of December 2014.

99. Comments to the author, background terms.

100. Barack Obama, "Remarks by the President at the National Defense University," White House, May 23, 2013, at http://www.whitehouse.gov/the-press-office/2013/05/23/remarks-president-national-defense-university.

101. Stanley McChrystal, My Share of the Task: A Memoir (New York: Portfolio Penguin, 2013), 310.

102. "Protocol Additional to the Geneva Conventions of 12 August 1949, and relating to the Protection of Victims of International Armed Conflicts (Protocol I)," ICRC, June 8, 1977, at http://www.icrc.org/ihl/COM/470-750044?OpenDocument.

CHAPTER 12

1. The infra-red camera gave away the heat signatures of those trying to hide.

2. Interview with the author, December 2013.

3. Interview with the author, Langley AFB, December 2013. Surname withheld at request of USAF.

4. Interview with the author, background terms.

5. David S. Cloud and David Zucchino, "Multiple Missteps Led to Drone Killing U.S. Troops in Afghanistan," Los Angeles Times, November 5, 2011, at http://articles.latimes.com/2011/nov/05/world/la-fg-drone-attack-20111106.

6. Interview with the author, January 2014.

7. Heather Linebaugh, "I Worked on the US Drone Program. The Public Should Know What Really Goes On," *Guardian*, December 29, 2013, at http://www.theguardian.com/commentisfree/2013/dec/29/drones-us-military.

8. DCGS was receiving 30 terabytes of data daily from ISR platforms. Email to the author ISAF ISR Agency, December 2013.

9. "As of Hubble's 24th anniversary in April 2014, Hubble observations have produced more than 100 terabytes of data." Hubble Facts, NASA, at http://www.nasa.gov/mission_pages/hubble/story/index.html#.UzSG7_l_vy0.

10. Interview with the author, Pentagon, December 2013.

11. Cited in Stew Magnuson, "Military 'Swimming in Sensors and Drowning in Data,'" *National Defense Magazine*, January 2010, at http://www.nationaldefensemagazine.org/archive/2010/January/Pages/Military%E2%80%98SwimmingInSensorsandDrowninginData%E2%80%99.aspx.

12. The Future of Air Force Motion Imagery Exploitation, Rand: Project Air Force, 2012, at http://www.rand.org/content/dam/rand/pubs/technical_reports/2012/RAND_TR1133.pdf.

13. The CIA Factbook identifies Somalia as the second-poorest nation internationally, with only the Democratic Republic of Congo seeing a lower average per capita income, at https://www.cia.gov/library/publications/the-world-factbook/geos/so.html.

14. Investigation into the Deaths of Abu Hafsa and Abu Uhud, Al Kataib Media, May 2013.

15. Abdi Guled, "Somali Militants Execute 3 Said to Inform CIA, MI6," Associated Press, July 22, 2012, at http://www.businessweek.com/ap/2012-07-22/somali-militants-execute-3-said-to-inform-cia-mi6.

16. See, for example, Mark Mazzetti and Helene Cooper, "Detective Work on Courier Led to Breakthrough on Bin Laden," *New York Times*, May 2, 2011, at http://www.nytimes.com/2011/05/02/world/asia/02reconstruct-capture-osama-bin-laden.html.

17. Audio commentary, Investigation into the Deaths of Abu Hafsa and Abu Uhud, Al Kataib Media, May 2013.

18. Declan Walsh, "Mysterious 'Chip' Is CIA's Latest Weapon against al-Qaida Targets Hiding in Pakistan's Tribal Belt," *Guardian*, May 31, 2009, at http://www.theguardian.com/world/2009/may/31/cia-drones-tribesmen-taliban-pakistan.

19. Hasnain Kazim, "Pakistani CIA Informant: 'Drone Attacks Are the Right Thing to Do,'" *Der Spiegel*, December 4, 2013, at http://www.spiegel.de/international/zeitgeist/interview-pakistani-cia-informant-on-drone-warfare-and-taliban-a-937045.html.

20. "'US Spy' Killed in Bajaur," *The News International*, November 3, 2006, at http://www.thenews.com.pk/TodaysPrintDetail.aspx?ID=4013&Cat=13&dt=11/3/2006.

21. Zia Khan, "Taliban Create Cell to Hunt 'Spies' Assisting US Drones," *Express Tribune*, March 28, 2011, at http://tribune.com.pk/story/138759/taliban-create-cell-to-hunt-spies-assisting-us-drones/.

22. David Rohde, "The Drone War," *Reuters Magazine*, January 17, 2012, at http://www.reuters.com/article/2012/01/26/us-david-rohde-drone-wars-idUSTRE80P11I20120126.

23. "Thousands Cheer as Pakistani Militants Decapitate, Shoot Afghans Accused of Spying for U.S.," Associated Press, June 27, 2008, at http://www.foxnews.com/story/2008/06/27/thousands-cheer-as-pakistani-militants-decapitate-shoot-afghans-accused-spying/.

24. Mark Lavie, "Palestinians Sentence Collaborators," Associated Press, August 1, 2001, archived at http://www.washingtonpost.com/wp-srv/aponline/20010802/aponline132112_001.htm.

25. "B'Tselem Strongly Condemns Executions of Individuals Suspected of Collaborating with Israel," B'Tselem press release, August 24, 2014, at http://www.btselem.org/press_releases/20140824_btselem_condemns_executions.

26. "Al-Qaeda Executes Alleged US Informer," AFP, March 6, 2014, at http://www.vanguardngr.com/2014/03/al-qaeda-executes-alleged-us-informer/.

27. Carol Grisanti and Mushtaq Yusufzai, "Taliban-Style Justice for Alleged U.S. Spies," NBC News, April 17, 2009, at http://worldblog.nbcnews.com/_news/2009/04/17/4376383-taliban-style-justice-for-alleged-us-spies?lite.

28. Declan Walsh and Eric Schmitt, "Drones at Issue as U.S. Rebuilds Ties to Pakistan," *New York Times*, March 18, 2012, at http://www.nytimes.com/2012/03/19/world/asia/drones-at-issue-as-pakistan-tries-to-mend-us-ties.html?pagewanted=all.

29. "Drone SIM—Taleban Claims," BBC Urdu, April 23, 2010, video at http://www.bbc.co.uk/urdu/pakistan/2010/04/100423_drone_sim_taleban_claim.shtml.

30. Zia Khan, ibid.

31. Gregory D. Johnsen, "Did an 8-Year-Old Spy for America?" *The Atlantic*, September 2013, at http://www.theatlantic.com/magazine/archive/2013/09/did-an-8-year-old-spy-for-america/309429/.

32. "The Al-Qaida Papers—Drones [English and Arabic]," Associated Press, February 21, 2013, at http://hosted.ap.org/specials/interactives/_international/_pdfs/al-qaida-papers-drones.pdf.

33. Interview with the author, November 2013.

34. Siobhan Gorman, Yochi Dreazen, and August Cole, "Insurgents Hack U.S. Drones," *Wall Street Journal*, December 17, 2009, at http://online.wsj.com/news/articles/SB126102247889095011.

35. Roee Nahmias, "Nasrallah Describes 1997 Ambush," YNet news, September 8, 2010, at http://www.ynetnews.com/articles/0,7340,L-3932886,00.htm.

36. "El Kaide üyeleri adliyede," Son Dakika, October 22, 2010, at http://www.sondakika.com/haber-el-kaide-uyeleri-adliyede-2332636/.

37. Craig Whitlock and Barton Gellman, "U.S. Documents Detail Al-Qaeda's Efforts to Fight Back against Drones," *Washington Post*, September 4, 2013, at http://www.washingtonpost.com/world/national-security/us-documents-detail-al-qaedas-efforts-to-fight-back-against-drones/2013/09/03/b83e7654-11c0-11e3-b630-36617ca6640f_story.html.

38. See, for example, Adam Rawnsley, "Iran's Alleged Drone Hack: Tough But Possible," December 16, 2011, at http://www.wired.com/2011/12/iran-drone-hack-gps/.

39. "Hamas Drone Plot against Israel Foiled by Palestinian Authority," *World Tribune*, October 28, 2013, at http://www.worldtribune.com/2013/10/28/hamas-drone-plot-against-israel-foiled-by-palestinian-authority/.

40. "100+ Wanted Arrested and Drones Workshop Seized," Aswat al-Iraq, August 20, 2013, at http://en.aswataliraq.info/(S(sihajrar2axj4n45ximygm55))/Default1.aspx/images/images/headers/Default1.aspx?page=article_page&id=154089&l=1.

41. Shakeel Anjum, "Capital Police Bust Al-Qaeda's Drone Project," *The News International*, October 12, 2013, at http://www.thenews.com.pk/Todays-News-13-26035-Capital-police-bust-al-Qaedas-drone-project.

42. Lynn E. Davis, Michael J. McNerney, James Chow, Thomas Hamilton, Sarah Harting, and Daniel Byman, "Armed and Dangerous? UAVs and US Security," Rand Corporation, May 1, 2012, at http://www.rand.org/content/dam/rand/pubs/research_reports/RR400/RR449/RAND_RR449.pdf.

43. Yaakov Lappin, "Israel Air Force Pilots Practice Shooting Down Enemy Drones in Massive Drill," *Jerusalem Post*, April 30, 2014, at http://www.jpost.com/Defense/Israel-Air-Force-pilots-practice-shooting-down-enemy-drones-in-massive-drill-350845.

44. Video archived at http://www.openanthropology.org/humamalbalawi.mp4.

45. Joby Warrick, *The Triple Agent: The Al-Qaeda Mole Who Infiltrated the CIA* (New York: Doubleday, 2011), 95–96.

46. "Troops End Attack on Karachi Naval Air Base," BBC News, May 23, 2011, at http://www.bbc.co.uk/news/world-south-asia-13495127.

47. John D. Gresham, "Attack on Camp Bastion: The Destruction of VMA-211," DefenseMediaNetwork, September 20, 2012, at http://www.defensemedianetwork.com/stories/attack-on-camp-bastion-the-destruction-of-vma-211/.

48. For a detailed listing of known crashes, see Drone Crash Database maintained by Drone Wars UK, at http://dronewars.net/drone-crash-database/.

49. "A Wedding that Became a Funeral: US Drone Attack on Marriage Procession in Yemen," Human Rights Watch, February 19, 2014, at http://www.hrw.org/sites/default/files/reports/yemen0214_ForUpload_0.pdf.

50. Ahmed Tolba and Sami Aboudi, "Al Qaeda claims it captured a US drone base in Yemen," Reuters, October 14, 2013, at http://www.csmonitor.com/World/Latest-News-Wires/2013/1014/Al-Qaeda-claims-it-captured-a-US-drone-base-in-Yemen.

51. Bill Roggio, "AQAP says assault on Yemen's Defense Ministry targeted US drone operations," Long War Journal, December 6, 2013, at http://www.longwarjournal.org/archives/2013/12/aqap_claims_assault.php.

52. Document 17, The bin Laden Files (English translation), West Point Counter-Terrorism Center, at http://www.ctc.usma.edu/posts/letters-from-abbottabad-bin-ladin-sidelined.

53. Document 15, from Osama bin Laden to unstated recipient October 2010, published by the West Point Counter-Terrorism Center, May 3, 2012, English

translation at http://www.ctc.usma.edu/posts/letters-from-abbottabad-bin-la din-sidelined.

54. Interview with the author, background terms.

55. Interview with the author, November 2013.

56. Ibid.

57. Interview with the author, September 2013.

58. Peter Olson, NATO Legal Representative, in letter to Judge P. Kirsch, Chair, United Nations International Commission of Inquiry on Libya, January 23, 2012, at http://www.nato.int/nato_static/assets/pdf/pdf_2012_05/ 20120514_120514-NATO_1st_ICIL_response.pdf.

59. "Libya: Obama Sanctions Use of US Predator Drones," Associated Press, April 21, 2011, at http://www.guardian.co.uk/world/2011/apr/21/us-obama-predator-drones-libya.

60. Anders Fogh Rasmussen, NATO Secretary General, "Monthly Press Briefing," November 3, 2011, at http://www.nato.int/cps/en/natolive/opinions_80247. htm.

61. See also C. J. Chivers and Eric Schmitt, "In Strikes on Libya by NATO, an Unspoken Civilian Toll," New York Times, December 17, 2011, at http:// www.nytimes.com/2011/12/18/world/africa/scores-of-unintended-casualties-in-nato-war-in-libya.html?pagewanted=all&_r=3&; "Libya: The Forgotten Victims of NATO Strikes," Amnesty International Report, March 2012, at https://www.amnesty.org/en/library/asset/MDE19/003/2012/ en/8982a094-60ff-4783-8aa8-8c80a4fd0b14/mde190032012en.pdf; and "Unacknowledged Deaths: Civilian Casualties in NATO's Air Campaign in Libya," Human Rights Watch Report, May 14, 2012, at http://www.hrw.org/ reports/2012/05/13/unacknowledged-deaths.

62. Report of the International Commission of Inquiry on Libya, Advanced Unedited Version, UNHRC March 8, 2012, at http://www.ohchr.org/Documents/ HRBodies/HRCouncil/RegularSession/Session19/A.HRC.19.68.pdf.

63. Marc Garlasco, "NATO's Lost Lessons from Libya," Washington Post, June 12, 2012, at http://www.washingtonpost.com/opinions/natos-lost-lessons-from-libya/2012/06/11/gJQAhkAoVV_story.html.

64. "Joint Resolution Concerning the War Powers of Congress and the President," passed November 7, 1973, archived at http://avalon.law.yale.edu/20th_century/ warpower.asp.

65. "United States Activity in Libya," White House Report to Congress, June 15, 2011, archived at http://www.washingtonpost.com/wp-srv/politics/ documents/united-states-activities-libya.html.

66. Interview with the author, April 2012.

67. Mazzetti alleged that in 2006 according to "three current and former intelligence officials" the United States secretly carried out a drone strike against alleged terrorist Umar Patek. This was denied by the Philippines military, which insisted it carried out the attack. Mark Mazzetti, The Way of the Knife: The CIA, a Secret Army, and a War at the Ends of the Earth (New York: Penguin Press, 2013), 133–134.

68. Thirty-four civilians died in a 2011Turkish airstrike based on intelligence provided by a US Predator. See Adam Entous and Joe Parkinson, "Turkey's Attack on Civilians Tied to U.S. Military Drone," *Wall Street Journal*, May 16, 2012, at http://online.wsj.com/news/articles/SB10001424052702303877604577380480677575646?mg=reno64-wsj&url=http%3A%2F%2Fonline.wsj.com%2Farticle%2FSB10001424052702303877604577380480677575646.htmll.

69. "U.S. Reaper drones have provided intelligence and targeting information that have led to nearly 60 French airstrikes [in Mali] in the past week alone . . . say French officials." Adam Entous, David Gauthier-Villars, and Drew Hinshaw, "U.S. Boosts War Role in Africa: American Drones Help French Target Militants in Mali, as Chad Claims Killings," *Wall Street Journal*, March 4, 2013, at http://online.wsj.com/article/SB10001424127887324539404578338590169579504.html.

70. Interview with the author, background terms.

71. The *Sunday Times* claimed a Hamas official was assassinated by an Israeli Hermes 450 near Port Sudan airport in January 2009. See Uzi Mahnaimi, "Israeli Drones Destroy Rocket-Smuggling Convoys in Sudan," *Sunday Times*, March 29, 2009, paywalled at http://www.thesundaytimes.co.uk/sto/news/world_news/article158293.ece.

72. In August 2012 Israeli, Egyptian, and Palestinian media outlets reported the targeted killing by an Israeli drone of an alleged militant 12 miles inside Egypt. However the IDF denied any knowledge of the attack. See Roi Kais, "Terrorist 'involved in attack on Israel' killed in Sinai," Y-Net News, August 26, 2012, at http://www.ynetnews.com/articles/0,7340,L-4273263,00.html.

73. "Mystery over Sudan 'air strike,'" BBC News, March 26, 2009, at http://news.bbc.co.uk/1/hi/world/africa/7966627.stm.

74. Tom Watson MP, "Official Communication: Complaint Regarding the UK's Response to the Report of Special Rapporteur Dated 28 February on Use of Drones in Extra-Territorial Lethal Counter-Terrorism Operations," May 2014, author's copy.

75. Ben Farmer, "'RAF Reaper Drones Bound for Iraq,'" *Daily Telegraph*, October 5, 2014, at http://www.telegraph.co.uk/news/worldnews/middleeast/iraq/11139751/RAF-Reaper-drones-bound-for-Iraq.html.

76. Interview with the author, March 2014.

77. American Civil Liberties Union versus Central Intelligence Agency, United States Court of Appeals: District of Columbia Circuit, Brief for Appellee, 34–35, May 2012, archived at http://www.lawfareblog.com/wp-content/uploads/2012/05/2012-05-21-ACLU-v-CIA-Appellee-Brief.pdf.

78. *New York Times v. US Department of Justice*: Memorandum of Law in Support of Defendants' Motion for Summary Judgment, June 20 2012, archived at https://www.aclu.org/files/assets/https____ecf.nysd_.uscourts.gov_cgi-bin_show_temp.pl_file10176016-0-17573.pdf.

79. Glenn Greenwald, "Obama DOJ Again Refuses to Tell a Court Whether CIA Drone Program Even Exists," *Guardian*, February 14, 2013, at http://www.theguardian.com/commentisfree/2013/feb/14/cia-aclu-drone-secrecy.

80. Mark Mazzetti, Charlie Savage, and Scott Shane, "How A US Citizen Came to Be in America's Cross Hairs," *New York Times*, March 9, 2013, at http://www.nytimes.com/2013/03/10/world/middleeast/anwar-al-awlaki-a-us-citizen-in-americas-cross-hairs.html.

81. *New York Times v. US Department of Justice* and *ACLU v. Department of Justice*, Department of Defense and Central Intelligence Agency: Judgment, US District Court, Southern District of New York, Judge Colleen McMahon, January 2, 2013, archived at https://www.documentcloud.org/documents/550539-dronedecision.html.

82. Cited in Kevin Johnson, "Federal Judge Questions Government Drone Program," *USA Today*, July 19, 2013, at http://www.usatoday.com/story/news/politics/2013/07/19/judge-aclu-drone-al-qaeda-al-awlaki-terrorism/2568667/.

83. *Nasser al-Awlaqi v. Leon Panetta et al.*, United States District Court for the District of Columbia, Civil Action No. 12-1192 (RMC), Judge Rosemary Collyer, April 4, 2014, archived at https://ecf.dcd.uscourts.gov/cgi-bin/show_public_doc?2012cv1192-36.

84. Dianne Feinstein, "Feinstein Statement on Intelligence Committee Oversight of Targeted Killings," February 13, 2013, at http://www.feinstein.senate.gov/public/index.cfm/press-releases?ID=5b8dbe0c-07b6-4714-b663-b01c7c9b99b8.

85. Michael Hirsh and Kristin Roberts, "What's in the Secret Drone Memos," *National Journal*, February 13, 2013, at http://www.nationaljournal.com/nationalsecurity/what-s-in-the-secret-drone-memos-20130222.

86. Jo Becker and Scott Shane, "Secret 'Kill List' Proves a Test of Obama's Principles and Will," May 29, 2012, at http://www.nytimes.com/2012/05/29/world/obamas-leadership-in-war-on-al-qaeda.html?pagewanted=all.

87. *New York Times v. US Department of Justice* and *ACLU v. Department of Justice*, Department of Defense and Central Intelligence Agency: Judgment, United States Court of Appeals Second Circuit, April 21, 2014, archived at https://www.aclu.org/sites/default/files/assets/targeted_killing_foia_appeal_ruling.pdf.

88. "Memorandum for the Attorney General" [redacted], US Department of Justice Office of Legal Counsel, July 16, 2010, archived at http://www.lawfareblog.com/wp-content/uploads/2014/06/6-23-14_Drone_Memo-Alone.pdf.

89. "A Thin Rationale for Drone Killings," *New York Times* Editorial Board, June 23, 2014, at http://www.nytimes.com/2014/06/24/opinion/a-thin-rationale-for-drone-killings.html.

90. Barack Obama, "Remarks by the President at the National Defense University," White House, May 23, 2013, at http://www.whitehouse.gov/the-press-office/2013/05/23/remarks-president-national-defense-university.

91. Mark Mazzetti, "As New Drone Policy Is Weighed, Few Practical Effects Are Seen," *New York Times*, March 21, 2013, at http://www.nytimes.com/2013/03/22/us/influential-ex-aide-to-obama-voices-concern-on-drone-strikes.html.

92 "Generation Kill: A Conversation with Stanley McChrystal," *Foreign Affairs*, February 11, 2013, at http://www.foreignaffairs.com/discussions/interviews/generation-kill.

93. Interview with the author, September 2013.
94. Correspondence with the author, December 2013.
95. Interview with the author, March 2014.
96. Michael E. Leiter, "Testimony before the United States Senate Committee on Foreign Relations Counterterrorism Policies and Priorities: Addressing the Evolving Threat," March 20, 2013, at http://www.foreign.senate.gov/imo/media/doc/Michael_Leiter_Testimony.pdf.
97. Correspondence with the author, December 2013.
98. "Chapter 1. Attitudes toward the United States," Pew Research Global Attitudes Project, July 18, 2013, at http://www.pewglobal.org/2013/07/18/chapter-1-attitudes-toward-the-united-states/#drone-strikes.
99. John Rizzo, *Company Man: Thirty Years of Controversy and Crisis at the CIA* (New York: Scribner, 2014), 300.
100. Some 645 executions were carried out by US states between 2002 and 2014. "Executions by Year since 1976," Death Penalty Info, at http://www.deathpenaltyinfo.org/executions-year.

BIBLIOGRAPHY

Aid, Matthew M. *Intel Wars: The Secret History of the Fight against Terror* (New York: Bloomsbury Press, 2012).

Allawi, Ali A. *The Occupation of Iraq: Winning the War, Losing the Peace* (New Haven, CT: Yale University Press, 2007).

Bamford, James. *The Shadow Factory: The Ultra-Secret NSA from 9/11 to the Eavesdropping on America* (New York: Random House, 2009).

Bashir, Shahzad, and Robert D. Crews, eds. *Under the Drones: Modern Living in the Afghanistan-Pakistan Borderlands* (Cambridge, MA: Harvard University Press, 2012).

Benjamin, Medea. *Drone Warfare: Killing by Remote Control* (New York: O R Books, 2012).

Bergen, Peter L. *The Longest War: The Enduring Conflict between America and Al-Qaeda* (New York: Simon and Schuster, 2010).

———. *Manhunt: From 9/11 to Abbottabad—The Ten Year Search for Osama bin Laden* (London: The Bodley Head, 2012).

Berntsen, Gary, with Ralph Pezzullo. *Jawbreaker: The Attack on bin Laden and Al Qaeda—A Personal Account by the CIA's Key Field Commander* (New York: Crown Publishers, 2005).

Bolt, Neville. *The Violent Image: Insurgent Propaganda and the New Revolutionaries* (London: Hurst, 2012).

Bright, Timothy. "Assessing Irregular Warfare." Unrestricted Warfare Symposium Proceedings, Johns Hopkins University, 2007.

Brown, Vahid, and Don Rassler. *Fountainhead of Jihad: The Haqqani Nexus 1973-2012* (London: Hurst, 2013).

Bush, George W. *Decision Points* (New York: Virgin Books, 2010).

Byman, Daniel. *A High Price: The Triumphs and Failures of Israeli Counterterrorism* (New York: Oxford University Press, 2011).

Caroe, Olaf Sir. *The Pathans* (Karachi: Oxford University Press, 1958, 2011).

Cavallaro, Jim, Sarah Knuckey, and Stephan Sonnenberg. "Living under Drones: Death, Injury and Trauma to Civilians from US Drone Practices in Pakistan." Stanford Law School and NYU School of Law, September

2012, at http://www.livingunderdrones.org/wp-content/uploads/2013/10/Stanford-NYU-Living-Under-Drones.pdf.

Chehab, Zaki. *Iraq Ablaze: Inside the Insurgency* (London: I. B. Tauris, 2006).

Christie, Thomas P. "Operational Test and Evaluation Report on the Predator Medium-Altitude Endurance Unmanned Aerial Vehicle (UAV)." OTE (September 2001).

Clarke, Richard A. *Against All Enemies: Inside America's War on Terror* (New York: Simon and Schuster, 2004).

Coll, Steve. *Ghost Wars: The Secret History of the CIA, Afghanistan, and Bin Laden, from the Soviet Invasion to September 10, 2001* (New York: Penguin, 2004).

Cortright, David, Rachel Fairhurst, and Kristen Wall, eds. *Drones and the Future of Armed Conflict: Ethical, Legal and Strategic Implications* (Chicago: University of Chicago Press, 2015).

Erhard, Thomas. "Air Force UAVs: The Secret History." The Mitchell Institute (July 2010).

Finkelstein, Claire, Jens David Ohlin, and Andrew Altman, eds. *Targeted Killings: Law and Morality in an Asymmetrical World* (Oxford: Oxford University Press, 2012).

Franks, Tommy. *American Soldier* (New York: Regan Books, 2004).

Gates, Robert M. *Duty: Memoirs of a Secretary of War* (New York: W. H. Allen, 2014).

Giustozzi, Antonio. *Decoding the New Taliban: Insights from the Afghan Field* (London: Oxford University Press, 2012).

Goldsmith, Jack. *Power and Constraint: The Accountable Presidency after 9/11* (New York: Norton, 2012).

Greenwald, Glenn. *No Place to Hide: Edward Snowden, the NSA and the Surveillance State* (London, New York: Hamish Hamilton, 2014).

Grey, Stephen. *Ghost Plane: The Inside Story of the CIA's Secret Rendition Programme* (London: Hurst, 2006).

Hansen, Stig Jarle. *Al-Shabaab in Somalia: The History and Ideology of a Militant Islamist Group 2005-2012* (London: Hurst, 2013).

Haqqani, Husain. *Magnificent Delusions: Pakistan, the United States, and an Epic History of Misunderstanding* (New York: Public Affairs, 2013).

———. *Pakistan: Between Mosque and Military* (Washington, DC: Carnegie Endowment for International Peace, 2005).

Hersh, Seymour M. *Chain of Command: The Road from 9/11 to Abu Ghraib* (New York: Allen Lane, 2004).

———. "King's Ransom: How Vulnerable Are the Saudi Royals?" *The New Yorker*, October 16, 2001.

Hirschberg, Michael J. "To Boldly Go Where No Unmanned Aircraft Has Gone Before: A Half-Century of DARPA's Contributions to Unmanned Aircraft." American Institute of Aeronautics and Astronautics (January 2010).

Johnsen, Gregory D. *The Last Refuge: Yemen, al-Qaeda and America's War in Arabia* (New York: Norton, 2013).

Kilcullen, David. *The Accidental Guerilla: Fighting Small Wars in the Midst of a Big One* (London: Hurst, 2009).

———. *Out of the Mountains: The Coming Age of the Urban Guerilla* (London: Hurst, 2013).

Kiriakou, John, with Michael Ruby. *The Reluctant Spy: My Secret Life in the CIA's War on Terror* (New York: Random House, 2009).

Klaidman, Daniel. *Kill or Capture: The War on Terror and the Soul of the Obama Presidency* (New York: Houghton Mifflin Harcourt, 2012).

Lambeth, Benjamin S. *Air Power Against Terror: America's Conduct of Operation Enduring Freedom* (Santa Monica, CA: Rand Corporation, 2005).

Leedham, Howard. *Ask Forgiveness Not Permission: The True Story of an Operation in Pakistan's Badlands* (London: Bene Factum Publishing, 2012).

Lieven, Anatol. *Pakistan: A Hard Country* (New York: Allen Lane, 2011).

Martin, Matt J., with Charles W. Sasser. *Predator: The Remote Control Air War over Iraq and Afghanistan—a Pilot's Story* (Minneapolis, MN: Zenith Press, 2010).

Martin, Mike. *An Intimate War: An Oral History of the Helmand Conflict* (London: Hurst, 2014).

Mayer, Jane. *The Dark Side: The Inside Story of How the War on Terror Turned into a War on American Ideals* (New York: Random House, 2009).

Mazzetti, Mark. *The Way of the Knife: The CIA, a Secret Army, and a War at the Ends of the Earth* (New York: Penguin Press, 2013).

McChrystal, Stanley. *My Share of the Task: A Memoir* (New York: Portfolio/Penguin, 2013).

McRaven, William H. *Spec Ops—Case Studies in Special Operations Warfare: Theory and Practice* (New York: Ballantine Books, 1995).

Morrison, J. Stephen, and Jennifer G. Cooke, "Africa Policy in the Clinton Years." Center for Strategic and International Studies (October 1, 2001).

Musharraf, Pervez. *In the Line of Fire: A Memoir* (New York: Simon & Schuster, 2006).

Owen, Mark, with Kevin Maurer. *No Easy Day: The Only First-Hand Account of the Navy SEAL Mission That Killed Osama bin Laden* (New York: Penguin, 2012).

Packer, George. *The Assassin's Gate: America in Iraq* (London: Faber and Faber, 2006).

Prince, Erik. *Civilian Warriors: The Inside Story of Blackwater* (New York: Portfolio/Penguin, 2013).

Rashid, Ahmed. *Descent into Chaos: Pakistan, Afghanistan and the Threat to Global Security* (New York: Penguin, 2008).

———. *Pakistan on the Brink: The Future of Pakistan, Afghanistan and the West* (New York: Allen Lane, 2012).

Risen, James. *State of War: The Secret History of the CIA and the Bush Administration* (London: Free Press, 2006).

Rizzo, John. *Company Man: Thirty Years of Controversy and Crisis at the CIA* (New York: Scribner, 2014).

Rodriguez, Jose A., Jr., with Bill Harlow. *Hard Measures: How Aggressive CIA Actions after 9/11 Saved American Lives* (New York: Threshold Editions, 2012).

Roe, Andrew M. *Waging War in Waziristan: The British Struggle in the Land of Bin Laden, 1849-1947* (Lawrence: University Press of Kansas, 2010).

Rumsfeld, Donald. *Known and Unknown: A Memoir* (New York: Sentinel, 2011).

Sanger, David E. *Confront and Conceal: Obama's Secret Wars and Surprising Use of American Power* (New York: Crown, 2012).

———. *The Inheritance: The World Obama Confronts and the Challenges to American Power* (New York: Random House, 2009).

Scahill, Jeremy. *Dirty Wars: The World Is a Battlefield* (London: Serpent's Tail, 2013).

Schmitt, Eric, and Thom Shanker. *Counter Strike: The Untold Story of America's Secret Campaign against Al Qaeda* (New York: Times Books, 2011).

Schroen, Gary C. *First In: An Insider's Account of How the CIA Spearheaded the War on Terror in Afghanistan* (New York: Ballantine Books, 2005).

Shaffer, Antony. *Operation Dark Heart: Spycraft and Special Operations on the Front Lines of Afghanistan* (New York: Thomas Dunne Books, 2010).

Shahzad, Syed Saleem. *Inside Al Qaeda and the Taliban: Beyond Bin Laden and 9/11* (London: Pluto Press, 2011).

Singer, P. W. *Wired for War: The Robotics Revolution and Conflict in the 21st Century* (New York: The Penguin Press, 2009).

Small, Thomas, and Jonathan Hacker. *Path of Blood: The Story of Al Qaeda's War on the House of Saud* (London: Simon & Schuster, 2014).

Spain, James W. *The Way of the Pathans* (Karachi: Oxford University Press, 1962, 2011).

Strickland, Frank. "The Early Evolution of the Predator Drone." Studies in Intelligence Vol. 57, No. 1 (Extracts, March 2013), CIA Library.

Strick van Linschoten, Alex, and Felix Kuehn. *An Enemy We Created: The Myth of the Taliban/Al Qaeda Merger in Afghanistan, 1970-2010* (London: Hurst, 2011).

Tankel, Stephen. *Storming the World Stage: The Story of Lashkar-e-Taiba* (London: Hurst, 2011).

Temple-Raston, Dina. *The Jihad Next Door: The Lackawanna Six and Rough Justice in the Age of Terror* (New York: Public Affairs, 2007).

Tenet, George. *At the Center of the Storm: My Years at the CIA* (New York: Harper Luxe, 2007).

Thirtle, Michael R., Robert V. Johnson, and John L. Bidder. *The Predator ACTD: A Case Study for Transition Planning to the Formal Acquisition Process.* (National Defense Research Institute/Rand, 1997).

Urban, Mark. *Task Force Black: The Explosive True Story of the SAS and the Secret War in Iraq* (London: Little, Brown, 2010).

Warrick, Joby. *The Triple Agent: The Al-Qaeda Mole Who Infiltrated the CIA* (New York: Doubleday, 2011).

Weizman, Eyal, ed. *Forensis: The Architecture of Public Truth* (London: Sternberg Press, 2014).

Whittle, Richard. "Predator's Big Safari." Mitchell Institute for Airpower Studies, 2011, archived at http://higherlogicdownload.s3.amazonaws.com/

AFA/6379b747-7730-4f82-9b45-a1c80d6c8fdb/UploadedImages/Mitchell%20 Publications/Predator%27s%20Big%20Safari.pdf.

————. *Predator: The Secret Origins of the Drone Revolution* (New York: Henry Holt, 2014).

Woodward, Bob. *Bush At War* (London: Simon & Schuster, 2003).

————. *Obama's Wars: The Inside Story* (London: Simon & Schuster, 2010).

————. *The War Within: A Secret White House History 2006-2008* (London: Simon & Schuster, 2009).

Yousufzai, Hassan M., and Ali Gohar. *Towards Understanding Pukhtoon Jirga* (Lahore: Sang-e-Meel Publications, 2012).

Zenko, Micah. *Between Threats and War: US Discrete Military Operations in the Post-Cold War World* (Stanford, CA: Stanford University Press, 2010).

INDEX

Note: Tables are indicated by "t" following page number. Surnames starting with "al-" or "ul" are alphabetized by the following part of the name.